The Power of Small Groups in Christian Education

Harley T. Atkinson

Evangel
Publishing House
Nappanee, Indiana 46550

Toll-Free Order Line: (800) 253-9315
Internet Website: www.evangel.publishing.com

Cover design by Ted Ferguson
Copyediting by Janine Petry and Helen Johns

Publisher's Cataloging-in-Publication Data

Atkinson, Harley.
    The power of small groups in Christian education / Harley T. Atkinson. – 1st ed.
        p. cm.
    Includes bibliographical references.
    LCCN 2001099441
    ISBN 1-928915-28-0

    1. Church group work. 2. Small groups–Religious aspects–Christianity. 3. Christian education.
    I. Title

BV652.2.A85 2002   253'.7
                              QBI02-200401

Printed in the United States of America
9 8 7 6 5 4 3 2 1

Table of Contents

Preface

This morning my alarm clock was set to go off at 6:30, giving me just enough time to get up, get dressed, prepare for the day, and rush off to meet with a group of five men. We ate breakfast and shared in some friendly chitchat before engaging in the more formal part of our meeting. At this point we discussed a portion of a book which talked about our identity in Jesus Christ and then shared some of our personal needs and struggles. One man shared about a family conflict; another talked about an upcoming court appearance that was of grave concern to him; a third revealed a sensitive interpersonal issue that had to be dealt with in his office. In each case we stopped and prayed for the individual and the particular situation. Although the names have changed and the group has evolved over time, this has been roughly the pattern that has unfolded almost every Tuesday morning over the past decade.

We are not alone. The men in this group belong to one of the tens of thousands of small groups currently existing in North America and around the world. Indeed, small groups of all kinds are proliferating: encounter groups, growth groups, support groups, study groups, and outreach groups. Many of us belong to one of the numerous Bible studies or Sunday school classes existing in our neighborhoods or parishes. Most of us have a friend or colleague who attends a support or recovery group such as Alcoholics Anonymous. Currently four out of every ten Americans belong to a small group of some sort.

The strong interest in small groups that pervades churches and parishes in America and around the world is not faddish in nature, as some might suggest. Biblical and historical sources give evidence that small groups are the most effective structures for the communication of the gospel and that small-cell communities are strategic in fostering renewal in the church. In an age when "big is beautiful," there is a corresponding notion that suggests small is indispensable in structuring for community, outreach, and education.

As the church moves in to the twenty-first century it faces tremendous challenges in presenting a 2,000-year-old message to contemporary and diverse cultures. Small groups can provide a fresh yet time-proven approach to these challenges. However, if leaders and strategists are not careful, small groups can succumb to the subtle pressures of secular culture and degenerate into self-serving assemblages obsessed with self rather than concern for and outreach to others. Furthermore, small-group discussions can be nothing more than a pooling of ignorance or fruitless pursuits of elusive rabbit trails.

The purpose of this book is to provide the reader with strong foundations for Christian education groups before offering solid and carefully researched principles and strategies for leading effective small-group discussions. My intent is to draw from various disciplines such as history, theology, education, and communications, in presenting a book on developing small groups and facilitating group discussions in the context of Christian education.

I mentioned earlier that currently I meet with a group of men on a weekly basis. These friends and colleagues have provided for me an exciting opportunity to learn and grow in the context of the small group. So to Brian, Ken, John, Lance, Glen, Jimmy, Kenny, Greg, James, and others who were at various times part of the group, I express my gratitude for being a source of encouragement and strength through good and difficult times, and for providing a context where personal growth can take place.

There is another small group I am a part of; a group that is far more intimate and of far greater value than the other. This group is my family, consisting of my wife Shirley and daughters Sarah and Hannah. Together we laugh, cry, encourage one another, play, and yes, even engage in conflict! It is not all good times. But it is the small-group context where the most significant growth and learning in my life has taken place. To members of this small group—Shirley, Sarah, and Hannah—I dedicate this book.

Finally, special words of appreciation are offered to Suzanne Rich for proofreading the manuscript. Thanks to James Davies for sharing some excellent ideas for the book. Thanks to Kenn Gangel, Bob Wetmore, Joe Sprinkle, Dan Evearitt, Randy Pruitt, and Jarvis Crosby for proofreading particular sections of the manuscript. And a sincere word of appreciation is offered to James Michael Lee for his diligent work in editing this manuscript.

Harley T. Atkinson
Toccoa Falls, Georgia

1

Understanding Small Groups

PEOPLE are communicators. In every moment of conscious existence we are communicating in some manner. Some of this communication is intrapersonal, or within the individual; some of it takes place in a two-person dyad, the smallest and simplest of groups.[1] However, a significant amount of our communication exists in the context of small groups: committees, study groups, sports teams, educational groups, religious groups, and informal friendship affiliations. Certainly everyone learns to communicate and interact in the framework of the family, the social unit that provides our initial and primary group affiliation and is basic to all other types of social organizations and groups.[2]

Small groups are all around us. In fact, social groups constitute the basic fabric of our familial, social, and work life. One of the most distinctive characteristics of humanity is that we are social creatures whose lives are inextricably intertwined with the lives of others. Most of our daily activities are performed in the presence or context of people—we are small-group beings.[3]

Groups are playing an increasingly integral role in the religious life of individuals in America and around the world.

---

[1]John E. Farley, *Sociology* (Englewood Cliffs, N.J.: Prentice Hall, 1990), 178; James M. Henslin, *Sociology: A Down-to-Earth Approach* (Boston: Allyn and Bacon, 1993), 155.

[2]Scott G. McNall, *The Sociological Experience*, 3rd ed. (Boston: Little, Brown, 1974), 259; David W. Johnson and Frank P. Johnson, *Joining Together*, 6th ed. (Boston: Allyn and Bacon, 1997), 5–6.

[3]Johnson and Johnson, *Joining Together*, 5.

In churches and parishes small groups have proliferated as pastors and Christian educators have intentionally developed a variety of small-group ministries as the core of their church life and Christian education programs.[4] Currently, four out of every ten Americans belong to a small group that meets regularly, providing some kind of care and support for its members. This means that if there are about 200 million adults in the United States, about 80 million are participating in some kind of a small group. And 60 percent of these members belong to groups formally affiliated with a synagogue or church: support groups, twelve-step recovery groups, Sunday school classes, Bible study groups, singles' groups, book discussion groups, and political or civic groups.[5]

WHY SMALL GROUPS?

Why are small groups so prevalent in contemporary America that almost half the adults in the country are involved in some sort of group? Why are they seen as the basic unit of church community and a popular option for doing Christian education? They are so pervasive that sociologist Robert Wuthnow is able to confidently pronounce that the small-group movement is "effecting a quiet revolution in American society."[6] Similarly, Jeffrey Arnold proposes that the small-group movement is a catalyst for a "quiet revolution that has slowly built from the ground up into a crescendo that is more and more difficult to ignore. It has influenced every church's ministry in one way or another, and affected many people's lives."[7]

Clearly, small groups are a powerful and significant religious and sociological force in American culture. And the

---

[4]Jim Plueddemann and Carol Plueddemann, *Pilgrims in Progress* (Wheaton, Ill.: Harold Shaw, 1990), 11.

[5]Rob Wuthnow, *Sharing the Journey* (New York: The Free Press, 1994), 4, 6; Robert Wuthnow, *I Come Away Stronger* (Grand Rapids, Mich.: Eerdmans, 1994), 369.

[6]Wuthnow, *Sharing the Journey*, 2.

[7]Jeffrey Arnold, *Starting Small Groups* (Nashville, Tenn.: Abingdon, 1997), 13.

impact of small groups is not limited to North America. There is an explosion of house church and cell group ministries that is altering the structure and impact of the church worldwide.[8]

Why has the dramatic growth of small groups in recent decades been so pronounced? What benefits do they hold for church ministries and Christian education? A careful scrutiny of biblical passages as well as a review of contemporary sources offer the following reasons as to why small groups are beneficial to churches and their Christian education ministries:

- they provide individuals with a sense of community;

- they assist people in their quest for spirituality;

- they are an ideal point of entry into the church;

- they provide a safe environment for learning;

- they are an ideal way to study and apply Scripture and church doctrine;

- they are an effective way of mobilizing the laity to ministry.

A Sense of Community

Robert Wuthnow proposes that an understanding of the dynamic growth and popularity of small groups since the 1960s can be explained only by understanding the social context from which it has risen. Contemporary American society, he says, is a victim of the breakdown of traditional support structures, such as the neighborhood and extended family, that once offered a sense of security and belonging. Many people today live anonymous lives, no longer remain in the same neighborhoods most of their lives, and often do not retain close ties with their families. Wuthnow describes many people today as psychologically and emotionally stranded and alone. Families are breaking down and neighbors have become churlish or

---

[8]Kirk Hadaway, Stuart A. Wright, and Francis M. Dubose, *Home Cell Groups and House Churches* (Nashville, Tenn.: Broadman, 1987), 51–4.

indifferent.[9] The advance of the small-group movement is rooted in the disintegration of these longlasting support structures and our innate desire for community; what noted sociologist Robert Nisbet describes as relationships characterized by "a high degree of personal intimacy, emotional depth, moral commitment, social cohesion, and continuity in time."[10]

Robert Bellah and his colleagues, in their compelling study on American life, argue that ours is a society in which "the individual can only rarely and with difficulty understand himself and his activities as interrelated in morally meaningful ways with those of other, different Americans."[11] But the dearth of genuine community prevails not only in society at large, it exists in the church as well. In his travels across the United States, M. Scott Peck observes that there is both a deep lack of community and a genuine thirst for community among Americans. But most disturbing to him is the lack of community in those places we would most expect to find it—in the churches.[12]

Why is genuine community, even Christian community, so difficult to find? Why, as Thomas Kirkpatrick begs, are there so few churches that evidence a contagious, alive, and attractive fellowship?[13] Bellah cites the words of the early Puritan leader John Winthrop as archetypal of an understanding of what life in America was meant to be: "We must delight in each other, make others' conditions our own, rejoice together, mourn together, labor and suffer together, always having before our eyes our community as members of the same body."[14] How-

---

[9]Wuthnow, *Sharing the Journey*, 5.

[10]Robert A. Nisbet, *The Sociological Tradition* (New Brunswick, N.J.: Transaction, 1993), 47.

[11]Robert N. Bellah, Richard Madsen, William M. Sullivan, Ann Swindler, and Steven M. Tipton, *Habits of the Heart* (New York: Harper and Row, 1985), 50.

[12]M. Scott Peck, *The Different Drum* (New York: Simon and Schuster, 1978), 27-8.

[13]Thomas G. Kirkpatrick, *Small Groups in the Church* (Washington, D.C.: Alban Institute, 1995), 10.

[14]Bellah et al., *Habits of the Heart*, 28.

ever, while not entirely lost to American culture, Winthrop's idealistic notion of Christian community has, to a large degree, been given over to a disconnected hyper-individualism. Nisbet, who calls the problem of lack of community the single most impressive fact of the twentieth-century Western society, suggests it is a relatively modern issue. For most of history, group life was a given, whereas today there is less reason to spend time together and there are fewer ways of knowing each other. Yet our need for close, interpersonal relationships remains constant.[15]

Indeed sociologists are in agreement in describing members of contemporary society as individualistic, rootless, alienated, fragmented, lonely, and lacking a sense of belonging.[16] But Alvin Toffler insists that any decent society must generate a sense of community. Among other things, community offsets loneliness and offers individuals a sense of belonging.[17] The solution to this fragmentation and individualism has been to start intentional groups of like-minded persons who can regain a sense of community.[18] Jim and Carol Plueddemann advocate that as human beings, we are born with a need for belonging and find ourselves drawn to groups where we can establish relationships and work on common tasks.[19]

In his insightful book on loneliness and spiritual growth, Samuel Natale argues that in the United States at least, loneliness exists as a serious and growing problem.[20] In an increasingly mobile and hostile world, where loneliness and alienation are universal sources of human suffering, settings where individu-

---

[15]Nisbit, *The Sociological Tradition*, 47.

[16]Wuthnow, *Sharing the Journey*, 33–6, 191; Bellah, *Habits of the Heart*, 142 ff.; Alvin Toffler, *The Third Wave* (New York: Bantam, 1981), 367–8.

[17]Toffler, *The Third Wave*, 367.

[18]Wuthnow, *Sharing the Journey*, 5.

[19]Plueddemann and Plueddemann, *Pilgrims in Progress*, 80–1.

[20]Samuel M. Natale, *Loneliness and Spiritual Growth* (Birmingham, Ala.: Religious Education Press, 1986, 141.

als can experience a sense of belonging and neededness are more important than ever. The group experience, emphasizes Natale, is a powerful tool for intervening in both chronic (inability to relate to others) and situational (disruption of social interrelationships) aspects of loneliness.[21]

Not only can the church provide solutions to the problems of alienation and fragmentation, it has an unparalleled opportunity and responsibility to respond to the pressing relational problems that a harried generation possesses. The church has the potential to be an alternative community that models God's intentions for relationship and fellowship.[22]

Indeed a unifying theme of the Old and New Testaments is God calling His people into a community of faith. At the very core of human nature as created by God, argues Ray Anderson, is community. Existence in co-humanity is logically prior to any occurrence as discrete individuals.[23] T.S. Eliot writes, "There is no life that is not in community. And no community not lived in praise of God."[24] Adds Gareth Icenogle, "Scripture begins and ends with God calling humanity into relationship with the divine community and with one another."[25]

However, while humankind was created for community, it suffered serious interpersonal consequences because of the Fall (Ge 3). The onset of sin brought with it adverse effects in virtually all relationships: estrangement from God (Ro 5:10a) and alienation in our interpersonal connectedness with fellow human beings (Gal 5:20).[26] Our failure takes

---

[21]Ibid., 159–60.

[22]Kirkpatrick, *Small Groups in the Church*, 11–12.

[23]Ray Anderson, *On Being Human* (Grand Rapids, Mich.: Eerdmans, 1982), 154.

[24]T. S. Eliot, "Choruses From 'The Rock,'" *Complete Poems and Plays* (New York: Harcourt and Brace, 1952), 73.

[25]Gareth Icenogle, *Biblical Foundations for Small Group Ministry* (Downers Grove, Ill.: InterVarsity, 1994), 21.

[26]In Galatians 5:20 the apostle Paul includes hatred, discord, jealousy, fits of rage, selfish ambition, dissensions, factions, and envy among the acts of the sinful nature.

from us the pleasures of community that God intended for us and leaves us alienated, isolated, lonely, and disconnected.

But even the Fall was not to leave us eternally doomed to live without relationship with either God or fellow human beings. Though seriously disrupted, the capacity for community with God was not totally destroyed. Eve praised God at the birth of Cain (Ge 4:1), and Cain and Abel both offered sacrifices unto God (4:3–4). Similarly, human relationships are depicted in the Genesis account. Adam and Eve continued to exist as husband and wife, and Cain eventually took unto himself a wife (Ge 4:17). Nonetheless, insists Hal Miller, the smug and arrogant protest by Cain that he is not his brother's keeper (4:9) reflects an attitude of indifference toward his brother rather than a spirit of intimacy.[27] The truth of the matter is, concludes Anderson, Cain surely is his brother's keeper because both he and his brother, Abel, bear the *imago Dei*.[28]

God's provision for severed relationships and alienation from others is through the person of Jesus Christ. Though we became God's enemies, Jesus became our reconciliation. Paul writes, "For if, when we were God's enemies, we were reconciled to him through the death of his Son, how much more, having been reconciled, shall we be saved through his life!" (Ro 5:10).

The reconciling work of Jesus was extended to human relationships as well: "You are all sons of God through faith in Christ, for all of you who were baptized into Christ have been clothed with Christ. There is neither Jew nor Greek, slave nor free, male nor female, for you are all one in Christ Jesus" (Gal 3:26–28). In Christ, all relational barriers were brought crashing down as Jesus came preaching a Gospel that has as its essence relationships.[29] "Love your enemies and pray for those who persecute you" (Mt 5:44); "Love your neighbor as your-

---

[27]Hal Miller, *Christian Community: Biblical or Optional?* (Ann Arbor, Mich.: Servant Books, 1979), 39.

[28]Anderson, *On Being Human*, 154.

[29]Julie A. Gorman, *Community that Is Christian* (Wheaton, Ill.: Victor, 1993), 45.

self" (Mt 22:39); "By this all men will know that you are my disciples if you love one another" (Jn 13:35). Christ's teaching, then, places community at the very heart and center of the Christian experience.[30] Paul Hanson rightly insists that from a biblical perspective, the notion and experience of being in the world "begins with supportive community, where the faithful can gather to celebrate all that is good and worthy in life as a gift of divine grace, and can commemorate the central events of their common spiritual history together, like the event of deliverance from slavery in the Jewish Passover, or the events of rebirth and atonement in Christian baptism and the Eucharist." It is the context for the individual's growth into full personhood and spiritual maturity.[31]

The challenge for churches and Christian education programs is to offer lonely and disconnected people a solution to alienation by providing opportunities for relationship building through small-group communities. The notion of community is not difficult to understand. It is "the relationship of people to one another and the sense of belonging and of obligation to the group."[32] It is the New Testament idea of *koinonia* (having that which is in common), the very heartbeat and core of the early church (Ac 2:42–47).

While it is easy to understand, however, community is much more difficult to experience. Paradoxically, while people desire community, they run from it. While they seek it, they are afraid of it and fear getting too close to others.[33] Nonetheless, community can be achieved through the intentional efforts of small groups. Unfortunately, argues Arnold, relatively few churches do much to equip small groups to become a commu-

---

[30]Thomas G. Kirkpatrick, *Small Groups in the Church* (Washington, D.C.: The Alban Institute, 1995), 5.

[31]Paul D. Hanson, *The People Called* (San Francisco: Harper and Row, 1986), 501.

[32]Roberta M. Berns, *Child, Family, Community* (New York: Holt, Rinehart, and Winston, 1985), 298.

[33]Kirkpatrick, *Small Groups in the Church*, 11.

nity. As a result, small groups often operate in the deficit of relationships.[34] The awesome task of the church and Christian education ministries is to provide a context whereby lonely and disconnected individuals can hope to regain a lost sense of community.

Spiritual Formation

A second major objective that has accelerated much of the small-group movement is the "quest for spirituality." From his study of small groups, Wuthnow observed that a majority of all small-group adherents joined groups because they wanted to deepen their faith.[35]

This pursuit for spirituality identified with the small-group movement parallels or is no doubt connected to a religious intensity that exists on a much grander scale. In 1990 John Naisbitt and Patricia Aburdene identified a worldwide multidenominational religious revival leading into the next millennium, a trend characterized by intense interest in traditional and nontraditional religions alike.[36] This heightened religious intensity is affirmed by Gary Collins, who says there is a new interest in spirituality that is invading our lives and engulfing the whole world at lightening speed. It is attracting teenagers, business executives, physicians, psychologists, academics, and homemakers. It is impacting worshipers in traditional churches as well as people seeking out alternative and New Age forms of spirituality.[37]

It is part of being human, of course, to be on a spiritual journey or on a quest to satisfy a deep inner hunger. Centuries ago the great church father Augustine wrote "You have made us for yourself, O Lord, and our hearts can never rest until they rest in you." Twentieth-century existential writers, like

---

[34]Arnold, *Starting Small Groups*, 23.

[35]Wuthnow, *Sharing the Journey*, 6.

[36]John Naisbitt and Patricia Aburdene, *Megatrends 2000* (New York: William Morrow, 1990), 270.

[37]Gary R. Collins, *The Soul Search* (Nashville: Thomas Nelson, 1998), 5.

Jean-Paul Sarte and Albert Camus, have written poignantly concerning the anxiety, anguish, alienation, emptiness, and loneliness that characterize lives lived without God.

But clearly, there is a "sea of change" that is characterized by a heightened awareness of spiritual matters. At the top of the *New York Times* hardcover best-seller list for eight weeks was *Care of the Soul*,[38] by Thomas Moore. A psychotherapist and former Catholic monk, Moore came to the conclusion that many people are hungering for some sort of spiritual life and often evidence a "loss of soul."[39] In his immensely popular book Moore offers his audience a unique blend of psychology and religion as a guide for examining the connection between spirituality and the problems of the individual and society. Apparently Moore struck a nerve in the lives of American people, who in recent years have decided that spirituality and the care of their souls is of supreme value.

Indeed, for many Americans, faith has become a significant part of their life, and they have sought out others with whom they can pray and share common spiritual interests.[40] Wuthnow observes that the contemporary small-group movement presupposes that individuals are concerned about developing their spirituality, but that spiritual development is not easy and requires encouragement and support. He likens developing one's spirituality to learning to play a musical instrument. Hard work, practice, and a commitment to follow certain techniques are required, and the company of others may be required to sustain that discipline. Furthermore, that instrument may be played alone, but its value will be magnified if it is performed in harmony with others. And

---

[38]Thomas Moore, *Care of the Soul* (New York: HarperCollins, 1992).

[39]For his definition of *soul*, Moore draws from the fifteenth-century writer Marsilio Ficino, who believed that the soul existed somewhere between the mind and the physical world. As such, the soul holds together the mind and the body, ideas and life, spirituality, and the body.

[40]Wuthnow, *Sharing the Journey*, 16–7.

so it is with spirituality, it can be "played" or "practiced" in private, but its worth will be multiplied if performed in the company of others.[41]

The Pleuddemanns agree and explain that spiritual growth, like emotional and intellectual growth, does not take place in a vacuum. Rather, they suggest, it is fostered and nurtured by interaction. God has given each of us gifts and abilities so that we can contribute to the growth of others. Unfortunately, these gifts and abilities often lie dormant. In small groups, however, Christians can help each other "fan into flame" the gifts God has given them.[42]

Iris Cully also proposes that spiritual life is nurtured within community. She goes on to add that the most immediate group that can enable individuals to grow in the spiritual life is the prayer group, where participants strengthen and reinforce one another in prayer, Bible study, and the reading of devotional books.[43]

A Point of Entry into the Church

Successful churches and parishes have discovered that small groups serve as an ideal point of entry into the church for the previously unchurched. Small-group expert Lyman Coleman suggests that groups are particularly well suited to draw into the church those who are outside of it or on the periphery. Referring primarily to support and recovery groups, Coleman has identified approximately 130 "doors" where people can enter the full life of a church.[44]

While primary points of entry into the church in the past have been, at different times, the Sunday evening service, Sunday school, or the morning worship service, people today

---

[41]Wuthnow, *I Come Away Stronger*, 347.

[42]Plueddemann and Plueddemann, *Pilgrims in Progress*, 80.

[43]Iris V. Cully, *Education for Spiritual Growth* (San Francisco: Harper and Row, 1984), 136, 161.

[44]Cited in Warren Bird, "The Great Small-Group Takeover," *Christianity Today* (February 7 1994), 28.

seem to be entering the church through midweek activities. Citing the work of Lyle Schaller, Leith Anderson says people born after 1950 are much more likely to enter a new church through something other than the Sunday morning worship service: perhaps a church-sponsored Bible-study class, a sports team, a divorce recovery workshop, or a young adult group.[45]

Likewise Wade Clark Roof, in his study of Baby Boomers, observes that members of this generation are often attracted to large churches because of the diversity of programs and the variety of ministries they offer. Much of the attraction, he proposes, has to do with the range of small groups, dealing with everything from Bible study and prayer, to eating disorders, family life, singles' activities, abortion counseling, exercise, and weight lifting.[46]

People who have reservations or fears of entering a church sanctuary may be willing to join a small group in a home or participate in a lay-led support group. The small group, often serving as a kind of a halfway house, provides a nonthreatening opportunity to become part of the church.

From the perspective of evangelism, small groups provide a soft-sell approach to sharing the Gospel of Jesus Christ with nonbelievers, or the unchurched. The most effective witness, suggests Richard Peace, often springs from the *community* of believers. Significant sharing of the Christian faith often occurs when a small group of Christians and non-Christians gather together to discuss issues related to Christianity.[47] The power of community in impacting unbelievers was clearly evidenced in the initial stages of the church. As the early believers met together in homes and temple courts for teaching, fellowship, breaking of bread,

---

[45]Leith Anderson, *Dying for Change* (Minneapolis, Minn.: Bethany House, 1990), 65.

[46]Wade Clark Roof, *A Generation of Seekers* (San Francisco: HarperSanFrancisco, 1993), 254.

[47]Richard Peace, *Small Group Evangelism* (Downers Grove, Ill.: InterVarsity, 1985), 66.

prayer, sharing of goods, and meeting everyone's needs, "the Lord added to their number daily those who were being saved" (Ac 2:42–47). The first fruit of rapid church growth was indeed a testimony to the compelling power of Holy Spirit-invigorated *koinonia*.

A Safe Environment For Learning

It is not uncommon for adults to harbor negative perceptions about their ability to learn, and their capabilities for learning are often underestimated and underused. Older adults are especially prone to this sort of anxiety, and to them any type of in-depth learning venture is a move into foreign and unknown territory.[48]

For adults, emotional or psychological safety in the learning environment is one of the salient principles for effective learning. Jane Vella argues that adults are ready and willing to learn only when the learning environment provides a sense of emotional safety for them.[49]

Renowned adult education expert Malcolm Knowles agrees with Vella and insists that adult learners actively seek psychological security, protection against threats to their self-respect and self-image. It is this need that causes them to be cautious and reserved in a setting that is unfamiliar to them. He goes on to suggest that "when the need for security is not satisfied or is violated, various behavioral symptoms are likely to result. In certain situations some adult learners will respond to feelings of insecurity by pulling into their shell—withdrawing from participation, playing it safe until they get their bearings. Others respond to the same feelings in exactly the opposite way: they seek to protect themselves by taking over, controlling, dominating."[50] Individuals who do not feel secure in a

---

[48]Raymond J. Wlodkowski, *Enhancing Adult Motivation to Learn* (San Francisco: Jossey-Bass, 1993), 90–1.

[49]Jane Vella, *Learning to Listen, Learning to Teach* (San Francisco: Jossey-Bass, 1994), 7–8.

[50]Malcolm Knowles, *The Modern Practice of Adult Education*, rev. ed. (Chicago: Follett, 1980), 85.

small-group setting will either refrain from participating in small groups or will experience such anxiety and reduced self-esteem that learning and performance will be severely hampered.[51]

There are ways, however, to alleviate fear of the learning experience and to nurture an environment that offers a sense of psychological and emotional security. Vella proposes that a sense of safety can be achieved when the following characteristics are made present in a small-group learning experience:

- when group members trust in the group leader or facilitator;

- when group members trust in the feasibility and relevance of the objectives of the small group;

- when group facilitators allow group members to voice their own expectations, hopes, and fears about the small-group learning experience;

- when participants trust the sequence of activities (i.e., facilitators begin with simple, less threatening activities before moving to more advanced, difficult, or complex learning activities);

- when there is a realization by participants that the environment is nonjudgmental.

Small groups should provide a safe environment where adult learners can feel free to ask questions, raise doubts, and explore possibilities without fear of ridicule, embarrassment, or competitiveness.[52] Large-group formats are not designed for such interaction, and most people are uncomfortable in raising questions or expressing doubts in front of too many people. But in a small circle of amiable peers where a sense of confidentiality, understanding, and support has been established,

---

[51]Wlodkowski, *Enhancing Adult Motivation to Learn*, 197.

[52]James R. Newby, *Gathering the Seekers* (Washington, D.C.: The Alban Institute, 1995), 16.

individuals will often feel freer to open up. Jesus modeled this type of small-group interaction with His disciples, as they were encouraged and offered the freedom to ask tough questions of Him and dialogue over issues that perplexed them.[53]

A Way to Study and Apply Scripture

The problem of biblical illiteracy among Americans has been well documented. The George H. Gallup International Institute of Research noted that only 12 percent of teen-agers read the Bible daily, a number that drops to 9 percent in the college years.[54] George Barna discovered that among those who consider themselves to be Christian, 58 percent say they read the Bible at least one time during the week. Of these adults, however, only 12 percent read it daily.[55]

Barna concludes that many American Christians lack an understanding of the basic fundamentals and teachings of the church. He cites the following empirical research findings as confirmation of his conclusion:[56]

- Forty percent believe Jesus made mistakes.

- Two out of three respondents do not hold to the notion of absolute truth.

- Three of five adults do not believe in Satan.

- Many cannot name half of the Ten Commandments or who preached the Sermon on the Mount.

While the Bible remains the world's best-selling book, Americans, at least, remain unfamiliar with even the most basic of biblical facts. And if biblical knowledge is weak, we can be certain that theology is even less understood or ap-

---

[53]John 13–16.

[54]*The Religious Life of Young Americans* (Princeton, N.J.: The George M. Gallup International Institute, 1991), 43.

[55]George Barna, *What Americans Believe* (Ventura, Calif.: Regal, 1991), 289.

[56]George Barna, *Absolute Confusion* (Ventura, Calif.: Regal, 1993), 139.

plied.[57] In a sharp rebuke on the evangelical wing of the American church, David Wells argues that theology has been displaced from the center of evangelical life, where it defined life, and relegated to the periphery.[58] Consequently, adds James Newby of the Alban Institute, church members have great difficulty connecting what they hear Sunday morning to what happens to them on Monday. The question he raises then is not whether or not we should teach more Bible and theology, but *How do we make the Bible and theological information meaningful and lifechanging on the farm, in the office, or in the classroom?*[59]

It is a premise of this book that one of the best ways to study, learn, and apply the Scriptures to daily living, or to address pertinent issues from a biblical perspective, is to study them with a small group of interested individuals. In small groups we can encourage and help each other discover and obey God's Word in ways that are simply impossible in large groups or when the whole church meets together.[60]

Mobilizing the Body to Ministry

A careful look at the New Testament reveals the nature of the church as essentially a lay movement. The apostle Paul indicates that it was Jesus Christ "who gave some to be apostles, some to be prophets, some to be evangelists, and some to be pastors and teachers, to prepare God's people for works of service, so that the body of Christ may be built up" (Eph 4:11–12). The scriptural pattern for the church then, is that clergy are to equip lay men and women to minister to the world. The prominent American Quaker, Elton Trueblood, has said, "The ministry is for all who are called to share in Christ's life, the pastorate is for those who possess the peculiar gift of being

---

[57]Newby, *Gathering the Seekers*, 8.

[58]David F. Wells, *No Place for Truth* (Grand Rapids, Mich.: 1993), 108.

[59]Newby, *Gathering the Seekers*, 10.

[60]Steve Barker, et al., *Good Things Come in Small Groups* (Downers Grove, Ill.: InterVarsity, 1985), 15.

able to help other men and women to practice any ministry to which they are called."[61]

Historically, however, the church (whether Protestant, Catholic, or Orthodox) has operated as an institution more resembling a top-down business corporation than a bottom-up organism shaped by the spiritual gifts and callings of the whole body of Christ.[62] Indeed, one of the rallying cries of the fifteenth-century reformers was for the "priesthood of all believers," meaning they wanted most distinctions between the clergy and the laity abolished. What remains is a difference in role or function. To recapture the New Testament concept of full body life, there must be a renewed emphasis on the pattern that sees the primary function of the pastor-teacher as an equipping ministry.[63]

The small-group structure, insists Greg Ogden, more than anything else has the potential for mobilizing lay members for ministry. He goes on to say that the beauty and value of small groups is that they are led by equipped lay members of the congregation who have a call to this ministry and the spiritual gifts to carry it out.[64] Small groups shift the work of the ministry from the pastor or clergy to the laity, fulfilling the prescribed pattern of Ephesians 4:11. Ogden suggests that a small group is the place to begin an equipping ministry. A successful and effective small-group ministry provides a foundation on which the rest of the equipping ministry can be built.[65]

---

[61]Elton Trueblood, *The Incendiary Fellowship* (New York: Harper and Row, 1967), 41.

[62]Greg Ogden, *The New Reformation* (Grand Rapids, Mich.: Zondervan, 1990), 56–7.

[63]Thomas J. Mullen, *The Renewal of the Ministry* (New York: Abingdon, 1953), 43; John Stott, *One People* (Harrisburg, Penn.: Christian Publications, 1982), 59-60; R. Paul Stevens, *Liberating the Laity* (Downers Grove, Ill.: InterVarsity, 1985), 33–4.

[64]Ogden, *The New Generation*, 126.

[65]Ibid., 135.

Corinne Ware also encourages the notion that small groups be a lay-member project. She suggests that group leadership is particularly adaptable to the gifts of the lay people and groups are more likely to flourish if leadership emerges from the grassroots rather than if it is directed from a church official. What, then, is the role of the clergy in small-group Christian education ministries? Their work, like that of the apostle Paul's, is to "equip the saints" to do the work of dynamic small-group ministry.[66]

There are winds of change blowing in the Roman Catholic Church as well. Catholic theologians Bernard Lee and Michael Cowan propose that a worldwide web of small-group communities is indeed reinventing the church in our own time. They describe the leadership that is emerging in house churches and base communities as follows: "Unlike professional managers, emerging community leaders are not professionals with a transferable set of competencies. Most of them are thoroughly local leaders, who are unlikely to move on to leadership roles in other localities. They are women and men who have assumed positions of community leadership largely because others within their communities respond to them as leaders and acknowledge them as such. Their leadership roles are granted to them by their followers, not mandated by institutional power and structure. They have emerged as leaders within particular communities."[67]

The phenomenal spread of Catholic Basic Christian Communities in Latin America is due in part to the impact of various lay movements and efforts of lay apostolates to bring about ecclesial and personal renewal.[68] Similarly, one of the major characteristics of the African small Christian communities is that the leadership of the groups comes from within its own ranks.[69]

---

[66]Corrine Ware, *Connecting to God* (Washington, D.C.: The Alban Institute, 1997), 8.

[67]Bernard J. Lee and Michael A. Cowan, *Dangerous Memories* (Kansas City, Mo.: Sheed and Ward, 1986), 182.

[68]John Paul Vandenakker, *Small Christian Communities and the Parish* (Kansas City, Mo.: Sheed and Ward, 1994), 100.

[69]Ibid., 117.

In the United States, John Vandenakker characterizes most Catholic groups as stressing the shared responsibility of members for the welfare of the small Christian community. Generally no single person is considered the leader of the group, and those who are designated as pastoral facilitators maintain the role of giving motion to the meetings and liaising with the parish priest or staff.[70]

WHAT IS A SMALL GROUP?

What, precisely, is a *small group*? John Cragen and David Wright define a small group as "a few people engaged in communication interaction over time, usually in face-to-face settings, who have common goals and norms and have developed a communication pattern for meeting their goals in an interdependent manner."[71] Johnson and Johnson define a small group as a "two or more individuals in face-to-face interaction, each aware of positive interdependence as they strive to achieve mutual goals, each aware of his or her membership in the group and each aware of the others who belong to the group."[72] Robert Perucci and Dean Knudsen understand a small group as "having (1) no more than fifteen people who (2) have some emotional commitment, (3) some intimacy, and (4) some face-to-face contact with one another."[73]

According to adult education expert Malcolm Knowles, six basic elements of small groups distinguish them from any other general collection of people: size, group consciousness, purpose, interdependence, interaction, and cohesiveness.[74] Each of these critical group components needs further clarification.

---

[70]Ibid., 174.

[71]John Cragan and David Wright, *Communication in Small Group Discussions*, 4th ed. (St. Paul, Minn.: West, 1995), 7.

[72]Johnson and Johnson, *Joining together*, 12.

[73]Robert Perrucci and Dean D. Knudsen, *Sociology* (St. Paul, Minn.: West, 1983), 119.

[74]Malcolm Knowles, *Introduction to Group Dynamics* (New York: Association Press, 1959), 39–40.

Size: While size is clearly one of the single most important criteria of a small group, group dynamics scholars cannot seem to agree on the most appropriate perimeters. What is certain is that size determines the nature of the interaction that takes place in a small group. The smaller the group, the more personal and intense the interaction; conversely, the more people in a group, the more impersonal the group becomes.[75] For maximum intimacy and group satisfaction, the number of participants must be small enough so that each member is aware of and able to have reaction to each other member.[76]

While most small-group experts agree that three is the minimal number for effective small-group communication, the upper limit may be more arbitrary in that the best number depends on the kind of group that is formed.[77] However, authorities on small-group communication tend to agree that once the group size is extended beyond twelve to fifteen, it becomes increasingly difficult to maintain effective interpersonal relationships and accomplish group goals.[78] Stewart Tubbs observes that the optimum group size appears to be five. This size is small enough for members to engage in meaningful interaction yet large enough to generate a sufficient number of ideas.[79]

Considerable research has been conducted regarding the effect size has on group interaction and member satisfaction. For example, Hackman and Vidmar note that as group size increases, the higher the levels of disagreement among group

---

[75]Ian Robertson, *Sociology*, 3rd ed. (New York, N.Y.: Worth Publishing, 1987), 139.

[76]John K. Brilhart and Gloria J. Galanes, *Effective Group Discussion*, 8th ed. (Dubuque, Iowa: Wm. C. Brown, 1995), 8.

[77]Cragan and Wright, *Communication in Small Group Discussions*, 10.

[78]Neal F. McBride, *How to Lead Small Groups* (Colorado Springs, Colo.: Navpress, 1990), 24; Brilhart and Galanes, *Effective Group Discussion*, 8.

[79]Stewart L. Tubbs, *A Systems Approach to Small Group Interaction*, 5th ed. (New York: McGraw-Hill, 1995), 102.

members.[80] Cartwright and Zander discovered that group members found participation more satisfying and group processes more effective in smaller groups than in larger ones.[81]

Group Consciousness: According to this criteria, group members think of themselves as a group. In other words, they have a conscious identification with each other. Group members should be able to identify themselves as members of a particular group because they share certain characteristics, interests, or values that help define the group.

One of the first sociologists to address the issue of distinctive social groupings was Ferdinand Toennies (1855-1936), who made a distinction between two types of groups: the *Gemeinschaft* and the *Gesellshaft*. According to Toennies the *Gemeinschaft* is a small community of people in which members know each other and interpersonal relationships are close. People share similar values and people are oriented towards the interests and activities of the group as a whole.

On the other hand, the *Gesellschaft* is made up of a larger population in which group members are strangers to one another. Relationships are impersonal, individuals are oriented towards personal rather than group goals, people do not necessarily hold to the same values, and tradition has little influence on behaviors.[82]

More recently sociologists have found it similarly helpful to classify groups as either *primary* or *secondary* according to their function in society.[83] Primary groups are characterized by intimate face-to-face interaction and cooperation. This type

---

[80]J. Richard Hackman and Neil Vidmar, "Effects of Size and Task Type on Group Performance and Member Reactions," *Interpersonal Behavior in Small Groups*, ed. Richard J. Ofshe (Englewood Cliffs, N.J.: Prentice-Hall, 1973), 285–99.

[81] Dorwin Cartwright and Alvin Zander, "The Structural Properties of Groups: Introduction," *Group Dynamics*, eds. Dorwin Cartwright and Alvin Zander (New York: Harper and Row, 1968), 485–502.

[82]Ferdinand Toennies, *Community and Society* (East Lansing, Mich.: Michigan State University, 1957).

[83]McNall, *The Sociological Experience*, 79-81.

of group is so termed because it comes first in an individual's life and is the source of morals for the individual and, ultimately, society. Primary groups exist to meet needs of inclusion and affection and are by their very nature characterized by warmth and spontaneity. Examples of primary groups include families, friendship groups, gangs, sororities and fraternities, cliques, and, of course, structured small groups.

Secondary groups, by contrast, are larger, more formal, and people are more distanced from one another in time and space. Members may know each other as adherents of the same organization but do not know each other personally. Group members tend not to engage in meaningful interaction nor are they particularly concerned about seeing change in each other's lives. Some task force groups or work groups serve as examples of the secondary group.

Del Birkey makes an interesting and helpful application of these sociological definitions to church structure and renewal. He posits that the house church that existed up to the fourth century was that of a primary group. It emphasized the church as a fellowship of individuals in significant relationship to one another. The church model that emerged and has dominated most forms of Christianity since the fourth century is that of a secondary group. It concentrates, he argues, more on outward structure, architecture, hierarchy, and organizational systems.[84] Every renewal movement with any lasting impact (such as Pietism and Methodism) has had incorporated into it primary group meetings of some sort. And Christians who cry out for revitalization of the contemporary church invariably call for the implementation of primary groups.[85]

Reflecting on this, Lee and Cowan remind us that for a small Christian community or house church to exhibit the New Testament notion of *koinonia* or community there must be a concern for each other's welfare, and members must have a

---

[84]Del Birkey, *The House Church* (Scottdale, Pa.: Herald Press, 1988), 64–5.

[85]For example, see Mullen, *The Renewal of the Ministry;* and Snyder, *Liberating the Church.*

sense of belonging to others who confess the same Jesus Christ.[86] Hanson portrays the first generation church as one which recognized the centrality of the abiding presence of the risen Christ, practiced forms of community such as the partaking of a common meal, encouraged the custom of sharing goods in common, and worked towards the disappearance of all human barriers.[87] As such, the early house churches evidenced a group consciousness similar in nature to that described by contemporary sociologists in their notion of primary groups.

Shared Purpose: A group is significantly different from a mere collection of individuals. Twenty or twenty-five people standing in line to purchase tickets for a movie or basketball game are not a group but merely an aggregation, since they do not *interact* with each other so as to collectively (i.e., as a group) achieve a **common purpose** or **goal**.[88] To be more than simply a collection of people that are grouped together through happenstance, there must be some state or condition that the majority of group members desire to see occur.[89] For example, the common goal of a committee might be to revise a constitution; a shared purpose of a support group for parents of teens might be to assist each other in the sometimes difficult task of parenting adolescents. Indeed, small groups are held together by members' need to cooperate in the achieving of group goals.[90] If these goals can be achieved in a manner independent of the group context, group cohesion may be lost.

The well-known clinical psychologist and interpersonal specialist Gerard Egan insists that only through the establishment of clear goals and carefully defined means for achieving these goals do small groups achieve a high degree of effectiveness.

---

[86]Lee and Cowan, *Dangerous Memories*, 24.

[87]Hanson, *The People Called*, 437.

[88]J. Dan Rothwell, *In Mixed Company*, 3rd ed. (Fort Worth, Tex.: Harcourt Brace, 1998), 55.

[89]Harvey J. Bertcher, *Group Participation: Techniques for Leaders and Members* (Beverly Hills, Calif.: Sage, 1979), 16.

[90]Cragan and Wright, *Communication in Small Group Discussions*, 12.

He also agrees that it is almost impossible for a group to begin goal-less. Either the sponsoring agency (such as the church or Christian education department) has identified certain goals before the group begins or participants have particular goals in mind before they even join a group. Consequently hidden goals abound. However, he reasons, it is important for groups to make sense out of goal confusion and ambiguity and clarify group expectations, processes, and goals.[91]

Interdependence: The story is told of two lepers observed planting peas in a field. One had no legs, while the other had no arms. The leper with legs and feet but no hands carried on his back the one with hands but no feet. The leper with hands carried the bag of seeds and dropped a seed in the ground every few inches, while the other pushed the seed into the ground with his feet. Thus they were able to complete the task of planting the peas; together managing the work of one man.[92]

Small-group members need the help of each other to accomplish the purpose or purposes for which they joined the group. Consider the scenario where three young boys band together to build and operate a lemonade stand. One boy joins the group because it affords him the opportunity to try out his new woodworking tools by building the stand; the second boy wants to earn enough money to buy a baseball glove; the third simply likes to be with the other two. Although the motivation of each of the boys is different, their common goal is to establish a lemonade stand, and to accomplish this they must be dependent on each other's special interests and expertise.[93]

The New Testament, with clarity and unequivocality, emphasizes the interdependence Christians are to have with one another. In his correspondence with the house churches in Rome, Corinth, Ephesus, and Colossae, Paul utilized the word

---

[91]Gerard Egan, *Face to Face* (Monterey, Calif.: Brooks/Cole, 1973), 22–3.

[92]Elon Foster, *6000 Sermon Illustrations* (Grand Rapids, Mich.: Baker, 1992), 309.

[93]Summarized from Dorwin Cartwright and Alvin Zander, *Group Dynamics: Research and Theory* (New York: Harper and Row, 1968), 404.

body (*soma*) more than thirty times to illustrate how the church should function. Half of the time he referred to the human, physical body with its many parts, as a metaphor of the church; elsewhere he applied the term to the church itself—the body of Christ.[94] Consider the following examples (italics added):

> "So in Christ we who are many form one *body*, and each member belongs to all the others" (Ro 12:5).

> "Now the *body* is not made up of one part but of many" (1Co 12:14).

> "There is one *body* and one Spirit" (Eph 4:4).

> "From Him [Christ] the whole *body*, joined and held together by every supporting ligament, grows and builds itself up in love, as each part does its work" (Eph 4:16).

> "And He [Christ] is head of the *body*, the church" (Col 1:18).

The notion of body life means that every member of the church (the body) of Christ is important and absolutely essential for maturity and effective growth to occur in the church.[95] Likewise, the success a small group (a microcosm of the church) has in reaching its goals or achieving its purposes is dependent, to a large degree, on the ability of group members to rely on one another for the achievement of those goals and purposes. Put another way, given a set of agreed-upon goals, an aggregation of individuals will not become a successful group until members can learn to operate interdependently and are willing to do as much.[96]

Face-to-face Interaction: The mere presence of a number of people sitting on a park bench may not alert us to the presence of

---

[94]Gene A. Getz, *Building Up One Another* (Wheaton, Ill.: Victor, 1983), 7.

[95]Gene A. Getz, *Sharpening the Focus of the Church* (Chicago: Moody, 1974), 116.

[96]Bertcher, *Group Participation: Techniques for Leaders and Members*, 18.

a small group, but interactive face-to-face communication among several people might. The notion that face-to-face contact or interaction must occur for a collection of people to become a group is fundamental to an understanding of small groups. It is essential in maintaining small-group membership since it is rather difficult to imagine group participants self-disclosing feelings of intimacy and commitment without face-to-face interaction.[97] Face-to-face community is what small groups are all about.[98]

Egan says that small groups have many names, but whatever the name, group members sit face-to-face and talk to one another. He goes on to emphasize the value of such an encounter or transaction with others in a small-group experience: "If they can forge themselves into a supportive and understanding community—a community in which the members are basically 'for' one another and come to see the world through one another's eyes—then they can train themselves to engage in the kinds of behavior that make for interpersonal growth: exploration of one's interpersonal style, a freer and more responsible expression of human emotion, a willingness to challenge others caringly and to be challenged."[99]

But, Egan cautions, "face-to-face interaction can facilitate interpersonal growth, or can retard it."[100] Or, as Icenogle suggests, "There is possibility or peril in every face-to-face encounter."[101] Icenogle identifies the benefits and detriments of small-group encounter and confrontation in the biblical example of Job and his three friends. In Job's unfortunate set of circumstances, his friends provided some helpful support and community. First, they gathered around him to support him in his time of crisis (Job 2:11). Second, they entered into theological reflection and dialogue concerning his painful predicament. Third, they empathized with Job by entering into the depths of his pain,

---

[97]Perrucci and Knudsen, *Sociology*, 120.

[98]Icenogle, *Biblical Foundations for Small Group Ministry*, 69.

[99]Egan, *Face to Face*, v.

[100]Ibid.

[101]Icenogle, *Biblical Foundations for Small Group Ministry*, 69.

suffering, and feelings: "They began to weep aloud, and they tore their robes and sprinkled dust on their heads" (Job 2:12b).[102] On the other hand, Job's "comforters" demonstrated the possible shortcomings of intentional face-to-face small-group encounters and confrontations. First, they determinedly and consistently rejected Job's perspective and responses concerning the nature and purpose of human suffering. Second, their dialogue was sometimes more of a mockery of Job's insights than a supportive and compassionate discussion (Job 17:2). And third, their supposed words of encouragement and sense of compassion eventually evolved into group intimidation and effort of the majority to dominate or intimidate the individual.[103] This pattern of group action whereby there is an attempt to force individuals to reflect the thoughts of the majority, is what Irving Janis calls *groupthink*.[104]

Groupthink, concludes Icenogle, is an abuse of God's call for humankind to enter into meaningful face-to-face community. Rather, healthy face-to-face community must reflect a balance between individual thought and interdependence of the whole group.[105]

There is also a somewhat pragmatic inference for small groups that emanates from the notion of face-to-face communication. Face-to-face community and interaction implies that small groups must be arranged in such a manner that each small-group member can see the faces of other group members. Thus U-shaped or circle arrangements are encouraged for small groups, rather than rows. It is rather difficult for three or four individuals sitting on a sofa to see each other's faces, making communication less personal. Furthermore it's important to remove vases or flower settings that would obstruct the view members have of one another.[106]

---

[102]Ibid., 71.

[103]Ibid., 72.

[104]Irving Janis, *Groupthink*, 2nd ed. (Dallas: Houghton Mifflin, 1982), 7–8.

[105]Icenogle, *Biblical Foundations for Small Group Ministry*, 73.

[106]Ibid., 77.

Cohesiveness: A sixth, yet absolutely vital element of a group is its ability to stick together.[107] A highly cohesive group reflects the motto of the Three Musketeers, "All for one and one for all." Cohesiveness is the "we" feeling of a group.[108] Johnson and Johnson define cohesion as "the mutual attraction among members of a group and the resulting desire to remain in the group."[109] Tubbs describes it as feelings of belonging.[110]

The level of cohesion is indicated in a number of ways: consistent attendance, arrival to meetings on time, the level of trust and support present among members, the amount of individuality accepted by the group, the amount of fun the group has, morale, team spirit, and the strength of attraction of the group for its members.[111]

How do we build cohesiveness in small groups? There are a number of ways to do this:[112]

- *By encouraging compatible relationships.* When group members enjoy one another and each other's company, cohesiveness is easily built. On the other hand, when difficult or disruptive members are part of a group, cohesiveness can suffer.

- *By developing common goals.* When group members are working and pulling together to achieve a goal valued by all members, cohesiveness increases.

- *By working together to accomplish tasks.* Groups tend to become more cohesive as a result of task accomplishment.

---

[107]Ernest G. Bormann and Nancy C. Bormann, *Effective Small Group Communication* (Minneapolis, Minn.: Burgess, 1976), 48.

[108]Malcolm Knowles, *Introduction to Group Dynamics* (New York: Assocation Press, 1959), 45.

[109]Johnson and Johnson, *Joining Together*, 113.

[110]Tubbs, *A Systems Approach to Small Group Interaction*, 293.

[111]Johnson and Johnson, *Joining Together*, 234; Knowles, *Introduction to Group Dynamics*, 45.

[112]Rothwell, *In Mixed Company*, 62–3.

- *By developing a cooperative spirit.* When group members work together in cooperation rather than in competition, cohesiveness will likely flourish.
- *By promoting acceptance.* Group cohesiveness will in crease if members make efforts to make each other feel valued through praise and encouragement.

CATEGORIES OF SMALL GROUPS

Any number of types or varieties of groups can fit within the above criteria of small groups: a prayer group, a Bible study group, a bowling team, a church elders board, or a unit of Christian volunteers who work in a soup kitchen. However, almost all of them can be further classified into one of four categories based on the *primary* focus or central reason for which the Christian education group exists.[113] Most Christian education small groups can be classified as: (1) process-oriented, (2) content-oriented, (3) task-oriented, or (4) need-oriented.[114]

Of course, no group is purely a process-, content-, task-, or content-oriented group. But group members should clearly understand the intent of the group, so that the group operates in accordance with its reason for being.

The Process-Oriented Group

In this type of group, the primary focus is on *being* a group. What the group does, its format, is secondary to the emphasis placed on the dynamics of relationships and group identity.[115] Friendships and home fellowship groups fall into this category.

The Friendship or Contact Group: Friendship or contact groups are designed to establish relationships, with the group setting the pace or type of interaction. For example, a group of businessmen may meet for discussion over lunch or a group of home-school mothers might gather at a park

---

[113]McBride, *How to Lead Small Groups*, 65.

[114]Ibid.

[115]Ibid.

on Friday afternoons and interact with one another while their children are engaged in monitored activity. These groups may vary in size or regularity of meetings, perhaps weekly or biweekly. Invited individuals are given an opportunity to meet others, often peers with similar interests or needs, in an unstructured environment where relatively little is required of them. Spiritual depth may come at a later point particularly if group members indicate such an interest.[116]

Home Fellowship/Share Groups: Home share groups are going to have a strong emphasis on relationships and fellowship (*koinonia*). Hadaway, Wright, and DuBose describe them as "organized attempts to combat impersonal, bureaucratic structures that obstruct the building of intimate relationships and the practice of brotherly/sisterly love."[117] Bible study may or may not be on the agenda of the members of home share groups; they may simply meet to share personal issues, pray for one another, or simply to enjoy shared interests and activities. Singing and/or worship may also be a part of this type of group experience. Another criteria of the home share group is that it often functions without a designated leader. In terms of leadership, Ralph Neighbor gives the following advice to these types of small groups: "The best suggestion for leading a small group is: DON'T! Don't be the 'leader'; don't have a teacher; you may not even need an 'expert.' Let the Lord do the work through the entire group."[118] Clearly, the home fellowship group is concerned with the practice of the biblical principles of love and community, not the mere cognitive emphasis of study.[119]

---

[116]John Mallison, *Building Small Groups* (West Ryde, N.S.W., Australia: Renewal Publications), 38.

[117]C. Kirk Hadaway, Stuart A. Wright, and Francis M. Dubose, *Home Cell Groups and House Churches* (Nashville, Tenn.: Broadman, 1987), 89.

[118]Ralph Neighbor, *Touch of the Spirit* (Nashville: Broadman, 1972), 89.

[119]Hadaway, Wright, and Dubose, *Home Cell Groups and House Churches*, 89.

The Content-Oriented Group

This category includes a variety of Bible study, discussion, and learning groups. The primary purpose for meeting is to learn or better understand subject matter that is of mutual relevance and interest to group members. In addition to Bible content, content-oriented Christian education groups might study church or denominational history, theological or doctrinal themes, or current events and issues. Occasionally, a videotaped news documentary can serve as a useful focus for discussion.

Bible Study Groups: The primary activity of a Bible study group, naturally, is to study the Scriptures. However a Bible study group should never be limited to cognitive, cerebral activity alone. The value of studying the Bible without relating it to real life situations is limited and must be called into question.

The emphasis of effective Bible study should be the dynamic interaction between daily living and the Word.[120] For this reason, Bible study groups should also spend a portion of their time on other spiritual disciplines such as prayer, fellowship, and ministry.

Discussion Groups: While the major source of study for most Christian education and church groups ought to be the Bible, books that consider biblical, theological, historical, sociological, psychological, and political issues can also be used as starting points for discussion.[121] Groups might study the classical works by writers such as Thomas à Kempis or St. Augustine, or current authors such as Charles Colson, J.I. Packer, Henri Nowen, Howard Snyder, Anthony Campolo, or Billy Graham. Contemporary movies or plays may also be studied by having group members view the production, examine the message, and discuss personal reactions and insights.

---

[120]Plueddemann and Plueddemann, *Pilgrims in Progress,*127.

[121]Mallison, *Building Small Groups,* 39; John Mallison, *Creative Ideas For Small Groups in the Christian Community* (West Ryde, N.S.W., Aust.: Renewal Publications, 1978), 22–23.

The Task-Oriented Group

The task group exists primarily for the purpose of completing a job.[122] Tasks are performed in groups for a number of reasons: (1) one person alone may not be able to perform the task; (2) the group provides for a division of labor so that different skills and abilities might be utilized; (3) people often prefer to work in groups for social reasons; (4) the presence of others is encouraging or stimulating so more work is accomplished;[123] and (5) problem solving (critical thinking) and decision making (creative thinking) tasks are often better carried out by multiple minds. There are a number of task-oriented groups that are employed by churches and Christian education departments.

Committees: While the majority of people seem to disdain them, virtually every church and Christian education department has them. The universal contempt for this type of group is reflected in numerous jokes and stories. For example, there is the well-known quip that a camel is a horse designed by a committee. And there is Winston Churchill's sardonic definition of a committee: "A committee is the organized result of a group of the incompetent who have been appointed by the uninformed to accomplish the unnecessary." Well, like them or not, they are an integral part of organizational processes.

Committees are task-oriented small groups concerned primarily with decision making and problem solving.[124] Although interpersonal relationships are a consideration, they are usually not deemed as important as the task at hand, and are often seen as merely a means to an end.[125] The Plueddemanns challenge this assumption, however, and insist that committees see themselves as ministry teams who are committed to each other, as

---

[122]Michael Argyle, "Five Kinds of Small Social Groups," *Small Group Communication*, 7th ed., eds. Robert S. Cathcart, Larry A. Samovar, and Linda D. Henman (Dubuque, Iowa: Brown and Benchmark, 1996), 25–32.

[123]Ibid.

[124]Ibid., 29.

[125]Tubbs, *A Systems Approach to Small Group Interaction*, 109.

well as to the task. One way committees can become more fo-cused on interpersonal relationships and caring for one another is by beginning meetings with focused sharing and prayer.[126]

Longstanding Work Groups: Most organizations have long-standing work groups that have performed at high levels of productivity over the years to the point that their traditions, practices, and pride transcend the passage of time and per-sonnel changes.[127] For example, college or university trustee boards are often characterized as "good old boys" clubs that ooze tradition and operate by patterns of communication that have been handed down over the years. In the local church or parish, the governing board or board of elders may be consid-ered a longstanding work group, as well as the Christian education committee.

While work groups of this nature are usually productive (that is why they continue to exist or perform), they have cer-tain obvious weaknesses. Because tradition is such a powerful force in longstanding work groups (meetings take on ritualis-tic, almost legalistic proportions) often it is difficult, if not impossible, to introduce change. Change for the sake of effi-ciency is often met with resistance, partially because rich traditions may have to be dropped in the change process.[128]

Evangelistic Groups: A powerful way to share the Christian message to the unchurched is through evangelistic Bible study groups. Many people are interested in knowing about Jesus Christ and spiritual reality but are threatened by the church and wary of institutionalized religion. They may, however, go to someone's home to dialog and study the Bible.[129]

Bible study appeals to many people—certainly most Chris-tians. But non-Christians or unchurched people may often be less interested in it or even intimidated by it. Therefore an

---

[126]Plueddemann and Plueddemann, *Pilgrims in Progress*, 132–3.

[127]Cragan and Wright, *Communication in Small Groups*, 13–15.

[128]Ibid., 14.

[129]A helpful source for small-group evangelism or outreach is Richard Peace, *Small Group Evangelism* (Downers Grove, Ill.: Intervarsity Press, 1985).

outreach group might take a different approach such as discussing the topic "Who Is Jesus?" or "Does God Exist?" or other issues related to the meaning of life. Or a discussion might be based on a movie such as *Chariots of Fire* or *The Mission*.[130]

Small groups provide a number of advantages for evangelism:

- *They are nonthreatening.* They offer a safe environment for individuals who are uncomfortable in crowds or large groups.

- *They are personal.* For individuals who may feel lonely and insignificant, small groups provide a setting where they may receive care, concern, and recognition.

- *They allow maximum participation.* Each individual has the opportunity to ask questions, participate in the discussion, and share feelings and ideas.

- *They are flexible.* The length, time, and nature of the meeting can be varied to meet the needs and interests of various types of people. They can be designed to appeal to single adults, senior adults, married couples, or youth.

Ministry groups: While all small groups should provide opportunity for mutual ministry (that is, group members should be encouraged to minister to one another during meetings and between meetings),[131] there are some groups whose focus is on a particular ministry or outreach that extends beyond the group itself.[132] Members of ministry groups are interested and committed to both an "inward and outward journey."[133]

---

[130]For additional ideas, see Peace, *Small Group Evangelism*, 80.

[131]Icenogle, *Biblical Foundations for Small Group Ministry*, 335.

[132]Plueddemann and Plueddemann, *Pilgrims in Progress*, 132–3.

[133]Ibid., 131.

Outreach opportunities for ministry groups are unlimited. Groups may sponsor a refugee family, work in a soup kitchen or downtown mission, correspond with a missionary, or do prison or hospital ministry.[134] Ministry groups may also meet for weekly Bible study, prayer, personal sharing, and strategizing for the implementation of their ministry project.[135]

The Need-Oriented Group

Need-oriented or influence groups are made up of people who admit they need change in their lives and are willing to subject themselves to the scrutiny and support of other like-minded people. Encounter groups, growth groups, support groups, recovery groups, and spiritual formation groups fit into this category of Christian education groups.

The Encounter Group: Encounter groups, sometimes known as personal-growth groups, are intended to help relatively healthy people improve their ability to better function in society on an interpersonal level. While counseling and therapy groups are aimed at dealing with particular personality and behavioral problems, encounter groups seek to enable members to realize their full potential in patterns of thinking, feeling, and acting. The important guidelines or ground rules for encounter groups are that the participants be open and honest with one another, and focus on their feelings and perceptions rather than intellectualization. Most encounter groups share the following goals:[136]

- to develop more positive attitudes towards one's self,

---

[134]For helpful ideas on service and outreach projects read Anthony Campolo, *Ideas for Social Action* (El Cajon, Calif.: Youth Specialties, 1983).

[135]Plueddemann and Plueddemann, *Pilgrims in Progress,* 131.

[136]See Gerald Corey and Marianne Schneider Corey, *Groups: Process and Practice,* 3rd ed. (Pacific Grove, Calif.: Brooks/Cole, 1987),11, and Gerald Corey, *Theory and Practice of Group Counseling,* 2nd ed. (Pacific Grove, Calif.: Brooks/Cole, 1981), 11, for helpful descriptions of encounter groups.

- to improve one's interpersonal skills,

- to facilitate personality change,

- to transfer behavior and skills developed in the group to situations beyond the group.

The name most synonymous with encounter groups is Carl Rogers, who first used the group experience to prepare counselors for dealing with the problems of returning World War II GI's. His groups were oriented primarily toward personal growth, as well as the development of interpersonal communication and relationships.[137] Coming from a humanistic perspective, Rogers believes that all human beings have the tendency to move towards actualization or the realizing of their full capabilities. Rogers has developed eight hypotheses which tend to be held in common by most encounter groups:[138]

1. A climate of safety must be met before group members will freely express themselves and lower theirdefenses.

2. When a psychological climate of trust is established, members will begin to share their feelings about them selves and other group members.

3. A climate of mutual trust evolves out of the personal disclosures that have been made.

4. As defenses give way, risk taking develops. Possibilities of change in attitude and behavior become less threatening.

5. With a reduction in defensive thinking, individuals listen to each other and learn from one to another to a greater degree.

---

[137]Carl Rogers, *Carl Rogers on Encounter Groups* (New York: Harper and Row, 1970), 3-4.

[138]Summarized from Rogers, *Carl Rogers on Encounter Groups*, 6-7 and Jeremiah Donigan and Richard Malnati, *Critical Incidents in Group Therapy* (Monterey, Calif.: Brooks/Cole, 1987), 13.

6. A process of feedback develops as members become more open in sharing information about how they perceive one another.

7. Group members become more creative and imaginative with ideas and concepts. Innovation is desirable rather than threatening.

8. Members are expected to transfer these newly learned behaviors into relationships with their spouse, children, students, peers, and fellow workers.

The Growth Group: Similar in nature to the encounter group is the growth group. Like encounter groups, growth groups are instruments designed to help individuals discover who they are and use more of their latent resources.[139] Growth groups are somewhat broader in their nature including, according to Howard Clinebell, preparation for marriage groups, marriage enrichment groups, spiritual growth groups, and study groups that focus on intellectual and interpersonal growth.[140]

Clinebell defines a growth group as any group, whatever its name, with the following three characteristics:[141]

1. A dominant, though not exclusive, purpose is the personal growth of its members—emotional, interpersonal, intellectual, or spiritual.

2. Leadership style is growth-facilitating in nature.

3. The emphasis is on the here-and-now effectiveness in living, as well as future goals, rather than on past failures and problems.

A good growth group aims for a balanced emphasis on three dimensions—inreach, outreach, and upreach. Inreach refers to

---

[139]Howard Clinebell, *Growth Groups* (Nashville, Tenn.: Abingdon, 1977), 3.

[140]Ibid., 11.

[141]Ibid., 3.

one's personal awareness or coming alive to oneself. Outreach means relating to others in a responsible and responsive manner. Upreach refers to the vertical dimension of one's relationship to God.[142]

Growth groups that focus on spiritual disciplines, Christian character, and Christlikeness are often called *discipleship* groups. In these groups knowing the Bible is only part of the process. More important is developing a godly lifestyle or putting into practice what has been learned from studying the Word.

The Support Group: Support groups can be formed around any number of particular interests or needs and may also function as study, fellowship, or prayer groups. Lyman Coleman and Marty Scales specify support groups as those groups designed to allow participants to share experiences that they have in common. Support groups might be formed for individuals such as single parents, parents of adolescents or toddlers, single adults, men or women going through mid-life, retirees, individuals going through divorce, or people suffering grief or loss, to name a few.[143]

There is no single format that characterizes support groups. Some of these groups gather simply to discuss issues of common interest, while others spend large amounts of time in Bible study and prayer. But whatever the process or design of the small group, a common purpose is to offer emotional and spiritual support to group members. Often the supportive element of these groups is enhanced by interaction and socializing that occurs before and after the formal meeting time and between meetings.[144]

The Twelve-Step Recovery Group: A particular type of support group that has gained immense popularity in the 1980s and 1990s is the twelve-step recovery group. Recovery groups

---

[142]Ibid., 5.

[143]Lyman Coleman and Marty Scales, *Serendipity Training Manual For Groups* (Littleton, Colo.: Serendipity, 1989), 79.

[144]Wuthnow, *Sharing the Journey*, 69.

are made up of individuals who share a common need and are looking for a support system that will help alleviate their stress and give them the incentive to change their lives. Recovery groups are usually led by nonprofessionals who may in fact be struggling with the same issues as the group members, although they often involve professionals as guest speakers or consultants.[145]

The twelve steps to recovery used by many support groups today were formulated and published in 1939 by Bill Wilson. Wilson's purpose for identifying these steps was to help alcoholics overcome their dependency on alcohol. The organization he spawned was called Alcoholics Anonymous.

While Alcoholics Anonymous is pluralistic in nature and is tolerant of all religious beliefs, the twelve steps are drawn broadly from the Christian tradition, and many churches adopt the twelve-step program for their purposes. In addition to AA, twelve-step groups have emerged to assist people with a plethora of other addictions and dysfunctions. Other groups include Al-Anon (for family members of alcoholics), Adult Children of Alcoholics (ACOA), Narcotics Anonymous (NA), Overeaters Anonymous (OA), Co-Dependents Anonymous (CODA), and Anorexic Bulimics Anonymous.[146]

The Spiritual Formation Group: A particular type of growth group is the spiritual formation group. Corinne Ware of The Alban Institute argues for the need to facilitate spiritual growth or development in the context of a group, rather than by the individual direction approach. She identifies three significant objectives for the spiritual formation group. The first objective is to create an atmosphere for listening to the call of God on members' lives. The second objective is to serve as a safeguard against false notions of what spiritual formation really is. The

---

[145]Corey, *Theory and Practice of Group Counseling*, 15.

[146]See Wuthnow, *Sharing the Journey*, 429 for a helpful summary of resources on self-help recovery. See also Bill Morris, *The Complete Handbook for Recovery Ministry in the Church* (Nashville, Tenn.: Thomas Nelson, 1993).

third objective is to create a community of believers whose task is to accompany each other, rather than coerce or persuade.[147]

A typical spiritual formation meeting should last from ninety minutes to two hours and consist of four activities. The first group task is *quieting* the inner chaos and distractions brought from the exterior life. The next activity is *prayer* (and learning about prayer) followed by a time spent in *study* or inquiry into a matter of group interest. The group session comes to a close by again quieting and receiving a short *benediction*.[148] Group members are encouraged to practice a rule or particular *daily pattern* outside the context of group meetings. *Rule* is a medieval term for "a specific daily pattern for maintaining spiritual awareness."[149] Ware suggests that adopting the Benedictine emphasis on work as a gift from God, individualized *study* of the Scriptures or devotional books, involvement in the *community* of other believers, and daily personal practice of prayer is a good way to begin to develop a life pattern of spiritual formation.[150]

The Combination Group

As mentioned earlier, most groups are not purely of only one type. In fact, some strategies are clearly designed to incorporate combinations of task, relationship building, influence, and/or content acquisition. For example, Intervarsity Christian Fellowship, a Christian organization that works with students on university and college campuses, suggests the small-group experience include four components: *nurture* (influence), *worship* (task), *community* (relational), and *mission*

---

[147]Corinne Ware, *Connecting to God: Nurturing Spirituality through Small Groups* (Washington, D.C.: Alban Institute, 1997), 7.

[148]Ibid., 26–8.

[149]Ibid., 76.

[150]Ibid., 78–85. Two excellent sources on the spiritual disciplines are Richard J. Foster, *Celebration of Discipline* (San Francisco: HarperSanFrancisco, 1988) and Donald S. Whitney, *Spiritual Disciplines for the Christian Life* (Colorado Springs, Colo.: Navpress, 1991). Foster includes a helpful bibliography of recent works on spirituality.

(task).[151] Serendipity, a Christian organization that publishes small-group curricula and sponsors seminars on small groups, insists a good church-related small group includes relation building (relational), study (content), and mission (task). Cell groups and the uniquely Catholic Small Christian Communities (SCC) are excellent models of combination groups.

Cell Groups: Cell groups are significantly more than another small-group meeting or program. For those churches built on cell ministry, cells are the very heart of the church and do all the things a church does: equipping, discipleship, evangelism, prayer, and worship. A helpful understanding of cells is offered by Joel Comiskey who defines them as "evangelism-focused small groups that are entwined into the life of the church. They meet weekly to build up each other as members of the body of Christ, and to spread the gospel to those who don't know Jesus. The ultimate goal of each cell is to multiply itself as the group grows through evangelism and then conversions. This is how new members are added to the church and to the kingdom of God. Members of cell groups also are encouraged to attend the celebration service of the entire church, where cells come together for worship."[152] The only real difference between cell groups and house churches is that cell groups are always linked to a central church which provides supervision and sponsorship.[153]

While many types of small groups are closed or restricted to new members, such an approach is unthinkable in cell-based churches. Carl George emphatically exclaims, "The notion of group members shutting themselves off in order to accomplish discipleship is a scourge that will destroy any church's missionary mandate."[154]

Another important characteristic of cell groups is that they are generally led by lay house group pastors. As such, explains

---

[151]Barker et al., *Small Group Leader's Handbook*, 25–47.

[152]Joel Comiskey, *Home Cell Group Explosion* (Houston, Tex.: Touch Publications, 1998), 17.

[153]Hadaway, Wright, and Dubose, *Home Cell Groups and House Churches*, 95.

[154]Carl George, *Prepare Your Church for the Future* (Grand Rapids, Mich.: Baker, 1991), 99.

Comiskey, ministry is taken out of the hands of a chosen few and dispersed to many who will fulfill every biblical principle of pastoral ministry:[155]

- caring for the sheep (Ac 20:28–29);

- knowing the sheep (Jn 10:14–15);

- seeking the sheep (Lk 15:4);

- feeding the sheep (Ps 23:1–3);

- watching out for the sheep (Jn 10:10).

Small Christian Communities: A small-group model that has emerged in the Roman Catholic Church is the Small Christian Community (SCC). A type of cell group, the four essential elements of an SCC meeting are: (1) prayer, (2) faith-sharing, (3) support, and (4) continued learning. In addition, most groups stress the importance of members participating in some form of wider social outreach or ministry. SCCs are encouraged to limit the size of their group to eight to twelve members, meet in homes, and come together at least twice a month. Shared responsibility for the welfare of the group is encouraged, although there should be a pastoral facilitator who maintains the role of animating the meetings and maintaining a connection to the parish by liaising regularly with the parish priest.[156]

LIMITATIONS OF SMALL GROUPS

While it can be argued that small groups serve as a valid form of Christian education and provide multiple benefits for the church as a body, there are some limitations and potential pitfalls.Group hate, groupthink, false teaching, cliquishness, conflict, inappropriate self-disclosure, and self-centeredness are some possible drawbacks of small groups.

---

[155]Joel Comiskey, *Home Cell Group Explosion*, 56–8.

[156]John Paul Vandenakker, *Small Christian Communities and the Parish* (Kansas City, Mo.: Sheed and Ward, 1994), 162. 172–4.

Group Hate

Groups are inescapable; they are at the very core of our social organization. As Rothwell rightly observes, they are unavoidable unless one plans to live on an isolated island or alone in a cave.[157] But not everyone has an appreciation for small groups. Sociologists have coined the term "group hate" to describe how distasteful the small group or the small-group experience is for many people.[158] Sometimes individuals are thrown into groups and the particular mix of people may not be ideal. Others find groups boring and have trouble focusing on the topic. Bormann and Bormann detected some evidence of boredom with small groups on behalf of participants. They discovered that "whether the groups were composed of women in a Lebanese college, Japanese graduate students, university undergraduates, first-line managers at IBM, or educators in public health nursing, the average attention span for all groups was about one minute."[159] Apparently small-group participants, no matter what the nature of the group was, demonstrated a certain amount of disinterest or ambivalence.

But groups are here to stay, and while not everyone will come to love small groups, I believe Christian education groups (even committee meetings) can be highly productive and positive experiences. Like many other life opportunities and experiences, small groups are boring and ineffective when we do not know how to work and communicate effectively in this context. Small groups, however, can be more productive and enjoyable if we learn how to be skillful and competent small-group communicators.

Errant Teaching

Many pastors are concerned that small groups without professional leadership may go astray theologically or worse yet

---

[157]Rothwell, *In Mixed Company*, 2.

[158]Ibid., 3.

[159]Bormann and Bormann, *Effective Small Group Communication*, 132.

become splinter groups. Some clergy, suggests Wuthnow, fear that their authority will be undermined by small groups.[160] Certainly this is a real danger, but the same could be said for entire churches that are led astray by an authoritarian pastor.[161] A well-thought-out plan of recruiting and training reliable and trustworthy group leaders, as well as a strategy for holding leaders accountable to the pastoral staff or director of small groups, can significantly reduce the possibility of heretical groups forming. This can be done simply by meeting with small-group leaders on a regular basis and having them report on the nature of the content of the groups, as well as on the group's development.

Groupthink

A particular problem for highly cohesive groups is what has been earlier referred to as groupthink.[162] Once again, Wuthnow observes that clergy fear that small groups are avenues for turning individuals into conformists who blindly follow current trends and fads rather than being interested in the aggregate wisdom of religious traditions.[163] To refresh memories, groupthink is the tendency for groups to conform to a norm and avoid critical examination of all dimensions or aspects of a decision, issue, or problem the group is addressing.[164] In addition to highly cohesive groups, groups with members who are in high need for affiliation and groups with autocratic leadership are likely candidates for groupthink.[165]

---

[160]Wuthnow, *Sharing the Journey*, 28.

[161]Plueddemann and Plueddemann, *Pilgrims in Progress*, 84.

[162]Janis, *Groupthink*, 7–8.

[163]Wuthnow, *Sharing the Journey*, 27.

[164]Gloria J. Galanes and John K. Brilhart, *Communicating in Groups: Applications and Skills*, 3rd ed. (Madison, Wis.: Brown and Benchmark, 1997), 225.

[165]Tubbs, *A Systems Approach to Small Group Interaction*, 161; Janis, Groupthink. 7–8.

There are at least three primary symptoms of a group suffering from groupthink:[166]

- *The group has an illusion of invulnerability.* Group members believe they are not capable of making mistakes.

- *Group members are close-minded.* They have a preferred course of action that ignores the insights and arguments that contradict their preferences;

- *Group members are pressured to conform.*

There are a number of precautions a group can take to prevent groupthink. First, a group should always banter a problem around before settling on a solution or conclusion. Second, the group might assign one member to play "devil's advocate" during a particular meeting. Third, leaders should be careful not to reveal their preferences at the end or the beginning of the discussion so as not to unduly influence other group members. And finally, group members should be encouraged to gain insights from people and sources outside the group and introduce insights gained from these resources to the small-group thought process.

Inappropriate Self-Disclosure

Self-disclosure is the act of revealing something about one's self to another person or persons. While disclosure is a salient dimension of small-group communication and carries with it certain benefits, such as releasing stress or drawing group members closer together, inappropriate self-disclosure may be counter-productive. Self-disclosure is inappropriate when that which is disclosed is too revealing, too intimate, or harmful to another person. Small-group leaders can encourage members to be appropriate in their self-disclosing. Some questions to ask concerning the disclosure are: "Is the amount and type of disclosure appropriate?"; "Is the disclo-

---

[166]Cragan and Wright, *Communication in Small Groups*, 211; Galanes and Brilhart, *Communicating in Groups: Applications and Skills*, 225–6.

sure relevant to the situation at hand?"; and, "Will the effect be constructive?"

Cliques

Another possible danger of small groups is the formation of cliques. Some small groups may turn inward to find enjoyment and interpersonal satisfaction at the exclusion of outsiders or others who may want to be involved in a small group. To avoid exclusiveness, some groups place an empty chair in the circle, symbolically reminding everyone in the group that there is always room for one more member. Then when the group gets too large, a new small group is spawned.

Interpersonal Conflicts

Any time people (including Christians) meet together in close proximity, there is not only the risk, but the likelihood of conflict. Some people are too talkative or domineering, while others may be too critical or dramatic. Some simply lack commitment to the group, are irregular attendees, or are always late. Friction is inevitable.[167] However, while conflict is never desirable, the key to handling conflict is to make a commitment to positive results through effective conflict resolution and understanding that conflict can lead to growth. A group that allows itself to experience a certain amount of conflict can be a healthier group.[168]

Self-Centered Motives

There is some concern from critics of the small-group movement that small groups nurture a kind of self-centeredness. Social observers, says Wuthnow, are concerned that the movement may be contributing to a narcissistic obsession with self rather than encouraging or nurturing greater concern for others.[169] Wuthnow himself argues that one of the clearest limitations of small groups is their promotion of what

---

[167]Ibid., 85.

[168]Julie A. Gorman, *Community that Is Christian* (Wheaton, Ill.: Victor, 1993), 193.

[169]Wuthnow, *Sharing the Journey*, 27.

he calls a "me-first religion." This occurs as a by-product of focusing faith on individuals rather than on larger social or moral issues.[170] Warren Bird suggests that church related small groups may be more concerned with the emotional state of the individual than with true spiritual formation.[171] Theologian J.I. Packer adds that small groups are too often not thought of as a way of seeking God, but as a way of seeking Christian friends. In other words, the vertical axis is not emphasized as much as the horizontal axis.[172]

CONCLUSION

While small groups, such as family or work groups, have always constituted the basic fabric of life, intentionally formed small groups have become a powerful sociological force in North America. About 40 percent of American adults belong to some type of small group that meets on a regular basis. Furthermore, churches and Christian educators are increasingly employing small groups to make the spiritual life of church members more meaningful.

---

[170]Wuthnow, *I Come Away Stronger*, 356.

[171]Bird, "The Great Small-Group Takeover," 29.

[172]Quoted by Bird, "The Great Small-Group Takeover," 29.

2

Foundations of Small Groups

WHILE some people point enthusiastically to small groups as an effective format for doing Christian education and nurturing spiritual development, others view them suspiciously as another modern fad that is sweeping through our churches. But small groups are not simply a recent trend or another voguish effort on behalf of churches to succumb to the whims of people. While it is true that there is a small-group movement that has emerged at this particular moment in history, and while it is evident that Americans have acquired a distinctive appeal to them, small groups are neither new nor are they without sound bases.[1] They are built on strong biblical, historical, sociological, and educational foundations. This chapter will examine these foundations on which small groups and the small-group movement are established.

BIBLICAL FOUNDATIONS
While countless books have been written on the psychology and practice of small groups, relatively few efforts have emphasized the biblical and theological foundations for small groups and small-group ministry.[2] However, as it is with other

---

[1]Robert Wuthnow, *Sharing the Journey* (New York: Free Press, 1994), 31.

[2]Two refreshing exceptions are Gareth Weldon Icenogle, *Biblical Foundations for Small Group Ministry* (Downers Grove, Ill.: InterVarsity, 1994) and Julie A. Gorman, *Community that Is Christian* (Wheaton, Ill.: Victor, 1993). Neal F. McBride, *How to Lead Small Groups* (Colorado Springs, Colo.: NavPress, 1990) includes a chapter on the biblical foundations for small groups as well.

dimensions of church ministry or Christian education, it is of utmost importance that small groups find firm grounding in sound biblical and theological principles.

Old Testament Foundations

The basis for small groups and community can be initially detected in the Old Testament. While the Old Testament itself reflects no explicit theology of small groups or small-group community, interpersonal groups indeed existed during that time frame. The Hebrew household unit, care groups mobilized by Moses, and the nature of God all serve as helpful models for understanding small-group community.

The Family: The concept of small-group community is most clearly evidenced in the Old Testament through the children of Israel, God's chosen people. The idea and practice of groups was closely interwoven into the holistic structure of the individual and corporate identities and lives of Hebrew people. From the entire nation down to the smallest household unit, there was a large- and small-group mentality that permeated Israelite existence and social structure.[3]

The primary unit of social and territorial organization in ancient Israel was the tribe (*sebet*). The children of Israel, from the point of their sojourn into Egypt on, were divided into twelve tribes or subgroups, and membership in the tribes was based on one's descent from the twelve sons of Jacob (Ge 49).[4]

However, while an individual's tribal identity was of importance, particularly in wartime when military enlistment was based on tribal affinity, the tribe held the least amount of significance in terms of social relevance and kinship.[5] More

---

[3] C.J.H. Wright, "Family," in *The Anchor Bible Dictionary,* vol. 2, ed. David Noel Freedman (New York: Doubleday, 1992), 761–66.

[4] Wright, "Family," 761; Johs. Pedersen, *Israel: Its Life and Culture,* vols. 1–2, trans. Aslaug Moller (London: Oxford University, 1926), 30; Roland de Vaux, *The Early History of Israel,* trans. David Smith (Philadelphia: Westminister, 1978), 717–49.

[5] Wright, "Family," 761.

relevant to social and family structure were the further subdivisions of the clans (extended families) and households.

The clans (*mishpahah*), or family in the broader sense, were secondary groups of relatives who were a connecting link between the larger tribes and smaller households (Nu 2:34).[6] These clans were made up of descendants of the heads of the twelve tribes, often comprised of quite a large number of families. Numbers 26, for example, chronicles the clans according to their respective tribes, including the grandchildren and great-grandchildren of Jacob.[7] There was a commonality of interest and duties among clan members and individuals were cognizant of a bloodline between them, calling each other "brothers" (1Sam 20:29).[8]

The clans were then divided into a third level of kinship structure, an extended family of relatives (*bayit/be-tab*) living in the same household or dwelling. The household, or "father's house" (translated from the Hebrew), included the head of the house, his wife (or wives), his sons and their wives, his grandsons and their wives, as well as nonrelated dependents and servants. For example, Genesis 50:8 refers to the *household* of Joseph. The household was the core of the Israelite nation and heart of Hebrew society, and the unit in which the individual Hebrew felt the most powerful sense of security, inclusion, identity, and responsibility.[9]

Joshua 7:16–18 helps illustrate the organized society and social order of the nation of Israel. In this biblical account, Joshua goes through the process of detecting the sin of 7:16–18after the failure of the Israelites to capture Ai. First, the search was narrowed to the *tribe* of Judah, then to the *clan* or family of the Zerahites, and finally the *household* of Zimri. While

---

[6]Pedersen, *Israel: Its Life and Culture*, 46.

[7]C.F. Keil and F. Delitzsch, *Commentary on the Old Testament: Vol. III*, trans. James Martin (Grand Rapids, Mich.: Eerdmans, 1980 reprint), 208.

[8]Roland de Vaux, *Ancient Israel*, Vol. 1 (New York: McGraw-Hill, 1965), 19.

[9]Pedersen, *Israel: Its Life and Culture*, 46; de Vaux, *Ancient Israel*, 20; Wright, "Family," 762.

Achan was the grandson of Zimri and had children himself, he was still considered a part of the larger household of Zimri.

The home, or family unit, was the smallest of communities and the prototype of every other Hebraic community.[10] It was the center of religious instruction and the vehicle for passing on the faith, history, law, and traditions from generation to generation. It was the context whereby the father would give explanations to the children regarding particular events, institutions, or memorials. Significant occasions, such as the Passover Feast and the consecration of the firstborn son, were held in households, providing opportunities for the children to inquire about the meaning of the rituals; thus the family had significant pedagogical, as well as symbolic, implications.[11]

After the destruction of the Temple in Jerusalem (586 B.C.) and the scattering of the Jewish nation into exile, the Rabbis referred to the home as a *miqdash me'at* or "small sanctuary."[12] As a small sanctuary it was set aside for the worship of God, study of the Torah, and serving of community needs.[13] In no other ancient society was there such solidarity as was found in the early families of Israel—a community of father, mother, daughters, sons, brothers, sisters, grandparents, other kinsmen, and servants.[14]

How does the ancient Hebrew family unit serve as a helpful model of small-group community? The family, as John Macmurray rightly argues, is the original and most fundamental human community, the basis and origin of all community.[15]

---

[10]David J. Goldberg and John D. Rayner, *The Jewish People* (London: Penguin, 1989), 304.

[11]Wright, "Family," 764–5.

[12]This is not an Old Testament account, but rather a reference to Judaism of post Old Testament times. However, the home seen as a "small sanctuary" is a logical extention of the Hebrew "father's house" which preceded it.

[13]Marvin R. Wilson, *Our Father Abraham* (Grand Rapids, Mich.: Eerdmans, 1989), 214–16.

[14]Edith Deen, *Family Living in the Bible* (New York: Harper & Row, 1963), 20.

[15]John Macmurray, *Persons in Relation* (London: Faber and Faber, 1961), 155.

The aforementioned Hebrew word for family, *mishpahah*, refers not only the nuclear family, but implies the inclusion of extended family members. This clan was a social unit that included parents, children, aunts, uncles, cousins, and grandparents, a hallmark of family solidarity that has survived as a powerful Jewish custom to the present day. Marvin Wilson describes the community nature of the *mishpahah* this way: "The *mishpahah* is a group concept implying togetherness, not fragmentation or isolation. The strength and encouragement provided by the *mishpahah* and larger community is an important concept for the Church to consider today."[16]

With the virtual disappearance of the extended family and the decay and fragmentation of the nuclear family today, people increasingly feel a sense of estrangement and alienation. Furthermore, technological advances, while making life easier in some ways, contribute to individualism and isolation. Suburbanites cocoon themselves in their cars, offices, and home entertainment centers; increased job mobility separates spouses from each other and their children; children and teenagers sit passionately, often alone, in front of television sets, electronic game stations, and computers for hours on end. Consequently young and old alike often have the impression that no one cares for their well-being or is in any way concerned about them. Loneliness, insists Samuel Natale, is an epidemic of our culture with as many as 25 percent of the population experiencing acute loneliness.[17]

But no one, Wilson reminds us, is strong enough to make it through life alone or without support. The Hebrew concept of *mishpahah* reminds us of this biblical value of communal support which is so critical for the sustenance of contemporary society, as well as the church and home.[18] Robert Wuthnow concludes that most everyone in American society desperately

---

[16]Wilson, *Our Father Abraham*, 210.

[17]Samuel M. Natale, *Loneliness and Spiritual Growth* (Birmingham, Ala.: Religious Education Press, 1986), 1.

[18]Wilson, *Our Father Abraham*, 210–1.

desires community, but most have a difficult time finding the manner they would like it to be present in their lives. While neighborhoods and workplaces do not entirely satisfy individual needs for intimate sharing and caring, many people are looking to small group communities to satisfy their needs for inclusion, solidarity, and sanctuary.[19]

Moses and Small Groups: The first biblical account of a conscious effort to mobilize small groups as a strategy comes in Exodus 18:13–17, where Moses is counseled by his father-in-law, Jethro, to share the leadership responsibilities of judging disputes with others. After the exodus of the children of Israel from Egypt, and during the wanderings in the wilderness, the multitudes had quickly become dependent on Moses to be judge of disputes and expert in matters of justice. From morning until evening people lined up to plead their cases and have Moses settle their issues.

When Jethro observed the manner in which Moses took it upon himself to carry out this ministry as a lone, isolated figure, he inquired of Moses, "Why do you alone sit as judge, while all these people stand around you from morning till evening?" (Ex 18:14). Moses responded, "Because the people come to me to seek God's will. Whenever they have a dispute, it is brought to me, and I decide between the parties and inform them of God's decrees and laws" (vv. 15–17). Jethro wisely advised Moses that he would soon suffer what we today call "burnout" if he did not share the burden with other capable leaders.

Jethro then recommended that Moses implement a strategy of shared ministry and leadership, whereby he would choose and equip able men to be leaders over thousands, hundreds, fifties, and tens. "Have them serve as judges for the people at all times, but have them bring every difficult case to you; the simple cases they can decide themselves. That will make your load lighter, because they will share it with you" (v. 22). Jethro counseled his son-in-law to break the nation into smaller, workable units, so as to entrust able people with the

---

[19]Robert Wuthnow, *Sharing the Journey* (New York: Free Press, 1994), 54.

responsibilities of administration, counseling, supervision, and problem solving that would occur within these subdivisions.[20] In this system of large and small groups, needs were better met, burdens were shared, capable men were equipped for leadership, and a team ministry was implemented.

What implications does Moses' organizational structure have for Christian education small groups? While it cannot be denied that the framework of units Moses implemented were designed for the purpose of administrative efficiency, evident connections can be made to Christian education as well as church ministry in the broader sense.

First, just as breaking the nation of Israel down into manageable units intersected the entire framework of ancient Hebrew living, small groups must be regarded as essential, foundational building blocks of the contemporary church and, more specifically, Christian education. It is in the face-to-face ministry of small groups of three to twelve people that people are discipled, taught, cared for, and equipped for ministry. It is in small relational units that believers interact over God's Word, disclose vulnerabilities in their personal journey towards maturity and faithfulness in Jesus Christ, and intercede for each other in their growth towards spiritual maturity.[21]

Second, more than any other structure, small groups have the capacity to mobilize the laity toward ministry. A significant dimension of the Christian education task is equipping lay individuals to do the work of ministry, as the apostle Paul instructed in Ephesians 4:11–12. Just as Moses entrusted subunits (groups as small as ten) to able men, so too can pastors and Christian education directors enlist and equip qualified men and women who sense a call to these types of overseer ministries. Enlisting lay individuals to facilitate and lead small groups multiplies the number of shepherds in the church and releases pastors and Christian educators from the responsibil-

---

[20]Greg Ogden, *The New Reformation* (Grand Rapids, Mich.: Zondervan, 1990), 126–7.

[21]Ibid.

ity of carrying the burden of pastoral ministry and Christian education alone.[22]

The Nature of God: In a sense, a theological notion of small group community is conceived in the very nature of God himself. One might say that God exists as a small group. Icenogle proposes that "God is described as existing in divine community, in dialogue with other members of the God-self, an *intra*communicating group who also created humanity to exist in group intracommunication."[23]

Historically, the Christian church has understood God as triune, existing as three persons in one. Although the word *Trinity* is not itself a biblical term, there is likely no other dogma that is as widely accepted by Christians, in all their diversity, as is the Trinitarian doctrine.[24] The doctrine declares that in the one essence of the Godhead there are three distinct persons, the Father, the Son, and the Holy Spirit, who are, in all their individuality and uniqueness, still coequally and coeternally God.[25]

Scriptural records in the initial chapter of Genesis offer us hints by which one might infer plurality within the Godhead. In the creation account, God says "Let us make man in our image, in our likeness" (Ge 1:26). Christian theologians have regularly understood the plural pronouns as alluding to the triune nature

---

[22]Ibid.

[23]Icenogle, *Biblical Foundations for Small Group Ministry,* 21.

[24]While the earliest church fathers had no clearly articulated conception of the Trinity, the church took steps to formulate the doctrine of the Trinity in the 4th century. The Council of Nicea (A.D. 325) affirmed that the essence of the Son was identical to the Father and the Council of Constantinople (A.D. 381) completed the doctrine of the Trinity by asserting the deity of the Holy Spirit. See Charles Joseph Hefele, *A History of the Christian Councils* (Edinburgh: Clark, 1894/1972) and Louis Berkhof, *The History of Christian Doctrines* (Grand Rapids, Mich.: Baker, 1937/1975), 83–93. For an excellent historical treatment on the dogma of the Trinity from a Roman Catholic perspective, see Bertrand de Margerie, *The Christian Trinity in History* (Still River, Mass.: St. Bede's Publications, 1982).

[25]Wayne Grudem, *Systematic Theology* (Grand Rapids, Mich.: Zondervan, 1994), 227.

of God.[26] While no numbers are given, and there is by no means anything close to a complete doctrine of the Trinity offered, in this verse one may reasonably deduce, especially in light of New Testament teaching about the Trinity, that there is an involvement of more than one divine person.[27] Genesis 1:26, then, may well imply "counsel within the Trinity, God speaking with Himself."[28] There appears to be interaction and united effort on behalf of God in the creation of human beings. At the same time, there is suggestion of the presence of individual persons. The Bible indicates that during the creation process "the Spirit of God was hovering over the waters" (Ge 1:2); and the apostle

---

[26]St. Augustine [St. Augustine, *The Literal Meaning of Genesis*, trans. John Hammond Taylor (New York: Newman, 1982), 95] and Martin Luther [Martin Luther, "Lecutures on Genesis Chapters 1–5," in *Luther's Works, vol. 1*, ed. Jaroslav Pelikan (St. Louis: Concorida, 1958), 57] held to the view that *us* indicates plurality of the Godhead: the Father, Son, and Holy Spirit. While not quite as pointed in his reference to plurality, John Calvin implies it by suggesting that God entered into *consultation* with himself concerning His creation of humankind [John Calvin, *A Commentary on Genesis*, trans. John King (London: The Banner of Truth Trust, 1554/1965), 91]. According to Keil and Delitzsch the church fathers and early theologians held almost exclusively to the view that the plural "We" was indicative of the Trinity. Many modern commentators, including Keil and Delitzsch themselves, regard the plurality as a *pluralis majestis*. This interpretation "comprehends in its deepest and most intensive form (God speaking of Himself and with Himself in the plural number. . . with reference to the fullness of the divine powers and essences which He possesses) the truth that lies at the foundation of the Trinitarian view. . . ." [C. F. Keil and F. Delitzsch, *Commentary on the Old Testament, Vol. I*, trans. James Martin (Grand Rapids, Mich.: Eerdmans, 1980 reprint), 62]. Nonetheless, Ray Anderson cautions against inferring from plurality a Trinitarian concept of God. However, he goes on to suggest that "there is at least an intentional correspondence in this text between the intrinsic plurality of human being as constituted male and female and the being of God in whose likeness and image this plurality exists. . . . It is thus quite natural and expected that God himself is also a 'we.'" [Ray Anderson, *On Being Human* (Grand Rapids, Mich.: Eerdmans, 1982), 73].

[27]Grudem, *Systematic Theology*, 227.

[28]Loraine Boettner, *Studies in Theology*, 8th ed. (Philadelphia, Pa.: Presbyterian and Reformed, 1967), 98.

Paul, in his letter to the Colossians, reminds his readers that the Son created all things (Col 1:16).

The notion of plurality within the Godhead is similarly suggested in other verses in Genesis (italics added):

> "The man has become like one of *us,* knowing good and evil" (Ge 3:22).

> "Come, let *us* go down and confuse their language so they will not understand each other" (Ge 11:7).

> "Whom shall I send? And who will go for *us?*" (Isa 6:8).

However, one is compelled to go to the New Testament to find explicit evidence for interaction among the Father, Son, and Holy Spirit. Consider the following passages that illustrate dialogue and interrelationship within the Trinity:

> "But I tell you the truth: It is for your good that I am going away. Unless I go away, the Counselor will not come to you; but if I go, I will send him to you" (Jn 16:7).

> "He will bring glory to me by taking from what is mine. . . . That is why I said the Spirit will take from what is mine and make it known to you" (Jn 16:14–15).

> "After Jesus said this, he looked toward heaven and prayed: 'Father, the time has come. Glorify your Son, that your Son may glorify you'" (Jn 17:1).

> "I have revealed you to those whom you gave me out of the world. They were yours; you gave them to me and they have obeyed your word. Now they know that everything you have given me comes from you. For I gave them the words you gave me and they accepted them. They knew with certainty that I came from you, and they believed that you sent me" (Jn 17:6–8).

> "Therefore God exalted him to the highest place and gave him the name that is above every name. . . . " (Phil 2:9).

As we seek to establish a theological reference for small groups it is helpful to fashion a concept of God, who operates and exists in a social relationship.[29] There is undeniable evidence that the divine "group" portrays interdependence and community, and exemplifies communication and cooperation in mission.[30] Indeed the Trinity models for us the essential concept of relationships within a group and "is brought to bear on the relation of men and women to God, to other people and to mankind as a whole."[31]

Jurgen Moltmann declares that "the three divine Persons exist in their unique natures in relationship to one another and, in fact, are determined through these relationships. It is in these relationships that they are persons. Being a person in this respect means existing-in-relationship."[32] The eminent neo-orthodox theologian Karl Barth, in his *Church Dogmatics*, likewise observes that God himself exists in relationships and not in isolation.[33] Following Barthian thought, Ray Anderson suggests that "God exists as a being who encounters and relates to himself."[34] John Macquarrie, arguing from the fact that the Hebrew word for God, *Elohim*, is a plural form, suggests

---

[29]Gorman, *Community That Is Christian*, 28.

[30]Icenogle, *Biblical Foundations for Small Group Ministry*, 22; Gorman, *Community That Is Christian*, 25.

[31]Jurgen Moltmann, *The Trinity and the Kingdom*, trans. Margaret Kohl (San Francisco: Harper & Row), 19.

[32]Ibid., 172.

[33]Karl Barth, *Church Dogmatics*, vol. 3.4 (Edinburgh: Clark, 1961), 117.

[34]Anderson, *On Being Human*, 73–4. Anderson notes that the doctrine of *imago Dei* does not play a very important part in the Bible; it does, on the other hand, emerge as a critical issue for theologians. For a concise, but helpful, historical survey of interpretation and thought of *imago Dei*, see his appendix (215–26). For additional sources on this doctrine see Karl Barth, *Church Dogmatics*, vol. 1 (Edinburgh: Clark, 1977), 238–40; Emil Bruner, *The Christian Doctrine of Creation and Redemption*, vol. 2 (Philadelphia: Westminster), 44–5, 57–61, 75–8; Walter Eichrodt, *Theology of the Old Testament*, vol. 2 (Philadelphia: Westminster, 1967), 122–31; and Hans Walter Wolff, *Anthropology of the Old Testament* (Philadelphia: Fortress, 1974), 159–65.

that in the one God there is something analogous to social existence.[35]

This biblical notion of a relational God provides for us, as Gorman puts it, "a paradigm for living and ministering as His people who resemble Him in community."[36] Stan Grentz argues that the part of the Genesis narrative that says "Let us make man in our image" implies that humans in relationship with one another mirror the divine image in a manner that solitary individuals are incapable of doing.[37] Ray Anderson adds that it is through encounter and relationships with other individuals that we bear the *imago Dei*.[38]

Contemporary Christian educators and small-group participants should recognize that our own use of groups and our need for community, to a certain extent, is a logical extension of the fact that God exists in the divine form of a small group.[39] And because God is community, we are in the image of God only as we participate with and enjoy the community of others; as we exist in fellowship with one another we reflect, or show evidence, of what God is like.[40] Consequently, one of the primary reasons for meeting in small groups is to build and nurture community and meaningful interpersonal relationships.[41] In fact it must be accentuated that relationships be at the heart of every type of Christian education small group.

New Testament Foundations

The New Testament provides sound theological foundations, as well as concrete models, for small groups. These

---

[35]John Macquarrie, *In Search of Humanity* (New York: Crossroad, 1983), 85.

[36]Gorman, *Community That is Christian*, 28.

[37]Stanley J. Grenz, *Created for Community*, 2nd ed. (Wheaton, Ill.: Bridgepoint, 1996), 79.

[38]Anderson, *On Being Human*, 74.

[39]McBride, *How to Lead Small Groups*, 14.

[40]Grenz, *Created for Community*, 79–80.

[41]Icenogle, *Biblical Foundations for Small Group Ministry*, 25.

models, or prototypes, include Jesus and His small group and the early church house groups.

THEOLOGICAL FOUNDATIONS: There are a number of theological principles found in the New Testament writings which seem to suggest or imply the need for intimate, relational gatherings or small-group communities. These foundations include:

1. the call to practice genuine fellowship,

2. the responsibility to demonstrate mutual care and concern for one another, and

3. the necessity of spiritual gifts in the community life of the church.

It must be clearly emphasized that while these principles are no doubt a call to Christian living and church community in the broader sense, it is maintained that they are best learned and lived out in the context of small groups. It is in small, intimate groups that Christians learn to practice meaningful fellowship, engage in caring acts of concern for one another, and exercise the spiritual gifts the Holy Spirit has given each believer.

The call to genuine fellowship: Fellowship is very much in vogue in churches today, yet there are those who feel the church is missing the New Testament ideal of what it really is. British author and theologian John Stott, for example, says that fellowship "seldom means more than a genial friendliness, what Methodists call a 'P.S.A.' (Pleasant Sunday Afternoon), or a good gossipy get-together over a nice cup of tea. As a result, we fall sadly short of the rich, deep, full fellowship envisaged in the New Testament."[42] John MacArthur adds, "There is much phony fellowship today, people getting together on all kinds of pretenses. This is not true Christian fellowship."[43]

---

[42]John R. Stott, *One People* (Harrisburg, Pa.: Christian Publications, 1982), 79.

[43]John MacArthur, *Body Dynamics* (Wheaton, Ill: Victor, 1982), 130.

What then is genuine fellowship? The basis for Christian fellowship is found in the Greek word *koinonia,* which embodies the idea of community and communion, or having a common ground.[44] At least two features stand out. First, there is what we share *in* together, our common inheritance. The grounds for true Christian fellowship is found in 1 John 1:3, which says, "We proclaim to you what we have seen and heard, so that you also may have fellowship with us. And our fellowship is with the Father and with his Son, Jesus Christ." *Koinonia* denotes accord and oneness brought about by the work and presence of the Holy Spirit.[45]

Second, *koinonia* is not only a sharing in, it is a sharing *with,* the nature of which is evidenced in the early church and described by the writer of Acts: "They devoted themselves to the apostles' teaching and to the fellowship, to the breaking of bread and to prayer. Everyone was filled with awe, and many wonders and miraculous signs were done by the apostles. All the believers were together and had everything in common. Selling their possessions and goods, they gave to anyone as he had need. Every day they continued to meet together in the temple courts. They broke bread in their homes and ate together with glad and sincere hearts, praising God and enjoying the favor of all people. And the Lord added to their number daily those who were being saved" (Ac 2:42–47).

In this newly formed community they had all things in common. In other words, they shared with each other that which they possessed.[46] This fellowship of giving and receiving took place primarily in the homes of the believers, groups of people who met together as a small community for shared prayer,

---

[44]John Paul Vandenakker, *Small Christian Communities and the Parish* (Kansas City, Mo.: Sheed and Ward, 1994), 5.

[45]J. Schattenmann, "Fellowship," in *The International Dictionary of New Testament Theology,* vol. 1, ed. Colin Brown (Grand Rapids, Mich.: Zondervan, 1975), 639-44.

[46]Fredrick J. Cwiekowski, *The Beginnings of the Church* (New York: Paulist, 1988), 77.

worship, the teaching of the Apostles, partaking in the Eucharist, and voluntary sharing of goods.

A true understanding of New Testament *koinonia* warrants a reflective look at how fellowship can and should be an expression of small groups in contemporary Christian education. If Christian *koinonia* is the bond which connects believers not only to Christ, but to each other, as William Barclay rightly indicates, how can fellowship be made a critical dimension of all Christian education small groups?[47] John Stott suggests a threefold ideal small groups should seek to fulfill in regards to fellowship. First, he advises every group concerned with *koinonia* to seek to give expression to, deepen, and enrich the shared life which members enjoy—a common Christian inheritance. The primary means to this end is reading of the Scriptures and prayer.[48] Second, fellowship groups should endeavor to balance "sharing in" with "reaching out." For example, they might engage in prayerful intercession for the world. Third, there must be a sharing with one another: loving, caring, knowing, and bearing responsibility for each other's burdens.[49]

The responsibility of mutual care and concern: Much of the New Testament is concerned with relationships, especially the responsibility we have one for another. This is reflected in the numerous "one another" verses found scattered throughout the New Testament Scriptures, some of which are identified below:

"Be devoted. . . .Honor one another above yourselves" (Ro 12:10).

"Accept one another" (Ro 15:7).

---

[47]William Barclay, *New Testament Words* (Philadelphia: Westminster, 1974), 173.

[48]In groups that are not Bible study classes, be careful that Scripture reading does not dominate the hour. It is not the leader's responsibility to lecture the group, but rather to enable the group participants to focus on Christ together through the reading of His Word.

[49]Stott, *One People,* 93–7.

"Care for one another" (1Co 12:25, NRSV).

"Bear one another's burdens" (Gal 6:2, NRSV).

"Forgiving each other" (Eph 4:32).

"Encourage . . . and build each other up" (1Th 5:11).

"Spur one another on toward love and good deeds" (Heb 10:24).

"Confess your sins to . . . and pray for each other" (Jas 5:16).

"Serve others" (1Pet 4:10).

"Love one another" (1Jn 4:11).

While these "one anothers" might be worked out in a variety of settings or situations, an ideal format for their expression is the small group. The small-group context naturally stresses caring, interpersonal relationships in an informal setting. The level of Christian life depicted in the "one anothers," reasons Howard Snyder, require frequent intimate gatherings. These passages seem to suggest, he advises, frequent gatherings for encouraging one another apart from the corporate worship celebration of the church. They point to times of meeting in smaller groups for nurture, discipline, and interpersonal contact among believers.[50] The small-group context provides ideal opportunities for these types of expression that evidence the outworkings of mutual care and concern.

The necessity of spiritual gifts in the community life of the church:[51] Spiritual gifts are manifestations of God's grace (*charisma*) in the lives of individual Christians for the life of the community.[52] It is important to note that the word *charisma* is

---

[50]Howard A. Snyder, *Liberating the Church* (Downers Grove, Ill.: InterVarsity, 1983), 87.

[51]Ibid., 89.

[52]H.H. Esser, "Grace," in *The International Dictionary of New Testament Theology,* vol. 2, ed. Colin Brown (Grand Rapids, Mich.: Zondervan, 1975), 115–24.

derived from the Greek noun *charis*, which means "grace."[53]
Snyder describes these gifts as God's grace working through
the personalities of believers, preparing and enabling them for
their unique and particular ministries, in order that the church
may be built up, that the kingdom of God may be established,
and that God may be glorified in all that is said and done.[54]

The key New Testament passages that deal with spiritual
gifts are Ephesians 4:4–16, Romans 12, and 1 Corinthians 12,
which identify gifts such as prophecy, service, teaching, exhor-
tation, wisdom, discernment, speaking in tongues, and the
interpretation of tongues. In each of the accounts a twofold
emphasis on unity and diversity is apparent. For example, in
Ephesians 4 the apostle Paul teaches that there is "one body
and one Spirit" (v. 4), quickly speaks of the variety of gifts (vv.
11–12), and then concludes his thoughts by describing a whole
body which, nonetheless, is comprised of a variety of parts (v.
16). In 1 Corinthians 12, Paul intertwines pictures of unity
and diversity: "There are different kinds of gifts, but the same
Spirit. There are different kinds of service, but the same Lord.
There are different kinds of working, but the same God works
all of them in all men" (vv. 4–6). And in Romans 12 he similarly exhorts, "Just as each of us has one body with many
members, and these members do not all have the same function, so in Christ we who are many form one body, and each
member belongs to all the others" (vv. 4–5).[55]

One of the salient principles gleaned from the key passages
on spiritual gifts is that they are dispensed for the benefit of
the Christian community and service of the church—they are
not apportioned for personal gain.[56] As spiritual gifts are recognized by individuals and put into practice by each member

---

[53]James Montgomery Boice, *Foundations of the Christian Faith* (Downers
Grove, Ill.: InterVarsity, 1986), 608.

[54]Snyder, *Liberating the Church*, 89.

[55]Boice, *Foundations of the Christian Faith*, 606–7.

[56]Ralph P. Martin, "Spiritual Gifts," in *The Anchor Bible Dictionary*, Vol.
2, ed. David Noel Freedman (New York: Doubleday, 1992), 1015–8.

of the church community, the body grows in unity and love. These gifts are nurtured and manifested in the church in at least three ways: (1) through teaching concerning the gifts of the Spirit, (2) when there is an expectation of God to awaken the gifts in the life of the congregation, and (3) as they grow out of the community life of the church. Thus, it is imperative that the church involve its members in various forms of small-group structures so that community can be nurtured and spiritual gifts can spring forth.[57]

JESUS AND HIS SMALL GROUP: One of the most persuasive rationales for implementing small groups in the Christian education program of the local church or parish is modeled by the earthly ministry of Jesus and His band of disciples. Jesus' activity was centered around a quintessential group of twelve men whom He chose to be with Him, to learn from Him, and to minister with Him.[58] Neal McBride suggests that all you need to know about Jesus as a small-group leader can be summarized in seven statements.[59]

First, *Jesus began His expanded earthly ministry by establishing His small group* (Mt 4:18–22; Mk 1:16–20). "Follow me," Jesus said to the fishermen brothers Simon Peter and Andrew, "and I will make you fishers of men" (Mt 4:19). With this brief summon, our Lord Jesus embarked on a new phase of ministry. The selection of the twelve disciples was a significant marker in the public ministry of Jesus, dividing it into two

---

[57]Snyder, *Liberating the Church,* 157.

[58]A number of authors have endeavored to draw a picture of the twelve disciples of Christ. These include the following: Alexander Balman Bruce, *The Training of the Twelve* (Grand Rapids, Mich.: Kregel, 1871/1988); William Barclay, *The Master's Men* (New York: Abingdon, 1959); William P. Barker, *Twelve Who Were Chosen* (Old Tappan, N.J.: Fleming H. Revell, 1957); William Sanford LaSor, *Great Personalities of the New Testament* (Westwood, N.J.: Fleming H. Revell, 1961); George Matheson, *Portraits of Bible Men* (Grand Rapids, Mich.: Kregel, 1987 reprint); Asbury Smith, *The Twelve Christ Chose* (New York: Harper & Brothers, 1958); James S. Stewart, *The Life and Teaching of Jesus Christ* (New York: Abingdon, n.d.), 55–63.

[59]McBride, *How to Lead Small Groups,*16–17.

relatively equal periods of time.[60] For roughly a year-and-a-half to two years, Jesus chose to remain in relative obscurity, laboring single-handedly, confining His miraculous works and ministry to a limited area, and restricting His ministry primarily to one-on-one encounters.

But after the unfriendly reception He encountered at His hometown of Nazareth (Lk 4:16–29), Jesus moved to the city of Capernaum and launched an expanded public ministry. By this time His ministry was taking on ever-growing proportions and the magnitude of followers was increasing rapidly. A.B. Bruce suggests that the numbers had likely multiplied to the point that they were an encumbrance and impediment to His movements and that it was virtually impossible for all who believed to follow Him in the literal sense.[61] In response to this sudden outgrowth, Jesus enlisted able men who would bear witness to Him, come alongside Him and assist Him in His task, and eventually carry out the ministry of the Gospel after His Ascension.[62]

With the selection of the Twelve, Jesus models for us a small-group approach that is a key instructional strategy for Christian education ministry.[63] Like Moses, who discovered it was virtually impossible to meet the needs of the children of Israel as a lone leader, Jesus anticipated the difficulties of teaching and ministering to the masses single-handedly. In response, He selected a small group of men who would be with Him at all times. They were, however, to be more than traveling companions. In the words of Bruce, "From the time of their being chosen, indeed the twelve entered on a regular apprenticeship for the great office of apostleship, in the course of which they were to learn, in the privacy of an intimate daily fellowship with their Master, what they should be, be-

---

[60]Bruce, *The Training of the Twelve*, 29.

[61]Ibid.

[62]Robert E. Coleman, *The Master Plan of Evangelism* (Old Tappan, N.J.: Fleming H. Revell, 1986), 21.

[63]Icenogle, *Biblical Foundations for Small Group Ministry,* 118.

lieve, and teach, as His witnesses and ambassadors to the world."[64]

It is in this particular Christian education context that we are able to identify a critical precept of instruction. It is what Robert Coleman calls the "principle of concentration." He describes it this way: "One can not transform a world except as individuals in the world are transformed, and individuals cannot be changed except as they are molded in the hands of the Master. The necessity is apparent not only to select a few layman, but to keep the group small enough to be able to work effectively with them."[65] Clearly, Jesus proportioned His time to those He wanted to instruct and equip for ministry. And this graphically depicts a fundamental principle of religious teaching, that all else being equal, the smaller the size of group being instructed, the greater the possibility for effective Christian education and equipping for ministry.[66]

Second, *Jesus ministered in the context of both small and large groups, as well as to individuals.* One would be in gross error to conjecture that in spending more time with a few, Jesus ignored either the masses or needy individuals.

The Gospels record that even after He recruited and commissioned the Twelve for ministry, He continued to teach the multitudes and to maintain a popular following to the end. Here are just a few examples of Jesus extending himself to the crowds:

- Jesus preaches the Sermon on the Mount to the multitudes (Mt 5:1–18).

- Jesus speaks parables to the masses from a boat (Mt 13:1–52).

- Jesus goes about the villages and cities teaching, proclaiming the gospel, and healing the sick. He expresses compassion for the multitudes because they are

---

[64]Bruce, *The Training of the Twelve*, 30.

[65]Coleman, *The Master Plan of Evangelism*, 24.

[66]Ibid., 26–7.

"harassed and helpless, like sheep without a shepherd" (Mt 9:35–36).

- He feeds the five thousand men, plus women and children, by miraculously multiplying five loaves of bread and two fish (Mt 14:15–21).

- He feeds four thousand men, plus women and children, with seven loaves of bread and a few fish. In this encounter Jesus shows compassion for the multitude because they have been with Him for three days with nothing to eat (Mt 15:32–38).

- On the triumphal entry of Jesus into Jerusalem, prior to His crucifixion, a great number of people spread their cloaks on the road, set forth branches before Him, and shout, "Hosanna to the Son of David! Blessed is he who comes in the name of the Lord! Hosanna in the highest!" (Mt 21:1–11).

However, Jesus did not find the end of His mission either in teaching the masses or discipling the Twelve. Throughout His public ministry Jesus was also careful to receive and seek out individuals, address their personal needs, and adapt His teaching style to the uniqueness of each person.[67] Herman Horne, in his excellent book on the teaching techniques of Jesus, reminds us that Christ cared more for individuals than crowds, and suggests that He spoke to the masses, perhaps, so that He might reach the individuals.[68]

Here are just a few examples of Christ extending himself to individuals:

- Jesus graciously receives Nicodemus, a devout Pharisee and leader of the Jews, and converses openly with him (Jn 3:1–21).

---

[67]Jeffrey James, *The Personal Ministry of the Son of Man,* 3d ed. (Cincinnati, Ohio, n.d.), 9.

[68]Herman Harrell Horne, *The Teaching Techniques of Jesus* (Grand Rapids, Kregel, 1920/1976), 205.

- Jesus engages himself in dialogue with the Samaritan woman who came to draw water from the well. He was ambivalent to the custom of the day that respectable men did not talk to women in public, nor Jews to the "half-breed" Samaritans (Jn 4:5–26).[69]

- He heals the royal official's son (Jn 4:46–54).

- He heals Peter's mother-in-law (Mt 8:14–17).

- He heals the leper, warning him not to tell anyone (Mt 8:2–4).

- Jesus brings to life the only son of a widow. When the Lord sees her He feels compassion for her and urges her not to weep. A sizable crowd is with her and begins glorifying Jesus (Lk 7:11–17).

- The disciples rebuke parents for bringing their children to Jesus, but Christ welcomes the little ones, saying: "Let the little children come to me and do not hinder them, for the kingdom of heaven belongs to such as these" (Mt 19:14).

It was not the intent of Jesus to set one strategy of instruction against the other or work exclusively in one context of Christian education. Likewise, the Christian educator should discern multiple purposes wrought by this three-fold approach to religious instruction. In teaching the multitudes, Jesus was delivering the gospel of the kingdom to the souls of men, women, and children. In enlisting and equipping the disciples, He was providing for the future of the church and ensuring that the Gospel message would continue to be proclaimed after His departure from this world.[70] And by touching the lives of particular people, He demonstrated a personalization of

---

[69] Rick Yount, "Jesus, the Master Teacher," in *The Teaching Ministry of the Church,* ed. Daryl Eldridge (Nashville, Tenn.: Broadman & Holman, 1995), 21–42.

[70] Henry Latham, *Pastor Pastorum* (Cambridge: Deighton Bell, 1901), 226.

ministry and an effort to meet the unique needs of individuals. To Jesus, personal relationships were a critical dimension of ministry.

Third, *the ministry of Jesus to large groups was usually preceded by, and proceeded out of, the context of the small group.* In discerning why Jesus commissioned a group of twelve, one motive is often passed over quickly, if not completely overlooked. Mark, in fact, offers two reasons for the appointment of the disciples. One is that they might preach and have authority to drive out demons. The other (and the one mentioned first), however, is "that they might be with Him" (Mk 3:14). This is a key phrase that helps us understand the strategy of Jesus, but one that may elude the casual reader. Why did the Master need the company and fellowship of other men? Why did the Creator of the universe, the second person of the Trinity, choose not to endure the rigors of His earthly ministry alone? It is at this juncture we must give recognition to the humanness of Jesus. Being human himself, He needed fellowship and human love. And while much of His public ministry was spent under the pressure of great crowds, the masses could not satisfy His need for the fellowship of a close community.[71] James Stewart describes the solace and support the Twelve provided: "Often when the world outside had been showing itself callous and hostile and contemptuous, often when the day had brought him sneers that stung or a studied indifference that was like a blow in the face, he would turn back at nightfall with a great relief to these twelve men who for all their faults and bungling did love him and did believe in him."[72]

A number of Gospel accounts describe scenarios whereby Jesus either retreated from the masses to be alone with His disciples or where their time together preceded large-group ministry:

- Jesus withdraws to the Sea of Galilee with His disciples; a great multitude follows them (Mk 3:7–12).

[71]Smith, *The Twelve Christ Chose*, 5.

[72]Stewart, *The Life and Teaching of Jesus Christ*, 57.

- Jesus leaves the multitudes and retreats to a house where He explains the meaning of certain parables to His disciples (Mt 13:36).

- Jesus tours Galilee with His disciples, going from one city and village to another, proclaiming and preaching the kingdom of God (Lk 8:1–3).

- Jesus withdraws with the disciples to Bethsaida to rest awhile (Mk 6:31–34; Lk 9:10–11).

- After feeding the four thousand, Jesus sends the multitudes away and gets into a boat with the disciples (Mk 8:10–12).

- Jesus and the disciples share the Passover meal in the upper room (Mt 26:17–29).

- Jesus brings His disciples to the Garden of Gethsemane to pray with Him, but they fall asleep (Mt 26:36–46).

Leaders are often the loneliest of people. Of his position as president of the United States, it is said that Harry Truman lamented, "This is a lonely job. Everybody who comes to see me wants me to do something for him. No one comes to me for fellowship."[73] In recognition of His need for human fellowship and encouragement, Jesus chose twelve men who would serve as His "support group." As that, they were often frail in their ability to provide helpful community for Him and were sometimes anything but supportive—He had to rebuke Peter at least once (Mk 8:33); they argued amongst themselves over who was greatest in the eyes of their Master (Mk 9:34); they fell asleep on Him in the Garden of Gethsemane when He needed their support the most (Lk 22:45); Judas literally betrayed Him to His enemies (Lk 22:47–48); and Peter denied Jesus three times shortly before His crucifixion (Lk 22:54–61). Nonetheless, these were the men whom Jesus chose to "be with Him" through all the pressures, burdens, and demands ministry placed on Him.

---

[73] Quoted by Smith, *The Twelve Christ Chose*, 5.

There is a profound lesson here for Christian educators, indeed for leaders of all types. If it was essential for Jesus, the master teacher, to surround himself with a support group, how much more critical for men and women who are entrusted with the ministries of teaching and leading to encircle themselves with others who are capable of providing support and encouragement? No individual, however capable or gifted, has the ability to reach his or her capacity in isolation from others; every individual must benefit from the action and reaction of supportive others.[74]

Fourth, *Jesus spent the majority of His time with His small group of disciples.* If one could somehow log the hours Jesus toiled with the Twelve, it would be discovered that He clearly shared more of His time with them than anyone else on the face of the earth. In fact, the personal attention He gave them was so overwhelmingly more than that given to others, one can only conclude it was a deliberate instructional strategy.[75] They ate together and walked the long, dusty roads in the company of one another. Jesus involved them in active ministry with Him; He explained truths to them that He withheld from the masses; they prayed together in the desert and mountains; they sailed and fished the Sea of Galilee together; and He retreated to quiet places with them. And as His crucifixion drew near, His time with the Twelve intensified, while He spent less and less time with the multitudes.

The Christian educator must ponder why Jesus gave priority to so few. Had He not quickly amassed a good-sized following after His pronouncement by John the Baptist? And could He not have multiplied that following into thousands if He had so chosen to focus more attention on the multitude? Why did He trade a potentially successful ministry to the masses for intensified time with a few men who often evidenced little potential for greatness and habitually disappointed Him?

---

[74]Ibid.

[75]Coleman, *The Master Plan of Evangelism*, 43.

Once again, the insights of Coleman are helpful in understanding the manner of Jesus' actions. He reminds us that Jesus was not simply trying to appeal to the masses or impress the crowds. Rather, it was His intent to usher in a kingdom[76] (Mk 1:15; Mt 12:28), and this meant that He needed able men who could lead and provide direction for the incalculable number of followers to come. "Hence," Coleman explains, "He concentrated himself upon those who were to be the beginning of this leadership. Though He did what He could do to help the multitudes, He had to devote himself to a few men, rather than the masses, in order that the masses could at last be saved. This was the genius of His strategy."[77]

Fifth, *human relationships, rather than organizations, were central in His ministry and method of Christian education.* Jesus formed no local church, though His disciples later did so, and He headed up no educational institute. Rather, as a practical demonstration of the gospel, Jesus chose to spend most of His time with people: caring, healing, listening, forgiving, encouraging, teaching, and preaching. Furthermore, He equipped His disciples primarily through personal association, seeing them as individuals, and addressing the needs of each.[78] Because of His emphasis on interpersonal relationships, not programs, the only organization that merited Jesus' continuing time and attention was His small group.

Even secular educators discern the predominant value of relationships in the education process. Thomas Gordon maintains that one factor contributes more than any other in the success of one's efforts to teach others—the degree that an individual is effective in establishing a meaningful relationship with a learner or learners. More crucial than content, methodology, or programs, is the quality of the teacher-learner relationship.[79] Joseph Lowman reviewed a number of studies

---

[76]See also Leonard F. Badia, *Jesus: Introducing His Life and Teaching* (New York: Paulist, 1985), 23–7.

[77]Coleman, *The Master Plan of Evangelism*, 33.

[78]Horne, *Teaching Techniques of Jesus*, 205.

[79]Thomas Gordon, *Teacher Effectiveness Training* (New York: David McKay, 1974), 2–3.

on college teaching effectiveness and discovered that two classifications of factors stood out. One set of factors concerned clarity of presentation, while the other reflected the quality of interpersonal relationships between the teacher and learners.[80]

Sixth, *Jesus used the informal small group to model and teach spiritual knowledge, attitudes, and behavior.* The twelve men Jesus chose as His ministry team were disciples or followers first, then apostles, or sent ones. At the time Christ walked the earth, a disciple, or *mathetes*, was one who bound himself to a teacher in order to acquire practical and theoretical knowledge from that individual.[81] It was not uncommon for philosophers, teachers, and rabbis to have men who would join their "school" and so become their disciples.[82] John the Baptist, for example, had his group of disciples (Mt 11:2) as did many of the Pharisees (Mt 22:16).

But whereas the disciples of the Jewish rabbis or pupils of the Greek philosophers attached themselves to their masters to receive objective teaching, Jesus took the initiative in choosing who His disciples would be. He then took on the unremitting task of instructing them. He rebuked them for their lack of faith (Mt 6:30); He explained parables to them (Mt 13:36); He sent them out into the countryside to carry out a ministry modeled on His (Lk 9:1–6); He taught them how to pray (Lk 11:1–4); and He shared with them the truths of the kingdom (Jn 14–16).

And in which learning setting did the Twelve receive most of their instruction and equipping? The disciples surely profited from the objective truths Jesus directed towards the masses, but it was in the context of the small group that they received the majority of their preparation. Living and traveling with Him, beholding Him in a variety of ministry situations, witnessing this miracles, and dialoging with Him in private, they

---

[80]Joseph Lowman, *Mastering the Techniques of Teaching* (San Francisco: Jossey-Bass, 1984), 9.

[81]D. Müller, "Disciple," in *Dictionary of New Testament Theology*, vol. 1, ed. Colin Brown (Grand Rapids, Mich.: Zondervan, 1975), 483–90.

[82]Ibid.

benefited from a small-group learning experience tutored by the Master Teacher himself.[83]

Finally, and perhaps most importantly, *the small group was Jesus' method for leadership preparation and equipping for future ministry.* While the Twelve were disciples, or followers, initially, they were eventually to become apostles or "sent ones" (Mt 10:2).[84] Bruce indicates that the Twelve arrived at this ultimate relationship, or fellowship, with the Master in stages. In the first stage, they were simply believers in Him as the Messiah, and occasionally companions at particular events. In the second stage, they entered into a relationship of "followership" whereby they abandoned their occupations and traveled with Him. In the third and highest stage of discipleship, they were chosen by their master from the masses to be formed as a select band so they might be equipped for the work of apostleship.[85] As apostles they were promised the power of the Holy Spirit (Ac 1:5, 8), given the command to evangelize (Ac 1:8), and through the event of Pentecost (Ac 2), they were made bearers of the Holy Spirit, mighty authorities of early Christianity who guarded the tradition of the historical Jesus.[86]

It was Jesus' strategy to select a small band of men to pour His life into, equip them for future ministry, and eventually send them out with all authority to carry out the work of the Gospel when He returned to His Father (Mt 10:1; 28:16–20). To this point Jesus alone had been the teacher, but at this pivotal juncture in history the disciples (now sent ones) assumed this role and became disciple makers themselves.[87] The small band of common men selected by Jesus, unlearned and igno-

---

[83]Stewart, *The Life and Teaching of Jesus Christ,* 57–8; Icenogle, *Biblical Foundations for Small Group Ministry,* 119.

[84]R.T. France, *Matthew* (Grand Rapids. Mich.: Eerdmans, 1985), 176.

[85]Bruce, *The Training of the Twelve,* 11–2.

[86]D. Müller, "Apostle," in *Dictionary of New Testament Theology,* Vol. 1, ed. Colin Brown (Grand Rapids, Mich.: Zondervan, 1975), 128–135.

[87]France, *Matthew,* 415.

rant by standards of man (Ac 4:13), were entrusted with the whole future of the ministry of Jesus.

Asbury Smith depicts the enduring impact one can have when his or her life and teachings are entrusted to others in the striking contrast between contemporaries George Whitefield and John Wesley: "George Whitefield was perhaps the greatest preacher of the eighteenth century. John Wesley, though not as great a preacher as Whitefield, knew how to prepare other men to preach. He organized classes with leaders; he set up societies and appointed local preachers. Whitefield was an orator; Wesley was a leader. Whitefield left a memory; Wesley left a church. The prophets of the Old Testament and the orders of the Roman Catholic Church illustrate the same truth."[88]

THE EARLY CHRISTIAN COMMUNITIES: Prior to His Ascension, the risen Christ left the disciples with the Great Commission, the command to make disciples by evangelizing, sealing through baptism, and instructing the new converts to observe His teachings (Mt 28:19–20). This sequence was very quickly realized at Pentecost and the days following.[89] After the outpouring of the Holy Spirit on the day of Pentecost and the powerful discourse of Peter, the church experienced explosive growth from 120 (Ac 1:15) to more than 3,000 (2:41). This rapid expansion continued as souls were added to the church daily (2:47).

The pattern of the apostles' teaching and ministry that emerged in the wake of the outpouring at Pentecost had a two-pronged approach. First, they proclaimed the truths of Jesus Christ in the temple courts, and second, they taught the new believers by going house to house (5:42). Several references to the temple or temple courts are scattered through the initial chapters of Acts, indicating that for the first believers this sacred edifice continued to be a place of corporate worship (2:46;

---

[88]Smith, *The Twelve Christ Chose*, 6.

[89]Everett F. Harrison, *The Apostolic Church* (Grand Rapids, Mich.: Eerdmans, 1985), 178.

3:1) and instruction (5:21) for a period of time.[90] Initially, Christianity probably appeared to be simply one more sect within Judaism that was already accustomed to diversity in religious practice and expression.[91]

However, while the apostolic Christians who lived in Jerusalem still worshiped in the temple and observed the Mosaic Law, they soon cultivated other customs unique to their religious life beyond this context. In addition to the worship and instruction that took place in the central gatherings, the home group communities provided fellowship, nurture, prayer, opportunities for outreach, baptism, the breaking of bread, and the sharing of goods (2:42–47).[92] These household gatherings quickly became the definitive expression of the church (*ekklesia*) and most pervasive form of church structure until the time of Constantine.

To gain deeper insights about the nature of the early Christian communities, one is compelled to investigate the churches that sprang up in the wake of Paul's missionary travels.[93] Virtually all of the New Testament churches that are mentioned in his letters as having specific locations were in private homes.[94] In fact, Paul's deliberate missionary strategy was to convert entire households to Christianity and then use the homes as the bases for further missionary and church growth activity.[95] His letters make note of these house churches (*oikon ekklesia*) on a number of occasions. For example, in 1 Corinthians 16:19 he refers to the couple Aquila and Priscilla and the "church that meets at their house." In Philemon, he greets

---

[90]Ibid., 181.

[91]Henry Chadwick, *The Early Church* (London: Penguin, 1967),13.

[92]Vandenakker, *Small Christian Communities and the Parish*, 5; Frederick J. Cwiekoski, *The Beginnings of the Church* (New York, N.Y.: Paulist), 76–9.

[93]Vandenakker, *Small Christian Communities and the Parish*, 10.

[94]Wayne A. Meeks, *The First Urban Christians* (New Haven, Conn.: Yale University, 1983), 75.

[95]Abraham Malherbe, *Social Aspects of Early Christianity* (Baton Rouge, La.: Louisiana State University, 1977), 69.

his fellow worker, Philemon, "Apphia our sister . . . Archippus our fellow soldier and to the church that meets in your home" (v. 2). Again in Romans, Paul mentions the church that meets in the home of Aquila and Priscilla (16:3–5). And in his letter to the Colossians, he sends his greetings to Nympha and the church in her house (4:15). Paul seems to distinguish these small household-based groups from the whole church, which might also gather together on occasion (1Co 14:23; Ro 16:23).[96]

The fact that Paul landed on a successful strategy for establishing household churches was probably not without careful thought and consideration of the social structure existing at that time. The emphasis on the home as the fundamental unit of society had been strong both in the Israelite and Roman culture and was no less basic in the contemporary Greco-Roman society. Michael Green insightfully proclaims that "sociologically speaking, the early Christians could not have hit on a sounder basis."[97] In the Roman Empire, the family was a complex institution, with the father serving as the undisputed head. In addition to the immediate relatives, the household was constituted of slaves, freedmen, hired workers, tenants, and sometimes trusted friends and business partners.[98] Consequently the apostle Paul and other church-planting missionaries made deliberate attempts to convert whole households, making them central to the Christian advance.[99]

The house churches Paul makes mention of, then, were usually comprised of more than just the immediate family members. Slaves, servants, freedmen, laborers, tenants, business associates, and certainly new converts would make themselves a part of a particular household community.[100] As

---

[96]Meeks, *The First Urban Christians,* 75.

[97]Michael Green, *Evangelism in the Early Church* (Grand Rapids, Mich.: Eerdmans, 1970), 208–9.

[98]Ibid., 209.

[99]Ibid., 210.

[100]Meeks, *The First Urban Christians,* 75; Malherbe, *Social Aspects of Early Christianity,* 69.

such, the New Testament household was considered a basic
political unit and offered security and a sense of belonging that
was lost to the larger social and political structures.[101] Furthermore, with the existing household as the nucleus, the house
church was the smallest unit and "basic cell" of the congregation in the very early years of the Christian movement.[102]

In what sense does the New Testament house church serve as
a helpful prototype of contemporary church-based small groups?
Wayne Meeks proposes that the early congregations indeed belong to the category that contemporary sociologists call small
groups.[103] Revisiting Cragan and Wright's definition of small
group, as cited in the first chapter, is helpful in making the connection: "a few people engaged in communication interaction over
time, usually in face-to-face settings, who have common goals and
norms and have developed a communication pattern for meeting
their goals in an interdependent manner."[104]

The size of the house churches: Concerning the size of these
early Christian meetings, Paul is not specific and one can only
surmise how small or large these gather-ings were. But the fact
that there both were smaller gatherings, consisting of a portion of the Christians in a city, and larger meetings, involving
the whole Christian population, puts a limit on the numbers
involved. Banks suggests that the entertaining room of a moderately well-to-do household could hold about thirty people
comfortably, and it is unlikely that a meeting of the whole
church could have exceeded forty or forty-five people. Either
type of meeting would have been small enough for relatively
intimate relationships to develop between members.[105] It ap-

---

[101]Malherbe, *Social Aspects of Early Christianity,* 69.

[102]Meeks, *The First Urban Christians,* 75; J. Goetzmann, "House," in *Dictionary of New Testament Theology,* Vol. 2, ed. Colin Brown (Grand Rapids, Mich.: Zondervan, 1975), 247-251.

[103] Meeks, *The First Urban Christians,* 74.

[104]John Cragan and David Wright, *Communication in Small Group Discussions,* 4th ed. (St. Paul, Minn.: West, 1995), 7.

[105]Robert Banks, *Paul's Idea of Community* (Grand Rapids, Mich.: Eerdmans, 1980), 41–2.

pears that the house belonging to Gaius was large enough to accommodate the Christians in Corinth (Ro 16:23).[106] As one of the more prominent men in city, it is not sur-prising that his home would be used for a gathering of the whole Christian community of Corinth.[107] John Vandenakker notes that the household communities were small enough to encourage a personally focused encounter of catechis and discipleship, something that was eventually lost to the greater Christian community.[108]

The life and activities of the house churches: The religious activities that took place in the house churches were various, but all conducive to small-group community. The book of Acts reveals to us that the homes were used for prayer meetings (2:42; 12:12), fellowship (2:42), communion (2:42, 46), evangelism (2:47), worship (2:47), and teaching (2:42; 5:42).

While numerous activities constituted the life of the house church, the teaching ministry was of utmost importance, for along with the evangelizing activity carried out by preaching, it provided for the very continuance of the church.[109] So the apostles carried on their daily ministry of teaching not only in the temple, but from house to house (Ac 5:42).

The apostolic Christians gathered in three types of meetings, each of which evidenced a measure of religious instruction, either explicitly or implicitly.[110] The first of these meetings was for the teaching of the Word for the purpose of

---

[106]Vandenakker, *Small Christian Communities and the Parish,* 10–11; Cwiekoski, *The Beginnings of the Church,* 119; Williston Walker, *A History of the Christian Church* (New York: Scribner's Sons, 1959), 22.

[107]Banks, *Paul's Idea of Community,* 38.

[108]Vandenakker, *Small Christian Communities and the Parish,* 12. For isometric drawings of meeting places of the early house-church communities see Del Birkey, *The House Church* (Scottdale, Pa.: Herald, 1988), 56–7).

[109]Everett F. Harrison, *The Apostolic Church* (Grand Rapids, Mich.: Eerdmans, 1985), 166.

[110]Lewis Joseph Sherrill, *The Rise of Christian Education* (New York: Macmillan, 1944), 144–153.

edification. Edification, or instruction for the purpose of building one another up, included prayers, hymns, the reading of apostolic letters, prophetic revelations, and teachings on the Scriptures.

A second type of meeting was the common meal, or love feast, which was followed by the observance of the Lord's supper. The common meal was a practical expression of Christian fellowship and care for one another. The Lord's Supper, or Eucharist, was primarily an act of worship, but maintained an element of instruction as believers were reminded of the provisions Christ made for them through His death on the cross. The final kind of meeting was for taking care of business matters. Included in the business meeting were matters of discipline, as the Christian community took it upon themselves to expel members becasuse of gross sin, forgive them when repentant, and restore them to fellowship.

The apostle Paul made an effectual utilization of his rented house in Rome for small-group ministries. When he was no longer able to publicly declare the Gospel of Christ, he invited the Jewish leaders to come to his house, where he talked to them and discussed religious issues. The account in Acts describes Paul's pattern of teaching this way: "For two whole years Paul stayed there in his own rented house and welcomed all who came to see him. Boldly and without hindrance he preached the kingdom of God and taught about the Lord Jesus Christ" (28:30–31). Apparently Paul had discovered house evangelism and teaching to be a remarkably fruitful and rewarding endeavor.[111]

A sense of community: It is particularly helpful to see the community aspect of the early house churches in the larger religious and social settings operative of those days. At that time the Roman Empire witnessed a proliferation of clubs, guilds, and associations.[112] These groups, many of which were relatively small in size, emerged as a response to the need for a sense of belonging that the *polis* (city/state) or *oikos* (home/family) could not or did not provide. Many people, such as

---

[111]Green, *Evangelism in the Early Church,* 218.

[112]Meeks, *The First Urban Christians,* 77.

slaves, unmarried adults, and outcasts of society, were unable to participate in either of these two types of communities. Furthermore, as the Roman Empire expanded, political power became narrowed to fewer and fewer hands, leaving many who had once claimed their identity with the *polis* now disenchanted with it.[113]

It was in this context that many individuals looked to something other than the *polis* or *oikos* for a personal point of reference or sense of belonging. Consequently a variety of associations emerged, usually revolving around a particular interest, vocation, or ideology: political, military, and sporting groups; professional, commercial, and artisan guilds; and philosophical and religious groups. These groups bound members together from varied backgrounds, and their principle of existence was *koinonia*, a voluntary sharing or partnership.[114]

There was nothing particularly unusual or novel, then, with the appearance of small Christian communities in the presence of the political, religious, and social organizations that proliferated at that time.[115] In retrospect, they might be viewed as part of a greater movement towards the spontaneous grouping of individuals within society, paralleling the Jewish and Hellenistic fellowships that were also growing in popularity.[116]

There were, according to Meeks, some significant differences between the Christian groups and other voluntary associations.[117] First, the Christian groups were more exclusive than other associations in the sense that "to be baptized into Christ Jesus" meant a complete resocialization for the individual to the extent that the Christian group was to supplant all other loyalties.

---

[113]Banks, *Paul's Idea of Community,* 15–7.

[114]Vandenakker, *Small Christian Communities and the Parish,* 13.

[115]Banks, *Paul's Idea of Community,* 22.

[116]Banks, *Paul's Idea of Community,* 22; Vandenakker, *Small Christian Communities and the Parish,* 13.

[117] Meeks, *The First Urban Christians,* 78–80.

Second, while the Christian groups were exclusive in one sense, they were much more inclusive in another. In terms of crossing social stratifications, Christian groups were heterogeneous in nature, while Roman groups tended to draw together people who were socially homogeneous. Finally, Christian groups were linked to the larger Christian movement, whereas associations tended to be self-contained local phenomena.

HISTORICAL FOUNDATIONS

From a historical perspective, the small group as a dimension of the church and format for Christian education can be traced from the early church through the Reformation, post-Reformation, and the rise of Methodism to the proliferation of small groups in the church in the twentieth century, and continuing into the twenty-first century. Throughout two millennia of church history, varieties of small Christian communities and groups have provided the basis for most religious orders as well as the context for many spiritual renewal movements.

The Early Church to the Middle Ages

The house church remained the most significant framework of ecclesial form and structure up to the latter part of the third century, when Christians began building sanctuaries resembling the Roman basilicas. Comments by the early church father, Justin Martyr (c. A.D.150), indicate evidence of homes being used as meeting places for both worship and instruction.

When Martyr was interrogated and subsequently put to death because of his Christian faith, the Roman official demanded Justin reveal to him where the Christians met. Justin responded, "Where each one chooses and can: for do you fancy that we all meet in the very same place?"

To that response the prefect became more specific: "Tell me where you assemble, or into what place do you collect your followers?"

To this query Justin replied emphatically, "I live above one Martinus, at the Timiotinian Bath; and during the whole time (and I am now living in Rome for the second time) I am unaware of any other meeting than his."[118]

Archaeological discoveries might shed some light on the house-church practice of the early church. Under the church of Saint Clement in Rome are the remains of a house church that was no doubt standing in the first century, possibly the first-century dwelling of Clement of Rome.[119] And the excavations at Dura-Europos, on the sands of the Syrian Desert, reveal the remains of a private house, in which a small chapel appears to have been an original part of the dwelling structure.[120]

The Catechumenate: Religious instruction played an integral role in the primitive house church. One unique form of adult Christian education was known as the *catechumenate.* Taught by presbyters and deacons known as *catechists,* the catechumenate was the systematic instruction to those converts preparing for baptism and church membership.[121] These classes were taught in the homes of believers, often in the households of the teachers themselves. Clement of Alexandria is known to have taught these types of discipleship classes, quite likely with his home as the focal point of assemblage.[122]

According to Lewis Joseph Sherrill, these classes had three educational purposes. The first was the discipling of the moral life. The second was to acquaint the *catechumen,* or adult

---

[118]Alexander Roberts and James Donaldson, editors, *The Anti-Nicene Fathers,* vol. 1, trans. M. Dods (Grand Rapids, Mich.: Eerdmans, 1989 reprint), 305.

[119]Floyd V. Filson, "The Significance of the Early House Churches," in *Journal of Biblical Literature* 58 (1939), 109–12.

[120]Filson, "The Significance of the Early House Churches," 109–12; H. Daniel-Rops, *The Church of Apostles and Martyrs,* trans. Audrey Butler (London: Dent & Sons, 1960), 222.

[121]Philip Schaff, *History of the Christian Church,* vol. 2 (Grand Rapids, Mich.: Eerdmans, 1952), 256–7.

[122]Donald Allen, *Barefoot in the Church* (Richmond, Va.: John Knox, 1972), 23.; J.G. Davies, *Daily Life in the Early Church* (London: Lutterworth, 1952), 25.

learner, with the Christian life. The third was to nurture a penetrating devotion to the Christian faith and lifestyle.[123]

The catechumens were of at least two classes or grades, the hearers and the *competentes*.[124] The hearers were individuals who took part in the first part of the service and received liturgical lessons and oral instruction. The competentes were those who had been hearers for a period of time and had proven themselves morally worthy, were approaching their time of baptism, and were receiving final teaching in preparation for this religious observance. The instruction the competentes received was separate from the service of worship, and included the private instruction of individuals or groups.[125]

The catechumenate declined in importance after the middle of the fifth century. With the onset of infant baptism, the need for education prior to baptism was minimized, and the church made no special effort to create an agency to instruct those born in the church and baptized as infants or children. Rather, parents were admonished to perform the task of teaching children in the home.

Constantine and the Decline of the House Church: Attendance to the house churches increased rapidly, and very soon the small house dwellings were not large enough to hold the burgeoning congregations. So, by the end of the second century, the buildings we refer to today as churches began to emerge in cities such as Rome, Edessa, Apamea, Alexandria, and Antioch.[126]

---

[123]Lewis Joseph Sherrill, *The Rise of Christian Education* (New York: Macmillan, 1944), 186.

[124]C.B. Eavey, *History of Christian Education* (Chicago: Moody, 1964), 85, describes three grades or classes as hearers, kneelers, and the chosen. However, the prevailing opinion is that only two grades of catechumens existed and Sherill suggests that the confusion over the number of grades exists for three reasons: (1) certain classes of penitents were mistaken for catechumens, (2) nontechnical descriptions in early sources can be interpreted in various ways, and (3) because variations were obscured by the assumption that Christians everywhere followed a uniform practice [Sherrill, *The Rise of Christian Education*, 189].

[125]Sherrill, *The Rise of Christian Education*, 190.

[126]Daniel-Rops, *The Church of Apostles and Martyrs,* 222.

One of the earliest references to a special building as a place of worship occurs in the writings of Clement of Alexandria (ca. A.D. 200), who indicated that the "church" could refer to the building or house of worship.[127] The first archaeological evidence of a church building dates back to about A.D. 256 in Dura-Europos, a city on the Euphrates River.[128]

The early house church essentially disappeared during the era of Constantine (the turn of the fourth century) when basilicas all but replaced the house church as the principle gathering place for believers.[129] Strong persecution of the Christians continued into the third and early fourth centuries under Roman emperors such as Decius and Diocletian, but by the fourth century Christianity had become so strong that it was increasingly difficult to subdue it. So in A.D. 311 an edict of toleration was issued, bearing the names of Galerius, Constantine, and Licinius.[130] It declared that since many Christians "still persist in their opinions, and since we have observed that they now neither show due reverence to the gods nor worship their own God, we therefore, with our wonted clemency in extending pardon to all, are pleased to grant indulgence to these men, allowing the Christians the right to exist again and to set up their places of worship; provided always that they do not offend against public order."[131]

This pronouncement was followed shortly by the famousEdict of Milan in A.D. 313, which simply reaffirmed what was said in the 311 edict of toleration and essentially

---

[127]Clement of Alexandria, "The Instructor," III, 11, in *The Ante-Nicene Fathers*, vol. 2, eds. Alexander Roberts and James Donaldson (Grand Rapids, Mich.: Eerdmans), 209-96.

[128]Walter Oetting, *The Church of the Catacombs* (Saint Louis, Mo.: Concordia, 1964), 26.

[129]Bernard J. Lee and Michael A. Cowan, *Dangerous Memories* (Kansas City, Mo.: Sheed & Ward, 1986), 23.

[130]Karl Bihlmeyer and Hermann Tuchle, *Church History*, vol. 1 (Westminster, Md.: Newman, 1960), 97.

[131]Quoted in Henry Bettenson, ed., *Documents of the Christian Faith*, 2d. ed. (London: Oxford University Press,1963), 15.

gave Christianity equal footing with other religions and pagan cults.[132] Concerning the Christians and Christianity, they announced that "all who choose that religion are to be permitted to continue therein, without any let or hindrance, and are not to be in any way troubled or molested. Note that at the same time all others are to be allowed the free and unrestricted practice of their religions; for it accords with the good order of the realm and the peacefulness of our times that each should have freedom to worship God after his own choice; and we do not intend to detract from the honor due to any religion or its followers."[133]

With the official recognition of their religion, Christians no longer had to be reticent in expressing their faith, and churches became public buildings.[134] These churches or basilicas, as they were called, were rectangular halls with semi-circular niches, or apses, at the front. The apse was reserved for the clergy, while those attendees not taking an active part in the service sat on a bench against the wall.[135] Hadaway, Wright, and Dubose posit that there was nothing that symbolized the historical transformation of Christianity coming into public favor as dramatically as the change from the house church to the basilica as the fundamental expression of church life and function.[136]

The emergence of basilicas, and later cathedrals, contributed significantly to the nature of the church in its practice of worship, community life, and Christian education. One erroneous perception that emerged was that the church was a building, not a body

---

[132]Bihlmeyer and Tuchle, *Church History,* 98, 206-7.

[133]Ibid., 16.

[134]Henry Chadwick, *The Early Church,* Vol. I (London: Penguin, 1967), 280.

[135]For pictures and description of basilicas, see Henry R. Sifton, "Building for Worship," in *Eerdman's Handbook to the History of Chrisianity,* ed. Tim Dowley(Grand Rapids, Mich.: Eerdmans, 1977), 150-4.

[136]C. Kirk Hadaway, Stuart Wright, and Francis Dubose, *Home Cell Groups and House Churches* (Nashville, Tenn.: Broadman, 1987), 70.

of people. And as the church became building-centered, worship shifted from being the corporate celebration of all the people to a clergy-performed ceremony with the laity serving only as spectators. This building-centered approach to religious life and function has dominated the Church ever since, including Roman Catholic, Orthodox, and Protestant denominations.[137]

This striking contrast in church structure and practice depicts the difference between that of a primary group and a secondary group. The early house church was a primary group that emphasized community and *koinonia*, and was characterized by intimacy and face-to-face interaction. The church model that began to emerge in the third century was that of a secondary group, focusing more on outward structure, architecture, and hierarchies.[138]

Remnants of the House Church Movement: However, while the house church or small group community was lost to the mainstream of religious life in the Middle Ages, it was not entirely absent. The monastic movement, at least in its inception, strongly resembled the house church movement at the point of its communal nature. Walker describes the earliest Christian monasteries as follows: "Here all the inmates were knit into a single body, having assigned work, regular hours of worship, similar dress, and cells close to one another—in a word, a life in common under an abbot."[139]

The house church also found expression in some of the sectarian groups that existed alongside the Medieval Church. Ernst Troeltsch describes these sects as "comparatively small groups; they aspire after personal inward perfection, and they aim at a direct personal fellowship between members of each group."[140] One such sect was the Waldenses, whose members were followers of Peter Waldo of Lyons, France (ca. 1140–

---

[137]Hadaway, Wright, and Dubose, *Home Cell Groups and House Churches*, 71.

[138]Birkey, *The House Church*, 64.

[139]Walker, *A History of the Christian Church*, 126.

[140]Ernst Troeltsch, *The Social Teaching of the Christian Churches*, Vol. I (Chicago: University of Chicago, 1911/1976), 331.

1218). The Waldensians were a pre-Reformation group of Christians who sought for a purified Christianity and claimed that they could trace their roots to the early Church. Branded as heretics, they encouraged laymen to study the Bible for themselves, and disputed many teachings of the Catholic church. In an attempt to maintain or recover the type of intimacy and people-centered worship of the pre-basilica era, the Waldensians met in smaller groups in the mountains, forests, and caves, as well as in villages.[141]

Persecution also forced the Waldensians to keep their faith alive in their homes and in clandestine night meetings in stables and back rooms of little shops. Their private meeting places were known as *schola*, the locations where worship, upbuilding in the faith, and instruction occurred.[142] The important role teaching played in the religious life of the Waldensians is reflected in the following quote of one of the members: "In our home, women teach as well as men, and one who has been a student for a week teaches another."[143]

The Reformation and Post-Reformation Times

Throughout history, house churches and small groups have accompanied almost every recorded revival or renewal movement. Whether it has been the pre-Reformation Waldensians, the Anabaptists during the Reformation, or the Pietist groups following the Reformation, there has been a striking similarity. Each group experienced the recovery of the priesthood of the believer, a blurring of the lines between clergy and laity, an emphasis on the unity and community of all the people of God, and a return to the house church.[144]

---

[141]Robert H. Brumback, *History of the Church Through the Ages* (St. Louis, Mo.: Mission Messenger, 1957), 107.

[142]Giorgio Tourn, *The Waldensians*, trans. Camillo P. Merlino (Turin, Italy: Pubbligrafica, 1980), 30, 39.

[143]Ibid., 39.

[144]Hadaway, Wright, and Dubose, *Home Cell Groups and House Churches*, 72.

The Anabaptists and House Groups: During the Reformation, the house-church movement was associated more with the Anabaptists[145] than with the Lutherans or Calvinists.[146] This may have been due, in part, to the persecution the Anabaptists experienced from Lutherans, Calvinists, and Catholics. However when persecution let up, they continued to meet in homes because this was more faithful to early church practice.[147] References to house meetings are not difficult to find in the historical writings on Anabaptists. Bax makes reference to a certain Wolfgang Woliman who convinced followers from St. Gallen, Switzerland to shun churches and meet in houses, fields, and woods.[148] Pike offers a picture of Anabaptist believers meeting in the home of the mother of Felix Manz, an early leader in the movement.[149] And Estep describes a small band of devoted Christians who met on a regular basis in the home of Felix Manz, where Manz took a prominent role, occasionally teaching the Bible from the Hebrew Scriptures.[150]

Religious instruction played a crucial role in many of the Anabaptist meetings as indicated by the comments of Ambrosius Spitemaier when questioned in 1527 on where they

---

[145]Anabaptists were radical reformers intent on renewing the church in a number of areas. The term *Anabaptists* (meaning "rebaptizers") was coined by their enemies in reference to the denial of the practice of infant baptism. More fundamental to the Anabaptist belief systems than the issue of baptism, however, was a love ethic that encouraged redistribution of wealth and the prohibiting of war, as well as an insistence upon the separation of church and state. Today's descendents of the Anabaptist movement include Mennonite, Brethren, Amish, and Hutterite Christians. See John H. Yoder and Alan Kreider, "The Anaptists," in *Eerdmans' Handbook to the History of Christianity,* ed. Tim Dowley (Grand Rapids, Mich.: Eerdmans, 1977), 399–401.

[146]Birkey, *The House Church,* 69.

[147]Plueddemann and Plueddemann, *Pilgrims in Progress,* 6–7.

[148]E. Belfort Bax, *Rise and Fall of the Anabaptists* (New York: American Scholar, 1903/1966), 55.

[149]E.P. Pike, *The Story of the Anabaptists* (London: Thomas Law, 1904), 38.

[150]William R. Estep, *The Anabaptist Story,* rev. ed. (Grand Rapids, Mich.: Eerdmans, 1975), 31.

met and what they did: "They have no special gathering places. When there is peace and unity and when none of those who have been baptized are scattered, they come together wherever the people are. They send messages to each other by a boy or girl. When they have come together they teach one other the divine Word and one asks the other: how do you understand this saying? Thus there is among them a diligent living according to the divine word."[151]

Luther and Small Groups: While house meetings played a lesser role in the Lutheran movement, Martin Luther himself expressed an interest in seeing Christians meet in homes for intimate gatherings. He envisioned such devout meetings as noted in the following comments: "Those who want to be Christians in earnest should sign their names and meet alone in a house somewhere to pray, to read, to baptize, to receive the sacrament, and to do other Christian works. According to this order, those who do not lead Christian lives could be known, reproved, corrected, cast out, or ex-communicated, according to the rule of Christ, in Matthew 18. Here one could also solicit benevolent gifts to be willingly given and distributed to the poor, according to St. Paul's example, in 2 Corinthians 9. Here would be no need of much and elaborate singing. Here one could set out a brief and neat order for baptism and the sacrament and center everything on the Word, prayer, and love."[152]

Unfortunately, Luther was forced to abandon his vision for the house church and intimate gatherings, and with wistful regret confessed that "As yet I neither can nor desire to begin such a congregation or assembly or to make rules for it. For I have not yet the people or persons for it, nor do I see many who want it."[153]

---

[151]Quoted in Lois Barrett, *Building the House Church* (Scottdale, Penn.: Herald, 1986), 22–3.

[152]Martin Luther, "The German Mass and Order of Service," in *Luther's Works,* vol. 53, ed. Ulrich S. Leupold, (Philadelphia: Fortress, 1965), 53–90.

[153]Ibid.

Nonetheless Martin Luther did engage his household in small-group discussions of sorts. After his marriage to Katherine von Bora, his spacious home was the gathering place for all varieties of people. In addition to students who regularly boarded there, there was a constant flow of clergymen, government officials, visitors from abroad, and colleagues of Luther such as his close friend Philip Melanchthon. The relaxed atmosphere of the home, and the late afternoon supper hour in particular, made for much small-group spiritual conversation.[154]

The nature of this "table talk," as it came to be known, is described by one John Mathesius, who was a frequent visitor to Luther's home: "

> When he wished to get us to talk he would throw out a question, "What's new?" The first time we let this remark pass, but if he repeated it—"You prelates, what's new in the land?"—the oldest ones at the table would start talking. Dr. Wolf Severus, who had been the tutor of his royal majesty of the Roman Empire, sat near the head of the table and, unless there was a stranger present (like a traveling courtier), he got something started.
>
> If the conversation was animated, it was nevertheless conducted with decent propriety and courtesy, and others would contribute their share until the doctor started to talk. Often good questions were put to him from the Bible, and he provided expert and concise answers. When at times somebody took exception to what had been said, the doctor was able to bear this patiently and refute him with a skillful answer. Reputable persons often came to the table from the university and from foreign places, and then very nice talks and stories were heard.[155]

---

[154]"Table Talk," *Luther's Works*, vol. 54, ed. and trans. Theodore G. Tappert (Philadelphia: Fortress, 1967), ix.

[155]Quoted in *Luther's Works*, vol. 54, x. Some of the men who listened to the table conversations began to take notes; eventually these notes were published as *Table Talk*. An English version is found in *Luther's Works*, vol. 54.

The Pietist Practice of House Meetings: In the post-Reformation period, the pattern of house groups continued within the Pietist movement. *Pietism* is the name given to a religious awakening within the Protestant churches of the seventeenth and eighteenth centuries, so termed because of the renewal groups implemented by Jacob Spener, called *Collegia Pietatis.* These house meetings included prayer, Bible study, and discussion. Each week Spener brought the parishioners together to talk about the sermon, to contribute their own insights, and to give them opportunities to ask questions. In one particular publication, Spener recommended the establishment of Bible study groups for spiritual development, with the idea that in each congregation a group of "experiential Christians should be gathered to nurture a stricter and warmer Christian life."[156]

The educational axis of these meetings is described by Spener:

> One person would not rise to preach (although this practice would be continued at other times), but others who have been blessed with gifts and knowledge would also speak and present their pious opinions on the proposed subject to the judgment of the rest, doing all this in such a way as to avoid disorder and strife. This might conveniently be done by having several ministers . . . meet together or by having several members of a congregation who have a fair knowledge of God or desire to increase their knowledge meet under the leadership of a minister, take up the Holy Scriptures, read aloud from them, and fraternally discuss each verse in order to discover its simple meaning and whatever may be useful for the edification of all. . . . Everything should be arranged with an eye to the glory of God, to the spiritual growth of the participants, and therefore also their limitations.[157]

Spener goes on to describe the benefits of such meetings:

---

[156]Bruce L. Shelley, *Church History in Plain Language* (Waco, Tex.: Word, 1982), 346.

[157] Philipp Jakob Spener, *Pia Desideria,* trans. Theodore G. Tappert (Philadelphia: Fortress, 1964), 89–90.

Preachers would learn to know the members of their own congregations and their weakness or growth in doctrine and piety, and a bond of confidence would be established between preachers and people which would serve the best interests of both. At the same time the people would have a splendid opportunity to exercise their diligence with respect to the Word of God and modestly to ask their questions. . . . In a short time they would experience personal growth and would also become capable of giving better religious instruction to their children and servants at home.[158]

However, Spener himself grew cautious of the *Collegia Pietatis*. In spite of safeguards, these conventicles gave rise to movements towards separation and withdrawal. He eventually questioned the value of such meetings and established no such small groups in his ministries in Dresden or Berlin.[159] Nonetheless, Pietism brought a renewed stress on the study and discussion of the Bible and its application to daily living. Furthermore, the influence of Spener and other pietists flowed through Count Zinzendorf, the founder of the Moravian movement. The Moravians followed in the spirit and practice of the Pietists, including the use of intimate fellowship groups for spiritual growth and religious instruction.[160]

John Wesley and Small Groups

One of the spiritual descendants of the Moravians was the founder of Methodism, John Wesley. Wesley encountered a group of Moravians on a trip to the colonies, and was so impressed with the power of their piety that he visited them in their Saxon homeland. While Wesley eventually distanced himself from the Moravians, he owed much to them, including their system of small groups for spiritual growth and religious instruction.[161]

---

[158]Ibid., 90.

[159]Dale Brown, *Understanding Pietism* (Nappanee, Ind.: Evangel, 1993), 61-2.

[160]Shelley, *Church History in Plain Language*, 355.

[161]David Lowes Watson, *Covenant Discipleship* (Nashville, Tenn.: Discipleship Resources, 1989), 29; Shelley, *Church History in Plain Language*, 355.

Many observers of church renewal movements credit the success of Wesley's revivals and movement to the implementation of small groups.[162] Three types of groups characterized the structure of Wesley's organization. The cornerstone of his methodology was the neighborhood class meeting. Following the example of the Moravians, Wesley divided his societies into smaller groups of twelve or so members which he called "classes." The term is derived from the Latin *classis*, which means "division," and carries no overtones of schools. Wesley initially used them to raise financial support, a penny a week for the work. However, he soon realized that the collector might also serve as a spiritual guide for the people, and that class members could encourage each other in their Christian experience. As a result, the "class meeting" emerged for testimonies, prayer, and spiritual encouragement, a successful and significant feature of the Methodist awakening.[163] At first leaders visited class members in their homes, but soon found this was not so expedient, in part because it was simply too time-consuming and in part because it did not allow for effective exhorting, comforting, or reproving. Upon all considerations, it was agreed that those of each class should meet together. Wesley reflects on the advantages of meeting together:

> Many now happily experienced that Christian fellowship of which they had not so much as an idea before. They began to "bear one another's burdens," and naturally to "care for each other." As they had daily a more intimate acquaintance with, so they had a more endeared affection for, each other. And "speaking the truth in love, they grew up into Him in all things, who is the Head, even Christ."[164]

---

[162]For example, see Howard A. Snyder, *The Radical Wesley* (Downers Grove, Ill.: Intervarsity Press, 1980), 162–3.

[163]John Wesley, *The Works of John Wesley*, vol. 8 (Salem, Ohio: Schmul, 1872), 269–71; Shelley, *Church History in Plain Language*, 358.

[164]Wesley, *The Works of John Wesley*, vol. 8, 253–4.

Another type of small group used by John Wesley was the band, also the notion of which was adopted from Count Zinzendorf and the Moravians. They were smaller and generally divided by age, gender, and marital status; members were expected to abstain from evil, to be zealous in good works, and to use all the means of grace.[165] Each band was composed of an average of six members, who met weekly to confess their faults to one another and to encourage spiritual progress. The bands were restricted to those who had the assurance that their sins were forgiven. Each person was examined by traveling preachers.[166] Wesley drew up the following rules for the bands:

> The design of our meeting is, to obey that command of God, "Confess your faults one to another, and pray for one another, that ye may be healed." To this end, we intend,—
>
> 1. To meet once a week, at the least.
>
> 2. To come punctually at the hour appointed, without some extra-ordinary reason.
>
> 3. To begin (those of us who are present) exactly at the hour, with singing or prayer.
>
> 4. To speak each of us in order, freely and plainly, the true state of our souls, with the faults we have committed in thought, word, or deed, and the temptations we have felt, since our last meeting.
>
> 5. To end every meeting with prayer, suited to the state of each person present.
>
> 6. To desire some person among us to speak his own state first, and then to ask the rest in order, as many and as

---

[165]Snyder, *The Radical Wesley*, 59; Wesley, *The Works of John Wesley*, 258.

[166]Gangel and Benson, *Christian Education: Its History and Philosophy*, 261.

searching questions as may be, concerning their state, sins, and temptations."[167]

Like the classes, Wesley saw the union of believers in bands as replete with advantages. He writes that "They prayed for one another, that they might be healed of the faults they had confessed; and it was so. The chains were broken, the bands were burst in sunder, and sin had no more dominion over them. Many were delivered from the temptations out of which, till then, they found no way to escape. They were built up in our most holy faith. They rejoiced in the Lord more abundantly. They were strengthened in love, and more effectually provoked to abound in every good work."[168]

One more group characterized Wesley's small-group religious instruction processes. The select society was an even more intimate cell group, designed for those "who appeared to be making marked progress toward inward and outward holiness. . . ."[169] Wesley laid down three rules for the select societies beyond the band rules:

1. Let nothing spoken in this Society be spoken again; no, not even to the members of it.

2. Every member agrees absolutely to submit to his Minister in all indifferent things.

3. Every member, till we can have all things common, will bring once a week, *bona fida,* all he can spare towards a common stock.[170]

The system of small groups instituted by Wesley continued successfully for over a hundred years. In England, the bands disappeared about 1880, while class meetings in both England and America survived into the twentieth century in some churches.[171]

---

[167]Wesley, *The Works of John Wesley,* vol.8, 272.

[168]Ibid., 259.

[169]Snyder, *The Radical Wesley,* 61.

[170]Ibid., 61–62.

[171]Ibid., 62. For a further description of Wesley's classes and bands see Watson, *Covenant Discipleship,* 29–58.

The Nineteenth and Twentieth Centuries

Since the time of Christ, Christian small groups or gatherings of Christians in homes have been normative. Many modern denominations can trace their origins to house meetings, including the Baptists and Disciples of Christ, as well as the Methodists. Likewise, the Holiness revival[172] of the nineteenth century and the modern Pentecostal[173] movement which began in the early part of the 20th century, had their genesis in home meetings.[174]

The Holiness Movement and Small Groups: The cell-group legacy of Wesley lived on in American Methodism from the 1830s through to the weekly meetings of Phoebe Palmer of New York city, who took over a home prayer meeting started in 1835 by her sister, Sarah Lankford.[175] The "Tuesday Meeting

---

[172]The Holiness movement grew from seeds planted in the 1830s by the revivals that encouraged Christians to believe in great spiritual possibilities such as the complete sanctification of believers. The movement drew support from a variety of denominations and religious traditions, although Methodists were most prominent amongst its leaders. The holiness movement eventually included a number of denominations including the Church of God (Anderson, Indiana), the Church of the Nazarene, The Salvation Army, the Wesleyan Methodist Church, the Free Methodist Church, the Brethren in Christ Church, and the Evangelical Friends. See H. E. Raser, "Holiness Movement," in *Dictionary of Christianity in America,* ed. Daniel G. Reid, (Downers Grove, Ill.: Intervarsity, 1990), 543–46; Sydney E. Ahlstrom, *A Religious History of the American People,* vol. 2 (Garden City, N. Y.: Image), 287–91.

[173]Pentecostalism is a modern Christian movement that emphasizes an experience of baptism in the Spirit subsequent to conversion that is evidenced by speaking in tongues. Pentecostal denominations include the Assemblies of God, the International Church of the Foursquare Gospel, the Church of God (Cleveland, Tennessee), the Church of God in Christ, the Pentecostal Holiness Church, and Pentecostal Assemblies of Canada. See R. G. Robbins, "Pentecostal Movement," in *Dictionary of Christianity in America,* ed. Daniel G. Reid, (Downers Grove, Ill.: Intervarsity, 1990),885–91; Sydney E. Ahlstrom, *A Religious History of the American People,* vol. 2 (Garden City, N. Y.: Image), 291–4; and John Thomas Nichol, *Pentecostalism* (New York: Harper and Row, 1966).

[174]Hadaway, Wright, and Dubose, *Home Cell Groups and House Churches,* 50.

[175]R.S. Ingersol, "Holiness Churches and Associations," in *Dictionary of Christianity in America,* ed. Daniel G. Reid, (Downers Grove, Ill.: Intervarsity, 1990), 541–3.

for the Promotion of Holiness," as it was known, was so popular it outlived her by thirty years and served as a model for home meetings throughout the United States. In the years following, similar groups were organized in Brunswick, Maine, Boston, Trenton, Philadelphia, Wilmington, and Baltimore. By the year 1886 over two hundred such groups, or bands as they were called, were in existence in the United States and around the world.[176]

The Influence of Psychology: The small-group movement in the church was influenced to a great extent by quite a different movement that sprung up within the field of psychology. In the 1940s and 1950s small groups, most commonly known as "T-groups" (the T standing for training), "encounter groups," and "sensitivity training" groups emerged in a variety of business, education, and counseling settings. Their origin is traced to Kurt Lewin, generally considered the founder of modern group dynamics.[177] Some time prior to 1947, Lewin found that certain methods of group discussion were superior to individual instruction and lecturing in changing social conduct and ideas. In group discussions, participants were able to learn more, not only about themselves, but about group dynamics in general.[178]

In 1947 the National Training Laboratory (NTL) was formed in order to study small groups and to organize training groups for industry and eventually for many areas outside of industry.[179] Carl Rogers describes these small groups as "training groups in human relations skills in which individuals were taught to observe the nature of their interactions with others and of the group process. From this, it was felt they

---

[176]Charles Edwin Jones, *Perfectionist Persuasion: The Holiness Movement and American Methodism, 1867-1936* (Metuchen, N.J.: Scarecrow Press, 1974), 2–3.

[177]Kurt Lewin, *A Dynamic Theory of Personality* (New York: McGraw-Hill, 1935); Kurt Lewin, *Principles of Topological Psychology* (New York: McGraw-Hill, 1936).

[178]Joseph Luft, *Group Processes* (Palo Alto, Calif.: Mayfield, 1970), 2–3.

[179]Luft, *Group Processes,* 1–4; William G. Dyer, ed., *Modern Theory and Method in Group Training* (New York: Van Nostrand Reinhold, 1972), v; Carl Rogers, *Carl Rogers on Encounter Groups* (New York: Harper & Row, 1970), 2–3.

would be better able to understand their own way of functioning in a group and on the job, the impact they had on others, and would become more competent in dealing with difficult interpersonal situations."[180]

About the same time, another phase of this small-group movement began to unfold at the University of Chicago where Carl Rogers and associates were involved in training counselors. These "encounter groups" were oriented more towards personal growth, including the development and improvement of interpersonal communication and relationships through an experiential process.[181]

In the 1960s the movement developed on a national scale, as businesses, religious institutions, retreat centers, and other organizations discovered (or rediscovered) small groups. But it was in the established churches and synagogues, says Robert Wuthnow, that small groups became especially prominent.[182] Why have small groups proliferated and spread so rapidly since the 1960s? Rogers credits their growth to an increasing dehumanization of the culture. There is a hunger for something the individual does not find in his work environment, in his church, in his school or college, nor even in modern family life.[183]

Small Groups Around the World: While the major development of the small-group movement in the church today has taken place in the second part of the twentieth century, there was some appearance of cell groups prior to the 1950s, and they were not confined to North America. One such form of the house church which continues to exist to this day is the Christian Ashram of India. The first Protestant Ashrams emerged in the 1920s, and the first Catholic Ashrams followed in the 1950s. The Ashrams are intentionally indigenous to India in style, structure, and purpose, although they have been strongly influenced by Western missionaries. The Ashrams

---

[180]Rogers, *Carl Rogers on Encounter Groups*, 3.

[181]Ibid., 4–5.

[182]Robert Wuthnow, *Sharing the Journey* (New York: The Free Press, 1994), 40.

[183]Rogers, *Carl Rogers on Encounter Groups*, 10–11.

range from the simple model of a disciplined community working for social change to those which are more spiritual in tone.
Both are Christian in nature and have a simple lifestyle in common. They differ in that the goals of the former (the community
working for social change) are more external and political in
nature while the goals of the latter (spiritual groups) are more
inwardly centered and communal.[184]

Similar to the Christian Ashrams of India, are the Basic
Christian Communities (BCC) of Latin America. These smaller
Roman Catholic house communities first emerged in Brazil
and from there spread quickly to other Latin American countries. Vandenakker points to three convergent forces which
spurred their initial development in the 1950s. The first force
was that of lay catechists being used to teach people about the
faith and gather them for liturgical services when a priest was
not available. A second force was educational movements designed to educate, evangelize, and address social concerns
especially by way of radios broadcasts. The third force came
from the impact of various lay movements that sought to bring
about ecclesial and personal revival.[185]

Basic Christian Communities usually meet in the homes
of the poor, and are somewhat of counter movement to the
traditional Roman Catholic Church in Latin America. Although they are diverse in nature, these basic communities
hold three things in common. First, they attend to the spiritual lives of people through prayer, worship, singing, and
exploration of the Scriptures. Second, they offer spiritual,
material, and emotional support to one another. And third,
members pool their resources and unite their commitments
toward the social transformation of unjust social structures.[186]

---

[184]Hadaway, Wright, and Dubose, *Home Cell Groups and House Churches*,
51; P.O. Phillips, "The Place of Ashrams in the Life of the Church," *International Review of Missions* 35 (1946), 265; E. Stanley Jones, *Along the Indian
Road* (New York: Abingdon, 1939), 181–213.

[185]Vandenakker, *Small Christian Communities and the Parish*, 100.

[186]Lee and Cowan, *Dangerous Memories*, 39.

The movement is, by and large, lay-oriented, although many priests and nuns are in sympathy with it and relate to it in an informal manner. The communities enjoy a growing acceptance among the leadership of the Catholic Church. Their faith is distinctly Roman Catholic and the home meetings are characterized by a strong liturgical flavor. The movement is, however, radical in its application of religious faith to the social issues related to poverty and oppression in Latin American countries. This model has inspired groups elsewhere, and the movement is now gaining momentum in Western Europe, Africa, and Asian countries.[187] It is estimated that in Brazil alone there are as many as eighty thousand such groups involving 1 to 1.5 million people.[188]

One of the most remarkable modern-day church movements has been the house church of mainland China. Threatened by the communist takeover and Cultural Revolution, the church in China was held together by thousands of house churches. These home churches survived and grew in spite of the severe persecution of the Cultural Revolution. There is a significant parallel to the first-century Christians who suffered and thrived under persecution by the Roman Empire. It is estimated that over fifty million Catholic and Protestant Christians attend thousands of house churches in mainland China.[189]

Christian and Missionary Alliance missionary Joel Comiskey has traveled extensively, studying what he calls "a worldwide home cell group explosion." He sees the contemporary cell group movement as a driving force in church growth and outreach around the world.[190] In Seoul, Korea, the Yoido Full Gospel Church has become the largest church in the world, with over 700,000 members. Un-

---

[187]Hadaway, Wright, and Dubose, *Home Cell Groups and House Churches,* 52; Lee and Cowan, *Dangerous Memories,* 39–45.

[188]Vandenakker, *Small Christian Communities and the Parish,* 100.

[189]Plueddemann and Plueddemann, *Pilgrims in Progress,* 9; Peter Brierley, ed. *World Churches Handbook* (London: Christian Research, 1997) np.

[190]Joel Comiskey, *Home Cell Group Explosion* (Houston, Tex.: Touch Publications, 1998), 24–26.

der the leadership of Paul Yonggi Cho, this church has successfully used home cell ministry for taking care of people's needs, Bible study, and prayer.[191] In Cho's model, a house group is formed in a local community or neighborhood with its own house group pastor, but is structurally tied to a central church. The church has approximately twenty-three thousand home cell groups.[192] The cell group strategy of the Full Gospel Church is described by pastor Cho in his book, *Successful Home Cell Groups*.[193]

Comiskey indicates that many other pastors have followed the lead of Cho and the Yoido Full Gospel Church. In Bogota, Colombia, the International Charismatic Mission has more than 10,000 cell groups penetrating every corner of the city. La Mision Cristiana Elim in San Salvador, El Salvador, has well over 100,000 people attending 5,300 cell groups. The Faith Baptist Church of Singapore began in 1986 with 600 people. Today the full-fledged cell church pastors 7,000 members in 500 active cell groups. Pastors and churches all over the world have effectively adapted Cho's cell-based model for their own situations and environments.[194]

The Recent Small-Group Movement in America: In America, small groups were dominated by the Sunday school movement in the first half of the twentieth century. This model was distinguished by certain characteristics: a single individual usually led the group, instruction was didactic in nature, and the class usually followed standardized lesson plans.[195] But by the 1960s and 1970s, Sunday school was on the decline while other forms of small groups were on the rise.[196] According to the careful

---

[191]J. Gregory Lawson, "The Utilization of Home Cell Groups," *Christian Education Journal* 13 (Spring 1993), 68.

[192]Hadaway, Wright, and Dubose, *Home Cell Groups and House Churches*, 80.

[193]Joel Comiskey, *Yoida Full Gospel Church*. http://celycecomiskey.tripod. com/yoido_full_gospel_church.htm

[194]Comiskey, *Home Cell Group Explosion*, 24–6.

[195]Wuthnow, *Sharing the Journey*, 42–3.

[196]Harold J. Westing, "Adult Sunday School," *in The Christian Educator's Handbook on Adult Education,* eds. Kenneth O. Gangel and James C. Wilhoit (Wheaton, Ill.: Victor, 1993), 289–99.

analysis of Robert Wuthnow, the small-group movement that began to take form in these two decades was built on the prototypes of the more traditional Sunday school classes described above. However, it differed from these meetings in a variety of significant ways:[197]

- Small groups were deliberately initiated as additions to the traditional church meetings and classes by clergy and lay leaders who felt the traditional meetings were not entirely effective in meeting the needs of the people in the parish or congregation.

- In addition to the instructional or task-oriented meetings (such as Bible lessons or prayer sessions) the new small groups focused on the affective nurturance of community, support, interpersonal relationships, sharing, and socializing.

- The new groups drew heavily on the research and ideas related to group dynamics and group process. Special attention was paid to mutual interaction as opposed to didactic techniques with an emphasis on greater self-awareness, inner healing, and life goals.

- The basis for forming small groups was expanded beyond age and gender to include broader sociological dimensions. Thus geographic location, marital status, personal issues (such as substance abuse, divorce, or single parenthood), and specialized concerns (such as poverty, racial integration, or peace and justice) became the impetus for forming many small groups.

As mentioned in chapter one, approximately 40 out of every 100 adults in the United States belong to some kind of formal small group. This means that approximately 80 million adult Americans are meeting regularly in some sort of

---

[197]Wuthnow, *Sharing the Journey*, 44–5.

small group (this number does not include all the groups that children and teenagers attend).[198] A further breakdown of church-related groups reveals the following statistics: 800,000 Sunday school classes involve 18–22 million people; 900,000 Bible-study groups involve 15-20 million people; 500,000 self-help groups have 8–10 million people; 250,000 political/current events groups have 5–10 million people; and 250,000 sports or hobby-event groups add another 5–10 million people.[199]

There is an increasing and ever-widening spectrum of religious groups and congregations experimenting with small groups. Vandenakker notes the proliferation of a variety of Small Christian Communities (SCCs) within the Roman Catholic Church.[200] For example, Catholic parishes that were involved in the Renew movement are turning to small groups as a way of maintaining their momentum.[201] Jewish groups are also experimenting with small, informal gatherings in homes, and many Protestant pastors are encouraging small groups as a way of nurturing church growth.[202]

Wuthnow suggests the small-group movement is so powerful it is beginning to alter American society. It is changing our understanding of community and redefining our spirituality. In other words, small groups are affecting the ways in which persons relate to each other and how they view God.[203]

---

[198]Robert Wuthnow, *I Come Away Stronger* (Grand Rapids, Mich.: Eerdmans, 1994), 369.

[199]Warren Bird, "The Great Small-Group Takeover," *Christianity Today,* February 7, 1994, 27.

[200]Vandenakker, *Small Christian Communities and the Parish,* 133-178.

[201]RENEW is a Roman Catholic spiritual renewal movement aimed at deepening personal faith and creating a new awareness of Christian community in the parish. See Vandenakker, *Small Christian Communities and the Parish,* 139-145.

[202]Wuthnow, *Sharing the Journey,* 44.

[203]Ibid., 3, 11–21.

The Influence of Para-church Organizations: The impact that certain para-church organizations have had on the small group movement must not be minimized. One such organization that has worked closely with churches is Serendipity House. Under the leadership of Lyman Coleman, Serendipity has published a number of curriculum booklets that cover basic biblical teachings, a number of life topics such as family, careers, stress, money, and singleness, as well as a wide variety of study guides concerned with addictions and codependency.[204] Coleman has further contributed to the small-group movement by leading seminars across the country on how to organize and lead small groups. In 1993, the last year he led these seminars, Coleman conducted nearly 100 nationwide, with a total attendance of more than 10,000 people from a multitude of Christian persuasions.[205]

Publishers affiliated with campus organizations, such as the Navigators (NavPress), Intervarsity Christian Fellowship (Intervarsity Press), and Campus Crusade for Christ, offer a wide variety of study books and leader guides. NavPress publishes the *Lifechange Bible Study Series*; Intervarsity Press offers the *Lifeguide Bible Study Series* and inductive Bible study guides on the Bible and other topical studies; Campus Crusade publishes a series of booklets designed for discipling young Christians.

Another source that has played an important role in the development of small groups is an organization called Neighborhood Bible Studies. This organization provides leadership training seminars, study guides, a newsletter, and yearly conferences on holding outreach Bible studies.[206]

The Future of the Small-Group Movement: Currently, small groups are proliferating as churches and parishes are intentionally developing varieties of small-group ministries, and

---

[204]Serendipity curricula for small groups are available from Serendipity, Box 1012, Littleton, CO 80160, or 1-800-525-9563.

[205]Wuthnow, *Sharing the Journey,* 103.

[206]For information on Neighborhood Bible Studies, Inc., write to Box 222, Dobbs Ferry, NY 10522 (914-693-3273).

pastors and Christian educators are encouraging church members to join these small groups. But what is the future of the small-group movement in Christian education? Many experts suggest that the cultural trends which led to fragmentation and impersonalness will continue to impact the movement as people look to small groups as a source of intimacy and community building.

Howard Snyder, as early as 1983, suggested that "the church of the next generation may resemble the church of the first-century Roman Empire or present-day China more than the American Protestantism of the 1950s and 1960s. Many indicators point in this direction. Clearly there is a thirst for closer community today and a growing recognition that the church must move in the direction of more intimate and responsible community life."[207]

Wuthnow observes that the social effects of the small group movement have been largely beneficial: "In responding to social and personal needs, this movement has been able to grow enormously. Consequently, it is now poised to exercise even greater influence on American society in the next decade than it has in the past two decades."[208] However, he suggests that the movement stands at an important crossroad—a turning point that will require it to choose one of two directions. It can continue to draw millions by making them feel good about themselves and by encouraging them to develop a pragmatic, domesticated form of spirituality. Or it can focus less on numbers and challenge members to make more serious commitments to others who are in need and serve the wider community.[209]

Warren Bird also raises some questions for the church to grapple with as it looks to the future. "Are small groups truly helping the church to pass on the faith, encourage biblical lit-

[207]Howard A. Snyder, *Liberating the Church* (Downers Grove, Ill.: Intervarsity Press, 1983), 36.

[208]Wuthnow, "How Small Groups Are Transforming Our Lives," *Christianity Today,* February 7, 1994, 24.

[209]Ibid.

eracy, and form committed disciples of Jesus Christ? How effective are they as a tool for outreach? And are they driven more by God's calling for his church or by the vagaries of our secular culture?"[210]

SOCIO-PSYCHOLOGICAL FOUNDATIONS

There are also strong socio-psychological foundations for small groups, as groups constitute the basic fabric of life itself. Human beings exist as members of families, clubs, work groups, and circles of friends. David and Frank Johnson suggest groups are incalculably important in the life of every human, and that skills in group functioning are absolutely essential to every individual. Belonging to groups, they add, is a most fundamental aspect of life, and the quality of one's life depends upon the effectiveness of the groups belonged to. Furthermore, this effectiveness is largely determined by personal skills and knowledge of group processes.[211] Several important points are considered in regards to the role of small groups in society.

Human Beings Are Social Creatures

Daniel Defoe's well-known fictional character, Robinson Crusoe, traveling the highs seas, found himself shipwrecked on a remote and desolate island for more than twenty-eight years. The prospect of living in a state of isolation indefinitely is reflected on early in the story: "I had great reason to consider it as a determination of Heaven that in this desolate place and in this desolate manner I should end my life. The tears would run plentifully down my face when I made these reflections, and sometimes I would expostulate with myself, why Providence should thus completely ruin his creatures, and render them so absolutely miserable, so without help abandoned, so entirely depressed, that it could hardly be rational to be thankful for such a life."[212] Crusoe would have learned from personal experience the reality of John Donne's fa-

---

[210]Bird, "The Great Small-Group Takeover," 26.

[211]David Johnson and Frank Johnson, *Joining Together* (Englewood Cliffs, N.J.: Prentice-Hall, 1975), 1.

[212]Daniel Defoe, *Robinson Crusoe* (n. c.: Landoll's, 1992 reprint), 55.

mous lines: "No man is an island, entire of itself; every man is a piece of the continent, a part of the main."[213] We were not created to live in isolation from one another.

Groups of various kinds play a strategic role in society because humans are social beings and have an inherent social nature. It is not in our nature to live or function in isolation, and survival without the social contact of others is problematic. Aristotle remarked that man is a social animal and emphatically declared, "To live alone, one must be either an animal or a god."[214] Robert Bierstedt contends that total ostracism from one's group is probably the cruelest punishment one can endure, short of death itself.[215] Consequently we live and function in groups; all sorts of groups. Each person is born into a group called the family, and it is in this group we spend the first years of our lives. We are socialized within the family and peer groups in ways of behaving and thinking; we are educated and taught in these groups to have a certain outlook on the world and ourselves. Virtually all of our time is spent interacting in groups. We are educated in groups, we work in groups, we worship in groups, and we play in groups.[216]

M. Scott Peck addresses the reality of the God-instilled need for meaningful connection with others with the following assertion: "We can never be completely whole in and of ourselves. . . . There is a point beyond which our sense of self-determination not only becomes inaccurate and prideful but increasingly self-defeating. . . . We are inevitably social creatures who desperately need each other not merely for sustenance, not merely for company, but for any meaning to our lives whatsoever."[217]

---

[213]From the writings John Donne called "Devotions Upon Emergent Occasions," included in Frank J. Warnke, *John Donne* (Boston: G. K. Hall, 1987), 101.

[214]Aristotle, *Politics*, i, 2.

[215]Robert Bierstedt, *The Social Order* (New York: McGraw-Hill, 1957), 289.

[216]Johnson and Johnson, *Joining Together*, 1.

[217]M. Scott Peck, *The Different Drum* (New York: Simon and Schuster, 1987), 54–5.

While it is highly unlikely any of us would experience alienation from other human beings in the manner Robinson Crusoe did, observers of American culture suggest that in the United States at least, there is a dangerous, self-centered individualism or isolationism that is increasingly pervading our manner of living. Robert Bellah and his colleagues suggest that individualism lies at the very core of American culture and has pursued personal rights and autonomy to ever new realms.[218] Allan Bloom, in a sweeping analysis of American college and university students, describes them as being preoccupied primarily with themselves.[219] Wuthnow observes that the evidence of community breakdown is all around us: "The smile and 'hello' that used to greet us at the grocery store have been replaced by the pallid face of an automaton who busily passes our items across a bar-code scanner. Work was once a place where people did the same things, knew the same skills, and shared a common destiny. Now the boss may be miles away, linked to us by satellite and computer networks, and our coworkers may have become our most bitter competitors. If we are lucky, we may have some close friends at work—after all, we spend an increasing share of our waking hours in the workplace. . . . Faced with impersonality, bureaucratic red tape, and incessant competition, we may be sorely tempted to launch a full-scale retreat from public life."[220]

What is the answer to this spiraling descent into the entrapment of individualism? How do members of a fragmented society disengage themselves from the harmful and erroneous notion that every person *is* an island? Wuthnow argues that rebuilding community in America is the challenge, and the yearning for community and meaningful relationships is the force behind the recent rise of the small-group movement.[221] We long for meaningful relationships and encounters

---

[218] Robert N. Bellah, et al., *Habits of the Heart* (New York: Harper & Row, 1985), 141–2.

[219] Allan Bloom, *The Closing of the American Mind* (New York: Simon and Schuster, 1987), 83.

[220] Robert Wuthnow, *Sharing the Journey* (New York: Free Press, 1994), 35.

[221] Ibid., 36.

with other human beings; at all stages of our lives there exists an undeniable need to belong. At the core of all Christian education groups must be a commitment of group members to interdependence and mutual caring.

Small Groups Are the Building Blocks of Society

Clovis Shepherd writes that the small group is "an essential mechanism of socialization and a primary source of social order."[222] As such, small groups are the major source of values, beliefs, norms and attitudes that define the basic institutions of society.[223] Shepherd goes on to say that there is little doubt that the roles children learn within the family and their play groups serve as the initial roles which they will take into other situations. The small group serves an important function of mediating between the individual and the society at large.[224] Simply put, the behaviors and beliefs of individuals are greatly influenced by the groups they belong to.

It will be particularly helpful, at this point, for Christian education group leaders to consider the difference between "formational" group experiences and "informational" group experiences. Icenogle describes the differences between the two experiences as follows: "Formation has to do with changing patterns. Information is what is needed to help the group understand why the formational process is so important. . . . Formation has to do with being in touch with real life—intellect, volition, emotion, and physical action."[225]

Dynamic Christian education does both—it provides information and it nurtures formation. Instruction in the truths of Scripture, for example, gives individuals the in-

---

[222]Clovis Shepherd, *Small Groups: Some Sociological Perspectives* (Scranton, Pa.: Chandler, 1964), 1.

[223]Robert Perrucci and Dean D. Knudsen, *Sociology* (St. Paul, Minn.: West, 1983), 132.

[224]Shepherd, *Small Groups: Some Sociological Perspectives*, 1.

[225]Gareth Weldon Icenoble, *Biblical Foundations for Small Group Ministry* (Downers Grove, Ill.: InterVarsity, 1994), 286–7.

formation and tools necessary for the formational experiences of spiritual growth and faith development. Thus, affirms Karl Barth, "It is rare in life to be able to separate form and content."[226] And James Michael Lee rhetorically asks, "Where is substantive content to be found if it is not within the realm of the learner's experiencing during the religious lesson?"[227]

Small groups will tend to emphasize either the informational or formational Christian education experiences but will not be exclusively one or the other. For example, study groups will, by their very nature, give emphasis to informational content (such as the Scriptures or doctrinal instruction), but it is imperative that it is imparted with the resolve of seeing formation take place in the lives of group members. Growth and recovery groups, on the other hand, are concerned first and foremost with formation (and transformation), but cannot be devoid of informational content. Lee iterates the fact that to emphasize *process* (transformation) in Christian education in no way implies that *doctrine* (information) thereby disappears.[228]

So just as little children learn societal roles in their family and peer groups as Shepherd suggests, thought patterns, behaviors, values, and attitudes of small group participants are influenced, formed, and transformed as they are in dynamic relationship with one another. Then, adds Icenogle, the maturing group will in turn have a transforming impact on the society at large in which it functions and has its being. "There is a direct relation between the maturity of a small group and its members' desire and courage to venture into an alienated world with the experience of *koinonia*."[229]

---

[226]Karl Barth, *Dogmatics in Outline,* trans. G.T. Thompson (New York: Harper & Row, 1959), 96.

[227]James Michael Lee, *The Content of Religious Instruction* (Birmingham, Ala.: Religious Education Press, 1985), 18.

[228]Ibid., 93.

[229]Icenoble, *Biblical Foundations for Small Group Ministry,* 285.

Groups Are Primary or Secondary in Nature

Sociologists have found it helpful to classify groups according to their function in society. One of the first to address the issue of distinctive social groupings, as mentioned in chapter one, was the German Ferdinand Toennies (1855–1936), who made a distinction between two types of groups: the *Gemeinschaft* and the *Gesellschaft*. According to Toennies, the *Gemeinschaft* is a small community of people in which members know each other and interpersonal relationships are close. People share similar values and people are oriented towards the interests and activities of the group as a whole. The neighborhood of the rural village is the picture of a *Gemeinschaft* community: "The proximity of dwellings, the communal fields, and even the mere contiguity of holdings necessitate many contacts of human beings and cause inurement to and intimate knowledge of one another."[230]

On the other hand, the *Gesellschaft* is made up of a larger population in which group members are strangers to one another. Relationships are impersonal, individuals are oriented towards personal rather than group goals, people do not necessarily hold to the same values, and tradition has little influence on behaviors. [231]

American sociologist Charles Horton Cooley, making a similar distinction at the turn of the twentieth century, introduced the notion of *primary* groups. By primary groups Cooley meant those groups "characterized by intimate face-to-face associations and cooperation." He identified only a few groups that fit his definition, but suggested that these were by no means the only ones: the family, the play group of children, and the neighborhood group of elders.[232] These are the groups in which

[230]Ferndinand Toennies, "Community and Society," in *Theories of Society,* Vol. I, eds. Talcott Parsons, Edward Shils, Kaspar D. Naegele, and Jesse R. Pitts (New York: Free Press of Glencoe, 1961), 191–201.

[231]Ibid.

[232]Charles H. Cooley, "Primary Groups," in *Theories of Society,* vol. 1, eds. Talcott Parsons, Edward Shils, Kaspar D. Naegele, and Jesse R. Pitts (New York: Free Press of Glencoe, 1961), 315–8.

we enjoy the most intimate kinds of relationships, where we sense a "we" feeling of belonging.

Secondary groups,[233] by contrast, are larger, more formal, and people are more distanced from one another in time and space. Members may know each other as adherents of the same organization but do not know each other personally. Group members tend not to engage in meaningful interaction nor are they particularly concerned about seeing change in each other's lives.

In the broader sense, the primary group has numerous consequences for our social life—"It molds our opinions, guides our affections, and subtly influences our actions."[234] But there are strong implications for specifically Christian education groups. One of the goals of many small groups is to provide closer, more intimate contact among church attenders who may not connect well with people in the larger church setting. In a sense small Christian education groups "make the big church small."[235] For these small Christian communities to exhibit the New Testament notion of *koinonia* or community, there must be a concern for each other's welfare and members must sense a belongingness to others who confess the same Jesus Christ.[236]

EDUCATIONAL FOUNDATIONS

It has been established that small groups have strong theological, historical, and sociological foundations. But before hastily instituting small groups as a strategy for Christian education or spiritual formation, the Christian educator must consider their soundness from an educational perspective. From the standpoint of the teaching-learning process, small-group activities provide

---

[233]Cooley himself did not use the term "secondary groups" in his analysis of social groups. It is a term that sociologists have used to contrast his primary group [R. Serge Denisoff and Ralph Wahrman, *An Introduction to Sociology* (New York Macmillan, 1975), 90; Bierstedt, *The Social Order,* 305].

[234]Bierstedt, *The Social Order,* 305.

[235]George M. Thomas and Douglas S. Jardine, "Jesus and Self in Everyday Life: Individual Spirituality Through a Small Group in a Large Church," in *I Come Away Stronger,* ed. Robert Wuthnow (Grand Rapids, Mich.: Eerdmans, 1994), 275–99.

[236]Lee and Cowan, *Dangerous Memories,* 24.

appealing alternatives to the more traditional lecture and classroom discussion formats. But do they serve as an effective teaching and learning strategy? A growing number of educators laud the instructional and nurturant benefits of group processes. For example, Joyce and Weil, in their strategic book *Models of Teaching,* propose that certain well-structured small-group methods can be a very efficient way of teaching academic knowledge as well as affective content, such as warmth and trust, respect for others, and independence in learning.[237] Elizabeth Cohen, while admitting that small groups are not a panacea for all instructional problems, argues that group work is a superior way to develop cognitive skills such as conceptual learning and problem solving, as well as social competencies such as cooperation, trust, and friendliness.[238]

Group Processes in Education

The grouping of students for the purpose of instruction is not a new educational strategy. In the fifth century B.C., teacher/philosopher Socrates employed a small-group teaching technique that came to bear his name, the "Socratic method." Contemporary educators reflect a keen interest in group processes in the classroom. At least two approaches to small-group learning can be identified in current educational research, theory, and practice. One line of thinking proposes that small groups be used within the traditional classroom to advance peer tutoring and student rehearsal of material presented by the teacher. This approach stresses cognitive learning found at the lower strata of Bloom's taxonomy,[239]

---

[237]Bruce Joyce and Marsha Weil, *Models of Teaching,* 3rd ed. (Engelwood Cliffs, N.J.: Prentice-Hall, 1986), 237.

[238]Elizabeth G. Cohen, *Designing Groupwork,* 2nd ed. (New York: Teachers College Press, 1994), 1, 6.

[239]Bloom's taxonomy is an effective system for classifying levels of cognitive activity and questions that enhance learner interest. Benjamin Bloom and colleauges identify six levels of learning as follows: knowledge, comprehension, application, analysis, synthesis, and evaluation. Knowledge and compehension are generally considered lower levels of cognitive activity, while

namely the acquisition of information and comprehension.[240]

A second, and currently more popular model, views "cooperative learning in small groups as a social context for task-oriented cooperation, communication, and intellectual exchange among peers."[241] This model, which emphasizes inquiry, problem solving, and the investigation of knowledge from multiple sources, finds its philosophical roots in the writings of the early twentieth-century American educator and philosopher, John Dewey. In *Democracy and Education*, Dewey proposed that the entire school be organized as a miniature democracy, where students could participate in the development of the social system. A central motif to his educational strategy was the creation of a democratic group that defined and encountered significant social problems.[242]

In the 1950s and 1960s the group-process trend in public education got a significant boost from the National Training Laboratory (NTL), and more specifically from educator Herbert Thelen, one of the founders of the NTL. Like Dewey, he emphasized the social nature of people and encouraged group inquiry into problems. Thelen recommended that group inquiry begin with a problem situation to which learners "can react and discover basic conflicts among their attitudes, ideas, and modes of perception. On the basis of this information, they identify the problem to be investigated, analyze the roles required to solve it, organize themselves to take these roles, act, report and evaluate these results. These steps are illuminated by reading, by personal investigation, and by consultation with experts. The group is concerned with its own effectiveness, and with

---

application, analysis, synthesis, and application are seen as higher levels of activity [Benjamin Bloom et al., *Taxonomy of Educational Objectives. Handbook 1: Cognitive Domain* (New York: David McKay, 1956].

[240]Shlomo Sharan, Zalman Ackerman, and Rachel Hertz-Lazarowitz, "Academic Ahievement of Elementary School Children in Small-Group Versus Whole-Class Instruction," in *Journal of Experimental Education* 48 (2:1980), 125–9.

[241]Ibid., 125.

[242]John Dewey, *Democracy and Education* (New York: MacMillan, 1916).

its discussion of its own process as related to the goals of investigation."[243] Briefly put, Thelen promoted experienced-based group learning situations, characterized by vigorous inquiry into specific problems that were easily transferred into subsequent life situations.[244]

The influence of the National Training Laboratory was evidenced in an increased emphasis on the utilization of group processes in the field of education. A notable contribution to the theoretical field of group learning was a publication by the National Society for the Study of Education titled, *The Dynamics of Instructional Groups: Sociopsychological Aspects of Teaching and Learning.* The edited book included titles such as "The Classroom Group as a Unique Social System," "The Sociopsychological Structure of the Instructional Group," and "Implications of the Dynamics of Instructional Groups."[245] In the initial chapter Gale Jenson reflected the conviction of the society by affirming that "at the heart of educational practice, at least in its present form, is the instructional group."[246] Subsequent to this landmark publication, books and articles focusing on the theory and practice of group processes in educational settings began to appear with increased frequency.[247]

---

[243]Herbert Thelen, *Education and the Human Quest* (New York: Harper and Row, 1960), 82.

[244]See also Herbert A. Thelen, *Classroom Grouping for Teachability* (New York: Wiley & Sons, 1968; Jacob W. Getzels and Herbert A. Thelen "The Classroom Group as a Unique Social System," in *The Dynamics of Instructional Groups,* ed. Nelson B. Henry (Chicago: National Society for the Study of Education, 1960), 53-82.

[245]Nelson B. Henry, ed., *The Dynamics of Instructional Groups,* (Chicago: National Society for the Study of Education, 1960).

[246]Gale Jensen, "The Classroom Group as a Unique Social System," in *The Dynamics of Instructional Groups,* ed. Nelson B. Henry (Chicago: National Society for the Study of Education, 1960), 3-10.

[247]For example see Mary A. Bany and Lois Vivian Johnson, *Classroom Group Behavior* (New York: Macmillan, 1964); Rita B. Johnson, ed., *Encounter Groups for Educators* (New York: Associated Educational Services Corporation, 1969); Richard A. Schmuck and Patricia A. Schmuck, *Group Processes in the Classroom* (W. C. Brown: Dubuque, Iowa, 1971); Shlomo Sharan, ed., *Handbook of Cooperative Learning Methods* (Westport, Conn.: Greenwood, 1994).

More recently, at least three lines of research have contributed significantly to the development of cooperative learning groups.[248] One is led by David and Roger Johnson of the Cooperative Learning Center.[249] A second is led by Robert Slavin of the Johns Hopkins University,[250] while a third is spearheaded by Shlomo Sharan of Israel.[251] The Johnsons have focused their efforts on outcomes of cooperation, cooperative strategies, and essential components of cooperative group learning. And based on extensive studies and reviews they have realized the following conclusions regarding cooperative group learning: (1) cooperative learning has been proven effective as an educational strategy; (2)cooperative learning can be used with some confidence at every age level, for any area of subject matter, and for any task; and (3)cooperative learning affects many different instructional outcomes simultaneously: achievement, reasoning, retention, motivation, friendships, prejudice, self-esteem, and moral reasoning, to name a few.[252]

Slavin's work essentially parallels the Johnsons' efforts and generally confirms their findings. In addition, Slavin has explored the possibilities of differentiating tasks whereby individual group members become experts or specialists in specific areas of the topic. For example, in his Jigsaw method, students work in four- or five-member teams whereby all members read a common narrative (book chapter, short story, or

---

[248]Joyce and Weil, *Models of Teaching*, 216.

[249]David W. Johnson, Roger T. Johnson, and Edythe J. Holubec, *Cooperative Learning in the Classroom* (Alexandria, Va.: Association for Supervision and Curriculum Development, 1994); David W. Johnson, Roger T. Johnson, and Edythe J. Holubec, *The New Circles of Learning* (Alexandria, Va.: Association for Supervision and Curriculum Development, 1994).

[250]Robert E. Slavin, *Cooperative Learning* (New York: Longman, 1983); Robert E. Slavin, *Cooperative Learning: Student Teams*, 2d ed. (Washington, D.C.: NEA, 1987).

[251]Sharan, Ackerman, and Hertz-Lazarowitz, "Academic Ahievement of Elementary School Children in Small-Group Versus Whole-Class Instruction," 125-9.

[252]Johnson, Johnson, and Holubec, *The New Circles of Learning*, 16-7.

biography). However, each member is assigned a more specific topic on which he or she is expected to become the specialist. Those with the same topics meet in expert groups to discuss them, then return to their original teams to share what they have learned with their groups.[253]

Sharan and his colleagues demonstrate a clear bias in favor of employing cooperative small groups as "the preferred instructional strategy for encouraging student involvement in learning within a social context."[254] Sharan's team has two main visions for the learner's classroom experience. The first, stemming from their rejection of the notion that the student is a passive learner, is a determination to increase students' sense of capability by teaching them to control more of their own learning opportunities by planning and carrying out activities as group members. The second vision for selecting learning techniques is embedded in the rationale that active learning—interacting with the environment—will help develop logical thinking and verbal communication skills.[255]

Educational Benefits of Small-Group Methods

Concerning the educational process, small group techniques and methods offer several benefits. But while small-group activities can be a helpful teaching-learning tool, they have certain disadvantages. The drawbacks of small-groups methods are that they are time-consuming, require the teacher to be knowledgeable in small-group processes, and are not very appropriate for the didactic dispensing of information.[256] Furthermore, small groups that are not properly structured, or where participants are poorly prepared concerning the substantive content, become

---

[253]Slavin, *Cooperative Learning: Student Teams*, 16; Judy Clark, "Pieces of the Puzzle: The Jigsaw Method," in *Handbook of Cooperative Learning Methods*, ed. Shlomo Sharan (Westport, Conn.: Greenwood, 1994), 34–50.

[254]Shlomo Sharan and Yael Sharan, *Small-Group Teaching* (Englewood Cliffs, N.J.: Educational Technology Publications, 1976), xiii.

[255]Ibid., x.

[256]Paul Westmeyer, *Effective Teaching in Adult and Higher Education* (Springfield, Ill.: Charles Thomas, 1988), 67.

nothing more than a "pooling of ignorance" and hardly undertake worthwhile learning activities. But if carefully planned and thoughtfully structured, small-group instructional techniques offer the Christian educator several benefits.

Active Learning: Perhaps the strongest benefit of group learning techniques is that they have the potential of *actively* engaging everyone in the learning process and giving larger numbers of students opportunities to voice their ideas.[257] Traditional classroom settings, where teachers speak and students passively receive information, tend to stifle student participation. Even when students are given opportunities to interact in large classroom settings there will be those who feel uncomfortable in speaking up. On the other hand, students who never participate in large classroom discussions will be more prone to participate in small groups. In so doing, argue Chet Meyers and Thomas Jones, they will gain confidence in their own abilities and the value of their ideas.[258] Small-group activities can incorporate several key elements of active learning such as listening, talking, reading, writing, and reflecting on alternative perspectives.[259]

Interpersonal Skills and Social Interaction: Another educational benefit of small-group activities is the development of critical interpersonal skills that will serve students well, not only in the small group, but in settings beyond the group. Meyers and Jones identify the skills a small-group participant might learn:

- good listening;
- ability to cooperate in a common task;
- giving and receiving helpful feedback;
- respecting differing opinions;

---

[257]Ibid.

[258]Chet Meyers and Thomas Jones, *Promoting Active Learning* (San Francisco, Calif.: Jossey-Bass, 1993), 62.

[259]Ibid., 60.

- supporting judgments with evidence;

- appreciating different points of view.[260]

Based on an extensive review of empirical research studies, Johnson, Johnson, and Holubec conclude that cooperative learning groups typically produce more positive relationships in students (including increased esprit de corps, caring and committed relationships, support for one another, valuing of diversity, and cohesion) than those involved in competitive and individualistic efforts.[261] Slavin, also basing his findings on a comprehensive survey of research, concludes that people who cooperate in small groups learn to like one another and are especially adept at appreciating and getting along with individuals outside their own ethnic group.[262]

Material Comprehension and Academic Achievement: Finally, small-group techniques are helpful in aiding students in comprehending material.[263] A burgeoning body of empirical research indicates that small-group methods enhance academic achievements. For example, Robert Borreson found that students studying statistics in small groups scored significantly higher on tests than did those working individually, studying the same content.[264] In a comparative study of elementary school children in small-group versus whole-class instruction, Sharan, Ackerman, and Hertz-Lazarowitz demonstrated that the students in cooperative small groups were able to achieve superior scores on tests which measured higher levels of cognitive functioning (according to Bloom's

---

[260]Ibid., 61.

[261]Johnson, Johnson, and Holubec, *Cooperative Learning in the Classroom,* 11-12.

[262]Slavin, *Cooperative Learning: Student Teams,* 21-2.

[263]For a helpful source on learning groups in higher education see Clark Burton and Rusel Y. Garth, eds., *Learning in Groups* (San Francisco: Jossey-Bass, 1983). The book is a collection of case studies in which group activity is the primary or exclusive process in a particular college course.

[264]C. Robert Borreson, "Success in Introductory Statistics with Small Groups," in *College Teaching* 38 (1:1990), 26–28.

taxonomy of thinking skills) than those in whole-class instruction. Achievement scores did not differ on items measuring low levels of cognitive functioning (knowledge acquisition and comprehension).[265]

In an extensive review of sixty-three empirical studies on the effects of cooperative group learning on achievement, Slavin discovered that thirty-six (57 percent) found significantly greater academic achievement in the learning groups than in whole classes. Twenty-six studies (41 percent) found no differences, and only in one study did the control group outperform the experimental group (the small group). Slavin concludes that when the classroom is structured in a manner that allows students to work cooperatively together in small groups on learning tasks, students benefit academically as well as socially.[266]

Keys to the Successful Use of Small-Group Instructional Techniques

Group teaching techniques are educationally sound only to the degree that certain procedures are followed. There are several keys to the successful use of small groups as a learning activity. One key is to have a clearly defined goal or objective for the group. In other words, the Christian educator must take precautions to insure the small-group participants know exactly what is to be accomplished by clearly stating the topic or problem, or thoroughly describing the task.[267]

Second, it is critical to understand the importance of what the groups are accomplishing in a broader context. The Christian educator might ask him or herself questions such as, What do I intend to do with the learner's findings, suggestions, or

---

[265]Sharan, Ackerman, and Hertz-Lazarowitz, "Academic Ahievement of Elementary School Children in Small-Group Versus Whole-Class Instruction," 125–9.

[266]Robert Slavin, *Cooperative Learning: Student Teams*, 2nd ed. (Washington, D. C.: National Education Association, 1987), 18–26.

[267]Peter J. Frederick, "Student Invovement: Active Learning in Large Classes," in ed. Maryellen Gleason Weimer, *Teaching Large Classes Well* (San Francisco: Jossey-Bass, 1987), 45–56.

ideas?, To what greater problem will the groups be contributing?, How do the small-group discussions fit into the overall pattern of the class?[268] Group members, observe Meyers and Jones, soon figure out if time spent in small groups is worthwhile, or simply a waste of time.[269]

Third, students must be prepared for small-group activities in two ways. They must be equipped with a certain amount of substantive content or knowledge of the issue so as to avoid pooling ignorance, as mentioned earlier. In addition they should be briefly instructed in group dynamics and small-group behavior. For example, students should be encouraged to form circles, to exercise good listening skills, to respect the thoughts and views of others, and to refrain from dominating the discussion.

Finally, the Christian educator must know when to bring the small-group discussions to closure. The learners may get so involved in the discussions that it seems counterproductive to conclude their interaction. But it is better to stop them while they are still actively dialoging and discovering rather than to wait until they have come to an uncomfortable silence or have moved on to chit-chat.

CONCLUSION

The mammoth church-based small-group movement that has emerged in the latter half of the twentieth century and continues into the next millennium is not embraced with enthusiasm by everyone. There are those who view church-related small groups as another short-lived trend or a faddish response to the whims of the masses. Christian education groups as a whole, however, are nothing of the sort and are built on solid theological, historical, sociological, and educational foundations. This chapter has been offered to provide a strong basis for using small groups for Christian education practice in local churches and parishes.

---

[268]Ibid.

[269]Meyers and Jones, *Promoting Active Learning*, 66.

3

Becoming a Group

Collections of people remain individuals until a single event or purpose or emotion molds them into groups, and then the group lives, feels, and thinks in a way of its own, superior in energy and intensity to the activity of any one of its members.[1] —Gilbert Highet

IN 1980, a team of young U.S. Olympians stunned the sports world by upsetting the powerful Soviet Union ice hockey team and going on to win the gold medal at the Lake Placid Winter Olympics. At that time, the United States was not considered an international amateur hockey power, and virtually no one considered them even a possibility to be a medal contender. The victory against the Soviet team was so unlikely that announcer Al Michaels screamed over the television broadcast, "Do you believe in miracles?" How did a ragtag collection of college kids peak at the appropriate time, defeat the then-most-powerful hockey team in the world, and go on to surprise the world by garnering a gold medal?

At the beginning of the season an athletic team comes together with the lofty hopes to reach a championship. Most likely the team launches the campaign as a group of individuals who do not work particularly well together, perhaps experience interpersonal tensions, or even express doubt as to the capabilities of the team or certain team members. But with effective leadership, a commitment to succeed, and hard work, the team will be shaped into a unit and can reasonably hope to have a successful season. If the team simply remains a group of individuals,

---

[1]Gilbert Highet, *The Art of Teaching* (New York: Vintage, 1950), 50.

if cohesion is not achieved, failure or limited success can be expected.

So it is with small groups. A small group goes through a process whereby a collection of individuals become a group. They experience tension, go through phases or stages, are made up of individuals with unique roles and behaviors, and eventually develop cohesiveness and unity. This chapter endeavors to answer the question, "How does a collection of unique individuals become a well-functioning small group?"

TENSION IN SMALL GROUPS

If a collection of individuals is to become a group that functions as a unit, one of the first issues it must address is how to manage the inescapable interpersonal tension that is a normal part of group development. Group development implies change, and as long as change is part of a system, tension will surely surface. But tension should not be viewed as an entirely negative force; in fact a certain amount of tension in many life experiences is desirable. Athletes are at their best when they find a balance between relaxation and anxiety. A certain amount of healthy anxiety motivates a student to study for an exam and thoughtfully respond to the questions. While too little or too much tension impairs our ability to think clearly or function with proper intensity, an optimum amount of tension usually enables us to perform at peak capacity. Just as individuals must learn how to handle tension productively, groups must learn how to deal with the social tensions they will experience.

One of the most widely used and helpful systems for the study of the small-group communication process was developed by Robert Bales and his associates at Harvard University. According to their investigations, twelve categories of interaction were sufficient to account for all verbal and non-verbal communication cues in a small group meeting. One of the categories the researchers identified was "Shows Tension."[2]

---

[2]Robert F. Bales, *Interaction Process Analysis* (Cambridge, Mass.: Addison-Wesley, 1951), 9.

Ernest Bormann, who studied small groups at the University of Minnesota for two decades, expanded on Bales's tension classification by dividing group tension into two categories: primary and secondary.[3] All Christian education groups experience both types.

Primary Tension

Harvey drove up and down the street anxiously looking for the house where the new singles group was supposed to meet. He was sure he had the right address, but the house just didn't seem to be on this street. He checked the address one more time—353 Cedar Court. That was it. He was on Cedar Court. "Why do they make the street layouts in these developments so confusing?" he muttered to himself. By now he was thoroughly frustrated to the point of going home and watching the basketball game. He always felt uncomfortable in groups anyway, especially when there were people there he didn't know.

Harvey finally found the house and, contrary to his better judgment, anxiously rang the doorbell. Sure enough, he was late, and as he was welcomed into the house his worst fears were realized. Not one person, except for the host, Jerry, did he know. Well it's too late now, he thought to himself, I can't leave now. However, as Harvey joined the circle of single adults he quickly realized that he was not the only one who felt uneasy. When Jerry left the room to get some refreshments there was an uncomfortable mood. At the end of the sofa, Dennis was explaining to the young man sitting beside him, in hushed words, how he ended up in this group. At the same time Sharon was saying "Hi" to an acquaintance sitting across the room. Most sat in awkward silence, not sure of what to do or say.

---

[3]Ernest Bormann, *Small Group Communication: Theory and Practice*, 3rd ed. (New York: Harper and Row, 1990),131; Ernest G. Bormann and Nancy C. Bormann, *Effective Small Group Communication*, 2nd ed. (Minneapolis, Minn.: Burgess, 1976), 73–4.

Primary tension refers to the interpersonal tension that usually occurs in the initial stages of a group's development, the kind of tension that Harvey and others experienced in the above scenario. Bormann and Bormann describe the primary tension a group will experience when they first meet: "They feel ill at ease. They do not know what to say or how to begin. The first meeting is tense and cold and must be warmed up. When groups experience primary tension, the people speak very softly; they sigh, and they are very polite. They seem bored and uninterested."[4] New members are worried about how the other members will perceive them, so they are careful not to say or do something that might alienate them from others. Individuals do not know what their contribution or that of the others will be. A number of questions may enter members' minds: Who will become the group's most influential members? Will I have a positive influence on the group? Will the other small-group members appreciate my contributions?[5] At this point members will try to avoid conflict or any behavior that would be disturbing to others, so group members tend to stick to an overly formal and polite style of interaction.

Once again, we must be reminded that primary tension is a normal occurrence in groups. Even groups that have a long-standing history should expect that tension of this nature will happen.[6] This is especially true if groups meet infrequently or when new members enter the group. Nonetheless, it is extremely important to manage tension of this nature, otherwise the group may get stuck in a stifling communication pattern of overpoliteness, formality, and reluctance to differ, which will unduly hinder critical thinking and healthy interaction.[7] If the

---

[4]Bormann and Bormann, *Effective Small Group Communication*, 73.

[5]Gloria J. Galanes and John K. Brilhart, *Communicating In Groups: Applications and Skills*, 3rd ed. (Madison, Wis.: Brown and Benchmark, 1991),120–1.

[6]J. Dan Rothwell, *In Mixed Company: Small Group Communication*, 3rd ed. (Fort Worth, Tex.: Harcourt Brace College, 1992), 69.

[7]John K. Brilhart and Gloria J. Galanes, *Effective Group Discussion*, 8th ed. (Madison, Wis.: Brown and Benchmark, 1995), 129.

Christian education group fails to diffuse primary tension early in its development, the whole style of future group meetings may be set in this awkward and stifling pattern.[8]

How can primary tension be reduced? Humor is one of the best ways to relieve this kind of tension. Bormann and Bormann advise that groups engage in laughing, joking, and socializing before getting down to business.[9] A more structured way to reduce primary tension is by taking the time to have members talk about themselves—their backgrounds, hobbies and interests, experiences—as well as their feelings about the group. The Christian educator can facilitate this kind of disclosing by preparing and asking nonthreatening questions, designed to help group members tell a little about themselves. Finally, it may be worthwhile for the group to plan for a party or a group meeting that has nothing on the agenda but social interaction and fun.

Secondary Tension

Secondary tension is work related and, like primary tension, is a normal part of group development. It results from the differences of opinion among members as they seek to carry out their tasks and from the need to make decisions as a group. For example, a learning group may disagree over the substantive content to be studied, the nature of the group, when it will meet, or where it might meet. And whether the disagreements are mild or intense, the group must resolve these secondary tensions *as a group*.[10]

Although the tendency is often to ignore secondary tension because dealing with it may be uncomfortable, groups that deal with such tensions have at least two advantages. First, attempts to ignore tension-producing issues simply do not work. If ignored, the issues will build up and impede any potential group growth or development. Second, groups that manage

---

[8]Bormann and Bormann, *Effective Small Group Communication*, 74.

[9]Ibid.

[10]Bormann, *Small Group Communication: Theory and Practice*, 135.

secondary tension experience a greater cohesiveness as a result of working through the tension together.[11]

Secondary tension can be managed or diffused in a variety of ways. Showing agreement is one way to reduce tension among members. The more often people are openly agreed with, the less defensive they become and the more they relax and communicate with each other in a positive manner.[12]

A second way the Christian educator can reduce unhealthy secondary tension is by facilitating group solidarity, helping members to indicate that they are committed to the group. Some ways to nurture solidarity are by encouraging group members to use *we* when referring to the group, to speak well of other small-group members, to offer to help each other, to express confidence in the group, and to talk about the importance of the group and its task. Promoting such actions encourages members to move away from patterns of self-centeredness and dissension.[13]

The Christian educator can also strive to diffuse secondary tension through the use of humor, as long as the humor does not ridicule or belittle other members. Humor can break uncomfortable tension, make it easier to listen, and move a group through an impasse.[14]

PHASES IN THE DEVELOPMENT OF SMALL GROUPS

A considerable body of research and theory has been amassed describing the stages, or phases, humans go through as they pass from birth to death. The development of a human being begins with the formation of a single-celled, fertilized egg at conception and arrives at birth as a complex organism. The individual then passes through early childhood, becomes a schoolchild with developing interests and abilities; an adolescent searching for identity; a young adult settling on a career

---

[11]Brilhart and Galanes, *Effective Group Discussion*, 130.

[12]Brilhart and Galanes, *Effective Group Discussion*, 130; Bormann and Bormann, *Effective Small Group Communication*, 74.

[13]Brilhart and Galanes, *Effective Group Discussion*, 130.

[14]Ibid.

and establishing a family; a parent and involved member of society; a grandparent and senior citizen. Human development is an amazingly complex and life-encompassing process.[15]

In a way, small groups are like people, in the sense that they go through identifiable phases or stages on their way to maturity. For example, just as an infant learns to crawl before walking, a group must resolve certain foundational issues before becoming productive and efficient. And a Christian education group that is concerned with tension that should have been expunged in its embrionic phase is expending mental and emotional energy that detracts from accomplishing the purposes or tasks for which the group exists.

A working knowledge of the phases a group will likely go through will be helpful to the Christian educator for a couple of reasons. First, an understanding of phases will assist the leader in nurturing development. Rather than standing by helplessly as a small group flounders or develops haphazardly, the facilitator can actively nurture the group towards outcomes that are mutually beneficial to all its members.[16] Second, knowledge about the development of a group is a practical tool in helping the small-group leader face—or avoid—many of the pitfalls or potential headaches that may be encountered. Being forewarned of potential problems takes the edge off the shock when a problem does appear, and prepares one to handle the situation accordingly.[17]

A number of small-group communication scholars have classified group development into specific phases, or stages. One of

---

[15]Human development is explored under a variety of categories including physical development; cognitive development [Jean Piaget and B. Inhelder, *The Early Growth of Logic in the Child* (New York: Harper and Row, 1964)]; moral development [Lawrence Kholberg, *The Philosophy of Moral Development* (San Francisco: Harper and Row, 1981); Carol Gilligan, *In a Different Voice* (Cambridge, Mass.: Harvard University,1982)]; psycho-social development [Erik H. Erikson, *Identity and the Life Cycle* (New York: W. W. Norton, 1980)], and faith development [James W. Fowler, *Stages of Faith* (San Francisco: Harper and Row, 1981)].

[16]Neal F. McBride, *How to Lead Small Groups* (Colorado Springs, Colo.: Navpress, 1990), 43.

[17]Ibid., 43–4.

the first researchers to investigate group stages was Robert Bales, who identified two developmental concerns with which any group must deal. Early in the development of the group, members must develop interpersonal relationships that provide harmony and stability and allow the group to function in a cooperative spirit. These, he called *socio-emotional* concerns. *Task* concerns involve the group's attention to its job and the completion of its particular assignment. Groups tend to cycle back and forth between these two concerns, focusing on one, then the other. Groups that resolve their socio-emotional concerns early, however, are quicker to shift their attention to task concerns.[18]

Bales also determined that laboratory groups that run for an hour or more go through an identifiable course of development. The first phase of a meeting is devoted largely to getting oriented to the problem the group faces. This is followed by a phase of analyzing and diagnosing the problem. Phase three might be devoted to choosing the means of controlling situational factors (e.g., the activities of the members) so as to bring about the desired goal of the group. Then a period of laughing and joking might appear, enabling the group to release and dissipate the various tensions that might have built up in the process. Finally a brief phase of reward, praise, and encouragement would knit the group together again and bring the meeting to successful closure.[19] While Bales's phases describe the process that occurs in a single meeting, Tuckman argues that groups that run for a period of a year follow a similar course of development.[20]

Tuckman himself formulated a small-group development model that identified four phases that groups go through. He cleverly identified the phases as forming (getting together), storming (period of tension), norming (determining standards and rules of conduct), and performing (goal achievement).[21] Other helpful

---

[18]Bales, *Interaction Process Analysis*, 8–10.

[19]Ibid., 11.

[20]Bruce Tuckman, "Developmental Sequences in Small Groups," in *Psychological Bulletin*, 63 (1965), 384–99.

[21]Ibid.

models that describe phases of group development are proposed by Fisher (orientation, conflict, emergence, and reinforcement)[22] and Johnson (exploration, transition, action, and termination. See Fig. 3:1).[23]

Phase One: Exploration[24]

> Jerry had been working for six months to get this single-adults group off the ground. He and his wife had correctly observed that there were a number of single adults in their church and that they, by and large, seemed to feel out of place in most of the classes, groups, and social activities available to them. As Jerry conversed with these important members of the church, he found that many of them expressed a desire to join some kind of a group that they would feel comfortable in. After a lot of time spent talking with single adults, and asking God for wisdom as to what direction to take, Jerry and his wife planned an initial meeting. Finally that time had come. The first meeting was designed to be informal, with the intent of exploring some important issues, such as the purpose of the group, the nature of the meetings, and securing details such as meeting days and times.

The initial activities of a Christian education group contribute to what is called the *exploration* phase. At this juncture of group development, interpersonal and socio-emotional concerns predominate and small-group members attempt to work out the kinds of relationships they will have with one other.[25] In drawing

---

[22]B.A. Fisher, "Decision Emergence: Phases in Group Decision Making," in *Speech Monographs*, 37 (1970), 53–66. A concise summary of the model is also found in John F. Cragan and David W. Wright, Communication in *Small Groups*, 4th ed. (St. Paul, Minn.: West, 1991), 32–4.

[23]Judy Johnson, "Stages of Small Groups," in *Small Group Leaders' Handbook*, ed. Ron Nicholas (Downers Grove, Ill.: InterVarsity, 1982), 50–61.

[24]The nomenclatures used for these phases, as well as some of the descriptions, are taken from Johnson, "Stages of Small Groups," 50–61.

[25]Brilhart and Galanes, *Effective Group Discussion*, 131.

an analogy to human development, McBride includes birthing and infancy as a part of this period. This phase begins before the group ever meets, when the initial idea to start a Christian education group is conceived.[26]

As one might expect, this phase is characterized by primary tension. Group members come to the initial meeting with a certain amount of apprehension, yet anticipating new and exciting opportunities for relationships and personal growth. Some of the questions members might ask at this point are: Do I belong to this group? Will I fit in? What are these other people like? What will this group be like? Is this group going to work? What will be expected of me? Can I place my trust in these people? There may also be a number of questions about the purpose of the group, meeting agendas, and so forth. Asking a lot of questions is important in getting the group oriented correctly. Small-group experts affirm that successful groups ask more questions than groups that are not successful.[27]

The level of interaction at this stage of the Christian education group tends to be superficial and conversation will be, by and large, on safe topics. Expectations of group members are expressed in guarded terms: ("I'm just looking for some good fellowship") and basic information is shared (occupations and where members are from). It is a time of getting to know group procedures and norms, as well as other group members.

While this phase may be relatively short, it is imperative that a proper foundation is set and early tensions are resolved so that attention can be shifted to the primary task of the group. During this initial phase, the group will be highly dependent on the leader to guide the processes and provide vital information for the successful formation of the group. The Christian educator should pay close attention to the following key leadership issues of the first phase:[28]

---

[26]McBride, *How to Lead Small Groups*, 44..

[27]John F. Cragan and David W. Wright, *Communication in Small Groups*, 4th ed. (St. Paul, Minn.: West, 1991), 32.

[28]Adapted from McBride, *How to Lead Small Groups*, 45.

- ensuring careful formation of the Christian education group;

- coordinating the initial meetings;

- clarifying the purpose or purposes of the group;

- providing an opportunity for each group member to share his or her personal story (for example: name, background, occupation, spiritual journey);

- identifying the expectations each member has for the group;

- helping members feel a sense of belonging;

- helping facilitate location and agenda details;

- clarifying format options.

It is possible that one or more members may withdraw from the Christian education group at this time because they do not feel comfortable with the nature or direction of the group. It is imperative that the facilitator take the time to clarify the reasons an individual may offer for leaving the group; on the other hand, it is important not to force anyone to remain in the small group.

Phase Two: Transition

"Jerry—phone call for you." Jerry shut down the lawn mower, muttering, "I'll never get this yard fixed up if I keep getting interrupted." It was Dennis, a young man in his early thirties who had been coming to the singles' Christian education group.

Dennis was rather abrupt and got right to the point. "I think I'm going to quit coming to the group, Jerry. I appreciate what you're trying to do with this group, giving us single adults a place where we can fit in. But that's just it. I don't fit into this group. I think the group has attracted a lot of whiners and complainers. They're always talking about their problems and nothing seems to go right for any of them. I'm sorry, but I think I've got my life pretty much in order and I don't need all that negative stuff. I just don't like the direction this group is going in." After patiently listening to Dennis unload, and urging him to consider staying as an encourager to other group members, Jerry hung up the phone, pretty much convinced Dennis wouldn't be back.

Jerry was discouraged and left wondering what the future of the group held. Dennis wasn't the only one to voice a complaint. In fact he was the third person this week to indicate dissatisfaction with the group. Jerry really thought that he and his wife could help meet a need in their church with this singles' group. But now he was wondering whether or not the group would really take off.

Clearly the most difficult and complex period of time a Christian education group will experience is the *transition* phase. While some groups may navigate this phase with relative ease, others may find it somewhat rocky. After the first month or two, members may become frustrated or disillusioned with one or more aspects of the small group and will experience the secondary tension (task-related tension) described earlier. Questioning and adjustment are two major tasks of the group in this phase. At this juncture in the small group's life, with some of the initial inhibitions are gone, members are beginning to feel free to call into question decisions and practices. Members find it a little bit easier to voice agreement or disagreement with relationships and activities.[29]

While the group leader (as well as some members) may become frustrated with this development, the wise Christian educator will recognize this phase as a necessary step in the growth to maturity. Bormann and Bormann note in their observations that successful groups establish ways to tolerate and even encourage disagreements without allowing these disagreements to strain the social fabric of the group. They build cohesiveness so that

---

[29]Ibid., 48.

they can afford to have disagreements and not break up. They joke and laugh; they demonstrate solidarity by encouraging one another with comments like, "That was a good meeting," or "We certainly accomplished something." They tell each other they are needed and that the group cannot effectively proceed without their help and participation.[30] Whether the group emerges from this transition stage stronger and more productive or not depends largely on the ability the Christian education leader has in developing cohesiveness.

The questions or comments that emerge at this point in the group's development will be similar to the following: This group is not quite what I wanted, needed, or anticipated! Who is in charge of this group? Is this group really going to work? Why are other group members not more committed? Why are we doing this? Why are we not doing this?

The level or nature of participation and interaction may reflect certain secondary tensions. It is that in-between time when individuals want openness and realness but are not willing to take the step themselves. There may be low enthusiasm, interpersonal tension, and impatience.

The real challenge facing the effective Christian educator is to manage the tension and conflict that characterizes the transition phase of the Christian education group. What can be done to help the group through this developmental stage? The first step is to reclarify the expectations and purpose of the group. Confusing points may have to be clarified and particular adjustments may have to be made. Perhaps there needs to be a change in the meeting time or alteration of the format. It might be necessary to spend time working through a particular relational issue.[31]

Second, the facilitator should model openness through self-disclosure, challenge individuals to a commitment to the group, and ask probing questions to find out what some underlying issues might be. This means that the Christian educator will

---

[30]Bormann and Bormann, *Effective Small Group Communication*, 75.

[31]McBride, *How to Lead Small Groups*, 49.

have to be an active listener, encouraging group members to share their opinions and feelings.[32]

And third, the Christian educator should tolerate, even encourage, disagreement and differences. Suppressing differences or frustrations will only contribute to increased tension and cultivate more conflict. The trick is to keep the disagreement or conflict within limits that are tolerable. One way to do this is to encourage group members to stick to the issue at hand and avoid drifting into irrelevant side issues that might stir up unnecessary contention.[33]

Some key issues for the Christian educator to remember during this developmental phase are:[34]

- allowing members to question the practices of the small group;

- accepting the need to make necessary adjustments or change;

- conducting evaluations;

- helping members accept responsibility for the group;

- changing where change is needed;

- encouraging group involvement in decision making.

Phase Three: Action

"Hey Jerry, how ya doin'?" It was Ben Thornton, a member of the singles' group that met every Tuesday evening. "I wanted to talk to you about some things concerning our group. First, thanks for the great leadership you're providing. The group has come to mean so much to me—I don't know what I'd do without it. Say, is it okay if I invite a friend from work? I've been talking about what we do to-

---

[32]Rothwell, *In Mixed Company*, 71.

[33]Ibid.

[34]Adapted from McBride, *How to Lead Small Groups*, 49.

gether and how the group has helped me, and he asked if there was room for one more. I said I'd check with you. Oh, one more thing. Your wife has been providing refreshments up till now. Do you think she would mind if I brought some donuts this week? It might save her a little work."

Jerry was flying high as he drove home from the mall. Just three weeks ago he thought the group was going to fold. Now everyone seems to be excited about what's going on. Members are volunteering to help in various ways, they are coming up with ideas to make the group better, and they are even inviting others to come out. "I wonder what happened to cause such a change?" he reflected.

Assuming the Christian education group does not self-destruct during the difficult transition period, it moves into the *action* phase. Galanes and Brilhart call this the *production* phase, the stage where the group is able to concentrate on its primary task or purposes.[35] McBride describes it as the performing stage, the point at which the small group functions with effectiveness and purpose and views itself as being successful.[36] This is the point at which the group reaches maturity; members come together and become more productive.

The types of questions participants may now be asking are more positive in nature: What can I do to be more involved? What can I do for the betterment of the group? How can we meet our goals? How can we better accomplish our tasks? Members are enthusiastic and cooperative. The level of interaction moves from the superficial and cautious to the point where deeper and more personal self-disclosure takes place. Interpersonal relationships are maturing and personal growth is happening. As group procedures gradually unfold more smoothly in the production stage, increasing amounts of time can be spent directly on task concerns and less on relational

---

[35]Galanes and Brilhart, *Communicating in Groups: Applications and Skills*, 126.

[36]McBride, *How to Lead Small Groups*, 49.

issues.[37] However, at no time can a group disregard interpersonal concerns and relationships.

It should be noted that a Christian education group can experience a sort of "mid-life crisis." A group could get bored with the routine, encounter unresolved conflicts or clashing schedules, develop ambiguous norms, or experience a lack of variety in meetings. When a crisis of this nature occurs, special effort by the Christian education leader is needed to identify the cause and satisfactorily resolve the issue.[38]

Key leadership issues for the Christian educator at the action phase are summarized as follows:[39]

- maintaining small-group relationships, procedures, and details;

- encouraging ongoing participation in the life of the group;

- enabling the group to be accountable and responsible for itself;

- assisting the group to deal with the ups and downs;

- conducting evaluations of the group and group development;

- making any necessary adjustments for improvement.

Phase Four: Termination

Jerry was carefully rehearsing the words he would have to share with the singles' group tonight. Three years have slipped by since they first met and a lot has happened since then. Interestingly, only three of the seven original members remain and others have come and gone. When the group got together tonight, he was going to suggest that it was time they disband and encourage members to get involved in other ministries or

---

[37]Brilhart and Galanes, *Effective Group Discussion*, 132.

[38]McBride, *How to Lead Small Groups*, 50.

[39]Adapted from McBride, *How to Lead Small Groups*, 50.

groups. There were several reasons for his thinking. First, he felt the group had grown stagnant and the current participants were reticent to including newcomers. This attitude was quite contrary to the spirit in which the group was started. Second, the church had developed other ministries and groups for singles that were doing a better job of meeting the emotional and spiritual needs of single adults. And third, he and his wife felt that they should move into another area of ministry. Their oldest daughter was thirteen, and they would like to get involved as volunteers in the youth group she was attending. Jerry realized that his proposal would be met with resistance and emotions would certainly get involved. But as far as he was concerned, this was the direction he—and they— had to go.

Every small group, no matter how successful, will eventually come to an end. This *termination* phase may occur by choice or through natural cause. Many groups are designed to last for a predetermined amount of time; others are open-ended and exist until something causes closure. Perhaps the leader moves away, or the purpose for which the group exists ceases to hold meaning.

This may be the most difficult time of the whole small group experience, and whatever the reason for termination, careful attention must be given to this final phase of development, ensuring the group ends on as positive a note as possible. Actually, a small group does not simply conclude on its final meeting; it is a process that takes place over a number of meetings.[40]

Depending on how meaningful and successful the group has been in meeting individual needs and nurturing interpersonal relationships, there will likely be a grieving process that takes place. Thus, one of the primary tasks of the leader will be to help group members deal with grieving that may accompany termination. In a situation where successful groups are required to disband in spite of their feelings or preferences, it is important that members are brought to understand the value inherent in this process.[41]

---

[40]Ibid., 51.

[41]Ibid.

Figure 3.1

Phases of Small Group Development

Phase	Description	Leadership Issues
Exploration	Formation stage. Group members have mixed feelings of anticipation and apprehension. Level of interaction is superficial and focused on safe topics.	Assure formation of group. Coordinate first meeting. Clarify purpose. Provide for storytelling. Deal with expectations. Help members belong. Facilitate establishment of format details.
Transition	Questioning and adjustment. Group often experiences tension and questioning of decisions and practices. Some members will become frustrated to the point of dropping out.	Allow questioning. Conduct evaluation. Make adjustments. Help group accept responsibility for itself. Affirm group invovlement in decision making.
Action	The production phase, where the group is able to concentrate on its task or purpose.	Maintain group relationships, prcedures, and details. Encourage continued participation. Help the group be responsible for itself. Assist the group to deal with ups and downs. Conduct formal evaluation. Make necessary adjustments or improvements.
Termination	Period of coming to an end. May be a very difficult time for some members.	Help group members through grieving. Help members understand the need or value of breaking up. Review and reflect on accomplishments. Show appreciation. Give thanks to God. Do a summative evaluation.

They might be reminded of the value of developing relationships with other members of the church, of the importance of new and fresh experiences, and of the dangers of cliques and ingrownness that often accompanies ongoing groups.

In addition, there are a number of procedures the Christian educator can do to help make termination a successful process. First, reviewing and reflecting on what God has accomplished in and through the group during its time together is vital. One or two of the final meetings should be set aside for this. These are times to laugh and cry together, to enjoy reminiscing, and to praise God for each other and the group as a whole.[42] Second, as a leader, demonstrate your personal appreciation to group members for their contributions to the success of the group and to the personal development of group members. Third, as a group, give thanks to God for what has happened in the period of time the group has been together. Fourth, it would be a formal process of gathering specific information to be used to make judgments and decisions about the group. This information then provides the basis for forming and nurturing future small groups, and for learning from group achievements and mistakes.[43]

RULES AND NORMS:
STANDARDS FOR SMALL-GROUP BEHAVIOR

When Captain James Cook, on his remarkable eighteenth-century voyage to the South Pacific, asked the Tahitian chiefs why they always ate alone and apart from each other, they simply responded, "Because it is right." If we ask Canadians and Americans why they sit at tables when they eat, or why they eat with knives and forks, or why they greet one another with handshakes, or why they applaud at concerts, we will most likely get similar, rather vague answers: "Because that's our custom." "Because that's the way

---

[42]Ibid.

[43]Ibid., 52.

we do it." "Just because its right." Or even, "I don't really know."

The reason for these, and countless other actions and patterns of social behavior, is that members of any society are influenced by shared standards and guidelines that prescribe appropriate behavior in a given situation. *Norms* are behavioral standards that describe how people "ought" to act in a particular society under certain circumstances.[44] For example, when we attend a symphony concert we behave according to a whole set of norms related to gatherings of this nature. We clap politely at certain points, refrain from loud talking while the orchestra is performing, and perhaps applaud more vigorously for an encore. If we were to attend a rock concert or the Grand Ole Opry, our expected behavior would be significantly different. A system of norms enables us to predict what people will do in particular situations and pattern our own behavior appropriately.[45]

The standards of behavior and procedures by which members of a small group operate are also governed by rules and norms. Rules and norms are important for a Christian education group in that they help group members know what is and is not acceptable behavior in a particular small-group setting.[46]

Group Rules

Rules are more formalized guidelines and may be constructed from two sources; external and internal. First, they may be prescribed by the church or the arm of the church responsible for establishing and monitoring Christian education small groups. For example, the director of Christian education may decree that all small groups meet for no longer than one year or that groups use a particular curriculum or format.

---

[44]Judson R. Landis, *Sociology: Concepts and Characteristics*, 10th ed. (Belmont, Calif.: Wadsworth, 1998), 76.

[45]Ibid., 77.

[46]Galanes and Brilhart, *Communicating in Groups: Applications and Skills*, 127.

A second source of formal rules is the group itself. For example, the small group may decide at what time meetings will start and finish, where the meetings will be held, what will be studied or discussed, what may be shared or not shared, and perhaps some guidelines on confidentiality. Sometimes these rules are articulated in the form of a covenant or contract that is written, agreed upon, and signed by members of the group. This is more appropriate in a closed group that involves a high level of accountability and commitment than it is in an open group where participants come and go more freely. More will be said of covenants shortly.

Group Norms

Small-group norms, or standards, are informal "rules" and are seldom written down. Rather, they are shared attitudes, values, beliefs, behaviors, and procedures related to the group's purpose that are usually agreed upon subconsciously by group members.[47] For example, urban gang members are clearly identified by a distinctive style of dress and unique argot. In a similar manner, members of a particular Christian education group are likely to display a noticeable homogeneity of values, behaviors, and attitudes. These norms are established in a variety of ways. Sometimes behaviors that occur early in the development of the group help establish enduring group norms. For example, to reduce tension at the initial meeting, a hostess serves coffee to members as they arrive. This could very well establish the norm, or standard operating procedure, that each meeting begins with a cup of coffee.

Norms, though typically unspoken, can also be established by explicit statements made by group leaders or other members. For example, a member may inform a new attender that a particular chair is usually reserved for the group facilitator. Or the group leader may remind members that while arriving to the meeting five minutes late is tolerated, it is generally not acceptable to ar-

---

[47]Dorwin Cartwright and Alvin Zander, eds., *Group Dynamics: Research and Theory*, 3rd ed. (New York: Harper and Row, 1968), 139.

rive much later than that since it is disruptive to the group discussion. There is no question that the expectations that individual members and groups exert on others result in uniform behavior patterns.[48]

Critical events or important happenings may also contribute to the development of group norms. Galanes and Brilhart describe a situation in which the group members of a small class came to trust each other to the point of revealing personal information with each other. "Two of the students told nonmembers some of what occurred in the class. When the other members discovered this, they felt angry. At the next meeting, members expressed their feelings of betrayal, and the group discussed nothing else during that class period. Whereas before the critical incident some members thought it was all right to reveal in-class information to selected outsiders, after the meeting it was clear to *all* members that such behavior was a serious violation of a group norm requiring confidentiality."[49]

Finally, norms are often a carry-over from the larger society or environment that small-group members belong to.[50] Common courtesy norms, such as not interrupting, refraining from telling rude or crude jokes that might offend someone, or not smoking, are examples of norms that are carried over from the larger culture. Difficulties arise, however, when group members come from different cultures. For example, students from certain Asian cultures often respond more passively in educational settings than do American students.[51]

---

[48]Leon Festinger, Stanley Schachter, and Kurt Back, "Operation of Group Standards," in *Group Dynamics: Research and Theory*, 3rd ed. Dorwin Cartwright and Alvin Zander, eds. (New York: Harper and Row, 1968), 152–164.

[49]Galanes and Brilhart, *Communicating In Groups: Applications and Skills*, 129.

[50]Cartwright and Zander, *Group Dynamics: Research and Theory*, 141.

[51]Galanes and Brilhart, *Communicating In Groups: Applications and Skills*, 129.

Small-Group Covenants

Sometimes Christian education groups set forth group expectations in the form of a covenant, a written contract that is agreed upon by all group members. Covenants not only establish what is expected of group members, they also assist the group in identifying and achieving its purpose, goals, and intentions. A solid understanding of small-group covenants will be enhanced by exploring the biblical notion of covenant, the use of learning contracts in adult education, and the use of learning covenants in Christian education.

The Biblical Notion of Covenant: A covenant is one way to verbalize and seal a commitment one person has for another. In the Old Testament, covenant refers to *a legally binding obligation.*[52] According to Robertson, the result of a covenant commitment is "the establishment of a relationship 'in connection with,' 'with' or 'between' people."[53] To Noah, God announces His covenantal intentions: "I will establish my covenant with you, and you will enter the ark. . . . I establish my covenant with you: Never again will all life be cut off by the waters of a flood; never again will there be a flood to destroy the earth" (Ge 6:18; 9:11). God's covenant with Noah involves not only Noah and his family, but is extended to all mankind and creation. God promises never again to curse the ground or destroy living creatures as He did in the Flood.[54]

To Abraham, God makes this binding promise: "As for me, this is my covenant with you: You will be the father of many nations. No longer will you be called Abram; your name will be Abraham, for I have made you a father of many nations" (Ge 17:4–5). This covenant, however, requires reciprocity: "As for you, you must keep my covenant, you and your descendants after you for the generations to come" (v. 9). Consequently, notes Waltke, there

---

[52]J. Barton Payne, *The Theology of the Older Testament* (Grand Rapids: Zondervan, 1962), 79.

[53]O. Palmer Robertson, *The Christ of the Covenants* (Philipsburg, N.J.: Presbyterian and Reformed, 1989), 6.

[54]Bruce K. Waltke, "The Phenomenon of Conditionality within Unconditional Covenants," in *Israel's Apostasy and Restoration*, Avraham Gileadi, ed. (Grand Rapids: Baker, 1988), 123-39.

is a connection between Abraham's faith and Yahweh's fulfillment of the covenant with Him.[55]

It is always, however, the almighty Yahweh who initiates and imposes the covenant—people do not earn it. McCarthy points out that this is so true that it is even possible for the human partner to be asleep when the covenant is made (Ge 15:9–12; 17–18).[56] It is Yahweh alone who establishes the conditions of the covenant.[57]

God's covenants with Noah and Abraham are forthright manifestations of His love and faithfulness to His people. Payne states that God's self-imposed obligation for the deliverance of sinners becomes an instrument for effectuating God's elective love.[58] In a similar manner, we create covenants in Christian education groups of various kinds as a way of solidifying our desire to love others.[59] Em Griffin favors initiating covenants in groups because it acknowledges our desire to love others in the same manner God loved us.[60] By the covenant, individuals become committed to one another.[61]

The Use of Learning Contracts in Adult Education: A learning contract,[62] as used in adult education situations, is a binding agreement between the adult learner (or learning group) and the instructor. It stipulates the precise ways in which to achieve and demonstrate the achievement of a particular educational

---

[55]Ibid., 128.

[56]Dennis J. McCarthy, *Old Testament Covenant* (Atlanta: John Knox, 1972), 3.

[57]Gustave Friedrich Oehler, *Theology of the Old Testament*, trans. E. D. Smith and S. Taylor (Grand Rapids: Zondervan, n.d.), 175.

[58]Payne, *The Theology of the Older Testament*, 79.

[59]Judy Johnson, "Making a Covenant," in *Small Group Leaders' Handbook*, ed. Ron Nicholas (Downers Grove, Ill.: InterVarsity, 1982), 85–94.

[60]Em Griffin, *Getting Together* (Downers Grove, Ill.: InterVarsity, 1982), 35.

[61]Robertson, *The Christ of the Covenants,* 7.

[62]*Contract* is another word describing a binding agreement, thus making it a synonym of *covenant*. In secular education, however, *contract* seems to be the preferred terminology when referring to an agreement between learner and teacher.

goal.[63] Stephen Brookfield has reviewed the literature on learning contracts and confirmed that they have been utilized in a variety of educational settings including adult education, higher education, educational training, and Christian education.[64]

The learning contract model was originally proposed by androgogy expert Malcolm Knowles, who proclaims that the learning contract is an ideal way to enable students to structure their own learning.[65] One of the greatest benefits of this technique, he suggests, is that it solves (or at least reduces) the problem of dealing with a wide variety of differences within a group of adult learners (e.g., educational backgrounds, experience, learning speeds, learning styles, interests, and outside commitments). Learners can articulate their objectives in their own terms and identify learning resources and strategies that work best with their particular learning styles.[66] A second benefit, he proposes, is that what adults learn on their own initiative they learn deeper and more permanently than when they are being taught by someone else.[67] Knowles specifies a clear-cut pattern for developing a learning contract:[68]

1. Diagnose your learning needs.
2. Specify your learning objectives.

---

[63]Raymond J. Wlodkowski, *Enhancing Adult Motivation to Learn* (San Francisco: JosseyBass, 1993), 103.

[64]Stephen D. Brookfield, *Understanding and Facilitating Adult Learning* (San Francisco: Jossey-Bass, 1986), 81.

[65]Malcom S. Knowles, *Self-Directed Learning* (New York: Cambridge, 1975), 129–135; Malcom S. Knowles, *The Modern Practice of Adult Education: From Pedagogy to Andragogy* (Chicago: Follett, 1980), 243; Malcom S. Knowles, *Using Learning Contracts: Practical Approaches to Individualizing and Structuring Learning* (San Francisco: Jossey-Bass, 1986).

[66]Knowles, *The Modern Practice of Adult Education*, 243.

[67]Knowles, *Self-Directed Learning*, 129.

[68]For a more exhaustive treatment of the steps for contract development see Knowles, *The Modern Practice of Adult Education*, 382–5 or Knowles, *Self-Directed Learning*, 130–5.

3. Identify the resources (material and human) you will use in accomplishing each objective and the strategies (techniques and tools) you will employ in utilizing them.
4. Specify target dates for completing each objective.
5. Describe the evidence to be collected as indicators of objective achievement.
6. Specify how the evidence is to be evaluated.
7. Review the learning contract with consultants.
8. Carry out the contract.
9. Evaluate the learning experience.

The Use of Learning Covenants in Christian Education: The learning contract, as proposed by Knowles, has been appropriately adapted by Wickett for adult Christian education practice. He changes the nomenclature, however (without any explanation), from *learning contract* to learning *covenant*.[69]

Wickett suggests the model can be effectively used with either individuals or groups and proposes a number of potential values for learning covenants in the Christian education context. First, there is a high level of commitment that develops in using this particular learning process. Second, a covenant establishes a definitive framework in which learning can occur. Third, upon completing a covenant, both the learner and facilitator know what to expect of the learner. Finally, a covenant can help provide clear evidence of what the learner has accomplished as a result of the Christian education experience. Wickett sees the model as being most helpful in the acquisition of ministry skills.[70]

---

[69]R.E.Y. Wickett, *Models of Adult Religious Education Practice* (Birmingham, Ala.: Religious Education Press, 1991), 100–10; R. E. Y. Wickett, "Specific Educational Procedures: Methods and Techniques," in *Handbook of Young Adult Religious Education*, Harley Atkinson, ed. (Birmingham, Ala.: Religious Education Press, 1997), 186–203.

[70]Wickett, *Models of Adult Religious Education Practice*, 102–3.

The following outline provides procedures for the Christian educator in developing the learning covenant:[71]

1. Ask the learner to review material related to the learning contract.

2. Have the learner consider his or her specific area of interest.

3. Provide a short explanation and clarification of the learner contract technique.

4. Ask the . . . adult learner to identify his or her particular interest, and discuss this for deeper understanding by both the . . . adult religious educator and learner.

5. Have the learner begin work on a draft of a written contract.

6. Review the draft with the learner, paying close attention to issues such as clarity, feasibility, and accessibility of resources. The covenant should include resources and process.

7. Make sure the learner leaves the second session with clear insight into what should be done to prepare a final written contract.

8. Review and approve the document in the third session. Make arrangements at this time for the monitoring of the contract.

9. Continue to provide support for the learner until the final session, when the learner brings closure to the experience through self evaluation and response from you, the religious educator.

Writing a Christian Education Small-Group Covenant: While there are similarities between learning contracts or covenants and small-group covenants, there is at least one distinct difference. A learning contract is a binding agreement between two parties (an adult learner or learning group and an instructor) that identifies the exact ways in which to achieve and

---

[71]Wickett, "Specific Educational Procedures: Methods and Techniques," 197–8.

demonstrate achievement of a particular learning goal. A small-group covenant may include an agreement with an instructor or Christian educator, but it is primarily concerned with the commitments group members have with one another and the intentions they set for themselves as a group.[72] A covenant of this nature assists the group in identifying and achieving its purpose and goals and enables them to resolve format and procedure questions.

One source suggests the following helpful steps in writing a covenant:[73]

1. Ask participants to identify their expectations for the small group.

2. As they share their expectations, write them so that the whole group can see them.

3. Have members identify what they liked and disliked about other small groups they have participated in.

4. Ask members what they are willing to commit themselves to as a group to meet their expectations. Make sure that each part is fully understood by all and everyone agrees with each statement.

5. State how long the covenant will be in effect and when it will be evaluated.

6. Print the covenant and have it signed by each group member.

7. Submit a copy to each individual.

What should be included in a covenant? Christian education small groups should consider including at least three componants: (1) purpose and goals, (2) format and procedures, and (3) expectations and standards for participation.

The first order of covenanting is to determine the purpose and goals of the small group. For what reason or reasons does

---

[72]Johnson, "Making a Covenant," 89.

[73]Adapted from Ron Nichols, editor, *Good Things Come in Small Groups* (Downers Grove, Ill.: Intervarsity Press, 1985), 142.

the group exist? What would the group like to accomplish? For example, a small group in one of my classes declared their purpose statement as follows: "It is our goal to build trust, character, and accountability in the lives of group members, and develop a proper understanding of God through prayer, Bible study, and fellowship." Another group identified four goals: (1) To encourage and build each other up; (2) to learn how to lead a small group; (3) to learn how to minister to others within the context of a small group; and (4) to understand God's will for our lives.

The next step in developing a small-group covenant is to determine the group format and operating procedures that govern the small group: what the Christian education group does when it meets and the details necessary to ensure that meetings unfold successfully. Some format and procedure questions that must be resolved are identified as follows:[74]

- When do you meet?

- Where do you meet?

- How long should the meetings be?

- What will be the length of time this group will be together?

- What do you do when you meet?

- How large or small should the group be?

- Is the group open (always willing to take in new members) or closed (does not take in new members)?

- Will the group be homogeneous (same gender, same age bracket, etc.) or heterogeneous (both genders, mixed ages, etc.)?

Finally, a small group should identify expectations and standards, the ground rules for small group participation. These are the "rules" one particular group agreed to follow (these

---

[74]Summarized from McBride, *How to Lead Small Groups*, 67ff.

were written for a particular kind of closed group, and serve only as an *example* of what the expectations and standards of a group might include):[75]

1. Be personal, not abstract, when sharing needs. Do not deal with theological abstractions, but with overt acts, attitudes and feelings.

2. Intellectual opinions play no part in our discussions, except as they may bear upon our own personal lives.

3. Each person has a right to his or her feelings. No one is condemned for having feelings and each person is encouraged to express those feelings, even though they may embarrass the other group members or the person's spouse. The task of the group is to protect the rights of each person.

4. While we always express our feelings, we are careful not to excuse one another or pass judgment on one another—especially our spouses. We are not called to confess one another's sins—only our own sins and deficiencies.

5. We agree to pray for one another daily.

6. We agree to try to set aside daily quiet time for study, meditation, and prayer.

7. What is spoken in the group remains in the group.

8. We agree we will not discuss church business except as it affects each of us personally.

In another covenant model, Em Griffin suggests the following ground rules be included:[76]

- *"Attendance:* I need everyone in the group in order to grow. One person's absence will affect the whole group. . . . Dealing with the stories or problems of those who are not here is helpful neither to them nor to us. . . .

---

[75]Quoted from *Buckingham Report* (vol. 1, no. 22, November 20, 1985), 1.

[76]Quoted from Em Griffin, *Getting Together* (Downers Grove, Ill.: Intervarsity, 1982), 35–7.

- *Affirmation:* There is nothing you have done or will do to cause us to/make me stop loving you. I may not agree with your actions, but I will love you unconditionally. It is more blessed to care than to cure. . . .

- *Confidentiality:* What's said here stays here! A permissive atmosphere flourishes when others are trustworthy. I will never repeat what another has said unless given special permission.

- *Openness:* I will strive to reveal who I am—my hopes, hurts, backgrounds, joys and struggles—as well as I am able. I'll share a story not a sermon. I can help others more by risking to be known and telling what is real to me than when I repeat a teaching I heard from someone else.

- *Honesty:* I will try to mirror back what I see others saying and doing. This way I will help you understand something you may want to change but were unaware of. You can help me in the same way. This may strain our relationship, but I will have confidence in your ability to hear the truth in love. I will try to express his honestly, to meter it, according to what I perceive the circumstances to be.

- *Sensitivity:* I will try to put myself in your shoes and understand what it is like to be you. I will try to hear you, see you and feel where you are, to draw you out of the pit of discouragement or withdrawal. But I recognize that you have the individual right to remain silent. Groups don't have rights; individuals do.

- *Accountability:* I am responsible for my own growth. I won't blame others for my feelings. None of us are trapped into behaviors that are unchangeable. I am accountable to myself, others and God to become what God has designed me to be in His loving creation. I will help you become what you can be.

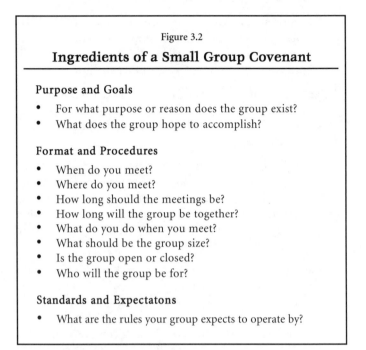

Figure 3.2

Ingredients of a Small Group Covenant

Purpose and Goals

* For what purpose or reason does the group exist?
* What does the group hope to accomplish?

Format and Procedures

* When do you meet?
* Where do you meet?
* How long should the meetings be?
* How long will the group be together?
* What do you do when you meet?
* What should be the group size?
* Is the group open or closed?
* Who will the group be for?

Standards and Expectatons

* What are the rules your group expects to operate by?

* *Prayer:* During the course of this group, I will pray for the other members and bask in the confidence that they are praying for me.

I do not propose that covenants be made mandatory for all Christian education groups, but it is important that people who join groups demonstrate a sense of commitment to that group. Covenanting is one way to demonstrate commitment. Covenants also help to develop member ownership, with each participant aware of his or her responsibilities. But most important, they remind us of God's faithful commitment to His people and help put love in action by assisting group members to be accountable to each other.[77]

---

[77]Wickett, "Specific Educational Procedures: Methods and Techniques," 197–8.

DEVELOPING GROUP COHESIVENESS

An indispensable dimension of small-group development and ultimate effectiveness is cohesiveness, the "we" orientation a small group has. In fact, cohesiveness has come to hold a principal position in most theories of group dynamics. For example, Johnson and Johnson include cohesion as an important aspect of group effectiveness and further describe group cohesiveness "as the sum of all the factors influencing members to stay in the group; it is the result of the positive forces of attraction toward the group outweighing the negative forces of repulsion away from the group."[78] Cartwright sees cohesiveness as the degree to which group members desire to remain a part of a particular group.[79] Rothwell defines it as the degree of attraction individuals have to a group and their desire to be a member,[80] and Shaw simply sees it as the "degree to which a group 'hangs together' as a unit."[81] The notion of cohesiveness as proposed by sociologists and small-group experts is somewhat likened to Paul's descriptive concept of the church as a *body*, which "joined and held together by every supporting ligament, grows and builds itself up in love, as each part does its work" (Eph 4:16).

What characterizes a highly cohesive group? A small group is high in cohesiveness if the relationships among small-group members are, for the most part, attractive to them and they have a high degree of togetherness and unity.[82] The level of group cohesiveness is evidenced in a number of ways: attendance by group members, arriving on time, trust and support group members have for one another, the amount

---

[78]David Johnson and Frank Johnson, *Joining Together* (Englewood Cliffs, N.J.: Prentice-Hall, 1975), 233.

[79]Dorwin Cartwright, "The Nature of Group Cohesiveness," in *Group Dynamics*, eds. Dorwin Cartwright and Alvin Zander (New York: Harper and Row, 1968), 91–109.

[80]Rothwell, *In Mixed Company: Small Group Communication*, 74.

[81]Marvin E. Shaw, "Group Composition and Group Cohesion," in *Small Group Communication*, 6th ed., eds. Robert S. Cathcart and Larry A. Samovar (Dubuque, Iowa: Brown), 214–220.

[82]Brilhart and Galanes, *Effective Group Discussion*, 143.

166 ❖ The Power of Small Groups in Christian Education

of individuality accepted by group members, how much fun
members have, [83] rates of interaction, positive feelings group
members express for one another, satisfaction with the group,
the ability to effectively cope with problems, and productivity.[84]

The Importance of Cohesiveness

Keeping the above definitions in mind, one can only surmise that cohesiveness is the "glue" that keeps a group together.
It is the affective variable which causes members to stay with
the group even when there are pressures or influences to leave
it.[85] However, early work by Cartwright and subsequent efforts
by Marvin Shaw identify several additional positive consequences of group cohesiveness.[86]

Maintenance of Group Membership: One of the positive consequences of group cohesiveness is the ability it provides the
group to retain members through group attractiveness. Thibaut
and Kelly formulated a helpful explanation to account for the
ability a group has in retaining or losing members. They proposed that the level of cohesiveness at any point in time is a
function of two types of forces affecting each member. *Cen-
tripetal* forces consist of materials and rewards the group
provides that attract or pull an individual into the group. *Cen-
trifugal* forces are made up of the costs or detriments that are
extracted from a group member. If the rewards a group offers
are greater than the drawbacks, group membership is maintained.[87] For example, if one of the rewards of belonging to a
Christian education group is maintaining several intimate
friendships, that person must examine the attraction of the

---

[83]Johnson and Johnson, *Joining Together*, 234.

[84]Brilhart and Galanes, *Effective Group Discussion*, 143–4.

[85]Robert S. Cathcart, Larry A. Samavor, and Linda D. Henman, *Small Group
Communication*, 7th ed. (Madison, Wis.: Brown and Benchmark, 1996), 179.

[86]Cartwright, "The Nature of Group Cohesiveness," 103–9; Shaw, "Group
Composition and Group Cohesion," 214.

[87]John W. Thibaut and Harold H. Kelly, *The Social Psychology of Groups*.
(New York: Wiley, 1959).

reward over the cost of time taken out of a schedule that affords him precious few free hours. If the need for relationships outweighs the need for time, he will most likely remain in the group.

Influence of a Group Over Members: The New Testament clearly and without reservation declares that Christians are members one of another (Rom 12:5). In three major passages, the apostle Paul makes extensive use of the analogy of the body (*soma*) to illustrate this concept (1Co 12; Ro 12; Eph 4). Just as there are many parts of the physical body, so the body of Christ is made up of many parts. Taking the analogy a step further, Paul teaches that each individual brings a gift or contribution to the effective building up of the body. No Christian can function adequately alone—we exist, at least in part, to influence and be influenced by one another.

The very nature of the Christian education group is such that it provides great opportunity to influence the lives of others. Highly cohesive small groups have the ability to exert a greater influence over group members than do low-cohesive groups. In a study of community groups, Festinger, Schachter, and Back found that the more cohesive the groups were, the more effectively they influenced their members. Further, they found that in more cohesive groups there were fewer deviants than in less cohesive groups.[88]

Achievement of Group Goals: High-cohesive groups are also more effective than low-cohesive groups in accomplishing tasks or achieving whatever goals group members have set for themselves.[89] Bormann and Bormann correctly observe that cohesive task groups accomplish more because participants take the initiative and assist one another. By contrast, members of groups that lack cohesion wait for assignments and do only what they

---

[88]Leon Festinger, Stanley Schachter, and Kurt Back, "Operation of Group Standards," in *Group Dynamics*, eds. Dorwin Cartwright and Alvin Zander (New York: Harper and Row, 1968), 152-64.

[89]Shaw, "Group Composition and Group Cohesion," 215.

are told to do.[90] Christian education groups that want to nur-ture cohesiveness will stress teamwork and ensure that group performance comes before personal glory or achievement.

Group Communication: It should come to no surprise to any-one that people who like each other and enjoy one another's company will engage in more verbal interaction than those who dislike each other. Empirical research indicates that the more co-hesive the group, the more efficient the communication within the group.[91] Cohesiveness encourages feedback, disagreements, questions, and interaction because group members know their places and are secure. By contrast, low-cohesive groups are quiet and apathetic, with little disagreement or give-and-take discus-sion.[92] Since a Christian education group, as does any small group, succeeds or fails based on its ability to communicate efficiently, it is imperative that group leaders build a cooperative atmosphere which will, in turn, enhance dynamic intragroup communication.

Building Cohesiveness in a Christian Education Group

So how then do Christian education groups build cohesive-ness? Ernest and Nancy Bormann suggest a group attend to at least five activities,[93] to which Brilhart and Galanes add a sixth.[94]

Develop Group Identity: One important step to greater group cohesiveness is group identity. The psychologist, Erik Erikson, made popular the term *identity* in his work related to psycho-social development. Erikson was concerned with the ability of the adolescent or young adult to develop an *ego* ("I") identity to help identify who he or she is in relationship to family and society.[95]

---

[90]Bormann and Bormann, *Effective Small Group Communication*, 48.

[91]Kurt W. Back, "Influence Through Social Communication," in *Journal of Abnormal and Social Psychology* 46:9–23; A.J. Lott and B.E. Lott, "Group Cohesiveness, Communication Level, and Conformity," in *Journal of Abnormal and Social Psychology* 62:408–12.

[92]Bormann and Bormann, *Effective Small Group Communication*, 48.

[93]Ibid., 70–2.

[94]Brilhart and Galanes, *Effective Group Discussion*, 145.

[95]Erik H. Erikson, *Identity and the Life Cycle* (New York: W. W. Norton, 1980).

Similarly, Christian education groups that desire cohesiveness should work towards identifying themselves as a unique group. Group members should speak of the group as *we*, not *you*. References should be made to *our* group and what *we* want to accomplish. The leader or facilitator should accentuate the *we* rather than the *I*. For example, he or she should avoid stressing personal statements like "I would like to see our group do. . . ." or "I would like to see our group reach this goal." Groups can also encourage identity formation by developing insignias, mascots, or nicknames that offer group members a special sense of belonging.

Build Group Tradition: "Tradition," declared the Jewish peasant Tevye in *Fiddler on the Roof,* "gives us balance." However, as a poor milkman trying to marry off five young daughters, he found that not everyone agreed with his time-honored value system. Even his daughters rebelled against certain religious and family traditions. We may not agree with Tevye's particular passion for tradition, but most of us would admit that there is at least some merit in maintaining tradition in our activities, institutions, and even small groups.

No sooner does a Christian education group begin, than special things occur. Somebody has a birthday, anniversary, or the birth of a new child—the group begins to have a history. Highly cohesive groups take the opportunity to celebrate these special happenings through traditional events, ceremonies, or rituals. Such traditional celebrations add meaning to group functionality and help build loyalty. Groups might also include opportunities to recall past events that were unusual, exciting, or humorous, so that they become part of the group's history and tradition.

Stress Teamwork: Highly cohesive groups avoid selfish attitudes, as well as emphasizing personal credits or accomplishments. The effective Christian educator will ensure that team performance comes before personal glory. One approach to group leadership that enhances teamwork, even with a designated leader, is distributing leadership responsibility among the group members. Although a considerable amount of responsibility is placed on the designated leader for coordinating and structuring the group's activities, all members can and should equally share the responsibility of group leadership. In addition to actually leading meetings, group members can share in responsibilities such as planning special activities, hosting meetings, arranging for refreshments, or coordinating prayer times.

Encourage and Recognize One Another's Efforts: The writer of Hebrews urges his readers to "encourage one another daily" (3:13) and to "consider how we may spur one another on toward love and good deeds" (10:25). Christian education groups can build cohesiveness by learning to praise and compliment one another. Low-status members (those who are quiet and nonparticipating) especially need positive reinforcement. If words of encouragement do not come easily to a particular group, the Christian educator might incorporate group activities that provide members with opportunities for building one another up. For example, a simple but effective procedure is to have each group member identify a spiritual gift or natural ability in the person to the left (or right) of him or her. Go in a circle and have each member share the affirmation with the rest of the group.

Set Group Goals: Working together to achieve short-term goals rewards a group and, consequently, helps build a sense of cohesiveness. Long-term goals may be helpful in some ways, but are often too vague for cohesion building. Goals set for the next meeting or next week are more likely to increase morale. What are some attainable goals Christian education group members might set for themselves? They might agree to read a particular book or a certain section of a book. Or they might set a goal to memorize a Scripture verse each week for the next few weeks.

CONFLICT IN SMALL GROUPS[96]

While most people have an aversion to conflict, few would disagree with the fact that it is an inevitable part of human relationships. Stewart Tubbs proposes that a relationship free of

---

[96]The benefits and drawbacks of conflict as well as ways of dealing with conflict or conflict resolution in the context of Christian education groups will be addressed in the following chapter on leadership.

conflict is probably a sign that there is no relationship at all.[97] Conflict is indeed a fact of life. And Griffin adds that it is not a matter of deciding whether or not you will allow the presence of conflict in your group—it is already there.[98] But while most people do not like conflict, since it often brings about undesirable results, it is not to be avoided entirely. In fact in some cases, is desirable in the small-group experience.

A number of definitions exist for conflict, but one of the most helpful is suggested by Joyce Hocker and William Wilmot. They say conflict is "an expressed struggle between at least two interdependent parties who perceive incompatible goals, scarce resources, and interference from the other party in achieving their goals."[99] Simply put, conflict exists when incompatibility occurs. Conflict in small groups originates from a number of sources, including (1) differences in information, beliefs, values, interests, or desires, (2) a scarcity of some resource such as time, space, or position, (3) rivalries in which one person competes with another, (4) difficulty of a task, (5) pressure to avoid failure, (6) the importance of an individual's or group's decision, (7) differences in skill or understanding level whereby the more skilled are irritated with the less skilled, and (8) personality differences.[100]

Conflict in most small groups will usually be one of three types: substantive, affective, or procedural. Task groups might also experience a fourth type of conflict stemming from inequity in the group. *Substantive* conflict involves *what* the group should do. It is a task-related disagreement over ideas, issues, and meanings. It is "the vehicle by which ideas, proposals, evidence, and reasoning are challenged and critically examined, doubts are brought into the open, and the group works to-

---

[97]Stewart L. Tubbs, *A Systems Approach to Small Group Interaction*, 5th ed. (New York: McGraw-Hill, 1995), 249.

[98]Griffin, *Getting Together*, 134.

[99]Joyce Hocker and William Wilmot, *Interpersonal Conflict*, 3rd ed. (Dubuque, Iowa: Wm. C. Brown, 1991), 12.

[100]Stewart L. Tubbs, *A Systems Approach to Small Group Interaction*, 250.

gether to find the best solution."[101] *Affective* conflict originates from interpersonal clashes. It is related to the *who* in small groups and is usually detrimental to its functioning. Some of this interpersonal conflict emerges from a struggle for power and position. *Procedural* conflict is a type of substantive conflict more specifically related to the procedures a group should follow in meeting or working towards its goals. This is disagreement as to the *how* of group function and interaction. Conflict over inequity or perceived inequity occurs when group members do not seem to have equal workloads or do not make equal contributions to the group.

CONCLUSION

This chapter discussed the process a small Christian education group goes through in becoming an entity with its own distinct personality. To establish a unique group identity, members experience different kinds of tension, go through distinct phases, identify and adhere to certain behavioral standards, develop cohesiveness, and engage in various levels of conflict.

---

[101]Brilhart and Galanes, *Effective Group Discussion*, 260–2.

4
Providing Leadership in Small Groups

Whoever wants to become great among you must be your servant, and whoever wants to be first must be your slave.
(Mt 20:26)

"LEADERSHIP is a universal human phenomenon," proclaim Stogdill and Bass. Regardless of culture—whether people are isolated Indian villagers, Eurasian nomads, or Polynesian fisherfolk—leadership appears.[1] And for centuries people have been seeking answers as to who becomes a leader, why certain individuals emerge as leaders, and what makes effective leadership. Plato contended that only a select few with superior wisdom become leaders; Aristotle proposed that from the moment of birth some individuals are marked for subservience, while others for command; Jesus expressed leadership in terms of servanthood (Mt 20:26); and the apostle Paul viewed leadership as a spiritual gift (Ro 12:8).

PERSPECTIVES ON EFFECTIVE LEADERSHIP

One of the most critical dimensions of Christian education small groups is leadership. According to Carl Larson and Frank LaFasto, the final ingredient for effective small-group performance is leadership, with the right person serving in the leadership role.[2]

---

[1] Ralph M. Stogdill and Bernard M. Bass, *Stogdill's Handbook of Leadership* (New York: Free Press, 1981), 5.

[2] Carl Larson and Frank LaFasto, *Teamwork: What Must Go Right/What Can Go Wrong* (Newbury Park, Calif.: Sage, 1989), 118.

173

Without leadership, says another source, groups "can easily flounder, get off course, go too far or not go far enough, lose sight of their mission and connection with other teams, lose confidence, get stymied by interpersonal conflict, and simply fall short of their enormous potential."[3] Gareth Icenogle advises that "the development of a healthy small group ministry structure has to do with the careful appointment and placement of key leadership."[4]

The Meanings of Leadership

Based on the number of definitions and manners of describing the notion, leadership appears to be a rather sophisticated concept. While the term *leader* appeared in the English language as early as 1300, the word *leadership* only emerged in the first half of the nineteenth century in writings concerning political influence and control of the British Parliament.[5] Since the onset of the notion of leadership, however, countless attempts have been made to define the concept. Bennis and Nanus state that decades of analysis have provided us with over 850 definitions of leadership.[6] All of this has prompted James Burns to declare: "Leadership is one of the most observed and least understood phenomena on earth."[7] Nonetheless, Bass and Stogdill have reviewed the countless definitions of leadership and completed the arduous task of constructing a helpful scheme of classification. Included in their many perceptions of leadership are the following categories:[8]

---

[3]John Zenger, Ed Musselwhite, Kathleen Hurson, and Craig Perrin, *Leading Teams* (Homewood, Ill.: Irwin, 1994), 15.

[4]Gareth Weldon Icenogle, *Biblical Foundations for Small Group Ministry* (Downers Grove, Ill: InterVarsity, 1994), 93.

[5]Stogdill and Bass, *Stogdill's Handbook of Leadership*, 7; David W. Johnson and Frank P. Johnson, *Joining Together*, 6th ed. (Boston: Allyn and Bacon, 1997), 178–9.

[6]Warren Bennis and Burt Nanus, *Leaders: Strategies for Taking Charge*, 2nd ed. (New York: HarperBusiness, 1997), 4.

[7]James MacGregor Burns, *Leadership* (New York: Harper and Row, 1978), 2.

[8]Ibid., 7–14.

- leadership as a focus of group change;
- leadership defined according to personality and character traits;
- leadership as the exercise of influence;
- leadership as power;
- leadership as an instrument of goal achievement;
- leadership as an effect of interaction.

Leadership as Focus of Group Change: Early definitions of leadership emphasized the role of the leader as the focus of group change, activity, and process. For example, Charles Cooley, a distinguished pioneer in American sociology, declared, "It is never the case that mankind move in any direction with an even front, but there are always those who go before and show the way."[9] Unfortunately, definitions of this nature often mistakenly placed the leader in a "particularly fortuitous, if not helpless, position in the inexorable progress of the group."[10] This relatively unsophisticated and passé approach to leadership seems to perceive leaders simply as individuals who are in the precarious position of being one step ahead of their followers so that they, as leaders, will not be run over.

Leadership as Personality and Character Traits: Leadership defined in terms of desirable traits of personality and character has long been a popular approach to the subject. But the attempts to discover the traits, or characteristics, that distinguish leaders from others have been rather disappointing to say the least. Charles Bird investigated the relevant research prior to 1940 and compiled an extensive list of traits which appeared to distinguish leaders from nonleaders. He discovered, however, that only a paltry 5 percent of the traits were common to four or more studies.[11]

---

[9]Charles Horton Cooley, *Human Nature and the Social Order* (New York: Schocken, 1902/1964), 357.

[10]Stogdill and Bass, *Stogdill's Handbook of Leadership*, 8.

[11]Charles Bird, *Social Psychology* (New York: Appleton-Century, 1940), 379-80.

Stogdill pursued a similar study of leadership traits and found some support for the notion that leaders, on average, exceed group members in intelligence, scholarship, dependability, social activity, and socio-economic status. He concluded, however, that effective leadership is not confined to the mere matter of possessing a certain combination of traits.[12]

Leadership as the Exercise of Influence: Of the innumerable definitions or meanings of leadership, the one most considered is that which identifies leadership as the exercise of interpersonal influence. Fiedler proposed that leadership is a "process of influencing others for the purpose of performing a shared task."[13] Similarly Tannenbaum, Weschler, and Massarik defined leadership as "interpersonal influence, exercised in a situation and directed, through the communication process, toward the attainment of a specified goal or goals."[14] And more recently, Hackman and Johnson identify it as "human communication which modifies the attitudes and behaviors of others in order to meet group goals and needs."[15] Bennis and Nanus simply see leadership as "influencing, guiding in direction, course, action, opinion."[16] According to Stogdill and Bass, the influence concept of leadership implies "a reciprocal relationship between leader and followers, but one not necessarily characterized by domination, control, or induction of compliance on the part of the leader."[17]

---

[12]Roger Stogdill, "Personal Factors Associated With Leadership: A Survey of the Literature," in *Journal of Psychology*, 25 (1948), 35–71.

[13]Fred E. Fiedler, "Personality and Situational Determinants of Leadership Effectiveness," in *Group Dynamics*, eds. Dorwin Cartwright and Alvin Zander (New York: Harper and Row, 1953), 362-80.

[14]Robert Tannenbaum, Irving Weschler, and Fred Massarik, *Leadership and Organizations: A Behavioral Science Approach* (New York: McGraw-Hill, 1961), 24.

[15]Michael Hackman and Craig Johnson, *Leadership: A Communication Perspective* (Prospect Heights, Ill.: Waveland, 1991), 11.

[16]Bennis and Nanus, *Leaders: Strategies for Taking Charge*, 20.

[17]Stogdill and Bass, *Stogdill's Handbook of Leadership*, 10.

Leadership as Power: In a landmark and often-cited empirical research study, French and Raven defined leadership in terms of disparate power relationships between leader and followers.[18] According to their findings, leaders can influence the conduct of others to the degree that they have power that is perceived and acknowledged by the followers. Five sources of power were postulated: *reward* power (the ability to reward followers with both tangible and intangible items); *coercive* power (the ability to gain compliance through threat or force); *legitimate* power (influence that exists because of a position or title); *referent* power (influence based on attraction or identification with followers); and *expert* power (influence based on knowledge or expertise).

Leadership as an Instrument of Goal Achievement: A number of theorists embrace the notion of goal achievement in their definition of leadership. Burns proposes that group leadership is measured "not only by the achievement of the task but by the extent to which the task embodies group values and the achievement furthers fundamental group goals."[19] According to Shaw, leadership is "an influence process which is directed toward goal achievement."[20] Wilson and Hanna agree with Shaw to the extent that the statement is amended to read, "Leadership is an influence process that is directed toward group goal achievement."[21]

Leadership as an Effect of Interaction: Some theorists view leadership as an effect of group action, rather than a merely a cause or control of it. For example, for Rothwell, leadership is a two-way influence process. Leaders influence followers, but "followers also influence leaders by making demands on them,

---

[18]John R.P. French and Bertram Raven, "The Bases of Social Power," in *Group Dynamics*, eds. Dorwin Cartwright and Alvin Zander (New York: Harper and Row, 1953), 259-69.

[19]Burns, *Leadership*, 295.

[20]Marvin E. Shaw, *Group Dynamics: The Psychology of Small Group Behavior* (New York: McGraw-Hill, 1981), 317.

[21]Gerald L. Wilson and Michael S. Hanna, *Groups in Context* (New York: Random, 1990).

requiring them to meet members' expectations, and evaluating their performance in light of these expectations."[22] Freiberg defines transformational leadership as a dynamic interaction between leaders and followers where they "become fused into a mutually bonded relationship where both continuously move each other and the organization to higher levels of motivation and performance."[23]

LEADERSHIP IN CHRISTIAN EDUCATION SMALL GROUPS

While definitions of leadership abound, most experts agree that small-group leadership, more than anything else, is understood as an interpersonal influence process.[24] Gareth Icenogle, for example, describes leadership in the context of small-groups as "the art of influence, of taking initiative, of showing others where to go, what to do, how to act and how to think."[25] In this sense, Jesus serves as a model, as He led His small group not only in word, but in action; in prayer and in planning. He called them to be like Him and to do that which He did (Mt 11:29; Jn 13:15).

Dynamics of Small-Group Leadership

The consensus that leadership, and small-group leadership in particular, is an influential process serves as a basis for suggesting that Christian education group leadership is grounded in four dynamics:

---

[22]J. Dan Rothwell, *In Mixed Company*, 3rd ed. (Fort Worth, Tex.: Harcourt Brace, 1998), 148–9.

[23]Kevin L. Freiberg, "Transformational Leadership," in *Small Group Communication,* 6th ed., eds. Robert S. Cathcart and Larry A. Samovar (Dubuque, Iowa: Wm. C. Brown, 1992), 523–33.

[24]For example, see John K. Brilhart and Gloria G. Galanes, *Effective Group Discussion*, 8th ed. (Madison, Wis.: Brown and Benchmark, 1995), 158; Rothwell, *In Mixed Company*, 148; Joseph Luft, *Group Processes* (Palo Alto, Calif.: Mayfield, 1970), 42–3; Robert L. Husband, "Leading in Organizational Groups," in *Small Group Communication*, 6th ed., eds. Robert S. Cathcart and Larry A. Samovar (Dubuque, Iowa: Wm. C. Brown, 1992), 464–76.

[25]Icenogle, *Biblical Foundations for Small Group Ministry*, 160.

- group goals;

- good communication;

- adaptability;

- influence.

Accomplishing Group Goals: Small-group leadership is directed towards the fulfilling or accomplishing of group goals. Typically, both group and leadership success are measured by the extent to which group goals are achieved and group values are embodied.[26] Consequently, effective leadership excludes behavior that endeavors to place personal goals over those of the group, or attempts in some way to sabotage the group goals. Christian education groups form for a cooperative purpose: to achieve goals that individuals could not accomplish in isolation from others. Thus, in order to be effective, groups must set goals that all members—including leaders—commit themselves to work together on achieving.[27] Accordingly, good small-group leadership, as Keating correctly reminds us, serves the needs of the whole group.[28] The test of good leadership is the ability to realize change or goals collectively acknowledged by the group leader as well as group members or followers.[29]

Good Communication: Effective small-group leadership is accomplished through cogent communication; not by means of coercion or manipulation of any sort. It is achieved through discussion, with the leader guiding and influencing the group in accomplishing its goals through the give-and-take of interpersonal communication.[30] Consequently, the communication competence of the small-group leader is cardinal to any discussion of leadership (chapter five is devoted to the theme of small-group communication).

---

[26]Burns, *Leadership,* 295.

[27]Ibid.

[28]Charles J. Keating, *The Leadership Book* (New York: Paulist, 1978), 13.

[29]Burns, *Leadership,* 295.

[30]Galanes and Brilhart, *Communicating in Groups: Applications and Skills,* 151.

Adaptability: Leadership is, to a large degree, situational, meaning it depends on the needs of the group members and even the leader himself or herself. The nature or style of leadership may change from group to group or from situation to situation.[31] But successful small-group leadership adapts to the situation. For instance, one particular Christian education group might consist of highly interactive individuals while another may include a couple of silent members. In the first group, the designated leader will no doubt have a relatively easy time involving all participants in dynamic discussion; in the latter, he or she will have to find ways to actively engage the silent members in the ongoing life of the group.

Furthermore, leadership, as well as group development itself, is a process. Since leadership is a process, it is not a static or a fixed set of behaviors; rather it is a dynamic course of exchanged behaviors between the leader and members in an ever-fluctuating context.[32] Events or behaviors can and do alter how one responds to or views others. For instance, members of a Christian education group can affect the quality of group interaction by their degree of interest in the substantive content or subject matter. Members may be disinterested one moment and highly intrigued another. Or a particular individual may come to a group meeting on an emotional high one week and depressed or discouraged the next. Ever-changing situations require the small-group leader to be adaptable.

Influence: Finally, we revisit the irrefutable notion that competent small-group leadership is, above all else, influence. Good leadership is not bullying, demanding, or coercing group members to accomplish goals or perform tasks. Rather, leadership is guiding, facilitating, and helping others to work toward the achieving of group goals or performance of tasks. Reflecting on their study of leadership in the twentieth century, Bennis and Nanus contend that skilled leaders lead "by pulling rather than by pushing; by inspiring rather than by ordering; by creating

---

[31]Keating, *The Leadership Book*, 13.

[32]Ibid., 152.

achievable, though challenging, expectations and rewarding progress toward them, rather than by manipulating; by enabling people to use their own initiative and experiences rather than by manipulating; by enabling people to use their own initiative rather than by denying or constraining their experiences and actions."[33]

Interpersonal Power and Sources of Influence

The term *power* elicits mixed responses from Christians. Henri Nouwen, for example, insists that historically, the root cause of almost every major crisis of the church is "power exercised by those who claim to be followers of the poor and powerless Jesus," and denounces any use of power claimed to be used in the service of God or for the benefit of others.[34] David Bickimer reasons that "power seduces many a leader in religious education much to the satisfaction of Satan, who is quite efficient in this regard.[35] Lawrence Richards and Clyde Hoeldke argue that while God gives human leaders authority, it does not rest on power in any way; it especially does not imply the right to control the actions or behaviors of others.[36] And Keating argues that if we are to accept the Gospel message we must view Christian leadership and power as mutually contradictory notions.[37]

Nouwen, in his helpful reflections on Christian leadership, reminds his readers that the third temptation of Jesus in the wilderness was the temptation of control or power: "The devil took him to a very high mountain and showed him all the kingdoms of the world and their splendor" (Mt 4:8).[38] He goes on to suggest

---

[33]Bennis and Nanus, Leaders: *Strategies for Taking Charge*, 209.

[34]Henri J.M.Nouwen, *In the Name of Jesus* (New York: Crossroad, 1991), 58–9

[35]David Arthur Bickimer, *Leadership in Religious Education* (Birmingham, Ala.: Religious Education Press, n.d.), 22.

[36]Lawrence O. Richards and Clyde Hoeldtke, *A Theology of Church Leadership* (Grand Rapids, Mich.: Zondervan, 1980), 136.

[37]Keating, *The Leadership Book*, 106.

[38]Nouwen, *In the Name of Jesus*, 57.

182 ❖ The Power of Small Groups in Christian Education

that the temptation for power is greatest when intimacy is a threat.[39] The intimacy of a small group may increase the temptation for a leader to be in control, to manipulate group process, or exercise autocratic authority in decision making.

Yet while we must unabashedly denounce leadership that relies on coercion or brute force, a functional approach to small-group leadership demands that an individual possess social or interpersonal power in order to, in turn, effectually exert influence that contributes to the operation of group functions. More succinctly put, it is the power to influence that enables an individual to perform acts of leadership.[40] Or stated another way, influence is perceived as the use of interpersonal power to modify or change the behavior, actions, or attitudes of others so as to achieve group goals.[41]

While Jesus condemned the Gentile rulers for misusing power and *lording* it over their followers (Mt 20:25), other biblical accounts chronicle the favorable use of power for the exertion of influence. Nehemiah provided leadership for the repairing of the walls of Jerusalem with the authoritative power conferred upon him by King Artaxerxes (Ne 2:1–10). Moses appointed leaders over groups of people and bestowed upon them the power to judge the people's disputes (Dt 1:9–18).

Icenogle contends that small groups cannot function in a healthy manner, in fact, unless there is a positive exercise of authority (a particular basis of power) and a shared movement of power between individuals.[42] Acts of Christian education leadership, in order to be effective, must rely on some basis of power. These bases are identified by French and Raven as: legitimate power, reward power, coercion power, expert power, and referent power.[43]

---

[39]Ibid., 60.

[40]Cartwright and Zander, *Group Dynamics*, 309.

[41]Galanes and Brilhart, *Communicating in Groups: Applications and Skills*, 152.

[42]Icenogle, *Biblical Foundations for Small Group Ministry*, 83.

[43]French and Raven, "The Bases of Social Power," 259–69.

Legitimate Power: Legitimate power refers to that influence that exists because of a position or title. The leader of a Christian education group may have been appointed by the parent or monitoring organization (such as the Christian Education Department), chosen by group members, or perhaps simply volunteered for the position. Being the legitimate or designated leader implies the authority to make certain decisions. With legitimate power, for instance, the group leader possesses the authority to cancel a meeting, call a meeting to order, or to bring a discussion to closure.

Reward Power: This refers to the ability of an individual to influence other group members through rewards. The small-group leader (or other group members, for that matter) may reward group members intangibly through smiles or praises, acknowledgment, compliments, or by tangibly giving them a responsibility to uphold or a task to carry out.

Coercion Power: Coercion power is the unethical and disrespectful tactic of using threats and force to make another group member comply with what one wants. Coercion should never be used in small-group leadership, as it only breeds the unhealthy characteristics of discontent, resentment, and uncooperation. It represents what Icenogle identifies as the dark side of leadership, leadership which not only controls, but destroys[44] and is described by Bennis and Nanus as perhaps the most damaging of all myths of what leadership actually is.[45]

Expert Power: Expert power is manifested as a result of obtaining expertise in a particular field or possessing a needed skill. For example, if a Christian education group desires to put on a skit or drama presentation for the church congregation, the individual who has acting experience emerges as the most influential person because he or she is perceived to have knowledge or skills vital to the success of the group's performance.

Referent Power: Power of this nature is often achieved when individuals are admired or respected by others. The more the

---

[44]Icenogle, *Biblical Foundations For Small Group Ministry*, 83.

[45]Bennis and Nanus, Leaders: *Strategies for Taking Charge*, 209.

Christian education leader is looked up to, the more group members are likely to imitate his or her behavior and the greater the power he or she has in influencing the group.

Usually a Christian education leader's influence stems from more than one source. The more bases from which the Christian educator draws, the more potential he or she has to influence a Christian education group. Furthermore, the more these bases of influence are distributed among group members, the more likely participation is to be shared, decision making to be cooperative, and satisfaction to be high.

Leadership Styles

Ever since the seminal work of Kurt Lewin and Ronald Lippitt on leadership, investigators of small groups have concentrated on leadership styles. Lewin and Lippitt differentiated between two polemic clusters of leadership behaviors and attitudes. On one hand they characterized *authoritarian* leaders as controlling and highly directive, while *democratic* leaders were depicted as nondirective and participatory.[46] Further investigation by White and Lippitt identified a third style called *laissez-faire*. This leadership style was portrayed as very nonparticipatory. According to this approach, leaders give the group complete freedom in decision making.[47]

Subsequent to the groundwork laid by Lewin and Lippitt, leadership style theory has been applied to small-group leadership by a variety of authors.[48] In Christian education groups, autocratic or authoritarian leaders are characterized as having a strong need to control small groups themselves; they may

---

[46]Kurt Lewin and Ronald Lippitt, "An Experimental Approach to the Study of Autocracy and Democracy: A Preliminary Note," in *Sociometry 1* (1938), 292–300.

[47]Ralph White and Ronald Lippitt, "Leader Behavior and Member Reaction in Three 'Social Climates,'" in *Group Dynamics*, eds. Dorwin Cartwright and Alvin Zander (New York: Harper and Row, 1953), 318–35.

[48]Rothwell, *In Mixed Company*, 160–3; Tubbs, *A Systems Approach to Small Group Interaction*, 142–6; Galenes and Brilhart, *Effective Group Discussion*, 163.

possibly even have an obsession for control.[49] They tend to be task-oriented leaders who like to make decisions for the Christian education group and to govern the group process. For the most part, an authoritarian leadership style is unacceptable in a Christian education setting. Even in small groups that exist to carry out or complete a task, the democratic style of leadership is likely to bring about better results.[50] Leadership which controls also destroys, and leadership tyranny is an abandonment of a healthy pattern for a small group on its way to community.[51]

Occasionally conditions will exist in the life of the Christian education group which make autocratic leadership effective or necessary. For example, when an urgent decision has to be made with little or no opportunity to consult group members, it may be appropriate for the designated leader to go ahead and implement the resolution on his or her own.

The philosophy of laissez-faire leadership in Christian education is "he who leads least leads best." According to this style, not only is there little desire for control, there is a lack of concern for direction, task accomplishment, and interpersonal relationships.[52] Conditions when laissez-faire leadership may be appropriate are when the Christian education group is committed to a decision, the group has the resources to implement decisions, and when members need relatively little input from the designated leader to work effectively.

Somewhere in the middle of the two extremes lies an appropriate leadership style for the Christian education group leader. The democratic leadership style represents this balanced approach. According to the democratic style of small-group leadership, the facilitator attempts to provide direction and performs both task and interpersonal leadership functions. At the same time, this type of leader endeavors to avoid dominating the group with his or

[49]Tubbs, *A Systems Approach to Small Group Interaction*, 144.

[50]Ibid., 145.

[51]Icenogle, *Biblical Foundations for Small Group Ministry*, 85.

[52]Tubbs, *A Systems Approach to Small Group Interaction*, 144-5.

her personal views.[53] Democratic leadership encourages group participation in decision making, tries to discover the wishes of group members, helps the group discover and achieve common goals, and tries to entertain all viewpoints in discussion and decision making.

The Designated Leader

The *designated leader* is the group's legitimate leader, an individual appointed or elected to the small group leadership position. Having a designated leader usually helps in providing stability to a Christian education group. Even though all group members share responsibility for the work and success of the group, the designated leader bears special responsibility for the organization and administration of a small group. The designated leader plays a critical role in assisting the group to get launched, to establish itself, and then to gain momentum.[54] In most small groups a designated leader will facilitate discussion and make sure the group begins and ends on time. Designated leadership may be undertaken by one person, or may be shared by two or more individuals. For example, a married couple may host and facilitate group activities. Or one couple might host, while another couple facilitates the meetings.

To achieve the goals or purposes of a small group, most successful group leaders carry out a number of tasks or responsibilities. While the nature of Christian education groups will vary (for example Bible study groups will differ significantly from support groups), most of the leader's tasks listed below, identified by McBride, will apply to each type of group:[55]

- *Listening:* being an effective listener.

- *Leading discussion:* guiding, or facilitating effective discussion and group interaction.

---

[53]Ibid., 145.

[54]Neal F. McBride, *How to Lead Small Groups* (Colorado Springs, Colo.: NavPress, 1990), 32.

[55]Adapted from McBride, *How to Lead Small Groups*, 33–4.

- *Facilitating group decision making:* helping the small group make important choices.

- *Understanding and leading group process:* being knowledgeable and skilled in facilitating group dynamics such as listening and responding.

- *Modeling openness and caring:* setting the example to other members by being honest, empathetic, and actively seeking ways to help group members.

- *Planning and leading the small-group meetings:* preparing for and conducting group sessions or helping other group members to plan and lead.

- *Resolving conflict:* helping the small group confront and resolve interpersonal conflict and general difficulties.

- *Meeting personal needs:* attending to group members at times apart from regular meetings.

- *Ongoing training:* participating in the training and organizational meetings of the group's overall program.

- *Evaluating:* making judgments and decisions about various elements of the group's existence, growth, and accomplishments.

Shared Leadership

To what degree does a small group depend on the power of a designated leader versus the shared leadership of all group members? The extreme of either type of leadership—the heavy hand of an individual leader or not having a designated leader at all—can be unhealthy. Most experts agree that even with a designated leader, a healthy small group distributes leadership responsibility among the group members. For instance, Brilhart and Galanes argue that although a considerable amount of responsibility is placed on the designated leader for coordinating and structuring the group's activities, all members can and should equally share the responsibility of group leadership.[56] Both Moses (Ex 18:14–26) and Jesus (Mt 10:1–40) modeled a shared leadership approach by selecting, equipping, and empowering other able men to participate in the flow of community or group operations. Leadership serves the needs of the group, so in this sense leadership can be exercised by any member of the Christian education group. In fact, urges Keating, the mark of good leadership is the success a designated leader has in encouraging other group members to participate in various leadership functions.[57]

Icenogle emphasizes the importance of balancing authority with shared leadership. He reasons that since every group member is unique and gifted differently, each person has the opportunity and responsibility to allow the power of God to flow through him or her into the group. When there is resistance to this kind of participation in mutual empowerment, essential leadership and direction is blocked for the whole group. When one member seeks to gather all the power or other members refuse to participate in the flow of power, a small group is prevented from becoming and doing all that God has gifted them to be and do.[58]

How can wise Christian education leaders successfully operate according to a shared approach to group leadership? It begins by recognizing that shared leadership is much more than rotated leadership. Leadership sharing is the intentional empowering of small-group members who are able and willing to take initiative in the group. The designated leader might empower and involve group members, for instance, as discussion leaders, hosts or hostesses, song leaders, or prayer leaders.

By contrast, rotated leadership is the passing of the leadership responsibility to group members whether or not they are

[56]Galanes and Brilhart, *Communicating in Groups: Applications and Skills*, 171.

[57]Keating, *The Leadership Book*, 13.

[58]Icenogle, *Biblical Foundations for Small Group Ministry*, 83.

able or willing to lead the small group. Sharing leadership brings out the brightest and the best the group members have to give; rotating leadership usually reduces the group to mediocrity.[59] Many individuals have neither the interest nor the expertise to effectively lead a small group and should not be burdened with responsibilities they are not prepared to handle.

Dan Williams describes leadership as exercising one's *gift* to produce an effect on others. By gifts he refers to everything a person has to offer: personality, spiritual gifts, abilities, background, and talent. From this perspective, Christian education group members have no option when it comes to leadership, for as they express who they are, they automatically lead. Even an individual with a quiet personality has an effect on other members and the small group as a whole. There is no such thing as a pure follower![60]

Effectively sharing leadership is contingent upon the openness of the designated leader and the expression of leadership from other group members.[61] The wise leader will recognize, evoke, nurture, and celebrate the gifts and abilities of others. On the other hand, the designated leader can discourage leadership of others or reduce their impact by cutting them off in different ways: by interrupting someone giving verbal leadership, ignoring members when they volunteer to do something, or being in charge of every process or project.[62]

A Christian education group might also practice what Williams calls *integrated* leadership.[63] By this he means that a group needs to recognize and implement the many different kinds of gifts and abilities members bring to the group (not just skills of leading a discussion) and recognize how they complement each other. For example, someone may be asked to pray or fa-

---

[59]Ibid., 84.

[60]Dan Williams, *Seven Myths about Small Groups* (Downers Grove, Ill.: Intervarsity, 1991), 74.

[61]Fred Keating, *The Leadership Book*, 13.

[62]Williams, *Seven Myths about Small Groups*, 74.

[63]Ibid.

cilitate a prayer time. Another, who has the gift of hospitality, may serve as a host or hostess for the small group. Or the leader might look for group members with unusual talents, such as a photographer who could take pictures and create a scrapbook for the group.[64]

Finally, the philosophy of shared leadership can be reflected in the term that is used for the designated leader. If the term leader implies that this individual does everything or plays all the important roles, perhaps a name change is in order. Using terms such as *facilitator* or *coordinator* might encourage group members to see leadership as something intrinsic in each member.

While Christian education groups are encouraged to practice shared leadership, they must be careful not to ignore the value of choosing or appointing an individual leader, for small groups also suffer if no individual takes the initiative to lead. "Leadership holds the group accountable to its covenantal life. It helps the group remember its faith history and celebrate its life together. Leadership provides a model for the group to imitate as it learns the disciplines of healthy community. Leadership nurtures more leadership."[65]

MAKING DECISIONS IN
CHRISTIAN EDUCATION GROUPS

The woman's study group that met each Wednesday evening in the fellowship room at Elmwood United Methodist Church was about to conclude. But before they wrapped up, Mary Stevenson, the discussion facilitator, had a small task to take care of. "We will be finished with our current curriculum in a few weeks and must decide on what to study next." Sharon, a young woman who had been part of this group since its inception a year ago responded quickly: "I think you should decide what we should use as our small-group curriculum. After all, you're the small-group expert

---

[64]Judy Hamlin, *The Small Group Leaders Training Course* (Colorado Springs, Colo.: NavPress, 1990), 126.

[65]Icenogle, *Biblical Foundations for Small Group Ministry*, 89.

and have been involved in Christian education in our church for a number of years. You know what's best." Mary *thought for a moment, carefully choosing her words. "I appreciate the confidence you have in me, but I think this is a decision we should all be involved in." "Okay,"* inter- *jected Beth, "why don't we have some suggestions, and then vote to see which topic or curriculum is the most popular choice?" "That will certainly involve everyone,"* replied *Mary, "but is it possible a majority vote will leave some feeling that they didn't really have a say in the issue? There is another way to make our choice. Why don't we bring some options to the table, spend some time discussing them, and try to come to a consensual decision; one that every one can affirm or at least live with."*

At various points in the life span of a Christian education small group, decisions will have to be made by the designated leader and group members. Some of these decisions may be trivial, such as whether to serve refreshments before, after, or during the small group discussion; or more consequential, such as the nature of the substantive content of a Christian education study group. How the designated leader handles decision making is critical to the well-being and effective development of the group.

Individual Versus Group Decision Making

Which is a more effective pattern for making decision: as groups or indivduals? The writer of Proverbs clearly indicates that there is immeasurable value in group, or team, decision making processes:

"For lack of guidance a nation falls, but many advisors make victory sure" (Pr 11:14).

"The first to present his case seems right, till another comes forward and questions him" (Pr 18:17).

"He who trusts in himself is a fool, but he who walks in wisdom is kept safe." (Pr 28:26).

Likewise, the social-science perspective is that, in most in- stances, group decision making and problem solving is superior to individual decision making.[66] For example, studies by Barnlund,[67] Shaw,[68] and Tuckman and Lorge,[69] propose that groups produce better decision or solutions to problems that do individuals. Herm Smith found empirical evidence for groups to be superior on conjunctive tasks, where each member possesses information necessary to solve a problem but no single member has all the needed information. Groups were not found to be superior at handling disjunctive tasks, tasks which require little coordination, thus enabling the most expert member to solve the problem without the help of others.[70]

Why are group decisions generally superior to those made by individuals? Johnson and Johnson offer several explanations:[71]

- Healthy interaction among group members results in ideas, insights, and strategies that individuals may not think of.

- In groups, poor decisions or incorrect solutions are more likely to be recognized and rejected than when individuals work in isolation.

- Groups have a greater ability to remember facts and events than do individuals.

- Groups provide a cooperative context in which group members can motivate one another to greater achievements.

---

[66]Irving Janis, *Groupthink*, 2nd ed. (Boston: Houghton Mifflin, 1982), 12.

[67]Dean C. Barnlund, "A Comparative Study of Individual, Majority, and Group Judgment," in *Journal of Abnormal and Social Psychology*, 58 (1959), 55–60.

[68]Marjorie E. Shaw, "A Comparison of Individuals and Small Groups in the Rational Solution of Complex Problems," in *American Journal of Psychology* 44 (1932): 491–504.

[69]Jacob Tuckman and Irving Lorge, "Individual Ability as a Determinant of Group Superiority," in *Human Relations* 15 (1962): 45–51.

[70]Herm W. Smith, "Group Versus Individual Problem Solving and Type of Problem Solved," in *Small Group Behavior* 20 (August 1989), 357–66.

[71]Johnson and Johnson, *Joining Together*, 231–3.

- Groups are more secure than individuals in taking risks or adopting more extreme positions.

Methods of Decision Making in Small Groups

Christian education groups use a variety of methods to make decisions. Each of the strategies has its own uses and is appropriate under certain circumstances. The circumstances or criteria that help a group determine which approach to take include the nature of the decision to be made, the amount of time and resources available, the nature of the task to be accomplished, and the type of setting the group is working in.[72] Four of the most common decision-making methods available to Christian education groups are as follows:

- the designated leader makes the decision;

- the Christian education group votes on a decision;

- the group member with the most expertise makes the decision;

- the group comes to a consensus through discussion.

The Designated Leader: One possibility for making a decision is that the designated leader thinks through the issue or problem alone and announces his decision. Generally, this is not the best pattern for a Christian education group to employ in decision making. Often the response from group members who have not been involved in the process is resentment, resulting in lowered cohesiveness, halfhearted support for the decision, and a reluctance to contribute to future decisions.[73] Thus, while this technique is a tempting trap, it should be avoided for the aforementioned reasons.

Is it ever appropriate for the designated leader to make decisions without consulting group members? The strategy can be applied to Christian education groups when simple, routine

---

[72]Ibid., 244.

[73]Brilhart and Galanes, *Effective Group Discussion*, 237.

decisions have to be made (such as not serving refreshments at a particular meeting); when relatively little time is available to make the decision (thirty minutes before the meeting starts, the leader finds out that most members cannot attend, and chooses to cancel); or when group members give the designated leader the freedom to make the decision (a support group gives the leader the authority to recruit and invite an expert guest for the next meeting).[74]

Majority Vote: Probably the most popular, though not necessarily the best, form of decision making in churches and Christian education small groups is the majority vote. This is done by a show of hands, by saying "aye," or by a written ballot. The majority vote seems to be most in keeping with persons having the democratic mentality of the United States and Canada. On the positive side, when using this method a decision is reached quickly, and each individual has an equal say and opportunity to influence the group decision. If the vote is unanimous, consensus (and thus harmony) is achieved. But with its advantages come one or two drawbacks. For example, if the vote is split, minority members ("the losers") may feel their needs and thoughts have not been recognized. As a result, the group may suffer from lowered cohesiveness and lack of commitment to the decision.[75] Furthermore, a majority decision may be in error, and a member of the minority may, in fact, have the best decision.

Voting itself assumes a competitive win-lose situation and offers a less-than-ideal environment for community growth.[76] This method of small-group decision making should be used only when time limits or prohibits consensus making, when the Christian education group has exhausted all possible ways of reaching a consensus, or when the decision is not so important that consensus must be achieved.[77]

---

[74]Johnson and Johnson, *Joining Together*, 231–3.

[75]Brilhart and Galanes, *Effective Group Discussion*, 237.

[76]Keating, *The Leadership Book*, 68.

[77]Galanes and Brilhart, *Communicating in Groups: Applications and Skills*, 209; Johnson and Johnson, *Joining Together*, 246.

Appointing an Expert: Small-group members may allow the group member with the most expertise to make the decision—either the designated leader or another expert in the group. This person (or persons) is given the authority to explore options, make a decision, and report back to the group.[78] Appointing a designated person to make a decision may be acceptable if the decision has a low effect on the group or, as Em Griffin suggests, it is a decision they do not see as central to who they are or what they are about.[79]

Consensus Decision: A particular decision-making method that is often viewed by work groups as being ideal is consensus.[80] It is usually the healthiest pattern for making decisions in Christian education groups, especially for serious, critical, and complex decisions that demand the commitment of all group members. For example, consensus would be desirable for a Christian education group in the process of choosing a curriculum for themselves; consensual agreement would be imperative for a group planning a mission trip to another country.

A consensus decision is one that is reached through discussion by all the group members, and one that all can agree to support or at least "live with." It does not mean that the final decision is each member's first choice, but it is the best decision that everyone in the Christian education group can support. Consensus may not be the most efficient way to make a group decision, but when a true consensus is reached, the results are usually a superior decision, with a high level of member satisfaction and general acceptance.[81]

The consensus method of decision making is illustrated on at least two occasions in the New Testament book of Acts. According to Acts 6:1–7 the Grecian Jews in the early church were complaining against those of the Aramaic-speaking com-

---

[78]McBride, *How to Lead Small Groups*, 87.

[79]Em Griffin, *Getting Together* (Downers Grove, Ill.: InterVarsity, 1982), 74.

[80]Kevin L. Sager and John Gastil, "Reaching Consensus on Consensus: A Study of the Relationships Between Individual Decision-Making Styles and Use of the Consensus Decision Rule," in *Communication Quarterly* 47 (Winter 1999): 67–79.

[81]Brilhart and Galanes, *Effective Group Discussion*, 238.

munity because their widows were being neglected. So the Twelve gathered together all the disciples and suggested they choose seven among them to take care of this matter. "This proposal *pleased the whole group*" (6:5) so *they* selected and appointed these men to the "apostles, who prayed and laid their hands on them" (6:6, italics added).

According to Acts 15 there were those who were preaching a gospel which said that unless the Gentiles were circumcised according to the custom of Moses, they could not be saved. This brought Paul and Barnabus into the dispute, and eventually other apostles and elders in the Jerusalem church. Finally, after days of exploring the issue, the council of leaders achieved consensus. In a letter to the Gentile believers that emerged from the council, the following words appear: "It seemed good to the Holy Spirit *and to us . . .*" (15:28, italics added). This is the heart, propose Richards and Hoeldtke, of consensus—a group of responsible individuals, using all the faculties God has given them to honestly and prayerfully explore an issue, and *come to one accord.*[82]

While decision making by consensus is supported by example biblically and is usually the most effective strategy, it has some drawbacks. The main weakness of the consensus approach is that it is more time-consuming than other procedures and occasionally consensus can never be reached, no matter how much time is spent wrestling with the issue. Another drawback of consensus is that a decision may be superficial when one or more members give in to or accommodate other members who may be "experts," people who express their views with force, a designated leader, or a large majority.[83] The following guidelines are helpful in making high-quality consensus decisions in Christian education small groups.[84]

1. *Group members should not argue stubbornly for their own positions.* Rather, participants should be encouraged to state their cases clearly and logically, being sure to care-

---

[82]Richards and Hoeldtke, *A Theology of Church Leadership*, 307.

[83]Brilhart and Galanes, *Effective Group Discussion*, 238.

[84]These guidelines are paraphrased from Brilhart and Galanes, *Effective Group Discussion*, 238–9 and Johnson and Johnson, *Joining Together*, 250.

fully listen to the reactions of others and to consider contrasting and or opposing viewpoints.

2. *Group members should not change their minds simply to avoid conflict or disagreement.* Conflict is likely to occur in the course of consensual decision making and can be helpful in encouraging critical thinking. One should yield only to arguments that have objective and logically sound bases.

3. *Groups should make every effort to avoid conflict-suppressing techniques such as majority vote or coin tossing.* Such techniques may suppress conflict, but they also discourage critical thinking and suppress constructive arguments.

4. *Every member of the Christian education group should be involved in the decision-making process.* Dennis Gouran proposes that the caliber of a group's decision is no better than the quality of interaction employed to come to that particular decision.[85] A superior decision will be reached if differences of opinion are sought out and there is a wider range of ideas and information.

5. *If a stalemate emerges, the group should seek the next best alternative acceptable to all.*

Effective Decision Making

Regardless of the method used to reach a decision—voting, consensus, or appointing an individual—there are steps a Christian education group can take to ensure the best possible results.[86]

1. *The Christian education group should clearly understand the issue or problem.* If group members are unclear about a par-

---

[85]Dennis S. Gouran, *Discussion: The Process of Group Decision-Making* (New York: Harper and Row, 1974), 158.

[86]These guidelines are paraphrased from Brilhart and Galanes, *Effective Group Discussion*, 242–3.

ticular issue, they may come to a decision that does not resolve the issue or one that addresses the symptoms rather than the root causes. Christian education groups that clearly understand the situation make better quality decisions.

2. *The Christian education group must carefully, and with clarity, establish the criteria for evaluating the decision.* Criteria are the standards and requirements that must be met when evaluating and choosing an alternative. For example, if the church or other parent organization says a small group must stay within a prescribed budget when selecting curriculum, the eventual decision must meet this criterion.

3. *It is critical the Christian education group evaluate all the options—using the established criteria to look at both the positive and negative consequences.* After listing all the possible options, group members should evaluate each in light of the possible consequences. Negative consequences should be anticipated, so as to eliminate the poorer options right off the bat.

4. *Finally, the group needs to select a single tentative option.* Once a tentative choice has been made, participants should go back over the decision as a group and reevaluate the decision. In so doing, the Christian education group is able to make additional improvements to the chosen alternative.

McBride offers these additional suggestions for effective decision making:[87]

1. *Adequate time must be set aside for the decision-making process.* Decisions that are rushed tend to be risky and are rarely the best resolutions.

2. *Group members should be encouraged to state their opinions convincingly.* After all, each individual is a member

---

[87]Paraphrased from McBride, *How to Lead Small Groups,* 88.

of the group. On the other hand, in effective decision making, participants must refrain from stubbornly demanding their own way.

3. *A group must be prepared to accept a stalemate.* If indeed this happens, the strategy is to find the next best alternative acceptable to each group member.

4. *A healthy group will endeavor to seek out varying opinions.* Different and contrasting opinions are useful in selecting alternative solutions and evaluating the best possible outcomes.

5. *It is imperative that a decision is supported by the entire group before it is implemented.* If group support is not achieved, any decision will be seen as a win-lose situation, a scenario that should be avoided at all costs.

6. *A Christian education group must learn to be flexible.* Decisions can be readily changed if the need arises and if the group is indeed agreeable to change.

HANDLING CONFLICT IN
CHRISTIAN EDUCATION SMALL GROUPS

Conflict, most would agree, is an inevitable part of relationships and relating to one another. Some would go so far as to say that a conflict-free relationship is likely an indication that there is really no relationship at all. Furthermore, conflict is most likely to occur where there are deep commitments to the Christian education group. The greater the degree of ownership and vested interest, the more the likelihood of conflict. Apathy is a surefire prevention for conflict.[88] Most of us do not like conflict, and perhaps try to avoid conflict at all cost. Yet, reflects Jeffrey Kottler, without conflict or "without disagreements of any kind, imagine how boring, predictable, and conventional your life would be. If you were

---

[88]Larry L. McSwain and William C. Treadwell, *Conflict Ministry in the Church* (Nashville, Tenn.: Broadman, 1981), 36.

to get everyone to agree with you all of the time, no one would ever challenge your thinking and actions. You alone would be responsible for all decisions without having your reasoning examined."[89]

A helpful definition of conflict is offered by Kenneth Boulding, who sees it as a situation of competition whereby individuals or parties are cognizant of the incompatibility of possible future positions or in which each party holds a position that is incompatible with the desires of another.[90] More simply, Morton Deutsch proposes that conflict exists any time incompatible activities occur.[91] Any person who leads a Christian education small group can be assured that he or she will encounter competition and incompatibility of positions, thus a measure of conflict. Furthermore, in Christian education groups conflict is an indispensable component of the decision- making and problem-solving processes. It is a very natural by-product of trying to come to an agreement over a problem or issue.[92]

Once again, conflict exists whenever incompatible activities occur or when differing ideas are expressed. Conflicts in Christian education groups may originate from a variety of sources including (1) differences in desires, interests, values, beliefs, or traditions; (2) a scarcity of a resource such as position, space, time, influence, or money; (3) rivalries in which one person competes with another; (4) difficulty of a task; (5) pressure to avoid failure; and (6) differences in skill levels which lead a more skilled individual to become frustrated at the less skilled.[93]

---

[89]Jeffrey Kottler, *Beyond Blame* (San Francisco: Jossey-Bass, 1994), 149.

[90]Kenneth E. Boulding, *Conflict and Defense* (New York: Harper and Row, 1962), 3–4; See also Donald E. Bossart, *Creative Conflict in Religious Education and Church Administration* (Birmingham, Ala.: Religious Education Press, 1980), 14.

[91]Morton Deutsch, *The Resolution of Conflict* (New Haven, Conn.: Yale University, 1973), 10.

[92]Brilhart and Galanes, *Effective Group Discussion*, 254.

[93]Tubbs, *A Systems Approach to Small Group Interaction*, 250.

It is most important to make a conceptual distinction between two very different types of conflict: *conflict of ideas* (cognitive conflict) and *conflict of feelings* (affective conflict).[94] Idea conflict is rooted in the substance of the task or issue and is generally considered a positive aspect of small groups. For example, a task-oriented Christian education group might experience idea conflict in the process of trying to achieve their group goals.[95] It is deemed to be of value because it discourages what we have already referred to as groupthink, the tendency for group members to uncritically share common assumptions, often leading to mistakes and poor decisions.

Unfortunately, idea conflict often evolves into conflict of feelings or interpersonal conflict, the kind of negative conflict that can be destructive or detrimental to the development and well-functioning of a Christian education group.[96] For example, one might find affective conflict in a Christian education group when group members are using the small group to satisfy self-centered desires or needs for dominance or status.[97]

Understanding Conflict Theologically

The reality of conflicts that erupt in Christian communities (whether between individuals, within a large congregation, or in a small group) will remain a mystery or perplexion unless a theological understanding of conflict is forged. At least four sequential theological themes should be addressed:

---

[94]Harold Guetzkow and John Gyr, "An Analysis of Conflict in Decision-Making Groups," in *Human Relations* 7 (May 1954): 367–81. Allen C. Amason and Kenneth R. Thompson, "Conflict: An Important Dimension in Successful Management Teams," in *Organizational Dynamics* 24 (Autumn 1995): 20–36.

[95]Guetzkow and Gyr, "An Analysis of Conflict in Decision-Making Groups," 367-81.

[96]Shaila M. Miranda and Robert P. Bostrom, "The Impact of Group Support Systems on Group Conflict and Conflict Management," in *Journal of Management Information Systems* 10 (Winter 1993–4): 63–95.

[97]Guetzkow and Gyr, "An Analysis of Conflict in Decision-Making Groups," 367-81.

- Creation and the harmony of human relationships;

- the fall of man and the introduction of conflict;

- redemption and reconciliation;

- the ministry of reconciliation.

Creation—Harmony: The biblical account of Creation indicates that from the very beginning, human relationship was created without conflict as a part of the life experience. C.F. Keil and F. Delitzsch describe Eden as a peaceful and conflict-free setting where man was endowed with everything essential for the natural development of his nature and attainment of his destiny: "In the fruit of the trees of the garden he had food for the sustenance of his life; in the care of the garden itself, a field of labor for the exercise of his physical strength; in the animal and vegetable kingdom, a capacious region for the expansion of his intellect; in the tree of knowledge, a positive law for the training of his moral nature; and in the woman associated with him, a suitable companion and help. In such circumstances as these he might have developed both his physical and spiritual nature in accordance with the will of God."[98]

According to Genesis 1 and 2, all indications point to a creation of harmony and peace. Upon completion of His creative acts God pronounced them as "very good" (Ge 1:31). Furthermore Adam and Eve stood before God and each other "and they felt no shame" (2:25). Neither the man nor the woman was guilty of sin, consequently neither was mindful of shame.[99] The Garden of Eden was a perfect communion between the Creator and His creation.

The Fall—Conflict: It is not until we come to the account in Genesis 3 that we see sin become part of the human dilemma and the creation vision for perfect harmony shattered. As a

---

[98]C.F. Keil and F. Delitzsch, *Commentary on the Old Testament*, vol. 1, trans. James Martin (Grand Rapids, Mich.: Eerdmans, 1980 reprint), 91.

[99]James Montgomery Boice, *Genesis*, vol. 1 (Grand Rapids, Mich.: Zondervan, 1982), 119.

result of sin, conflict immediately enters into virtually every dimension of human existence:[100]

- Adam and Eve broke fellowship with their Creator; consequently all of humanity from this point on is in a state of conflict with God. The Apostle Paul describes the state of humanity as follows: "There is no one righteous, not even one; there is no one who understands, no one who seeks God. All have turned away, they have together become worthless; there is no one who does good, not even one" (Ro 3:10–12).

- The seeds of interpersonal conflict were planted as Adam quickly blamed Eve for the dilemma they found themselves in (Ge 3:12). Subsequently interpersonal conflict remains a significant theme throughout Scripture: between Abraham and Lot (13:5–12); Jacob and Esau (Ge 27); David and Saul (1Sa 19); Paul and Barnabas (Ac 15:36-41); Paul and Peter (Gal 2:11–21).

- Nature, or "the ground," would no longer be as productive as it once was: "Cursed is the ground because of you; through painful toil you will eat of it all the days of your life. It will produce thorns and thistles for you, and you will eat the plants of the field. By the sweat of your brow you will eat your food" (Ge 3:17b-19a). Nature itself has turned against humankind and even elements of the environment have become poisonous and destructive.[101]

- The spiritual battle between humans and Satan is set in motion. To the serpent (Satan) God says, "I will put enmity between you and the woman, and between your offspring" (Ge 3:15). Paul characterizes spiritual conflict as a struggle "not against flesh and blood, but

[100]Kenneth O. Gangel and Samuel L. Canine, *Communication and Conflict Management* (Nashville, Tenn.: Broadman, 1992), 155.

[101]Keil and Delitzsch, *Commentary on the Old Testament*, Vol. 1, 104.

against the rulers, against the authorities, against the powers of this dark world and against the spiritual forces of evil in the heavenly realms" (Eph 6:12). This conflict will not be terminated until Satan is eternally consigned to his place in the lake of fire (Rev 20:10).

- Finally, the most entrapping conflict is that which every human being experiences internally. With the Fall, a sinful nature would become intrinsic to each and every individual. Paul describes the inner conflict that exists because of the sin nature within: "I know that nothing good lives in me, that is, in my sinful nature. For I have the desire to do what is good, but I cannot carry it out. For what I do is not the good I want to do; no, the evil I do not want to do—this I keep on doing" (Ro 7:18–19).

Redemption—Reconciliation Made Available: The third theological distinction related to conflict is, in the words of Bossart, "an all-powerful, transcendent God reaching out to an alienated humanity which needs . . . reunion with the Creator."[102] God's work of redemption, accomplished through the atonement of Christ, provides reconciliation not only between God and sinners (Col 1:21–2; 2Co 5:18–20) but between believing sinners who are in need of reconciliation one to another (Eph 2:14–18).[103] In his *Theology of Hope,* Jurgen Moltmann argues that the hope of the gospel finds relevance in the practical lives of men and women and to the relationships in which these lives are lived. The peace that is promised in the kingdom of God is expressed in terms of relationship and accordingly has to do with the relationships of humans to each other.[104]

The Ministry of Reconciliation—Conflict Resolution: The incarnation of Jesus Christ represents God's ultimate initiative for

---

[102]Bossart, *Creative Conflict in Religious Education and Church Administration,* 76.

[103]Gordon R. Lewis and Bruce Demarest, *Integrative Theology,* vol. 2 (Grand Rapids, Mich.: Zondervan, 1990), 406.

[104]Jurgen Moltmann, *Theology of Hope,* trans. James W. Leitch (New York: Harper and Row, 1967), 330.

seeking peace for mankind. Thrust into a world full of violence, hatred, opposition, and conflict, Jesus encountered competition over position (Lk 22:24–27), conflict over values (Jn 12:1–8), theological and intellectual debate (Lk 20:27–40), and family conflict (Lk 12:13–15). Furthermore Jesus addresses numerous conflict situations in the Sermon on the Mount. He warns against unresolved anger towards a brother (Mt 5:22); He demands reconciliation to a brother who has offended (5:23–24); He insists one settles matters quickly with an adversary (5:25); He preaches against adultery and divorce (5:27–31); He teaches the principle of turning the other cheek (5:38–39); and finally, He instructs His listeners to love their enemies and pray for those who persecute them (5:43–48).

Likewise, in Christian education every follower of Christ must practice a ministry of reconciliation that is, in the words of McSwain and Treadwell, a "living encounter with conflict in all of its forms."[105] How is this possible in Christian education groups? Conflict has the destructive power to alienate and divide individuals in discussion and support groups, thwart effective progress in task groups, and frustrate the development of Christian community in fellowship groups. Or it can be of productive assistance in working through critical issues and forging bonds among group members.[106] What is often lacking in small group conflicts, however, is the understanding of conflict and related conflict resolution skills crucial to reconciliation. It is imperative that small-group leaders and facilitators develop appropriate skills suited to utilizing conflict creatively in Christian education groups.

Myths That Shape Our Attitude Toward Conflict

Joyce Hocker and William Wilmot illustrate how we can sometimes entertain confused and contradicting thoughts concerning conflict in North American culture: "Conflicts with peers are all right if you have been stepped on and you are a boy, but talking back to parents when they step on you is not

---

[105]McSwain and Treadwell, *Conflict Ministry in the Church*, 25.

[106]Bossart, *Creative Conflict in Religious Education and Church Administration*, 229.

all right. Having a conflict over a promotion is acceptable, but openly vying for recognition is not. Competing over a girl (if you're a boy) is admirable, but having conflict over a boy (if you are a girl) is catty. . . . Thus, persons emerge with a mixed feeling about conflict, and many simply learn to avoid the whole subject."[107]

A better understanding of conflict and the ministry of reconciliation in Christian education groups begins with an awareness of the myths that fashion our perceptions and attitudes towards conflict. Frequently, even the topic of conflict is seen as controversial in nature and is often avoided at all cost because of the myths or dysfunctional generalizations associated with it. Some prevailing myths held concerning conflict are identified as follows:[108]

- harmony is normal, conflict is abnormal;

- conflict must be a win-lose situation;

- conflict is the result of personality clashes;

- all conflict is negative;

- Christians must never be in conflict;

- the Christian way to handle conflict is to give in.

Harmony Is Normal; Conflict Is Abnormal: This erroneous assumption suggests that when conflict does occur, it is unusual or in some manner unfitting. However, an observation of people in relationships shows that conflict is inevitable. In actuality, conflict alternates with harmony in a life pattern of ebb and flow.[109] It is an indisputable and unavoidable dimension of life and existence as thinking, feeling, and communicating beings. It occurs

---

[107]Joyce Hocker and William Wilmot, *Interpersonal Conflict*, 2nd ed. (Dubuque, Ia.: Brown, 1985), 6–7.

[108]Gorman, *Community That Is Christian*, 191–3.

[109]Hocker and Wilmot, *Interpersonal Conflict*, 7.

between individuals, between groups, within groups, and even within an individual.[110]

Clearly, the writers of the Scriptures make no attempt to conceal the reality of conflict.[111] Conflict, in fact, makes up a considerable dimension of the earliest Christian communities: Hellenistic Jews complained that their widows were being ignored (Ac 6:1–7); a very serious conflict emerged between the Judaizers and non-Judaizers over the issue of circumcision (Ac 15:1–35); Paul and Barnabus parted company over the issue of involving John Mark in a missionary journey (Ac 15:36–41); and Paul opposed Peter over theological issues (Gal 2:11–21).

And it should be no surprise that small groups, including Christian education groups, will experience a certain measure of conflict.[112] In fact, conflict may be present even before they come together for interaction.[113] For example, members of a task force group formulated to select a new pastor may have very different notions as to how the selection process should proceed or what they are looking for in a new pastor.

Conflict Is Always a Win-Lose Situation: It is assumed, according to this myth, that with every conflict someone will be a winner and someone will be a loser. Even "friendly competition" is expected to produce both winners and losers. But there are some serious detrimental consequences to resolving conflict in a win-lose pattern. The winner gains the rewards, but usually at the

---

[110]Robert J. Doolittle, *Orientations to Communication and Conflict* (Chicago: Science Research Associates, 1976), 1; Alex Boulter and C.W. Von Bergen, "Conflict Resolution: An Abbreviated Review of Current Literature with Suggestions for Counselors," in *Education* 116 (Fall 1995): 93–8.

[111]For further readings on the theme of conflict in New Testament writings see Jack Dean Kingsbury, *Conflict in Luke: Jesus, Authorities, Disciples* (Minneapolis: Fortress, 1991); Theodore J. Weeden, *Mark: Traditions on Conflict* (Philadelphia: Fortress, 1971); Ben Witherington, *Conflict and Community in Corinth* (Grand Rapids, Mich.: Eerdmans, 1995).

[112]John M. Levine and Leigh Thompson, "Conflict in Groups," in *Social Psychology: Handbook of Basic Principles*, eds. E. Tory Higgins and Arie W. Kruglanski (New York: Guilford, 1996), 745–76.

[113]Doolittle, *Orientations to Communication and Conflict*, 1.

expense of the loser; the loser may be damaged economically, socially, psychologically, or physically.[114]

In competitive sports, such as football, basketball, tennis, or hockey a win-lose attitude is necessary if the game is to mean anything. But in many types of conflict, mutually exclusive goals are not necessarily an actuality; rather there may exist varying degrees of differences and commonality. Serious conflict may arise when differences are perceived to be mutually exclusive and an unfortunate and unhealthy win-lose mentality subsequently emerges.[115] Effective conflict resolution, with an attitude of reconciliation seeks a win-win solution. This may mean compromise on behalf of each faction whereby each party will give up something in order to gain something more important—among other things, group cohesiveness and unity.[116]

Conflict Is the Result of Personality Clashes: As with all myths, there is an element of truth in this one in that personality clashes may be one source of conflict. It is erroneous thinking, however, to assume that all conflict occurs because people simply cannot get along or have clashing personalities. Conflict often occurs whenever incompatible *actions* occur and may originate from a variety of sources including differences in beliefs and ideologies. Conflict may also occur in Christian education groups over disagreements concerning how procedures should be followed in pursuing its goals or making decisions.[117]

All Conflict Is Negative: Early research on interpersonal conflict generally treated it as destructive, but more recently this orientation has shifted to include a positive view of conflict.[118]

---

[114]Ibid., 6.

[115]Keating, *The Leadership Book*, 43.

[116]Bossart, *Creative Conflict in Religious Education and Church Administration,* 1980; Alan C. Filley, "Conflict Resolution: The Ethic of the Good Loser," in *Readings in Interpersonal and Organizational Communication,* eds. Richard C. Huseman, Cal M. Logue, and Dwight L. Freshley (Boston: Holbrook, 1977), 234–52.

[117]Doolittle, *Orientations to Communication and Conflict,* 28.

[118]William P. McFarland, "Counselors Teaching Peaceful Conflict Resolution," in *Journal of Counseling and Development* 71 (Sept./Oct. 1992): 18–21.

Of course, some conflict is negative, even harmful and wrong. But sociologists agree that conflict serves a number of useful purposes for groups.[119] A distinction was made earlier between conflict of ideas and conflict of feelings. Feeling-based conflict is targeted at individual members of the Christian education group, detracts from the issue or task at hand, and can be detrimental to group functioning. Idea or issue-based conflict, on the other hand, focuses on problems or tasks and is desirable in that it lowers the possibility of groupthink and helps group make better decisions.[120] Conflict also affects a Christian education group positively when it advances cohesiveness and teamwork, when it enhances member understanding, and when it leads to satisfaction with both the process and the product.[121]

Christians Must Never Be in Conflict: The apostle Paul clearly commands believers to "Live in harmony with one another. . . . If is at all possible, as far as it depends on you, live at peace with everyone" (Ro 12:16, 18). The phrase "if it at all possible" indicates that it may not always be possible to be at peace with others.[122] Furthermore, suggests Gorman, Paul is talking about living positively with differences, not necessarily being uniform in thinking. In regard to Christian education groups, "When harmony is interpreted as everyone being alike, groups cultivate a pseudoharmony that gives the impression of peace and togetherness but which in actuality declares that Christians cannot be honest and real in their differences."[123]

---

[119]Levine and Thompson, "Conflict in Groups," 745–76; Doolittle, *Orientations to Communication and Conflict*, 3–5.

[120]Miranda and Bostrom, "The Impact of Group Support Systems on Group Conflict and Conflict Management," 63–9.

[121]Brilhart and Galanes, *Effective Group Discussion*, 257.

[122]John Murray, *The Epistle to the Romans* (Grand Rapids, Mich.: Eerdmans, 1968), 139.

[123]Gorman, *Community That Is Christian*, 19.

The Christian Way to Handle Conflict Is to Give In: While the teachings of Jesus include the mandate to yield one's personal wants and desires for the sake of others (Mt 5:40–42), Scripture also indicates that in certain situations it is important to stand firm in our conviction. For instance, in his confrontation with Peter over important doctrinal truths, Paul was convinced he was right and was determined to win his cause (Gal 2:11–21). Jesus further instructs, "If your brother sins against you, go and show him his fault. If he listens to you, you have won your brother over" (Mt 18:15).

Em Griffin notes that while giving in makes sense in some cases, it is not always appropriate. Concerning people who try to smooth every conflict, he says, "They give up the courage of their convictions in order not to ruffle the relationship. It makes you wonder how solid the friendship is if it could be shattered by a touch of disagreement. And aren't some issues worth fighting for?"[124]

The Value of Conflict

While it is granted that conflict is unavoidable, it is generally considered to be negative: the source of wars, divorces, broken friendships, bloody noses, and even church splits. No doubt certain types of conflict—especially those in which weapons are employed, or where verbal and physical abuse are exhibited—are indeed destructive and leave a string of casualties in their aftermath. But as mentioned above, most communication and small-group experts agree that a certain amount of conflict is desirable, productive, and healthy.

Conflict Often Produces a Better Understanding of Issues: All too often we assume that others feel as we do about issues and see things the way we do. One empirical study, however, found that when students discovered others holding differing opinions on an issue, they became more uncertain about where they stood, actively sought to find more information about the issue, were more able to take

---

[124]Griffin, *Getting Together*, 145.

the perspective of the other students, and were better able to retain information.[125]

If conflict is avoided entirely we may never get to the heart of the issue or really understand how others feel or think about a particular issue. Griffin adds "It is only when thoughts see the light of day in the free marketplace of ideas that they can be examined for their biblical soundness. This means conflict, for you may have noticed that not all Christians agree."[126]

Conflict Increases Motivation: When people do not care, they will expend little energy on an issue. But when small group members engage themselves in a conflict issue, they become actively involved. "When people care," says Gorman, "they get involved risking greater investment of themselves in the group."[127] At the point of conflict members become interested, excited, pay closer attention, and consequently learn more about the issue or subject matter. For example, a group member may not be able to agree with a particular theological belief held by another. This may motivate the individual to dig and research in order to defend her position or counter the argument. Her findings may be beneficial, not only to the individual doing the digging, but to all group members as they are shared and evaluated in the next small group study.

Conflict Usually Produces Better Decisions: Conflict management experts tend to be in agreement concerning the value of issue-based conflict in producing better decisions.[128] Amason and Thompson, for instance, studied the use of conflict in management teams and discovered that how teams managed conflict was the crux of team effectiveness. They found that successful teams employed conflict to their advan-

---

[125] Karl Smith, David W. Johnson, and Roger T. Johnson, "Can Conflict be Constructive? Controversy versus Concurrence Seeking in Learning Groups," *Journal of Educational Psychology* 73 (1981): 654–63.

[126]Griffin, *Getting Together*, 135.

[127]Gorman, *Community That Is Christian*, 194.

[128]See, for example, Miranda and Bostrom, "The Impact of Group Support Systems on Group Conflict and Conflict Management," 63–95; Janis, *Groupthink*, 1982.

tage by using it to arouse discussion and stimulate creative thinking. By contrast, less successful teams did a poor job of managing conflict and found conflict burdensome—something to be avoided. Avoidance consequently led to poor decisions and lessened group effectiveness.[129]

Through issue-oriented conflict, Christian education group members discover first that others disagree with them, then why they disagree. Participants find holes in arguments, flaws in reasoning, factors that other members failed to consider, or implications that were ignored. Thus, conflict can cause a group to become more creative and productive, producing decisions that are better. Gorman suggests that challenging the status quo or working through a dilemma means that group members must look for new or improved conditions and solutions, and the result will probably be a better group. Christian education groups with members who are willing to differ expand the boundaries that often limit and confine solutions.[130]

Conflict Can Produce Group Cohesiveness: Research has also determined that conflict can promote group cohesiveness.[131] When a small group successfully resolves conflict and overcomes interpersonal differences, it often can experience a special closeness that comes with "making up." Griffin reasons that openly dealing with conflict can be therapeutic. When it is dealt with constructively, conflict will draw people together into a cohesive whole.[132] The process of working through difficulties together binds members to each other. "Just knowing that they like each other and the group enough to reveal and work through issues of deep emotional ownership develops a feeling of commitment to others who shared in that revelation and process."[133]

---

[129]Amason and Thompson, "Conflict: An Important Dimension in Successful Management Teams," 20–36.

[130]Gorman, *Community That is Christian*, 195.

[131]Lewis A. Coser, *The Functions of Social Conflict* (Glencoe, Ill.: Free Press, 1964).

[132]Griffin, *Getting Together*, 135.

[133]Gorman, *Community That Is Christian*, 194.

The Negative Effects of Conflict

Conflict, however, is a two-edged sword. While a certain amount of issues-related conflict can be beneficial and even a necessary instrument for the critical evaluation of ideas, there is no doubt that interpersonal or affective conflict can be extremely harmful, especially if it is not dealt with in an appropriate manner. Once conflict escalates to the point where it is no longer under control, a group will usually yield negative effects. These negative outcomes include hurt feelings, lack of cohesiveness, diminished productivity, and group breakup.

Conflict Can Contribute to Poor Feelings Between Group Members: Interpersonal or affective conflict is usually directed toward specific group members and is manifested in negative emotions such as anger and resentment. Such conflict, if not managed correctly, lowers the effectiveness of the small group by cultivating hostility, distrust, cynicism, and apathy among group members.[134]

Conflicts in Christian education groups may find their genesis in the sphere of ideas or issues but forthwith transpire into interpersonal encounters. In conflict of this nature, remarks are often biting, even hostile. When conflict over issues and ideas are carried on over a long period of time or when feelings are hurt, group members will dread coming to meetings and eventually withdraw from the Christian education group. For example, a study group might engage in a heated debate over a particular theological issue or the appropriate Christian response to a social issue, like abortion. What begins as a discussion concerning a critical issue evolves into a conflict of ideas, and quickly degenerates into heated interpersonal conflict as participants become angry, defensive, and attack each other rather than the issue.

Conflict Can Lower Group Cohesiveness: Group unity or cohesiveness is often a dividend of judiciously managed conflict, when issue-related conflict in Christian education groups is prolonged or if it involves personal attacks, cohesiveness will

---

[134]Amason and Thompson, "Conflict: An Important Dimension in Successful Management Teams," 20–36.

likely be lowered. For example, Amason and Thompson noted that in one of the task groups they studied, when differences of opinions transformed into personalized disagreements, some group members would simply "throw up their hands and walk away from the decision." Frustrated group members ceased to actively participate in the decision-making process. "Not only did the team lose the value of their input, but the members lost the desire to work vigorously for the accomplishment of whatever decision was reached."[135]

Conflict Can Lower Group Productivity and Effectiveness: When conflict occurs too frequently or inappropriately, productivity in any type of Christian education group is hindered and work simply does not get done. As Christian education groups experience affective or interpersonal conflict, they tend to become less effective in achieving their desired results.[136] Simply put, they spend more time brooding and fighting, rather than nurturing one another and learning.[137] Jandt and Gillette observe that when conflict is not effectively resolved at the social-emotional level, groups suffer several destructive consequences: (1) group members suffer from stress and the debilitating effects of stress; (2) the small group misallocates personal and group resources as members devote their time, thoughts, and materials to doing battle rather than accomplishing the task for which the Christian education group exists; and (3) the group experiences diminished overall performance as participants allow conflict to deplete them of energy, determination, and dedication.[138]

Conflict Can Cause Group Dissolution: At worst, conflict can literally divide a Christian education group or cause a group to die. Interpersonal conflict that endures for an extended period of time or is too intense can eventually destroy relationships to the

---

[135]Ibid.

[136]Amason and Thompson, "Conflict: An Important Dimension in Successful Management Teams," 20–36.

[137] Johnson and Johnson, *Joining Together*, 336.

[138]Fred Edmund Jandt and Paul Gillette, *Win-Win Negotiating: Turning Conflict into Agreement* (New York: John Wiley, 1985), 101.

point that individuals will eventually leave the group and perhaps look for a different Christian education group in which they are better accepted.

Strategies for Managing Conflict in Small Groups

Individuals differ markedly in how they respond in the midst of conflict. Similarly, group facilitators demonstrate a variety of conflict management techniques that reflect their personalities, family backgrounds, past experiences with conflict, and theology of conflict. Johnson and Johnson describe this diversity with the following illustration: "Dealing with conflict of interests is like going swimming in a cold lake. Some people like to test the water, stick their foot in, and enter slowly. Such people want to get used to the cold gradually. Other people like to take a running start and leap in. They want to get the cold shock over quickly. Similarly, different people use different strategies for managing conflicts. Usually, we learn these strategies in childhood so that later they seem to function automatically on a preconscious level. We must do whatever seems to come naturally. But we do have a personal strategy and, because it was learned, we can always change it by learning new and more effective ways of managing conflict."[139]

When managing conflict in Christian education groups, two major concerns must be taken into account:[140]

1. *Reaching a decision that satisfies the needs of the group and helps the group achieve its goals.* The Christian education group is in tension because one or more of the group members has a goal or interest that conflicts with that of another. For example, John pushes to have the group meet on Thursday evening rather than Tuesday because he works late Tuesday and has trouble making it to the meeting on time. Sandy and Brad, on the other hand, can come only on Tuesday evenings.

2. *Maintaining appropriate relationships with other members of the group.* While John desires to see the group move its

---

[139]Johnson and Johnson, *Joining Together*, 339–40.

[140]Ibid., 340.

216 ❖ The Power of Small Groups in Christian Education

meeting time to Thursday, he does not want to jeopardize his relationships with Sandy and Brad or create any undue tension in the group by pressing for his preference.

In an effort improve our abilities to manage conflict, Blake and Moulton proposed a conflict grid, taking into consideration the two concerns of producing good results (task) and maintaining healthy interpersonal relationships.[141] Kilman and Thomas adapted Blake and Moulton's conflict grid and identified five conflict management styles: accommodating, avoiding, competing, compromising, and collaborating.[142] Figure 4.1 illustrates how the two underlying dimensions of tasks and relationships produce the five conflict management styles.

With conflicts that emerge in Christian education groups, the facilitator and group participants must decide how important group goals are and, likewise, how important relationships are. Given these two concerns the facilitator may choose one of the five strategies to manage or resolve group conflicts.

Avoidance: One strategy for conflict resolution is avoidance, a nonconfrontational or hands-off approach. For example, Lance, a high school basketball coach chooses to walk away from an encounter with a fan because the issue is not important enough to fight for, and because the other individual is not significant in his life.

While avoidance sometimes appears to be the most prudent and easiest way to deal with an issue of contention, it is a poor conflict resolution pattern to fall into. This passive approach provides no opportunity to explore options relevant to the issue, nor does it allow conflicting parties to reconcile. Since healthy relationships are germane to the success of a Christian education small group, the avoidance style of conflict management is almost never a suitable style of conflict resolution.

---

[141]Robert R. Blake and Jane S. Mouton, "The Fifth Achievement," *Journal of Applied Behavioral Sciences* 6 (1977): 413–26.

[142] R. Kilman and K. Thomas, "Interpersonal Conflict-Handling Behavior as Reflections of Jungian Personality Dimensions," in *Psychological Reports* 37(1975): 153–70.

Avoidance may be appropriate in Christian education groups when:[143]

- the issue or problem is so insignificant it will have little or no affect on long-range goals;

- the problem or issue is not the group or leader's responsibility;

- differences are so irreconcilable that confrontation will accomplish very little (for example it may be prudent

Figure 4.1

High	**Accommodating** A highly cooperative style whereby disagreements are smoothed over so that surface harmony is maintained. A high concern for relationships, but ideas and goals are compromised.	**Collaborating** A cooperative and assertive style of conflict management that combines a concern for people and a desire to confront the issues; encourages everyone to work toward a solution that pleases everyone.
Concern for People		**Compromising** Demonstrates a moderate concern for both relationships and task. Each party is willing to give up something to achieve peace; no one loses, but no one wins.
	Avoiding A passive approach that provides no opportunity to explore relevant options or to reconcile conflicting parties.	**Competing** An aggressive, uncooperative, win-lose approach to managing conflict; goals and ideas take precedence over relationships.
Low	*Concern for Task*	**High**

---

[143]Palmer, *Managing Conflict Creatively*, 26.

to avoid debate or argument over certain deeply held theological convictions or traditions);

- when participating individuals are in some way emotionally unstable, or their level of maturity will not allow for effective management of the conflict.

Accommodation: Accommodation, or giving, in is a highly cooperative style that demonstrates a high concern for the relationship but low concern for the group goal or idea. In this case a small group member tends to set aside his or her own views on the issue or problem at hand to reduce interpersonal tensions. For instance, John, willing to work around his scheduling problems, withdraws his request to have the group study meet on a different evening, for the sake of maintaining good relationships with other group members.

It is not advisable to give in to another party simply to end a conflict, for the resentment that may emerge as a result of accommodation could harm the relationship anyway. Accommodation is an appropriate style for conflict resolution in groups when:[144]

- the issue is temporary in nature or is of relatively little significance;

- an individual feels unsure about his or her position and senses his or her argument is weak;

- the long-term relationship is more important than the issue at hand;

- several equally good positions are proposed or are being considered.

Competition: If accommodation sacrifices the idea or task to save the relationship, competition sacrifices the relationship in order to preserve the conviction or complete the task. In this case, John fights to have the group meet on Thursday,

---

[144]Ibid., 28.

even if it means damaging his relationships with Sandy and Brad or losing them to the group altogether.

Competition is an aggressive, uncooperative approach to managing and resolving conflict. For competitive individuals, goals are highly important while relationships are of lesser significance. They seek to achieve their goals at all costs and are not concerned with the needs of others. Winning gives them a sense of pride and achievement, while losing brings feelings of weakness, inadequacy, and failure.[145]

A competition-driven style of conflict resolution is appropriate in groups when:[146]

- a decision must be made and acted on quickly;

- an unpopular but necessary decision must be made by the group leader or facilitator;

- when an individual is absolutely convinced that his solution or idea is correct or best for the Christian education group.

Compromise: Compromisers are moderately concerned with their relationships with others as well as with their convictions and goals. This style of conflict resolution assumes each party involved in the conflict will give up something to achieve peace and gain something greater. According to this style, the Christian education group might continue to meet on Tuesday evening, but meet at eight o'clock rather than at seven. The later time may not be entirely satisfactory for everyone, but allows John to make it to the meeting on time and Brad and Sandy can continue to attend.

This attitude says "I may not gain everything I had hoped for, but I can live with it." While there is a healthy spirit of cooperation here compromise entails only partial satisfaction for all

---

[145]Gorman, *Community That is Christian*, 201.

[146]Donald C. Palmer, *Managing Conflict Creatively: A Guide for Missionaries and Christian Workers* (Waynesboro, Ga.: Gabriel Resources, 1991), 26.

concerned, some losses for both parties, and a danger of settling for a less than ideal solution.[147]

Compromise is appropriate when:[148]

- opposing parties are of equal strength and are equally committed to different goals, ideas, or solutions;

- the goals and solutions are equally valid and the differences are not worth engaging in conflict over;

- the urgency for a solution does not allow for consideration of better solutions or the time needed for a consensus decision;

- there is something that can be divided or exchanged (consequently compromise will rarely work when deeply held theological convictions, values, or traditions are at stake).

Collaboration: A cooperative and assertive style that combines a concern and care for the other person, as well as an honest confronting of the issue that divides the parties is collaboration. Also known as negotiation and problem solving, collaboration encourages all members to work together for a solution that meets everyone's needs.[149]

For instance, the Sunday school department is faced with the unenviable task of securing more classroom space for a growing Sunday school program. The decision-making body is an ad hoc committee made up of representatives of the early childhood, children, youth, and adult departments. Options include dividing rooms, building an addition, creating new classes, and having an adult class meet in a nearby restaurant. Emotions run high as committee members endeavor to repre-

---

[147]Robert S. Cathcart, Larry A. Samovar, and Linda D. Henman, eds., *Small Group Communication*, 7th ed. (Madison, Wis.: Brown and Benchmark, 1996), 181.

[148]Palmer, *Managing Conflict Creatively*, 30.

[149]Brilhart and Galanes, *Effective Group Discussion*, 271.

sent their respective departments, explore the feasibility of each possibility, and wrestle with personal preferences and biases. The leader must be firm, yet sensitive to everyone's feelings. She must insist that each party give clear messages as to their preferences, ideas, and goals. She must guide the decision-making process in such a manner that ensures fairness and avoids personal attacks and intimidation. The collaborative style works in a manner that seeks each participant's good, a decision that is owned by all involved, and a resolution that is most helpful.[150]

Em Griffin uses the term "carefronting" to describe such an approach and describes it as follows: "People who enter into conflict situations with [this] kind of commitment see disagreements among people as neutral, neither good nor bad. Differences are merely the occasion for creativity while demonstrating our solidarity with others."[151] Collaboration is viewed as an ideal way of dealing with small-group conflict because all members involved can feel they have won without others feeling they have lost. It is most appropriate and the preferred style of conflict resolution when the conflict involves long-term goals and important relationships.

The drawback is that this style is often more time and energy consuming than other approaches, a factor that causes many groups to opt for a quicker solution. Christian education groups implementing the collaborative style of conflict resolution will be most effective when participants:[152]

- build on areas of mutual agreement;

- agree on the use of terms or definitions;

- clearly identify the specific changes necessary for a satisfactory resolution;

- stick to the issue at hand and do not let side issues or hidden agendas motivate them;

---

[150]Palmer, *Managing Conflict Creatively*, 30.

[151]Griffin, *Getting Together*, 148.

[152]Summarized from Tubbs, *A Systems Approach to Small Group Interaction*, 250; Brilhart and Galanes, *Effective Group Discussion*, 272–3.

- avoid personal attacks by disagreeing with ideas but never criticizing another individual;

- express their disagreements so that the group is not deprived of potentially valuable information;

- are sensitive and perceptive, and express their disagreements by selecting words that will not connote negative images;

- base their disagreement on substantial evidence and clear reasoning, at the same time avoiding rumors, innuendoes, unsubstantiated information, and emotionalism.

- react to disagreement with spirits of inquiry rather than defensiveness, and at the same time remain open to the ideas, evaluations, and suggestions of each group member.

- stay calm and speak reasonably even when attacked;

- respond to attacking members calmly and reasonably; work towards a win-win situation, using their energy to search for solutions that integrate each member's needs.

CONCLUSION

This chapter dealt with issues related to the sophisticated concept of leadership, perhaps the most important ingredient in the effective functioning of a Christian education group. Above all else, small-group leadership is influence, and includes the critical tasks of administration, facilitation of discussion, decision making, and conflict resolution.

5
Communicating in Small Groups

HISTORIANS and sociologists are fond of coining phrases intended to capture the essence or ethos of the age to which they are referring. The Age of Reason, the Age of Enlightenment, the Age of Ideology, the Atomic Age, the Space Age, the Age of Technology, and the Age of Information are but a few examples of their efforts. We live in an Age of Communication, a period of time when people, perhaps more than at any other point in history, are engaging in talk with one another. Communication plays a critical role in helping individuals meet the basic needs in family, work, education, and social relationships. And fundamental to all Christian education small groups is the process of communication.

SMALL-GROUP COMMUNICATION DEFINED
Whether one is communicating with another individual, in a small group, or to a large audience, the same basic process takes place. Thoughts, ideas, and feelings are shared with each other in commonly understandable ways.[1] But communication in small groups is both similar and dissimilar to communication in other milieus (such as large group or one-on-one settings). Communication in small groups is a two-way process whereby verbal or nonverbal symbols generated by the sender are received and responded to by other members.[2] While

---

[1]Cheryl Hamilton and Cordell Parker, *Communicating for Results* (Belmont, Calif.: Wadsworth, 1987), 4–5.

[2]Brilhart and Galanes, *Effective Group Discussion*, 42.

this definition is relatively simple, small-group communication itself is not, as can be demonstrated by the following concepts.[3] First, group communication is a complex process, more than nouns and verbs. It involves three or more people, includes the expression of both verbal and nonverbal symbols, and engages human senses, emotions, and feelings.

Second, group communication is a two-way process, including a sender and at least two receivers. If there is no audience, no communication takes place. If an individual speaks but no one is listening, communication has not occurred.

Third, communication in groups is primarily a receiver phenomenon. In a healthy small-group discussion, each individual will spend more time engaged in listening than speaking. Simple math tells us that if group members participate equally, in a four-person group an individual member will listen approximately 75 percent of the time; in a group of ten, 90 percent of the time, and so forth. In small-group communication then, receiving the message (listening) is just as important, if not more important, than sending the message. The level of understanding among group members is more contingent on how they listen and respond, than on how they speak. If Christian education group members want to be better communicators then it is of consequence that they pay more heed to the art of listening than to how they speak, as important as that may be.

Finally, communication in Christian education groups involves the sending and receiving of both verbal and nonverbal messages. We generally think of face-to-face discussion in terms of exchanging words. However, verbal and nonverbal signals operate in harmony with one another to create meaning in group interaction. Often nonverbal signals carry more influence in small-group communication, as they modify, supplement, reinforce, override, emphasize, or contradict verbal signals.

---

[3]Ibid., 81–3.

EFFECTIVE LISTENING IN
CHRISTIAN EDUCATION GROUPS

Be quick to listen, slow to speak.—James 1:19

Urge your local school to teach listening—a necessity in today's world.—Sperry Corporation[4]

The pervasiveness of listening in daily activities is well documented. Among the early researchers on communication, Paul Rankin stands out as most noteworthy. In 1926 he discovered that adults spent 70 percent of their waking day in some form of communication. He further analyzed his data and found that nearly half of that communication occurred in the form of listening.[5] Communication expert Lyman Steil insists that listening is the *primary* communication activity utilized by individuals throughout the world, essential to the personal, professional, familial, social, and educational success of every productive person.[6]

Successful businesses embrace the notion that the dynamic of listening is one of the most consequential ingredients in communication. For example, Weinrauch and Swanda argue that "the most important factor for successful communication is not only the ability to use language well or to speak well or to present one's own point of view; it is rather the ability to listen well to the other person's point of view."[7] In the popular business-related book *In Search of Excellence*, Peters and

---

[4]Part of a national advertising campaign of the Sperry Corporation, cited in "Speaking/Listening: Much Used, Little Taught," *Curriculum Report* 14 (December 1984).

[5]Cited in Lyman K. Steil, Larry L. Barker, and Kittie W. Watson, *Effective Listening: Key to Your Success* (New York: Random, 1983), 3.

[6]Lyman K. Steil, *Listening Training and Development* (St. Paul, Minn.: Communication Development, 1982), 39.

[7]J. Donald Weinrauch and John R. Swanda, "Examining the Significance of Listening: An Exploratory Study of Contemporary Management," *The Journal of Business Communication* 13 (February 1975): 25–32.

Waterman propose that excellent companies, in addition to offering service, quality, and reliability to their customers, are also better listeners. That is, they pay close attention to what their customers want and what they are saying about their products.[8] And in a review of twenty-five studies identifying the communication demands students will encounter when entering various organizational contexts, listening was identified as one of the necessary skills listed most frequently.[9]

The need for good listening extends beyond the context of business organization. Thomas Gordon, in his enormously popular *Teacher Effectiveness Training*, enumerates the values of active listening in the classroom: It makes students feel that they are understood and respected, fosters further communication, helps defuse strong feelings, facilitates the identification of problems, and puts students in the framework of wanting to listen to teachers.[10] Research also indicates that in sports, coaches who are the most successful interact with their players more and possess better listening skills.[11]

The Benefits of Listening

Lucrative monetary rewards are often offered to those who have gained a reputation of being good public speakers, or because of their expertise in a particular field. Well-known personalities can demand up to $60,000 or more for a public speaking engagement. Effective listeners, on the other hand, can make no such exorbitant demands. There are, nonetheless, invaluable benefits available to good listeners, including more modest monetary rewards. The salesperson, for example,

---

[8]Thomas J. Peters and Robert H. Waterman, *In Search of Excellence* (New York: Warner, 1982), 196.

[9]Vincent S. Disalvo, "A Summary of Current Research Identifying Communication Skills in Various Organizational Contexts," *Communication Education* 29 (July 1980): 283–90.

[10]Thomas Gordon, *Teacher Effectiveness Training* (New York: McKay, 1974), 88–9.

[11]Christopher L. Saffici, "Coaches: Listening to Your Players," *Physical Educator* 53 (Fall 1996): 164–8.

who listens attentively to the needs and interests of a prospective customer is more likely to be rewarded with more satisfied customers and increased sales than the salesman who assumes that selling primarily involves the skill of talking.

The gains of effective listening, however, are extended far beyond financial gain. Consider the following benefits to attentive listening in Christian education groups:[12]

Information and Understanding are Acquired Through Listening: Clearly the most obvious benefit of careful listening is the acquisition of information, and subsequently a better understanding of issues. While people often prefer to talk while engaging in interpersonal communication, it is important to remember that learning comes not so much from talking, but from listening. Solomon, the sagacious king of Israel, advised that the wise listen, and so add to their learning (Pr 1:5). Students listen in classes so as to learn the subject matter; employees listen carefully to find out what work has to be done; people listen to the news to find out what is happening in the world. And through careful listening in Christian education groups, participants become more informed of the subject matter and of the issues or needs of fellow group members. Having a broader information base, the good listener is then better equipped to contribute to group decisions, engage in group discussions, assist in conflict resolution and problem solving, and fulfill assignments.

Good Listeners Are Well Liked: Undoubtedly, one of the best-selling and most popular books of all time is Dale Carnegie's *How to Win Friends and Influence People.* In one section of his book, Carnegie identifies six ways to get people to like you. One of the important rules he proposes is to "be a good listener."[13] Conversely, his recipe for making people shun you and perhaps even despise you is rendered as follows: "Talk incessantly about yourself. If you have an idea while the other

[12]Andrew Wolvin and Carolyn Gwynn Coakley, *Listening,* 4th ed. (Dubuque, Ia.: Wm. C. Brown, 1992), 27–31.

[13]Dale Carnegie, *How to Win Friends and Influence People* (New York: Simon and Schuster, 1964), 88.

fellow is talking, don't wait for him to finish. He isn't as smart as you. Why waste your time listening to his idle chatter? Bust right in and interrupt him in the middle of a sentence."[14]

Listening Improves Interpersonal Relationships: Another reward of attentive listening is improved interpersonal relationships, best illustrated, perhaps, in family relations. Numerous books and publications stress the value of listening for improving not only husband and wife relationships, but parent-child relationships as well.[15] When individuals feel they have been truly listened to, they feel acknowledged, affirmed, understood, appreciated, and loved. Nichols goes so far as to propose that "the power of empathic listening is the power to transform relationships. When deeply felt but unexpressed feelings take shape in words that are shared and come back clarified, the result is a reassuring sense of being understood and a grateful feeling of shared humanness with the one who understands."[16] Listening surely strengthens relationships between Christian education group members by cementing their connections with one another.

Listening Contributes to the Growth of Self and Others: When Christian education group members truly listen to one another—to both verbal and nonverbal messages, feelings, and emotions—they understand themselves better and feel understood. Nichols notes, "In the presence of a receptive listener, we're able to clarify what we think and discover what we feel. Thus, in giving an account of our experience to someone who listens, we are better able to listen to ourselves. Our lives are co-authored in dialogue."[17]

---

[14]Ibid., 87.

[15]Michael P. Nichols, *The Lost Art of Listening: How Learning to Listen Can Improve Relationships* (New York: Guilford, 1995), 196–7; Thomas Gordon, *Parent Effectiveness Training* (New York: Peter H. Wyden, 1970), 49–61; Charles E. Schaefer and Howard L. Millman, *How to Help Children With Common Problems* (New York: Van Nostrand Reinhold, 1981), 114.

[16]Nichols, *The Lost Art of Listening: How Learning to Listen Can Improve Relationships,* 10.

[17]Ibid.

Hearing Versus Listening

Unfortunately, in spite of the tremendous rewards for listening, most people are not very good listeners. This is illustrated by a study presented to the American Psychological Association. According to the research, if you were to interrupt the average college lecture and ask students to encode their thoughts at that moment, you would discover that:[18]

- about 20 percent are pursuing erotic thoughts,

- about 20 percent are reminiscing about something,

- only 20 percent are actually paying attention to the speaker, while 12 percent are actively listening.

The remaining students are worrying, daydreaming, thinking about lunch, or thinking about religion.

Critical to the discussion of listening is the distinction between listening and hearing. Hearing is the reception by the ear of sound waves and transformation of these waves into auditory nerve signals.[19] But hearing is only one dimension of listening. A person who has acute hearing may be a poor listener who does not interpret or respond appropriately to statements made by other people. On the other hand, someone with significant hearing loss may be an excellent listener who is motivated to understand what other people are saying. These individuals attend closely to the dialogue, ask others to speak up, and interpret messages accurately despite loss of hearing.[20] Listening is defined as a "selective process of attending to, hearing, understanding and remembering aural (and at times visual) symbols."[21] Thus the small-group leader or participant may hear words (that is, receive sound waves)

---

[18]Cited by Ronald B. Adler and Neil Towne, *Looking Out Looking In,* 6th ed. (Fort Worth, Tex.: Holt, Rinehart and Winston, 1990), 251.

[19]Carol A. Roach and Nancy J. Wyatt, *Successful Listening* (New York: Harper and Row, 1988),13–4.

[20]Brilhart and Galanes, *Effective Group Discussion,* 50

[21]Larry Barker, *Listening Behavior* (Englewood Cliffs, N.J.: Prentice-Hall, 1971), 17.

but not engage in the total listening process by mentally tuning out the speaker.

Active Listening

> *"Epictetus, I have often come desiring to hear you speak, and you have never given me any answer; now if possible, I entreat you, say something to me."*
>
> *"Is there, do you think," replied Epictetus, "an art of speaking as of other things, if it is to be done skillfully and with profit to the hearer?"*
>
> *"Yes."*
>
> *"And are all profited by what they hear, or only some among them? So that it seems there is an art of hearing as well as of speaking. …To make a statue needs skill: to view a statue aright needs skill also."*
>
> *"Admitted."*
>
> *"And I think all will allow that one who proposes to hear philosophers speak needs a considerable training in hearing. Is that not so? Then tell me on what subject you are able to hear me."*
>
> —*Dialogue between Epictetus and another*[22]

At first glance, listening appears to be a passive act of taking in another person's verbal utterances. But an important distinction between hearing and listening is that while hearing is a natural process, listening is a purposeful and, at times, laborious task. In reality, listening is anything but passive, and involves a very active process of responding to the sender of the message.[23] Nichols describes the demands of good listening in this manner: "Listening puts a burden on the listener. Not only do we have to suspend the needs of the self; we also

---

[22]"The Golden Sayings of Epictetus," trans. Hastings Crossley, in Charles W. Elit, ed., *The Harvard Classics* (Danbury, Conn.: Grolier, 1980), 117–82.

[23]Lawrence M. Brammer, *The Helping Relationship: Process and Skills*

feel the weight of the other person's need to be heard. Attention must be paid."[24]

Active listening describes a listening technique whereby an individual endeavors to understand what a speaker means by paying close attention to both the verbal and nonverbal messages. In order to be an active listener, the Christian education group leader or participant should become competent at several communication skills including: attending, responding, and reading nonverbal messages.[25]

Attending: Attending is the nonverbal listening skill of letting the speaker know that you are with him or her. Gerard Egan describes it as the way one orients him or herself both physically and psychologically to the other person or persons.[26] He goes on to suggest that careful attending can invite or encourage others to trust you, open up to you, and disclose personal information. In contrast, poor attending can promote distrust and lead other group members into a reluctance to reveal themselves to you. In addition, the quality of attending, both physical and psychological, influences the quality of one's perceptiveness.[27]

Attending consists of a number of subcomponents, summarized by the acronym SOLER.[28]

- *Facing the speaker **Squarely**.* Facing the speaker in such a manner usually indicates involvement. It tells the other person that "I am with you" or "I am available to you." Conversely, turning away from a person sends the message of disinterest. When one places his or her body in such a position as to exclude another person (facing away from), he or she is clearly communicat-

---

[24]Nichols, *The Lost Art of Listening: How Learning to Listen Can Improve Relationships,* 64.

[25]Brammer, *The Helping Relationship: Process and Skills,* 81–6.

[26]Gerard Egan, *The Skilled Helper* (Monterey, Calif.: Brooks/Cole, 1982), 59.

[27]Ibid.

[28]Summarized from Egan, *The Skilled Helper,* 60–1.

ing intent to close off interaction with that individual.[29] In a small group circle it is not always possible to literally face the speaker squarely, but one should in some way turn toward the person who is speaking so that the message of involvement is conveyed.

- *Adopting an **Open** posture.* Crossed legs and arms can be signs of lessened involvement with the speaker. On the other hand, the folding of arms and crossing of legs in a small group setting often simply represent a less formal posture stance and can indicate relaxation.[30] It is important that the group facilitator carefully considers to what degree his or her posture communicates viability and openness to the other members and to what degree open communication qualities are reciprocated.

- *Leaning toward the speaker from time to time.* In North American culture, leaning slightly toward another person indicates interest in what is being said.[31] Leaning back, especially in a slouch, often suggests disinterest or boredom. Albert Mehrabian confirms this in his experimental research. His findings suggest that the forward lean of the trunk towards the speaker communicates a more positive attitude to the addressee than does a backward lean.[32] Of course, an individual must be careful not to lean forward too much, as this can be taken as demanding too much intimacy or closeness.

---

[29]Albert E. Scheflen, *Body Language and the Social Order: Communication as Behavioral Control* (Engelwood Cliffs, N.J.: Prentice-Hall, 1972), 81.

[30]Albert Mehrabian, "Inference of Attitudes From the Posture Orientation, and Distance of a Communicator," *Journal of Consulting and Clinical Psychology* 32 (1968): 296–308.

[31]Albert Mehrabian, *Silent Messages* (Belmont, Calif.: Wadsworth, 1971), 2.

[32]Mehrabian, "Inference of Attitudes From the Posture Orientation, and Distance of a Communicator," 296–308.

- *Maintaining good Eye contact.* Good eye contact is a crucial communication tool, vision being one of two primary ways human beings receive messages (the other primary channel is hearing). In small Christian education groups, eye contact is generally an invitation to communicate verbally; conversely, avoidance of eye contact indicates a likely reluctance to dialogue with the other person.[33] Whether one looks at a speaker or looks away is also a measure of the interest in what is being said.[34] However, an occasional look away is acceptable, if not suggested, since staring at another person is not a permissible practice in North American culture.

- *Remaining Relaxed, yet alert.* This means two things. First, it means avoiding nervous fidgeting or engaging in distracting facial expressions; second, it means becoming comfortable with the body as a vehicle of contact and expression. A tense posture, characterized by tightly clasped hands, clenched fists, or hands in motion (e.g., drumming fingers) communicates a negative attitude towards other group members.[35]

These guidelines should be handled with caution. It should first be remembered that people differ individually and culturally in how they demonstrate attentiveness. For example, it does not always mean that an individual is less involved with another person if his arms are crossed. The SOLER acronym is not a collection of concrete rules to be applied rigidly; what is important is that the listener be careful to orient him or herself physically to the speaker.

---

[33]Mark L. Knapp, *Essentials of Nonverbal Communication* (New York: Holt, Rinehart and Winston, 1980), 185.

[34]Mehrabian, *Silent Messages,* 2.

[35]Mehrabian, "Inference of Attitudes From the Posture Orientation, and Distance of a Communicator," 296–308.

Figure 5.1

SOLER Attending Skills

S   Face the speaker *Squarely.*
O   Adopt an *Open* posture.
L   *Lean* toward the speaker slightly.
E   Maintain good *Eye* contact.
R   Stay *Relaxed.*

Responding: Responding is a verbal activity that accomplishes at least two tasks. First, it demonstrates to the speaker that the receiver is indeed listening carefully and, second, it assists both the speaker and listener to better understand what is being said. Responding in Christian education groups includes the subelements of clarification, paraphrasing, verbal comments, and summarizing.

- *Clarification.* When the intended meaning of the speaker is unclear, it is important to ask for clarification. Here are some examples of clarification questions a discussion facilitator might use in a Christian education group:

  "Sandy, I am not sure what you mean by that. I wonder if you would you restate your comment and tell the group a little bit more?"

  "Lance, you said you would like the members of this support group to be more honest in addressing certain issues? What do you mean by that?"

  "Brian, you keep saying God is unfair. In what ways do you feel God treats us unfairly?"

- *Paraphrasing.* Paraphrasing occurs when the listener puts into what the original speaker said into his or

her own words.[36] It is imperative that the listener paraphrase, not repeat word for word, what the speaker
said since repetition does not demonstrate understanding. Once the listener paraphrases what has been
said, the original speaker can reply to the paraphrase
by accepting or revising the statement, whereby the
active listener may try again. Only when the speaker
is satisfied that the listener has understood accurately
what has been said should the speaker proceed with
more information. Effective paraphrasing in a Christian education group includes reflecting both the
thoughts and the emotions of the verbal message. For
example:

Group member: "I can't believe the work my profes-
sors are piling on. The assignments keep coming; I'll
never be able to get all my assignments in on time. At
the same time I've got a half-time job, and my wife
and children demand my attention."

Discussion facilitator: "It sounds like you have an extremely busy schedule, and you're not able to give each
of the areas the attention they need."

Group member: "I'm beginning to wonder if taking a
full load of classes is worth the stress they bring to
myself and my family."

Discussion facilitator: "So are you considering quitting college?"

Group member: "Well, maybe not right now, but I
think I will reconsider coming back after this semes-
ter is over."

• *Verbal Comments.* Verbal comments are short phrases
such as "That's interesting" or "I'll bet that hurt," or
even simple utterances such as "yes" and "uh-huh." The

---

[36]Schmuck and Schmuck, *Group Processes in the Classroom,* 97.

purpose of verbal comments is simply to let the speaker know that you are with him or her, and to encourage the speaker to continue. For example:

Group member: "I've been paying a lot of attention to the news lately, and consequently I'm spending a lot of time thinking about the atrocities that occur around the world. I'm wondering why God. . . ." (pause).

Discussion facilitator: "Yes, go on."

- Summarizing. At some point it may be helpful to stop and summarize what has been said. This technique differs from paraphrasing in that paraphrasing is for the purpose of clarification. Summarizing, on the other hand, is helpful for reviewing and highlighting what has been said. A summarizing statement in a Christian education group discussion might begin: "Let's see, you've mentioned . . ." or "Let me see if I can summarize what you said to this point."

Reading Nonverbal Behavior: As a listening participant in a Christian education group, it is of extreme importance to realize the significance of nonverbal behavior. As mentioned earlier, often the nonverbal messages communicated by a sender are of greater consequence than the words themselves. Small-group participants who want to be effective listeners should learn how to listen and read nonverbal actions such as body movements, gestures, facial expressions, and voice-related behaviors.[37] (Nonverbal behavior will be dealt with to a greater degree in a subsequent section.)

Pitfalls to Effective Listening

Unfortunately, listening in Christian education groups is often rendered ineffective as a result of tiredness, preoccupation with unrelated issues, hearing problems, or background noise and activity. However, even when bothered by other con-

---

[37]Egan, *The Skilled Helper*, 64.

cerns, participants may listen poorly as a result of bad habits they are unaware of. Following are seven patterns that significantly interfere with good listening in groups.[38] In a sense they could be characterized as types of nonlistening.

Pseudolistening: Pseudolistening refers to the practice of appearing to listen by giving the speaker the attention good listeners do such as nodding, smiling, and uttering polite responses. In reality, the person is "faking listening" and is more likely daydreaming, thinking of a personal problem, or thinking of an argument against the speaker. Pseudolisteners may ignore the speaker because they have something else on their mind, are bored, or already heard what is being said. For example:

> Sarah appears to be giving the discussion leader and other participating group members her undivided attention when they speak. She smiles, nods her head, and even utters the occasional "uh-huh." But she was engaged in a severe argument with her husband about an hour before the group met, and in reality her mind keeps going back to that confrontation. She cannot recall even the most basic points made in the group discussion.

Silent Arguing: Sometimes the listener forms a quick initial judgment about the speaker's statement or idea, without hearing him or her out completely. Without fully understanding the position, the individual develops a silent argument against what was said. The quality of listening is often reduced when significant time is spent considering what is going to be said and when it will be said. For example:

> Ruth: "I need to share something with this group that I don't feel at liberty to talk about with anyone else. I really need the support of my friends in this small group— I don't know what else to do. Most of you know my sixteen-

---

[38]Summarized from Brilhart and Galanes, *Effective Group Discussion,* 51–2; Galanes and Brilhart, *Communicating in Groups: Applications and Skills,* 57–8; and Adler and Towne, *Looking Out Looking In,* 250–2.

year-old daughter Ashley. Well, she got pregnant and con-fessed to me that she had an abortion. I really want to. . . ."

John: (to himself) "An abortion! What on earth does she expect us to do? She must certainly know how all of us feel about that. Abortion is wrong. The Bible says that. . . ."

Premature Replying: Replying prematurely can take on two forms. Often members of a small group get to know each other so well they anticipate what the other participants are going to say and they say it before the speaker completes the thought. A more common instance of premature replying is the situation where an individual responds before fully hearing or under-standing a statement or question being offered. The result is misunderstandings, frustrations on the part of the interrupted speaker, and disjointed discussions. The writer of Proverbs says "He who answers before listening—that is his folly and his shame" (18:13). Consider the following exchange of interrup-tive behaviors:

Jack: "And then he suggested that my business might do better if I implemented certain biblical principles that. . . ."

Henry: "Oh, I know what he's talking about. I once owned and managed a restaurant in a small town in Kansas. . . ."

Jack: "Well that's the Midwest. Things are different here in Los Angeles. This is the big city and people in the city. . . ."

Henry: "No, when it comes to the restaurant business, there are some things that are the same everywhere. . . ."

Jack: "Well, anyway, my friend suggested. . . ."

Interruptions not only demonstrate disrespect to the speaker, they indicate disinterest and an unwillingness to listen carefully. Edmund Addeo and Robert Burger describe this type of nonlistening in the following manner: "The reason that no one listens, usually, is that our egos get in the way, in the sense that we're mentally formulating what *we're* going to say when the other person gets through speaking. Instead of digesting the other person's information, we are most often busy thinking only of how best we can impress him with our next statement. The result is what we call *EgoSpeak*."[39] This type of interruptive communication behavior does not lead to very effective small-group dialogue.

Focusing on Distractions and Irrelevancies: This occurs when a listener pays more attention to things other than what is being said, such as dialect, dress, word choice, posture, or happenings in the small-group environment. For instance, a distraction in a Christian education group might be a ringing phone or a barking dog. Or a group member may be so distracted by the irrelevant fact that someone is wearing a sweater that does not match his or her shirt that the message of the speaker is missed.

Sidetracking: Sidetracking occurs when a group member says something that triggers a memory or idea in the mind of another and that individual goes off on a mental tangent. Several important discussion points are missed as the person's mind wanders or is caught up in a daydream. For instance:

> Fred: "You know, living the Christian life is a lot like a football game. Just when you. . . ."

> Brad: (to himself) "Ahh, football. What a game. Boy, the Superbowl isn't far off. Let see, who's left after this past weekend—Dallas, Miami, Seattle. And Jacksonville—boy, if they go all the way. . . ."

Defensive Listening: When a group member feels psychologically threatened by something another participant says, he or she may quit listening. An individual may feel defensive about an idea, concept or belief, or a certain "hot button" may

---

[39]Edmond G. Addeo and Robert E. Burger, *EgoSpeak* (Radnor, Pa.: Chilton, 1973), xii.

be pushed. Defensive listeners may also take innocent comments as personal attacks. For example:

> Jason: "I really believe war is wrong. How can we justify the atrocities and killing that occur in any war? I really feel that Christians should take more of a stand against our country being involved in war."
>
> Phil: (to himself) "This kind of thinking really makes me angry. I risked my life to serve my country in Viet Nam so guys like him could live in freedom. I wish people would just shut up about war. Nobody likes it, but there's nothing we can do about it. Sometimes you just have to stand up for what you believe—even if it means going to war."

Improving Listening Skills in Christian Education Groups

The aforementioned problems or pitfalls to effective listening are not present in every Christian education group experience, but nonetheless, all small-group group participants should take stock of their listening habits and make efforts to improve them. Following are several attitudes and behaviors that can improve listening in Christian education small groups.

Refraining from Too Much Talking: This principle is simple enough to understand, but may be more difficult for facilitators and participants to practice. Many individuals are not good listeners simply because they expend too much time and effort speaking. The Scriptures, however, admonish us to "be quick to listen, slow to speak" (Jas 1:19). Many times in small-group discussion, though, people reverse that order and are quick to speak but slow to listen. Because a small group typically involves more than three people, each participant will (or should) spend the majority of time listening. For example, as previously mentioned, in a four-member group an individual member will listen approximately 75 percent of the time; in a ten-person group, 90 percent of the time.[40] The responsibility falls on the group facilitator to

---

[40]Wolvin and Coakley, *Listening,* 405.

carefully regulate group interaction so as to ensure no one individual dominates the discussion.

Asking Questions: Effective listeners demonstrate to other Christian education group members that they are interested in them and what they are saying by asking questions. Most helpful are the types of questions that encourage other group members to develop their ideas and thoughts or those which are asked when the meaning or intent of the speaker's statement is unclear. Here are two examples:

> "Lori, you indicated that you believe that divorce is acceptable under certain circumstances. In what situations do feel divorce is okay?"

> "Jan, I think I heard you say that this group should be more involved in outreach activities. What do you mean by that?"

Listening to the Entire Message: Good listening in small-group discussion means withholding judgment until the speaker's entire message is heard. Although a listener may think he or she knows the direction in which a speaker is headed, the speaker may introduce new information at the end of the message that will require the listener to reconsider. People who interrupt before a speaker is finished may begin their sentence with something like "Yeah, I know just what you mean. . . ." although they do not know exactly how the speaker intended to finish. By reserving judgment, listeners give themselves a chance to reflect on their own data related to the message.[41]

Avoiding Distractions: Distractions can be of two types— mental or environmental. Mental distractions are irrelevant thoughts that occupy one's mind and can usually be rid through conscious efforts. Environmental distractions are outside disturbances that can be anything from an individual tapping his or her fingers on the table, to lack of light which hinders reading, to a television blaring in another room. Environmental distractions are not necessarily limited to sounds. If a group

---

[41]William Gorden, *Communication: Personal and Public* (Sherman Oaks, Calif: Alfred, n.d.), 124; Roach and Wyatt, *Successful Listening,* 30.

meets in a public place, such as a restaurant where people are coming and going, members may find they are naturally drawn to the movements of people. To the extent that a group has control over the physical environment, listening problems caused by outside distractions should be alleviated as much as possible.[42] For instance, televisions and radios should be turned off, pets should be taken care of, the drapes might be drawn on windows, lighting should be appropriate, and the temperature should be set at a level that is comfortable to the majority.

Being Aware of Biases and Poor Attitudes: Sometimes listeners have biases to messages, due to their own prejudices or value judgments. However, each group member deserves the chance to tell share what he or she knows about a topic, even though others may hold differing opinions.[43] Small group participants can also tune out a messenger for attitudinal reasons. For instance, an issue may be of no interest or is boring to an individual; a topic may appear to be too complex or difficult for a particular group member to understand; or a listener may simply not care for the person who is speaking. In any of these cases the individual will automatically pay less attention, and his or her listening will consequently be less effective.[44]

Acknowledging the Speaker: Attentive listening occurs when the listener responds to the speaker with both verbal and non-verbal cues.[45] Three helpful ways the listener can acknowledge involvement are: (1) by making good eye contact with the speaker; (2) by nodding or offering affirming facial expressions such as a smile; and (3) by using comments or vocal prompts such as "go on," or "uh-huh."

Understanding the Intent of the Speaker: It is essential that the group members understand clearly the speaker's ideas before judging them. Too often listeners form premature

---

[42]Roach and Wyatt, *Successful Listening,* 24–5.

[43]Gorden, *Communication: Personal and Public,* 124.

[44]Roach and Wyatt, *Successful Listening,* 31–2.

[45]Barbara Gross Davis, *Tools for Teaching* (San Francisco, Calif.: Jossey-Bass, 1993), 78.

conclusions before hearing the speaker out; or, as mentioned earlier, they form their own conclusions as to what an individual means by what is said. This can often lead to misunderstandings, miscommunication, and unnecessary interpersonal conflict.

NONVERBAL COMMUNICATION IN SMALL GROUPS

If you were able to observe a small group from behind a one-way mirror without hearing them, you would realize a considerable amount of communication was taking place in the form of nonverbal cues. The importance of nonverbal communication in small groups cannot be emphasized enough. In fact, most communication experts agree that nonverbal communication has more impact on listeners than verbal messages.[46] The impact and power of nonverbal signals is well captured in Edward Sapir's quote: "We respond to gestures with an extreme alertness and, one might almost say, in accordance with an elaborate and secret code that is written nowhere, known to none, and understood by all!"[47]

Even early writers were cognizant of the impact of nonverbal messages. The sixteenth-century essayist Francis Bacon (1561–1626) quotes the Latin poet Ovid, *"Nec vultu destrue verba tuo"* ("Contradict not your words by your look") and then adds his own words: "For a man may absolutely cancel and betray the force of speech by his countenance."[48]

---

[46]For example, see Peter Andersen, "Nonverbal Communication in the Small Group," in *Small Group Communication*, 6th ed., eds. Robert S. Cathcart and Larry A. Samovar, (Dubuque, Ia.: Wm. C. Brown, 1992), 272–86; Galanes and Brilhart, *Communicating in Groups*, 80; Adler and Towne, *Looking Out Looking In*, 196.

[47]Edward Sapir, "The Unconscious Patterning of Behavior in Society," in David G. Mandelbaum, ed., *Selected Writings of Edward Sapir in Language, Culture and Personality* (Berkeley, Calif.: University of California Press, 1986), 544–59.

[48]Francis Bacon, *Advancement of Learning* (New York: P. F. Collier, 1911), 338.

Research indicates that 93 percent of the emotional impact of a message comes from nonverbal expressions, whereas only 7 percent comes from what is said verbally.[49] Since nonverbal cues contribute so overwhelmingly to the conveyance of a message, it stands to reason that it is of great consequence that Christian education small-group leaders and participants develop the critical skills of noticing, understanding, and sending nonverbal messages.

Nonverbal communication consists of messages expressed by nonlinguistic means such as distance, touch, body posture and orientation, facial and eye expressions, body movement, voice characteristics, clothing, and physical environment. Nonverbal behavior can affect communication in small groups at least four ways:[50]

- nonverbal behavior can repeat or confirm what is said verbally;

- nonverbal behavior can confuse or deny the verbal message;

- nonverbal behavior can emphasize or strengthen that which is said;

- nonverbal cues are used to regulate or control what occurs in a group discussion.

First, nonverbal behavior can *repeat* or *confirm* what is being said verbally.[51] For example, if in giving directions an individual verbally instructs another to turn right at the end of the block, and simultaneously points in the direction that person should turn, the nonverbal behavior is confirming the verbal message. Or a speaker desires to make three points, so consequently holds up three fingers to confirm his verbal utterance.

Second, nonverbal behavior can *confuse* or *deny* the verbal message. When nonverbal behavior fails to match the verbal

---

[49]Mehrabian, *Silent Messages,* 44.

[50]Egan, *The Skilled Helper,* 65.

[51]Mark L. Knapp, *Essentials of Nonverbal Communication* (New York: Holt, Rinehart, and Winston, 1980), 11.

content, we experience what Mehrabian calls "inconsistent communications," those communications in which contradictory messages are conveyed concurrently by words and nonverbal behaviors such as posture, facial expression, tone of voice, or gestures.[52] For example, Albert Mehrabian and Morton Wiener found that the effects of the tone of the voice tend to be stronger than the effects of the verbal content. For instance, when the attitude communicated in the verbal content was contradicted by a negative tone, the overall message was considered as communicating a negative attitude.[53]

If in giving directions an individual instructs one to turn right but points in the opposite direction, the message has been confused. Or if in group interaction the phrase "That's just great" is said with a negative tone, the message will be interpreted as "That's bad!" or "That's not good" (even though the words themselves connote a positive message) because the vocal expression overrides the words themselves.

Third, nonverbal behavior can *emphasize* or *strengthen* that which is being said. If a group member raises his voice and pounds his fist on the table while saying "I will not be a part of such activities!" he is emphasizing his message with nonverbals (raised voice and fist pounding). In such a case the nonverbal behavior adds emotion and intensity to the message. It is demonstrated. Redundancy of messages in various behaviors (verbal and nonverbal) intensifies the impact of the desired message.[54]

Finally, nonverbal cues are often used to *regulate* or control what happens in a Christian education group.[55] In other words, they help control the back-and-forth flow of discussion or dia-

[52]Mehrabian, *Silent Messages,* 42.

[53]Albert Mehrabian and Morton Wiener, "Decoding of Inconsistent Communications," *Journal of Personality and Social Psychology* 6 (1:1967): 109–14.

[54]Mehrabian, *Silent Messages,* 56.

[55]Peter Bull, *Body Movement and Interpersonal Communication* (New York: John Wiley and Sons, 1983), 68–76; Dale G. Leathers, *Nonverbal Communication Systems* (Boston: Allyn and Bacon, 1976), 207.

logue.[56] For instance, eye contact with another group member may indicate readiness to listen to that person and conversely avoiding eye contact indicates disinterest or exclusion. A raised eyebrow or particular facial expression may indicate a desire to join the group interaction.

Failure to pay close attention to nonverbal cues and behaviors in a Christian education group may mean that one misunderstands and overlooks important information or attitudes that are being transmitted. Consequently effective listening is enhanced by learning to read nonverbal signals.

Principles of Nonverbal Communication

There are several principles concerning nonverbal communication that help Christian education group participants understand what happens when members send and receive nonverbal signals:[57]

- an individual cannot stop sending nonverbal messages;

- nonverbal messages, by themselves, are highly ambiguous;

- the major determinants of meaning in interpersonal communication are nonverbal cues;

- nonverbal communication is culture-bound;

- nonverbal signals are primarily affective in nature.

First, an individual *cannot stop sending nonverbal messages* in a small group. It is commonly said that "you cannot *not* communicate." Verbals occur some of the time, Lee reminds the Christian educator, while nonverbal messages occur virtually all of the time.[58] How powerful or pervasive are nonverbal mes-

---

[56]Richard Heslin and Miles L. Patterson, *Nonverbal Behavior and Social Psychology* (New York: Plenum, 1982), 88.

[57]Summarized from Adler and Towne, *Looking Out Looking In,* 197–205, and Brilhart and Galanes, *Effective Group Discussion,* 8th ed., 72–3.

[58]James Michael Lee, *The Content of Religious Instruction* (Birmingham, Ala.: Religious Education Press, 1985), 392.

sages? "Even when the nonverbal expression of emotion is unintended, it can send a clear message to a receiver. Indeed, emotions so automatically generate communicative displays that they can be problematic for the maintenance of competent self-presentations during interaction, particularly when negative emotions are unwittingly revealed."[59]

We automatically form distinct first impressions of people we meet; we judge them to be extroverted, introverted, domineering, obnoxious, self-assured, argumentative, hostile, or bland according to their appearance and actions. There is something about each individual, a penetrating or pervasive manner, that relates to almost everything he or she does and allows us to created an impression before any encounter of verbal dialogue.[60] Imagine a young lady who attends a small group but refuses to dialogue with other members because she is afraid to disclose anything about herself or is in some way fearful of people getting to know her. Whether she acknowledges it or not, the other participants will get to know her—or at least pass judgment on her—through her nonverbal messages. They might correctly assume she has a fear of self-disclosing, or perhaps they will wrongly assume she is shy, snobbish, or uncaring. The message may be misinterpreted, but nonetheless a message is sent and interpreted.

Second, nonverbal messages by themselves are *highly ambiguous,* thus sometimes difficult to interpret. In a study by Joel and Lois Davitz, one speaker's vocal cues were identified only 23 percent of the time, whereas another speaker's expressions were correctly recognized over 50 percent of the time.[61] It is critical, therefore, that to prevent misunderstandings about issues and relationships, nonverbal messages are accompanied with verbal explanations. The nonverbal activity of repeatedly looking at one's watch, for instance, could indicate boredom, nervousness, or anxiety. How should one handle ambiguous cues? Rather than jumping to inaccurate conclusions about the meaning

---

[60]Mehrabian, *Silent Messages,* 57.

[61]Joel R. Davitz and Lois J. Davitz, "The Communication of Feelings by Content-Free Speech," in *The Journal of Communication* 9 (March, 1959): 6–13; Joel R. Davitz and Lois J. Davitz, "Nonverbal Vocal Communication of Feeling," in *The Journal of Communication* 11 (1961): 81–86.

of a nonverbal signal such as a sigh, frown, slammed door, or yawn, it is far better to consider such messages as clues to be further investigated by asking questions or by careful observation of other nonverbals.[62]

Are some people more skillful at reading nonverbal signals than others? Adler and Towne suggest the most perceptive readers are those who are better senders of nonverbal messages. Furthermore, they indicate that women are better than men, that extroverts are relatively good judges of nonverbal behavior while dogmatists are not, and that the ability to read nonverbals increases with age and training.[63]

Third, the *major determinants of meaning* in interpersonal communication are nonverbal cues.[64] Ray Birdwhistle proposes that no more than 30 to 35 percent of the social meaning of a conversation is portrayed in the words themselves.[65] Mehrabian goes even further and insists that only 7 percent of one's message can be attributed to actual words; vocal expressions account for 38 percent of the message and facial expressions account for about 55 percent.[66] Furthermore, when verbal and nonverbal signals seem to contradict one another, the listener will usually listen to the nonverbal cues. We have all been in the almost humorous encounter where an individual shouts, **"I am not angry!"** while clenching his fist and turning red in the face. Which message do you listen to: the verbal message which argues he is not angry, or the nonverbal message which seems to indicate he is? The research of Mehrabian and Morton indicates that the nonverbal indicator, *tone,* can indeed override verbal content. They observed that when the attitude communicated in verbal content was contradicted by the attitude communicated in a negative tone, the entire message

---

[62]Adler and Towne, *Looking Out Looking In,* 204.

[63]Ibid., 204–5.

[64]Leathers, *Nonverbal Communication Systems,* 4; Michael Argyle, *Bodily Communication,* 2nd. ed. (London: Methuen, 1988), 303.

[65]Ray L. Birdwhistle, *Kinesics and Context* (Philadelphia: University of Philadelphia Press, 1970), 158.

[66]Mehrabian, *Silent Messages,* 44.

was judged as communicating a negative attitude.[67] Likewise, non-verbal expert Judee Burgoon asserts that reliance on nonverbal cues is greatest when the verbal and nonverbal messages are incongruent.[68]

The tendency for listeners is to pay attention to the nonverbal cues because these reactions are subject to little or no conscious control. Few people can curb their blood pressure, sweating, tension levels in muscles of internal organs, pupil dilation, blushing, and so forth. Simply put, we have considerable control over what we say, but limited control over many of our nonverbals. The general rule for understanding the effects of inconsistent messages, or when nonverbal actions contradict spoken words, is to rely more heavily on the actions to infer one's feelings.[69] However, if a listener is confused because the sender is sending mixed messages, it is in the best interest of both parties for the receiver to say so, in order that the speaker can clarify the intent of the message.

Fourth, nonverbal communication is *bound by culture*.[70] Just as cultures have different verbal languages, they have diverse nonverbal communication patterns.[71] While some nonverbal cues, such as the smile or frown, are universal in the sense that they send the same message in virtually all societies,[72] most nonverbals

---

[67]Mehrabian and Wiener, "Decoding of Inconsistent Communications," 109–14.

[68]Judee K. Burgoon, "Nonverbal Signals," in Mark L. Knapp and Gerald R. Miller, eds., *Handbook of Personal Communication* (Beverly Hills, Calif.: Sage, 1985), 344–90.

[69]Mehrabian, *Silent Messages*, 56.

[70]Leathers, *Nonverbal Communication Systems*, 47–8; Abne M. Eisenberg and Ralph R. Smith, *Nonverbal Communication* (Indianapolis, Ind.: Bobbs-Merril, 1971), 75–91.

[71]Martin S. Remland, Tricia S. Jones, and Heidi Brinkman, "Interpersonal Distance, Body Orientation, and Touch: Effects of Culture, Gender, and Age," *Journal of Social Psychology* 135 (3:1995): 281–97.

[72]Cenita Kupperbusch et al., "Cultural Influences on Nonverbal Expressions of Emotion," in Pierre Philippot, Robert S. Feldman, and Erik J. Coats, editors, *The Social Context of Nonverbal Behavior* (Cambridge, UK: Cambridge University Press, 1999), 17–44.

mean different things in different cultures. All cultures have distinctive nonverbal styles and cues.[73] For example, during research interviews with international students studying in the United States, Michael Watson indicated that the generally acceptable American habit of putting one's feet up on tables would be condemned as impolite or disrespectful in every country represented in the sample. One Arab student suggested that in his country it would be taken as an intentional insult by peers, while a Norwegian said that if one of his countryman put his feet on the table it would be seen as a sign of undue self-assurance, and the offender would "probably be trying to tell everyone he had been to America."[74]

Edward T. Hall, who has carefully studied space as a dimension of nonverbal communication, points out that people from North America like to conduct business at roughly a four-foot distance, while those from the Middle East stand much closer together.[75] This observation was confirmed a decade later by Watson in his study of foreign students attending university in the United States.[76]

Fifth, nonverbal signals are primarily *affective in nature.*[77] While words are adequate at conveying ideas and thoughts, as well as attitudes and feelings, nonverbal communication is

---

[73]For a helpful description of cultural differences in bodily communication see Argyle, *Bodily Communication,* 49-70. For a helpful discussion on the findings concerning cultural similarities and differences in nonverbal expressions see Kupperbusch et al., "Cultural Influences on Nonverbal Expressions of Emotion," 17-41.

[74]O. Michael Watson, *Proxemic Behavior: A Cross-Cultural Study* (The Hague, Netherlands: Moulton, 1970), 104.

[75]Edward T. Hall, *The Hidden Dimension* (New York: Anchor, 1969).

[76]Watson, *Proxemic Behavior: A Cross-Cultural Study,* 104.

[77]Leathers, *Nonverbal Communication Systems,* 1978. For more on nonverbal communication and emotions see Paul Ekman and Wallace V. Friesen, "Research on Facial Expressions of Emotion," in Albert M. Katz and Virginia T. Katz, *Foundations of Nonverbal Communication* (Carbondale, Ill.: Southern Illinois University, 1983), 97-107; Bull, *Body Movement and Interpersonal Communication,* 24-57; Richard Healin, Nonverbal Behavior and Social Psychology (New York: Plenum, 1982), 97-114.

primarily attitudinal.[78] For example it is easy to express tiredness, anger, joy, or love through nonverbal messages, but
difficult if not impossible to nonverbally express your thoughts
or beliefs (unless you use written symbols) about abortion,
capital punishment, or prayer in the classroom. Not only are
nonverbal messages the richest conveyor of emotional states,
they are reliable and stable indicators in portraying emotional
states.[79] Signals like pupil dilation, tone of voice, and perspira-
tion are normally difficult to control because they need to be
controlled by the emotional state itself, which is more difficult
than modifying bodily functions.[80]

Types of Nonverbal Signals

There are several types of nonverbal behaviors that small
group participants should be attuned to. Failure to respond to
these behaviors, or an inability to read and understand them,
may seriously hinder the group member both as sender or receiver. Physical appearance, space, eye movement, facial
expressions, body movements, voice, time, and touch are
among the key nonverbal categories the small group participant should be familiar with.[81]

Physical Appearance: Initial judgments small-group members
make about each other are based on physical appearance. The most
accurate information transmitted is gender and race. But rightly
or wrongly, other attributes, such as income and financial status,
social status, educational background, and whether or not one is
a friendly person, are inferred. These judgments may or may not
be accurate, but nonetheless, virtually everyone forms powerful
initial impressions based on physical appearance.[82]

---

[78]Burgoon, "Nonverbal Signals," 347.

[79]Leathers, *Nonverbal Communication Systems,* 4; Argyle, *Bodily Communication,* 306.

[80]Argyle, *Bodily Communication,* 306.

[81]For an exhaustive coverage of kinesic behavior as it relates to various
dimensions of religious education (including small groups) see Lee, *The Content of Religious Education,* 423–41.

[82]Andersen, "Nonverbal Communication in the Small Group," 273.

Dress, along with hair style and items of adornment influence initial judgments of others. Dress conveys a variety of meanings: decorative functions (fashionability or lack thereof), gender roles (concern for femininity or masculinity), formality (appropriateness for formal or informal occasions), conformity (uniform or similarity of dress to others), as well as comfort and economy.[83] Furthermore, dress and appearance affect the behavior of others. For example, in an intriguing study on the effect of dress, Lefkowitz, Blake, and Mouton found that pedestrians violated instructions given by a traffic signal light more often when an individual violated it ahead of them. Most important, however, was their finding that there were significantly more violations when the original violator was dressed to represent a high-status person than when dressed to represent a lower-status individual.[84]

James Fortenberry and colleagues conducted a similar study on the effect of dress on behavioral responses. The researchers compared two settings each involving one male and one female standing in a corridor at a conversation distance three feet apart. The arrangements were such that passers-by had to either pass through the conversationalists or avoid going through the area entirely. In one setting the conversationalists were dressed in formal daytime dress (the male in a business suit, shirt and tie; the female in a two-piece suit with high-heeled shoes). In the second scene, the conversationalists were dressed in casual attire (tennis shoes, jeans, and T-shirts). The researchers found a notable difference in the behaviors observed when formal dress was worn and when casual attire was worn. Significantly more positive deferential behaviors were observed under the formal dress condition, and more negative deferential behaviors were noted under the casual dress condition.[85]

---

[83]Gorden, *Communication: Personal and Public*, 64.

[84]Monroe Lefkowitz, Robert R. Blake, and Jane Srygley Mouton, "Status Factors in Pedestrian Violation of Traffic Signals," in *Journal of Abnormal and Social Psychology* 51 (1974): 704–6.

[85]James H. Fortenberry, Joyce MacLean, Priscilla Morris, and Michael O'Conner, "Mode of Dress as a Perceptual Cue to Deference," in *The Journal of Social Psychology* 104 (1978): 139–40.

While appearance is important, not everyone intentionally dresses to communicate. Some people dress to please themselves, for comfort, to maintain a certain self-image, or to be fashionable.[86] For this reason, judgments based on appearance are not always correct, and the Christian education group member should be careful to interpret such nonverbal messages with caution. On the other hand, small-group participants should remember that their dress makes an important statement to the group.

Body shape—height, weight, and physique—also affects the way people view others.[87] Judgments made about a person based on how he or she looks is called *somatyping*, and body shapes are generally classified into three basic types. *Endomorphs* are rounded, heavy people, who are often perceived as stupid, lazy, undependable, slow, socially undesirable, but happy, jolly, and easy to get along with. In American culture much discrimination occurs against this body type. *Ectomorphs* are tall and thin. They are perceived negatively as frail, sickly, and nervous, while positively as studious and intelligent. *Mesomorphs* are muscular, athletic types, are usually perceived more positively than the other types, and are more likely to be chosen as leaders. While there may be a small measure of validity for stereotyping according to body type, naturally, no human being falls neatly or completely into any one of these three categories. The perceptive group leader will view this as a weak and undependable practice. It is advisable to wait and make further observations of verbal and nonverbal behaviors before making evaluations of the personality of an individual.

Space and Seating: Significant attention is given to how we use space and distance in small-group communication, the study of which is called *proxemics*. A considerable number of experimental studies found that the space individuals give themselves in regards to other group members may give off a variety of nonver-

[86]Andersen, "Nonverbal Communication in the Small Group," 273.

[87]Brilhart and Galanes, *Effective Group Discussion*, 8th ed. 77, Andersen, "Nonverbal Communication in the Small Group," 273; and Eisenberg and Smith, *Nonverbal Communication*, 105.

bal cues. Thus seating position and the distance individuals afford each other have a direct influence on the pattern and frequency of small-group interaction.

One of the most widely known scholars of proxemics is Edward Hall, whose research has already been mentioned. Hall identifies four general distance categories whereby we conduct interpersonal communication. The first category is *intimate distance*. This distance, the closest of proxemic relationships, is reserved for the most personal or private of interactions, such as love-making, comforting, and protecting. Informal contact between friends is conducted at *personal distance*, between one and one-half and four feet. Most small-group communication is carried on at this distance. Acquaintances normally communicate at a range of four to twelve feet, the *social distance*, while formal communicators enter the *public distance* zone of twelve feet or more.[88]

A number of subsequent empirical research studies help to explain seating behaviors in small groups. An early study by Steinzor found that individuals seated in a circle tended to talk to those opposite them. Or, put another way, the greater the seating distance between two people, the greater the chance they will interact with each other verbally.[89] Hare and Bales observed that while in task-oriented groups this pattern holds true, in social sessions, members tend to talk more to the person next to them. They also found that more dominant subjects tend to select the central seats and do most of the talking.[90]

Gordon Hearn replicated Steinzor's study and found the following results:[91]

---

[88]Hall, *The Hidden Dimension*, 116–25.

[89]Bernard Steinzor, "The Spatial Factor in Face to Face Discussion Groups," in *Journal of Abnormal and Social Psychology* 45 (July, 1950), 552–5.

[90]A. Paul Hare and Robert F. Bales, "Seating Position and Small Group Interaction," in *Sociometry* 26 (1963): 480–6.

[91]Gordon Hearn, "Leadership and the Spatial Factor in Small Groups," in *Journal of Abnormal and social Psychology* 54 (1957); 269–72.

- in groups with no designated leadership, members will direct more comments to those opposite them than those sitting beside them;

- in groups where there is strong leadership, members will direct more comments to those beside than to those sitting opposite them; and

- where direction is shared equally between members and designated leadership there is no observable pattern.

Robert Sommer found that group leaders preferred the end positions at tables, and when they did not occupy the head position other people sat opposite or across rather than alongside them.[92]

The manipulation of objects in relation to spacing needs is what Eisenberg and Smith call *property management*.[93] Burgoon identifies some ways fixed features (permanent structures such as walls and doorways) dictate proxemic patterns of people. Volume of available space is one major influence. People who meet in large halls may take on close seating positions in the center of the room but distribute themselves evenly within the space. Groups that meet in smaller rooms may apportion themselves unevenly and closer to the walls to maximize their spatial freedom. The informality associated with the room may encourage more informal seating arrangements, while a formal setting such as a church sanctuary may cause people to cluster closer together.[94]

Lee proposes that Christian educators (including small-group facilitators) who wish to enhance the effectiveness of

---

[92]Robert Sommer, "Leadership and Group Geography," in *Sociometry* 24 (June 1961): 99–110.

[93]Eisenberg and Smith, *Nonverbal Communication,* 29.

[94]Judee K. Burgoon, "Spatial Relationships in Small Groups," in Robert S. Cathcart and Larry A. Samovar, eds., *Small Group Communication,* 6th ed. (Dubuque, Ia.: Wm. C. Brown, 1992), 287–300.

their teaching-learning activities would do well to grant due importance to the proxemics in the setting in which they teach.[95] Andersen argues that many small-group members, group leaders, and teachers fail to stimulate interaction or facilitate group participation effectively because of their insensitivity to proxemic communication.[96]

What, then, can Christian education small-group leaders do to demonstrate sensitivity to proxemics? First, they should be sensitive enough to *identify signs of discomfort* on behalf of participants due to either too little or too much space. Appropriate adjustments can then be made by rearranging the room or finding a more suitable space for meeting.

Second, group leaders must recognize that *small groups operate best in a circle or U-shaped format,* so that eye contact can be made with each other member of the group. Seating arrangement is also closely tied to leadership emergence. Consequently, discussion facilitators should choose positions that are more central, such as at the head of a table or across from as many group members as possible. Often other members will avoid sitting next to the designated leader, thus the setting will resemble a U or a semicircle rather than a circle. This will reinforce the leader's position and give the leader a comprehensive view of the group. Sommer suggests that a knowledge of how groups arrange themselves will assist in nurturing or diminishing group spirit. If a small-group facilitator desires to enhance group spirit or decrease the possibility of isolating someone, he or she might use a round or square table rather than a long, rectangular one.[97]

Third, small-group leaders would do well to *pay attention to where specific people sit in a group.* The group leader, for example, might make efforts to have a rather expressive individual sit opposite a quiet person, since there is a tendency for group members to talk to those directly opposite them. Or the facili-

---

[95]Lee, *The Content of Religious Instruction,* 444.

[96]Andersen, "Nonverbal Communication in the Small Group," 284.

[97]Sommer, "Leadership and Group Geography," 109.

tator might have two people who tend to monopolize conversation in a group sit next to each other, in order to decrease interaction between these two members.[98]

Eye Contact and Signals: "He speaketh not; and yet there lies a conversation his eyes." So penned the great American poet, Henry Wadsworth Longfellow, on the effects of eye behavior. And Francis Bacon eloquently proclaimed that "there lie concealed certain more subtle motions and action of the eyes, face, looks . . . by which the gate, as it were, of the mind is unlocked and thrown open."[99] The preoccupation with eyes and the perceived impact eye conduct has on human communication and behavior is also reflected in these popular phrases: "The look that kills," "He looks right through you," "The icy stare," "That certain look," "If looks could kill," "We see eye to eye," "Her eyes shot daggers," and "She has fire in her eyes." When it comes to expressing desires or relating feelings, eyes clearly serve as powerful tools.

The study of how the eye sends messages is called *occulesics,* the most important aspects of which are eye contact and gazing. Andersen notes that there is a subtle difference between eye contact and gazing. Eye contact is when two individuals look into one another's eyes, while gazing occurs when one individual looks at another.[100] The most fundamental meaning of gaze, according to Argyle and Cook, is that one is attending; that his or her visual channel is open.[101] Visual behavior is also an important tool for regulating the flow of communication. For most people, establishing eye contact is an invitation to communicate verbally; conversely, avoidance or diminishing of eye contact discourages interaction.[102]

---

[98]Steinzor, "The Spatial Factor in Face to Face Discussion Groups," 254–5.

[99]Francis Bacon, *Advancement of Learning* (New York: P. F. Collier, 1911), 365.

[100]Peter Andersen, *Nonverbal Communication: Forms and Functions* (Mountain View, Calif.: Mayfield, 1999), 40.

[101]Michael Argyle and Mark Cook, *Gaze and Mutual Gaze* (Cambridge: Cambridge University Press, 1976), 96.

[102]Knapp, *Essentials of Nonverbal Communication,* 185; James Michael Lee, *The Content of Religious Instruction* (Birmingham, Ala.: Religious Education Press, 1985), 419.

In small groups, eye contact is an invitation to interaction or dialogue, especially when it involves the group leader. Returning the leader's eye contact signals an interest to participate, while avoiding the leader's gaze indicates a desire to avoid interaction. Eye contact on behalf of the listener indicates an interest in the speaker and what the speaker is saying. Furthermore, eye movements are important nonverbal cues in that they can signal disgust, dislike, superiority, inferiority, and liking.[103] There is an aversion to gaze under negative conditions of embarrassment, guilt, and sorrow, perhaps an avoidance of unpleasant stimuli.[104]

Visual behavior has several practical consequences for small-group communication. Since eye contact invites interaction it is important that for maximum results in small-group communication, members sit in a circular or U-shaped arrangement so that eye contact with any particular individual can be effectively made with as many people as possible.[105] If a group member is set back from the group or it is apparent he or she has trouble making eye contact with other participants, the facilitator should have that person move to a more appropriate seating position. Perhaps the individual just needs to pull his or her chair up a bit, or another group member needs to move back slightly.

Group facilitators must be particularly alert to the primacy of eye contact. Silverstein and Stang note that group members with visual centrality speak more than those who have more difficulty making eye contact with all members.[106] Thus in order to encourage balanced group participation, the facilitator must have visual access to all of the other members of the group.[107]

---

[103]Andersen, "Nonverbal Communication in the Small Group," 274; Albert Mehrabian, "Relationship of Attitude to Seated Posture, Orientation, and Distance," *Journal of Personality and Social Psychology* 10 (1:1968): 26–30.

[104]Argyle and Cook, *Gaze and Mutual Gaze,* 81.

[105]Ibid.

[106]C.H. Silverstein and D.J. Stang, "Seating Position and Interaction in Triads: A Field Study," *Sociometry* 39 (1976), 166–70.

[107]Andersen, "Nonverbal Communication in the Small Group," 274.

Body Language: The study of how we communicate through body movement is referred to as *kinesics.* Categories of body language that are of concern to nonverbal communication experts include facial expressions, posture, body and hand gestures, and total body movement.[108]

Clearly the part of the human body richest in kinesic cues is the face, the most important nonverbal channel of communication.[109] William Shakespeare understood the revealing power of the face and was prompted to write:

"Your face, my thane, is as a book where men may read strange matters."[110]

People can make a variety of faces, but experts in nonverbal communication identify six major emotional expressions: happiness, surprise, fear, sadness, anger, and disgust/contempt.[111] And while physiologists have estimated that there are over twenty thousand somatically possible facial expressions, Birdwhistle isolated thirty-two basic elements, or *kinemes,* of these. For example, there are four kinemes of brow behavior: lifted brow, lowered brow, knit brow, and single brow movement.[112]

We look to the face, advises Knapp, as a principal source of information regarding other individuals, and no doubt make judgments about the personalities of others by characteristics clearly evident in their faces.[113] In addition, the personal use of facial expression can be a valuable tool in impacting others.

---

[108]David F. Cragan and David W. Wright, *Communication in Small Group Discussion,* 3rd ed. (St. Paul, Minn.: West, 1995), 150.

[109]Argyle, *Bodily Communication,* 121; Knapp, *Essentials of Nonverbal Communication,* 167.

[110]William Shakespeare, *Macbeth,* Act 1.

[111] Argyle, *Bodily Communication,* 121; Paul Ekman, *Emotion in the Human Face,* 2nd ed. (Cambridge: Cambridge University Press, 1982); Knapp, *Essentials of Nonverbal Communication,* 167; Ekman and Friesen, "Research on Facial Expressions of Emotion," 97–107.

[112]Birdwhistle, *Kinesics and Context,* 99–100.

[113]Knapp, *Essentials of Nonverbal Communication,* 162.

For example, empirical research has proven the smile to have a powerful influence on the perception others have of an individual.[114]

However, while facial expressions may often be good indicators of emotional states, research has revealed that facial cues are only partially accurate or reliable. For instance, when one looks into the face of a group member and perceives that person is angry, is he or she correct?[115] Sometimes we exaggerate or de-emphasize facial behaviors to hide our true feelings.[116] People who hide their feelings or reactions through their facial expressions are said to have "poker faces." When group members express few facial expressions, it is helpful to look for other nonverbal signals that may be more revealing. For example, people who display little emotion in their face tend to display other responses such as sweating.[117]

In addition to communicating a wide variety of emotions, facial expressions are used to facilitate interaction in at least three ways. First, they are employed to open and close channels of communication. For example, a desire to speak may be evidenced by opening the mouth in readiness to talk, accompanied by taking a quick breath. Second, the face is used to complement and qualify other communication behaviors. In normal conversation thoughts or comments are often underscored or emphasized by a facial expression. Sometimes a teasing remark, accompanied by a wink or a smile, is used to temper a remark that might be interpreted negatively. Finally, facial expressions are used to replace speech entirely. One rolls his or her eyeballs to express a measure of disgust or incredu-

---

[114]Emma Otta, et al., "The Effect of Smiling and of Head Tilting on Person Perception," *Journal of Psychology* 128 (May 1994): 323–31; Elizabeth Cashdan, "Smiles, Speech, and Body Posture: How Women and Men Display Sociometric Status and Power," *Journal of Nonverbal Behavior* 22 (Winter 1998): 209–28.

[115]Ekman and Friesen, "Research on Facial Expressions of Emotion," 97–107.

[116] Loretta Malandro and Larry Barker, *Nonverbal Communication* (New York: Random House, 1983), 153–4.

[117]Andersen, "Nonverbal Communication in the Small Group," 285.

lity. The eyebrows may express doubt or puzzlement, while opening one's eyes wide displays surprise.[118]

What does all of this mean to the small-group leader or facilitator? Certainly the most significant implication is that understanding the meanings of facial expressions is of primary importance. More specifically, the small-group leader must ask two pertinent questions: What can I tell about the small-group member from the facial expressions he or she uses? and What do I communicate to small-group participants when I use particular facial expressions?[119] The perceptive facilitator will learn to decode the nonverbal messages emitted by small-group participants: the furrowed eyebrow revealing puzzlement; the look of surprised joy that comes when a new truth is discovered; or the normal emotions of discouragement, anger, happiness, disinterest, or frustration, to name a few. It is then the responsibility of the leader to allow or encourage individuals to respond verbally to what they are displaying facially.

Another important form of body language is posture, the position or carriage of the body. Posture will often reflect a group member's level of interest or attentiveness to the subject matter at hand. If, for example, a member is sitting straight up in his or her seat or leaning towards the speaker slightly, it probably shows interest. On the other hand, slouching or an over-relaxed behavior likely indicates a nonchalant attitude.[120] Posture-related body movements such as shifting around in a chair, swinging a foot, or drumming fingers may reflect tension, frustration, impatience, or annoyance.[121]

The messages emanated from posture can sometimes be interpreted or understood in terms of Mehrabian's *immediacy principle,* which says that people are drawn toward people or things they like, prefer, or evaluate highly and move away from

---

[118]Knapp, *Essentials of Nonverbal Communication,* 162.

[119]Adapted from Lee, *The Content of Religious Education,* 411–2, who asks these questions in regards to the religious educator.

[120]Cragan and Wright, *Communication in Small Group Discussion,* 150.

[121]Brilhart and Galanes, *Effective Group Discussion,* 80.

or avoid people they dislike or do not prefer.[122] Consequently, Meharabian found that a forward lean of the upper body towards one's addressee coupled with a shorter distance to that person communicated a more positive attitude to that person than a backward lean and a greater distance.[123]

Posture can also be used as a regulator of interpersonal communication. Scheflen maintains that speakers often change head and eye positions and shift their posture to communicate their intent to limit or avoid interaction with another person. Likewise, when a receiver leans forward it may be a signal to the speaker that he or she wants a turn to speak.[124]

Hand and arm gestures are pervasive vehicles for nonverbal communication that are often categorized as either emblems or illustrators. Emblems are publicly understood, culturally determined actions, such as a shrug of the shoulders or shaking of the fist, that carry an entire thought and can be substituted for a verbal statement. On the other hand, illustrators occur in the context of ongoing vocal activity and can repeat, describe, or augment that which is provided for verbally (e.g., drawing a circle or a spiral staircase).[125] Hand and arm gestures can aid small group members in following the flow of speech and can be used by speakers in a positive way to emphasize verbal statements. Gestures often reflect the enthusiasm an individual has for the subject matter.[126]

---

[122]Mehrabian, *Silent Messages,* 1.

[123]Mehrabian, "Inference of Attitudes From the Posture Orientation, and Distance of a Communicator," 296–308; Mehrabian, "Relationship of Attitude to Seated Posture, Orientation, and Distance," 26–30.

[124]Scheflen, *Body Language and the Social Order: Communication as Behavioral Control,* 50.

[125]Peter Wolff and Joyce Gutstein, "Effects of Induced Motor Gestures on Vocal Output," *Journal of Communication* 22 (September 1972): 277–88; Paul Ekman and Wallace V. Friesen, "The Repertoire of Nonverbal Behavior: Categories, Origins, Usage, and coding," *Semiotica* 1 (1969), 49–98; Lee, *The Content of Religious Education,* 426–8; Argyle, *Bodily Communication,* 188-202.

[126]Andersen, "Nonverbal Communication in The Small Group," 272–86.

Voice: Paralanguage is the technical term given to the study of vocal cues, utterance, and voice characteristics other than the words themselves. The sound attributes that are generally included as significant senders of nonverbal messages include volume, pitch, rate, inflection, quality, tone, and silence. Sounds are also described according to labels such as breathy, nasal, throaty, resonant, clipped, harsh, or warm.[127]

Voice is highly significant in how an individual is accepted by listeners. For example, people who use vocal cues such as loudness, pitch changes, and a forceful tone to signal strong feelings on a particular issue are likely to be more persuasive than those who are more soft-spoken with little animation.[128] A soft, low, breathy voice might indicate a person is warm and affectionate, while a hurried, blaring voice tends to imply impatience.[129]

The emotional state of a communicator can be inferred from many of these paralanguage qualities.[130] Some of the findings are as follows:

- *joy and elation:* raised pitch, intensity, increased rate, and pitch variability;

- *anxiety:* raised pitch, faster rate of speech, silent pauses, breathy voice quality, more and longer silent pauses;

- *fear:* raised pitch, wider limits of pitch range, high energy at higher pitches;

- *anger:* raised pitch in rage, lowered pitch in cold anger, raised intensity, harsh quality of voice, and greater speech rate.

---

[127]Michael Argyle, "Nonverbal Vocalizations," in *The Nonverbal Communication Reader,* 2nd ed., eds. Laura K. Guerrero, Joseph A. DeVito, and Michael L. Hecht (Prospect Heights, Ill.: Waveland, 1999), 136.

[128]Argyle, *Bodily Communication,* 146.

[129]Lee, *The Content of Religious Education,* 423–4.

[130]Blaine Goss and Dan O'Hair, *Communicating in Interpersonal Relationships* (New York: Macmillan, 1988), 76.

Touch: Tactile communication, or *haptics,* refers to the action of touching, one of the primary types of nonverbal behavior. Perhaps no other form of nonverbal communication is as intimate as touch. Touch has the power to repel, arouse, disgust, soothe, threaten, affirm, reassure, and love. While research indicates that all human beings need and want some form of touch, the intensity and frequency of touch that one is willing to give is determined by age, gender, personality, and culture.[131] For example, high contact people groups include Arabs, Latin Americans, and Southern Europeans, while non-contact cultures include many Asians, Indians and Pakistanis, and Northern Europeans.[132] According to most studies, females initiate touch more than males.[133]

Touch can transmit a variety of messages. For example, it can communicate an emotion (grabbing someone you are angry with), or interpersonal attitude (patting someone so as to demonstrate inclusion). Touch in a small group may foster teamwork, sharing, or solidarity.[134] A widely held notion associated with nonverbal behavior is that a light touch can be persuasive in inducing another person to comply with a request or to volunteer needed assistance.[135] However, since people vary widely in the extent to which they receive and give touches, it is critical that group members touch each other only when they sense they are accepting of both touch and of each other.

---

[131]Malandro and Barker, *Nonverbal Communication,* 24; Martin S. Remland, Tricia S. Jones, and Heidi Brinkman, "Interpersonal Distance, Body Orientation, and Touch: Effects of Culture, Gender, and Age," *Journal of Social Psychology* 135 (3:1995): 281–97.

[132]Argyle, *Bodily Communication,* 59–61.

[133]Ibid., 231.

[134]Andersen, "Nonverbal Communication in the Small Group," 280.

[135]Martin S. Remland and Tricia S. Jones, "The Influence of Vocal Intensity and Touch on Compliance Gaining," *Journal of Social Psychology* 134 (February 1994): 89–97.

Interpreting Nonverbal Behavior

By now the reader is well aware of the powerful impact nonverbal cues have in the communication process. The ability to decode or read nonverbal messages is also related to relational well-being. In other words, individuals with skills in nonverbal communication are able to engage in more satisfying interpersonal relationships,[136] a quality highly valued in Christian education small groups. However, detecting, reading, and interpreting nonverbal behavior are sometimes difficult, as nonverbals are often open to a number of interpretations. Then there are those who Mehrabian calls "the nonverbally handicapped," those individuals who have difficulty reading the actions of others. For example, consider the annoying experience of being with someone who fails to pick up the subtle cues of our desire to terminate the conversation or to be left alone.[137]

The first responsibility of the Christian education small-group facilitator in regards to nonverbal communication is to develop a working knowledge of the various nonverbal behaviors and their possible meanings. A second task is to translate that understanding into a sensitivity to behavioral cues and an ability to read their meanings in a given situation.

Since nonverbal behaviors are open to interpretation, how does one know what they mean? The key, according to Egan, is context. Effective listeners read the entire context of the situation, and do not become fixated on details of behavior.[138] Rather, nonverbal gestures and movements should be interpreted in combination with other cues. It is helpful to look for clusters of gestures and movements that make up the nonverbal message.[139]

---

[136]John S. Carton, Emily A. Kessler, and Christina L. Pape, "Nonverbal Decoding Skills and Relationship Well-being in Adults," *Journal of Nonverbal Behavior* 23 (Spring 1999): 91–100.

[137]Mehrabian, *Silent Messages*, 130.

[138]Egan, *The Skilled Helper*, 67.

[139]Gorden, *Communication: Personal and Public*, 75.

Sending Nonverbals

Just as the ability to read and interpret nonverbal cues is critical to effective listening, it is important to be aware of the nonverbal communication being sent. One can convey positiveness through nonverbal behavior such as facial and vocal expressions, posture and gestures, eye contact, and body movement. Conversely people can send silent negative messages that discourage others from liking them or from developing relationships with them.[140]

An understanding of nonverbal communication can increase the group leader's awareness of his or her own nonverbal behavior. Often individuals who are students of nonverbal communication begin to examine critically and to change their own patterns of communicating.[141] An effective Christian education group leader or participant nurtures positive responses to himself or herself by radiating silent messages that are affirming, inviting, and pleasurable.

CONCLUSION

This chapter discussed communication in Christian education small groups. The skills of listening and reading nonverbal behavior were emphasized. Good listening means employing the skills of attending, responding, and reading nonverbal cues. It has been determined in this chapter that nonverbal communication has more impact on listeners than verbal messages. Nonverbal behavior is use to confirm, strengthen, or regulate what has been transmitted verbally. Conversely, it can confuse or deny the verbal message.

---

[140]Mehrabian, *Silent Messages*, 128–9

[141]Andersen, "Nonverbal Communication in the Small Group," 285.

6

Leading Dynamic Group Discussions

ANYONE familiar with modern business organization and industry is well aware of the increased use of small groups and group discussions in the decision-making process.[1] John Cragan and David Wright argue that America's democratic tradition has made public discussion of affairs of state a moral obligation, a privilege that is not afforded citizens of many other countries. So our towns and neighborhoods, they go on to say, are beehives of group discussions about relevant issues such as pollution, nuclear energy, inflation and the fast-food store that might endanger our children with increased traffic.[2]

Christian educators who understand that learning is something more than the accumulation of factual information recognize the value of discussion in the faith development and spiritual formation of youth and adults. Discussion provides individuals with the rich opportunity to better understand the relationship between facts and personal development, to learn to express themselves in such a manner that they enhance the spiritual and social life of one another, and to develop the skill of critical reflection so as to more intelligently wrestle with difficult ethical and theological issues.

This chapter deals with what most small groups are all about—discussion. Whether the Christian education group is a committee, study group, or support group, discussion is the core of what occurs. It is, suggests Neal McBride, "the proce-

---

[1]Tubbs, *A Systems Approach to Small Group Interaction*, 6; Cragan and Wright, *Communication in Small Groups*, 5.

[2]Cragan and Wright, *Communication in Small Groups*, 4–5.

dural glue that holds a group together. It is the method by which we exchange ideas, opinions, and feelings. It serves as a path for making group decisions and facilitating interpersonal sharing."[3] Thus, the ability to lead or facilitate small-group discussion is one of the most important skills a Christian education group leader can possess.

COMPONENTS OF DYNAMIC DISCUSSION IN CHRISTIAN EDUCATION GROUPS

Good interaction and discussion in Christian education groups does not just happen. Rather, it is the result of careful planning, the use of carefully crafted questions, active listening, and the capable facilitation of dialogue. To facilitate dynamic small-group discussion and maximize balanced group participation, the leader of a Christian education group must pay careful attention to at least six components:

- purpose,

- content structure,

- leadership role,

- communication,

- group involvement, and

- climate.

The Purpose of the Discussion

Discussion as an instructional method can be traced to Socrates, who first maintained that teaching meant not pouring new information or ideas into an empty brain, but drawing out universal truths which were already embedded and concealed in the mind. All of his teaching was done through conversation; he merely asked questions. To his critics and mere observers, his teaching may have appeared to be without form; random queries that angered some and were met with disinterest by others. But while his instructional objective may not

---

[3]McBride, *How To Lead Small Groups*, 90.

have been clearly evident to his pupils or observers, Socrates asked questions with purpose and direction. Gilbert Highet describes the discussion strategy of Socrates as follows: "He had a positive end in view. . . . He wanted to make every pupil realize that truth was in the pupil's own power to find, if he searched long enough and hard enough. . . . And he himself had a very clear, though very broad, idea of where the truth lay. His questions always steered the pupil, slowly and imperceptibly, with frequent failures and digressions, and pauses to meet sudden objections, towards that region. In the combination of these two, the critical method and the positive purpose, lies the essence of the tutorial system."[4]

For a Christian education small group to function effectively as a discussion group, the purpose or direction of the discussion must be clearly evident to all members. Untrained discussion leaders who allow an unprepared group to sit in a circle and talk aimlessly are more than likely wasting everyone's time through the pooling of ignorance.[5] The facilitator must ask himself or herself the question: How do I want the members of my group to change because of this session?

The response to this pedagogical question comes in the form of an objective or goal.[6] Robert Mager, in his seminal work on instructional objectives, defines an objective as "an intent communicated by a statement describing a proposed change in a learner—a statement of what the learner is to be like when he has successfully completed a learning experience."[7]

---

[4]Highet, *The Art of Teaching*, 108.

[5]Paul Bergevin and John McKinley, *Participation Training for Adult Education* (St. Louis, Mo.: Bethany, 1965), 82.

[6]In education, the terms *goals* and *objectives* are used interchangeably in describing learning outcomes. For example, see Robert F. Mager, *Preparing Instructional Objectives* (Palo Alto, Calif.: Fearon, 1962), 3; Leroy Ford, *A Curriculum Design Manual for Theological Education* (Nashville, Tenn.: Broadman, 1991), 154; and Bergevin and McKinley, *Participation Training for Adult Education,* 37. Lawrence O. Richards and Gary J. Bredfeldt, *Creative Bible Teaching* (Chicago: Moody, 1998), 135, use the term *aim.*

[7]Mager, *Preparing Instructional Objectives* (Palo Alto, Calif.: Fearon, 1962),

In Christian education groups, objectives can be expressed in the context of three learning domains: *cognitive* (thinking and knowing), *affective* (feelings, values, and attitudes), and *behavioral* (actions and skills).[8] The apostle Paul's charge to the Philippians indicates a target for potential change in each of these three areas: "Finally, brothers, whatever is true, whatever is noble, whatever is right, whatever is pure, whatever is lovely, whatever is admirable—if anything is excellent or praiseworthy—think about such things. Whatever you have learned or received or heard from me, or seen in me—put into practice. And the God of peace will be with you" (4:8–9). First, Paul taught that his audience had to consider, and change if necessary, their thought processes—to think on those things that are true, noble, right, pure, lovely, and admirable (cognitive). Second, he instructed them to put into practice the teachings they had heard and processed cognitively (behavior). And third, when their behavior was in line with correct thinking and knowledge, they would experience the peace of God (affective).

In Christian education discussion groups, there are several criteria for constructing learning objectives. Objectives must be:[9]

- written in terms of desired change in members' behavior,

- attainable or reachable,

- specific, and

- shared by all the participants.

It is especially important that objectives are stated in terms of desirable change in the lives of *group members,* not in regard to what the facilitator wants to accomplish with the participants. For example, the objective, *To help group mem-*

---

[8]Bergevin and McKinley, *Participation Training for Adult Education,* 37; Richards and Bredfeldt, *Creative Bible Teaching,* 136.

[9]Bergevin and McKinley, *Participation Training for Adult Education,* 37–8.

bers understand the implications of the death and resurrection of Jesus Christ, states the aim of the discussion leader.

Discussion leaders should also be alerted to the tendency for beginning groups, at least, to set goals that focus on increased knowledge and understanding, and avoid those that are concerned with feelings or behavior change. Bergevin and McKinley identify three obstacles which may appear when a Christian education group leader tries to set goals related to behavior change:[10]

- group members are often reticent to pledge themselves to make an effort to change unless they know and trust their fellow group members;

- group members may be unable to agree upon desirable changes beyond their understanding;

- individuals cannot always anticipate a need for change in a given area unless more information is explored and better understood.

Finally, it must be reiterated that for the group to effectively engage in discussion, each member must be able to recognize and adhere to the group objective. Consider the following scenario. A group of Christian education leaders and teachers in a local church meet to discuss ways to incorporate mission awareness in the Christian education program; but individual members have varied interpretations of the purpose of the discussion. One participant assumes the purpose is to debate certain issues in missiology while another has apparently come to refute the necessity of missions awareness. The dialogue degenerates into a state of haphazard argument as the original purpose of the discussion is lost. As long as a discussion facilitator permits group members to be guided by individual biases and self-centered goals the group may be unable to attain the intended purposes for discussion.[11]

---

[10]Ibid., 39.

Here are examples of small-group objectives based on the above criteria:

- *Cognitive objective:* Group members will learn what it means to "love your enemies" (Mt 5:44).

- *Affective objective:* Group members will share personal experiences where they loved another individual or were loved by another person as Jesus commanded.

- *Behavioral objective:* Group members will identify ways they can express love to others and commit to the group to carry out at least one of those actions during the following week.

Content Structure

The facilitator can also ensure that a discussion has direction by developing content structure. Bible study discussions, for example, might follow the Serendipity format (or something similar) of *Open* (introductory or opening questions), *Dig* ("What does the passage say?" or "What does the passage mean?"), and *Reflect* (application or personal reflection questions).[12] For example, for a discussion of Philippians 3:1–11 consider the following questions.[13]

- *Open question:* "If you had to brag about what you can do better than others, what would it be?"

- *Dig question:* "If this problem with those promoting circumcision had gone unchallenged, how would the Gospel been affected?"

- *Reflect question:* "How much merit would you assign to each 'confidence in the flesh': Good looks? Good works? Reputation? Christian tradition?"

---

[11]Ronald L. Applbaum, *Fundamentals of Group Discussion* (Chicago: Science Research Associates, 1976), 2–3.

[12]*Serendipity New Testament, 10th Anniversary Edition* (Littleton, Colo.: Serendipity House, 1996), 6.

[13]Ibid., 352.

Lawrence Richards and Gary Bredfeldt propose a discussion format that includes a similar four-step pattern: *Hook, Book, Look,* and *Took.* The *Hook* is a question or strategy that gets the attention of group members, sets a goal for the discussion, and leads participants into the particular study. In the *Book* section of the discussion, group members try to understand the information related to the topic or issue. The *Look* section gives the discussion group the opportunity to gain insights about the relationship between the information and life. Finally, in the *Took,* group members are led into response, an opportunity to reflect on ways they can apply truths learned or discovered to everyday living.[14] Following are examples of each type of question regarding the topic of persecution based on Philippians 1:12–30:

- *Hook Question:* "Does the persecution of Christians still occur today?" or "Have you or do you know anyone who has been persecuted for being a Christian?"

- *Book Questions:* "What is Paul's overriding attitude towards suffering for the cause of Christ?"

- *Look Questions:* "What difference has your personal faith in Jesus Christ made in your attitude toward suffering or being persecuted for His sake?"

- *Took Question:* "What are some ways you might experience persecution in your daily living? How will you respond to these situations in light of Paul's instructions?"

The facilitator can help the Christian education group maintain content structure and keep the discussion orderly, logical, and intact by:[15]

- pointing out the significance of the issue or topic early in the discussion;

---

[14]Richards and Bredfeldt, *Creative Bible Teaching*, 108–10

[15]Applbaum, *Fundamentals of Group Discussion*, 22.

- clearly defining the problem or goal and making sure it is understood by all participants;

- suggesting and exploring all possible solutions or answers;

- carefully analyzing or testing the facts, evidence, and reasoning;

- calling attention to fallacies in reasoning;

- avoiding sidetracking as much as possible;

- providing for frequent and accurate summaries to show the progress of the discussion, making sure the summaries reflect the thinking of group members;

- reminding group members of the main topic or issue from time to time;

- making clear transitions from one point or thought to another;

- pointing out areas of agreement and disagreement.

Leadership Role

It must be re-emphasized that in group discussion, the role of the leader is not so much didactic teacher as facilitator. *Webster's New Collegiate Dictionary* defines the word *facilitate* simply as "to make easier." Consequently the task for a small-group Christian education leader or facilitator is to *make it easier* for small-group members to engage in dialogue or discussion. Bergevin and McKinley assert that the discussion leader is not necessarily the individual who knows the most about the topic. Rather, he or she provides the kind of leadership that puts the responsibility for learning and change where it belongs—on each member of the group.[16]

As a discussion facilitator, the small-group leader performs several critical roles.[17] As a *catalyst* he or she causes members

---

[16]Bergevin and McKinley, *Participation Training for Adult Education,* 25.

[17]Ed Stewart and Nina Fishwick, *Group Talk!* (Ventura, Calif.: Regal,

to think individually and then interact with others. This strategy can be pursued by raising root questions in at least four directions:[18]

- *The origin of the thought or idea:* "How did you come to this idea or thought?"; "How did you come to think in this manner?"; "Can you recall the circumstances that led you to believe this way?"

- *Support for the idea:* "Why do you hold to this view?"; "What evidence to you have for this view?"; "What are some reasons people hold to this train of thought?"; "In holding to this view point, aren't you assuming that . . . is true?"; "Do you believe that is a sound assumption?"

- *Conflict with other thoughts:* "Others may object to your position by arguing. . . . What would you say to them?"; "What do you think of the contrasting view that says. . . .'"; "What would you say to the objection that. . . .'"

- *Implications and consequences of the view.* "What do you see as the consequences of holding to that view?"; "What would we have to do to implement this idea?"

As a *guide,* the leader keeps the discussion on track. For instance, when a group member attempts to take the group away from the chosen direction of the discussion, the leader might respond with something like, "Jonas brings up an interesting point, and I wish we could pursue it. However I think that the most pertinent issue right here is. . . . Let's address that right now, then if we have time we can come back to Jonas's comment about. . . ."

As a *clarifier,* the leader assists group members in understanding questions and comments. For example, if Pat asks a question or makes a comment that is apparently unclear to the

---

[18]Richard Paul, *Critical Thinking,* 2nd ed. (Santa Rosa, Calif.: Foundation for Critical Thinking, 1992), 315.

other group members, the facilitator might ask Pat to rephrase the question or comment. Or the facilitator might try to clarify it: "I think what Pat is saying is. . . . Is that right, Pat?"

And finally, as an *affirmer,* the discussion leader encourages members to recognize the value in every person and their contributions, and enables every group member to participate. For instance, in response to a statement made by a group member, the facilitator might say something like: "That's a very insightful comment, I've never thought of it quite that way before. What do the rest of you think about what Les just said?"

Christian education group discussions are more satisfying and beneficial when the facilitator allows participants to share what is on their minds or what *they* are learning and discovering. A small-group discussion is not to be viewed as an opportunity to pontificate, preach, or indoctrinate; it is designed to get people to talk, to think critically, and to explore possibilities.[19] This means that as a facilitator, the small-group leader minimizes the amount of talking he or she does.

Dominating leaders often try to use the small-group discussion as a place to practice a didactic teaching technique. They believe have information to impart or preconceived ideas concerning the topic and attempt to persuade group members to accept their ideas. Bergevin and McKinley identify some signs of dominating leadership as follows:[20]

- when a leader keeps discussions proceeding in a particular direction or along certain lines without inquiring into the feelings of other participants;

- when a discussion leader rewords contributions to fit his or her outline or preferred conclusions, or continually points members toward the particular "truth" he is trying to emphasize;

---

[19]It is *not* to be implied that either didactic teaching or preaching as information giving techniques are wrong in and of themselves. The suggestion here, is that information-giving is best kept to a minimum in discussion groups.

[20]Bergevin and McKinley, *Participation Training for Adult Education,* 83.

- when a discussion leader rapidly asks questions in an attempt to secure a particular answer, without exploring the significance of the answers he rejects;

- when a leader abandons his neutrality and becomes an information-giver and teacher;

- when a discussion leader blatantly judges the worth of participant's contributions by praising some and overlooking others;

- when a leader will not deviate from the outline he or she has prepared.

When a discussion leader dominates a discussion session in the manner described above, group members will quit talking simply because they do not have ample opportunity to share or because their contributions are overlooked. Eventually participants will become unmotivated, lose their interest in contributing, and assume they do not have anything of value to say. Then the leader usually resorts to instructive teaching rather than facilitating group dialog and interaction.[21]

Communication

Another critical component of group discussion is communication. From the perspective of the Christian education discussion leader, effective small-group communication is characterized by at least three skills: attending, asking questions, and responding.

Attending: The ability to attend, or listen attentively, is significantly more important in being a small-group discussion leader than is the ability to talk. The discussion leader will stimulate much better learning in a Christian education group by listening to what participants have to say, than by talking to them.[22]

---

[21]Pat J. Sikora, *Small Group Bible Studies* (Cincinnati, Ohio: Standard, 1991), 140.

[22]Ibid., 141.

For a more extensive coverage of small-group listening skills, the reader is referred to the previous chapter. However, some key behaviors related to the skill of listening are summarized as follows:

- reading nonverbal as well as verbal messages;

- reserving judgment on a contributor until the entire message is heard;

- avoiding both environmental and mental distractions;

- not biasing a message through personal prejudices or value judgments;

- acknowledging the speaker through verbal and non-verbal responses;

- listening carefully to the intent of the speaker.

Asking Good Questions: One of the keys to stimulating effective discussion in small groups is asking good questions, the question being one of the primary tools of the discussion facilitator.[23] The philosopher Socrates so mastered the art of asking higher-order questions that the ancient method is still looked upon by education experts today as a teaching technique to be emulated.[24] In Socratic questioning, the Christian education facilitator or leader probes the meaning, justification, logic, or strength of a claim, position, or line of reasoning.[25] It is helpful for the adept discussion facilitator to recognize that there are identifiable categories of Socratic questions to draw from:[26]

---

[23]Thomas P. Kasulis, "Questioning," in Margaret Morganroth, ed., *The Art and Craft of Teaching* (Cambridge, Mass.: Harvard University Press, 1984), 38–48.

[24]For example, see Highet, *The Art of Teaching*, 107–11; Paul, *Critical Thinking*, 315-6.

[25]Paul, *Critical Thinking*, 666. See also 360–91 of the same book for additional descriptions of the Socratic method.

[26]Ibid., 367–8.

- *questions of clarification*: "What do you mean when you say . . . ?"; "Could you give us an example?"; "Explain that a little further."

- *questions that probe assumptions*: "It seems that you are assuming. . . . Is that correct?"; "Is this always the case?"

- *questions that investigate reasons and evidence*: "What would be an example of . . . ?"; "What evidence do you have for your comment that people are less religious today than thirty years ago?"; "How do you know that . . . ?"; "How did you come to that conclusion?"

- *questions related to viewpoints*: "Does anyone in the group see this differently?"; "What alternatives are there to this view on capital punishment?"; "How are Ben's and Diana's ideas similar? Or different?"

- *questions that explore implications*: "If we say that lying is always unethical, what about the cases where certain Christians lied during World War II to protect Jews from the Nazis?"; "If we were to love our neighbors in that manner, what might the results be?"

- *questions in response to a question*: "How can we find an answer to that question?"; "Why is this question so critical to understanding the nature of God?"; "What is the question behind this question?"

Herman Harrell Horne, in his classic book, *Jesus—The Master Teacher*, suggests that while Jesus came to answer questions, His primary aim as the Great Teacher was to ask provocative and unsettling questions; the technique of asking questions was at the heart of His teaching methodology.[27] Horne may have overstated this notion slightly, but his point is well taken—questions played an integral part of the teaching strategy of Jesus. Consider some of His questions:

[27]Herman Harrell Horne, *Jesus—The Master Teacher* (New York: Association Press, 1920), 45, 51.

"Who then is the faithful and wise servant, whom the master has put in charge of the servants . . . ?" (Mt 24:45);
"Which is lawful on the Sabbath: to do good or to do evil, to save life or to kill?" (Mk 3:4);

- "How can Satan drive out Satan?" (Mk 3:23);

- "Who are my mothers and my brothers?" (Mk 3:33);

- "Who do the crowds say that I am?" (Lk 9:18);

- "Who do you say that I am?" (Lk 9:20);

- "Will you really lay down your life for me?" (Jn 13:38).

In advocating that Christian education group facilitators prepare carefully for discussion and provide structure, I want to make it clear that the facilitator should not predetermine what the outcome of the small-group discussion should be. As soon as group members sense the discussion is moving towards the point the group leader has in mind, interest will waver, and the discussion will become an exercise in manipulation rather than an experience in authentic dialog.[28] The key to leading provocative small-group discussions is providing guidance through the use of good questions, while preserving the opportunity for discovery and self-learning for group participants.[29]

What constitutes a good query? In the broadest sense, a good question is one that generates healthy and lively group interaction. But what kind of questions stimulate or generate good discussion? The following list of suggestions can serve as a pattern for choosing or developing discussion questions that rouse vigorous and impelling group discussions. Good questions:

- are clear and concise,

- are not leading,

---

[28]Stephen D. Brookfield, *The Skillful Teacher* (San Francisco: Jossey-Bass, 1990), 90.

[29]Maryellen Weimer, *Improving Your Classroom Teaching* (Newbury Park, Calif.: Sage, 1993), 56.

- are open-ended,

- are relevant,

- are of interest,

- encourage independent thinking.

First, *good questions are clear and concise.*[30] Questions that are succinctly stated, to the point, and clearly understood by group members work best. As noted above, Jesus' questions were most always very brief and to the point. Questions that are complex and hard to follow will only lead to frustration and silence. Words that are flowery or academic and are not a part of the group's vocabulary only hinder the opportunity for good discussion. If a discussion leader has to read or ask a question several times before group members understand it, chances are the question is not clear. If group members must work to decipher the query, the likelihood that they will respond to it is reduced.[31] Here's an example of a clear and concise question: "What does Paul mean by circumcision of the heart in Romans 2:29?"

Second, *good questions are not leading.*[32] Leading questions are those which look for a specific answer or are asked in a manner that predetermines the answer. For example, a question like "God would not look favorably on us if we treated our neighbor like that, would He?" is a leading question and would not likely lead to a gainful and open discussion on the Christian's responsibility to love his or her neighbor. The effective facilitator will frame questions in such a manner that they enable participants to gain insights, examine relationships,

---

[30]Barbara Gross Davis, *Tools for Teaching* (San Francisco: Jossey-Bass, 1993), 86; D. Bruce Lockerbie, *Asking Questions* (Milford, Mich.: Mott Media. 1980), 26.

[31]John R. Verduin, Harry G. Miller, and Charles E. Greer, *Adults Teaching Adults* (San Diego: Learning Concepts, 1977), 132; Joseph Lowman, *Mastering the Techniques of Teaching* (San Francisco: Jossey-Bass, 1984), 135.

[32]Davis, *Tools for Teaching*, 86.

[33]Lowman, *Mastering the Techniques of Teaching*, 133.

and develop their own conclusions.[33] A more fruitful and nonleading question related to the responsibility Christians have for their neighbors is, "According to Matthew 22:37–40, how is loving God related to loving our neighbors?"

Third, *good questions are open-ended.*[34] Meeting this criterion is probably the key to good questioning. Open-ended questions are those which have a variety of possible responses or encourage the exploration of possible answers. In contrast, closed-ended questions ask for one word answers or yes or no responses. Closed-ended questions are limiting in that they provide no, or minimal, opportunity for discussion. Such queries call for bifurcated thinking and hinder participants from exploring the gray areas or those problem issues to which there are no known, clear answers.[35] Examples of an open-ended question are "Why do you think this might be true?" and "In what ways would this attitude affect one's relationship with God?" Examples of a closed-ended question are "Do you agree with that?" and "Should a person lie to protect a loved one?" Often a closed question can be quickly turned into an open-ended inquiry simply by asking, "Why?"

Fourth, *good questions are relevant.* They are clearly related to the issue being discussed or the topic being studied. Does the question move you toward your goal or fit in with the flow of discussion? Will the question lead to a clearer understanding of the issue or passage being studied? Sikora adds these helpful insights: "Relevancy may also relate to where you are in the study. We need to build precept upon precept. We need to be careful not to come out of left field with a question for which we haven't yet laid the foundation. Watch the flow of your questions."[36]

Fifth, *good questions are of interest.* In order to be effective in facilitating discussion, the leader should ask questions

---

[34]Davis, *Tools for Teaching,* 85; Lowman, *Mastering the Techniques of Teaching,* 135; Richards and Bredfeldt, *Creative Bible Teaching,* 191.

[35]Bergevin and McKinley, *Participation Training for Adult Education,* 91.

[36]Sikora, *Small Group Bible Studies,* 151.

that are geared to the interest and needs level of the small-group members. To help formulate more stimulating questions the leader of a Christian group should make a con-centrated effort to understand the age-level or life-span issues and needs of group members. For example, early adults (college-age men and women) are most likely wres-tling with the problems of starting careers, finding marriage partners, or breaking ties with parents. Middle-aged adults are faced with mid-life crises, caring for aging parents, pos-sible career changes, and planning for retirement. By contrast, those in the senior adult age bracket may be strug-gling with retirement, loss of loved ones, or financial insecurities.[37]

Finally, *good questions encourage independent and reflective thinking.*[38] Carefully worded and well thought-out questions can be used to nurture and instigate critical thinking.[39] While a number of conceptual schemes have been used as the basis for developing questions that lead to higher-order thinking, the best known is the one developed by Benjamin Bloom and associates.[40] Originally designed as a system for classifying edu-

---

[37]For more complete taxonomies of tasks and concerns related to the vari-ous stages of life see: Karen Ann Szentkeresti and Jeanne Tighe, *Rethinking Adult Religious Education* (New York: Paulist, 1986), 10–24; Malcolm S. Knowles, *The Modern Practice of Adult Education: From Pedagogy to Andragogy,* rev. ed. (Chicago: Follett, 1980), 263–4; Robert J. Havinghurst, *Developmental Tasks and Education,* 3rd ed. (New York: David McKay, 1972).

[38]Verduin, Miller, and Greer, *Adults Teaching Adults,* 131; Stephen D. Brookfield, *Developing Critical Thinkers* (San Francisco: Jossey-Bass, 1987), 92–3.

[39]See chapter seven for more on small groups and critical thinking.

[40]Benjamin Bloom et al., *Taxonomy of Educational Objectives* (New York: David McKay), 1974.

[41]For example, see Norris M. Sanders, *Classroom Questions: What Kinds?* (New York: Harper, 1966); Davis, *Tools for Teaching,* 84; C. Bobbi Hansen, "Questioning Techniques for the Active Classroom," in Diane F. Halpern, ed., *Changing College Classrooms* (San Francisco: Jossey-Bass, 1994), 93–106; Glenn Ross Johnson, *First Steps to Excellence in College Teaching,* 3rd ed. (Madison, Wis.: Magna, 1995), 59.

cational objectives, other educators have adapted the taxonomy for use in planning discussion questions.[41]

The six levels of cognitive functions along with the operational behavior expected (in parentheses) are identified as follows from lower to higher levels of thinking:[42] (See Fig. 6.1.)

- *knowledge* (remembering or recalling information);

- *comprehension* (rephrasing the information, giving a description in one's own words);

- *application* (applying previously learned information to solve a problem or determine a correct answer);

- *analysis* (identifying motives, reasons, or causes; using available information to reach a conclusion);

- *synthesis* (producing original communication, making predictions);

- *evaluation* (judging the merit of an idea or an aesthetic work, based on specific criteria).

By asking group members questions that move them beyond the knowledge and comprehension levels, the discussion facilitator enables them to probe, reflect, and think critically about issues, their personal walk with God, their faith, and personal beliefs and values.[43]

Responding to Group Members: How a facilitator responds to comments and discussion patterns of group members is critical. The following strategies can assist the Christian education

---

[42]Harley Atkinson, *Ministry with Youth in Crisis* (Birmingham, Ala.: Religious Education Press, 1997), 50–51.

[43]For other helpful classification schemes for questions see Verduin, Miller, and Greer, *Adults Teaching Adults*, 131; Richard L. Carner, "Levels of Questioning," in James Raths, John R. Pancella, and James S. Van Ness, eds., *Studying Teaching* (Englewood Cliffs, N.J.: Prentice-Hall, 1967), 182-186.

[44]Davis, *Tools for Teaching*, 86.

Figure 6.1

Bloom's Taxonomy of Objectives and Discussion Questions

Level	Type of Skill	Sample Question
Knowledge	Remembering Recalling Recognizing	Could you recite the definition of faith given at last week's discussion?
Comprehension	Understanding Describing	Explain faith in your own words. What do you think Jesus means when he says...?
Application	Implementing Solving	How could you apply Jesus' principle "love your enemy" to a situation at work?
Analysis	Identifying Concluding	What evidence can you find that supports the idea "money is the root of all kinds of evil"?
Synthesis	Producing Predicting	Construct a collage of pictures that represent your ideas, feelings and values concerning.... What would it be like if...?
	Judging	Which is better...? Why would you favor...?

group discussion leader in being more effective in interacting with group members.

First, it is important to *allow for silence.*[44] It is sometimes difficult for a small-group facilitator to endure prolonged silence after he or she has asked a discussion question. Silence can be threatening, often causing leaders to answer their own questions without giving other group members opportunity to respond.

[45]Two helpful essays on silence as a component of the communication process are Adam Jaworski, "The Power of Silence in Communication," and Charles A. Braithwaite, "Cultural Uses and Interpretations of Silence." Both appear in *The Nonverbal Communication Reader,* 2nd ed., eds. Laura K. Guerrero, Joseph A. DeVito, and Michael L. Hecht (Prospect Heights, Ill.: Waveland, 1999), 156–62,163–72.

However, it is very important to give everyone sufficient time to reflect on the question before responding.

There are usually good reasons for silence in small-group discussions.[45] Perhaps a particular query poses a difficult question and the response demands some reflective thinking. Or maybe the potential responses are risky or sensitive, and participants want to be careful how they word their answers. It is also possible that the discussion members do not understand the question. If this happens, the leader may receive puzzled or blank looks. If a prolonged silence continues, the facilitator should ask the group what the silence indicates: "Everyone has been silent for a while—why?" Or the group leader could encourage participants by saying something like, "I know it may not be easy to respond to this question." Lowman suggests that ten seconds is not too long to wait in silence, although it may seem like an eternity. Counting out ten seconds silently can help mark the passage of time.[46]

Second, the discussion facilitator *must not always be satisfied with the first answer given in response to a discussion question.* Since an initial comment is often difficult to obtain, there may be the tendency to be content with that response and move on. However the effective discussion leader will follow up initial responses with some additional probing. Probing questions are follow-up questions that ask group members to examine more closely the ideas or assumptions implicit in their initial statement, help them explore and express what they know about the issue,[47] and encourage them to think above the recall and comprehension levels.[48] Examples of probing questions are "Why do you say that?" and "What, exactly, do you mean by that statement?"

A Christian education group facilitator should also appeal to other group members by encouraging them to respond to

---

[46]Lowman, *Mastering the Techniques of Teaching*, 136.

[47]Davis, *Tools for Teaching*, 87.

[48]Johnson, *First Steps to Excellence in College Teaching*, 59.

[49]Kasulis, "Questioning," 45.

statements. For example, after an individual makes a response to a particular question, the facilitator might say, "How do the rest of you feel about the comment Kirk made?" Or "Do you agree with Kirk's statement that . . . ?" This type of question also encourages group interaction.[49]

Third, the facilitator should try to *avoid the temptation of making personal comment on each remark made by group participants*. Rather, it is important to allow group members to develop their own ideas and respond to each other. Often a discussion leader feels constrained to provide commentary or reflect on each statement offered by group members. Some group leaders talk too much and turn a discussion into a one-way presentation.[50] This practice can get monotonous and fosters the notion that the leader is the *expert*.

It may be helpful from time to time to summarize a remark to make sure every member grasped or received the information. However, these summaries should be very brief. Personal comments or reflections should be kept to a minimum unless the facilitator desires to shift the focus of discussion or bring it to closure.[51] For example, after a fruitful and exhaustive discussion on a particular area of subject matter, the facilitator might say something like this: "Several critical comments were made to this point concerning. . . . In light of what was said, I'd like to change the direction of our discussion slightly and address the issue of. . . ."

Fourth, the discussion facilitator can enhance discussion by *throwing questions back to the group*. Many time Christian education group members ask the leaders questions and all too often leaders feel compelled to try to furnish an answer to each question. Small-group facilitators can nurture full-membership participation by throwing questions back to the discussion group.[52] For instance:

---

[50]Davis, *Tools for Teaching,* 76

[51]Lowman, *Mastering the Techniques of Teaching,* 137.

[52]Davis, *Tools for Teaching,* 78.

Phil: "Of course, lying is an unethical practice and not compatible with a Christian style of living. But what about lying to protect your family, say in the case that an intruder, intent on harming your family, asks you where your wife and children are? Is it appropriate to lie then?"

Facilitator: "Boy, that's a tough one. Would anyone like to respond to Phil's question about lying in that particular kind of situation?"

Once again, this strategy discourages members from holding to the idea that the leader is the resident expert and final authority on every issue. Often individuals other than the leader have valuable insights and worthy responses to inquiries. Furthermore this is a great opportunity for the leader to stimulate group interaction and to encourage reflective thinking on behalf of the entire group.

Group Participation[53]

One of the difficult tasks of a leader is attaining optimum participation and involvement from all group members, an essential ingredients for good discussion. The quality of the group discussion depends as much on group participation and members accepting this responsibility as it does upon the discussion leader.[54] However, Christian education groups may suffer from a number of communication problems that hinder or diminish balanced participation, such as silence, lack of acceptance, defensiveness, or misunderstanding.

Sometimes groups include individuals who exhibit characteristics that reduce group productivity: the apathetic, the quiet and shy, or the psychologically withdrawn. On the other hand, there may be those members who tend to dominate or monopolize group interaction. It is the difficult, yet necessary, task of the facilitator to regulate participation and

---

[53]The following chapter deals exclusively with group participation.

[54]Bergevin and McKinley, *Participation Training for Adult Education*, 29; Davis, *Tools for Teaching*, 75.

endeavor to give each individual an equal opportunity to be involved.

Perhaps here more than at any other point, a discussion leader must use sensitivity and tact. The leader should be particularly sensitive in curbing a dominator or encouraging a silent member to interact. The discussion facilitator can regulate participation and secure involvement of group discussion members by doing the following:[55]

- *being especially sensitive to participants attempting to enter the discussion* (members who are shy or hesitant may never get a chance to enter the discussion without some help from the leader):[56] "Sandy, I noticed you sort of reacted when Don commented on the difficulty he has speaking in public. Did you want to interject something here?"

- *encouraging informal, spontaneous, multi-directional participation*[57] (members should know that it is not necessary to raise their hands or look for permission from the leader each time they desire to say something): "I want to remind you that you're all welcome to respond to anyone at any time—you don't need my special consent to jump into the discussion."

- *avoiding directing questions to shy or sensitive people unless they appear to be interested in contributing to the group discussion*: "Sue, did you want to respond to that last comment by Tonya?"

- *being cautious in curbing talkative or dominant members*[58] (avoid embarrassing them or making them look

---

[55]R. Victor Harnack and Thorrel B. Fest, *Group Discussion: Theory and Technique* (New York: Appleton-Century-Crofts, 1964), 324–5; Applbaum, *Fundamentals of Group Discussion*, 21.

[56]Davis, *Tools for Teaching*, 78.

[57]Ibid.

[58]Davis, *Tools for Teaching*, 79.

bad in front of other group members): "I'd like to hear from others in the group."

- *recognizing the individual who has not talked over the one who has*: "Dave, I appreciate the comments you've made in our discussion, and now I'm interested in hearing what Michele has to say on this issue."

- *avoiding leader-member interaction only* (participation between group members should be encouraged): "How do the rest of you feel about the comment Doug just made?"

- *guarding against overly lengthy contributions by individual group members and working toward the goal of giving all a chance to participate in the discussion*: "Jonathan, I notice that our time is moving on. Let's set a thirty-second limitation on everybody's comments."

Climate

Climate refers to the environmental atmosphere or conditions prevailing in the discussion setting. According to adult education expert Malcolm Knowles, climate is the most crucial element in a learning experience. If the climate in the whole process is not conducive to learning, then all the other elements in the process are jeopardized.[59] The atmosphere of a discussion group should be one that excites group members' interest and encourages their participation. Climate or envi-

---

[59]Malcom Knowles, *The Adult Learner: A Neglected Species,* 2nd ed. (Houston: Gulf, 1978), 109–15.

[60]A number of sources emphasize the importance of learning environment: James Michael Lee, *The Flow of Religious Instruction* (Birmingham, Ala.: Religious Education Press, 1973), 65–73; William R. Yount, *Created to Learn* (Nashville, Tenn.: Broadman and Holman, 1996), 295–315; Malcom S. Knowles, *The Modern Practice of Adult Education* (Chicago: Follett, 1980), 46-7; Knowles, *The Adult Learner: A Neglected Species,* 109-15; J.R. Kidd, *How Adults Learn* (New York: Association Press, 1973), 234-40.

[61]Luft, *Group Processes,* 17.

ronment is generally considered to consists of two dimensions: physical and emotional.[60]

Create a Comfortable Physical Environment: The physical environment can have a powerful effect on the life and activity of a Christian education group.[61] By taking the time to create interesting and warm physical surroundings, a leader can enhance group discussion enormously. Lee advises that interaction among members of a group is significantly affected by the design of a room as well as the arrangement of the physical environment in which the discussion is carried on.[62] Knowles contends that instructors and leaders of educational opportunities all too often take for granted the physical setting of the learning experience, and wrongly ignore many of the simple things they can do to improve the impact it can have on the social climate of their activity.[63] The following strategies will help energize the physical environment for dynamic small-group discussions:

- meeting in a small room;

- avoiding the use of sofas and easy chairs;

- sitting in a circular or U-shape fashion;

- avoiding environmental distractions; and

- paying close attention to group size.

By *meeting in a small room,* the facilitator has a better chance of creating an emotionally warm climate than if the group meets in a larger, more impersonal room. An auditorium, gymnasium, church basement, or even a church sanctuary is not usually the most practical setting for a small-group discussion; there is something about the bigness and openness that diminishes closeness or intimacy and hinders stimulating

---

[62]Lee, *The Flow of Religious Instruction,* 71.

[63]Knowles, *The Modern Practice of Adult Education,* 224.

[64]William A. Draves, *Energizing the Learning Environment* (Manhattan, Kans.: Learning Resources Network, 1995), 25–6.

interaction. On the other hand, argues William Draves, living rooms in homes, and often living room-like arrangements in other buildings, are highly desirable and most effective for discussion, ideas, creativity, feelings, honesty, problem-solving, or an informal presentation of information.[64]

If a Christian education group is forced to meet in a larger hall or auditorium, efforts can be made to rearrange the room into a more appropriate small-group setting. It is not necessary to accept the space as it is; one can make an effort to create a subsection of the room that will create a more intimate and personal meeting space. Are their partitions available that could be used to divide the room? Are there bulletin boards that might serve as partitions? Can a curtain be strung from wall to wall? Are there pieces of furniture that could be used to psychologically mark off an area of the room?[65]

It might also be helpful to *avoid the use of sofas and easy chairs.* While a group leader will want to create a relaxed and warm climate, it is not good if group members become too comfortable. Participants must be alert and aware of what is happening. Sofas and easy chairs tend to cause participants to "kick back" and get too relaxed, to the point, perhaps, of dozing or drifting off mentally. Furthermore, when an individual sits back in a comfortable easy chair, he or she is alienated, in a sense, from other group members. Good eye contact is lost, and posture and other nonverbal messages may indicate aloofness or a lack of interest.

It is important that participants in Christian education discussion groups *sit in a circular or U-shaped fashion.* Seating arrangement is an extremely important factor in making group discussion dynamic and achieving optimum participation from members.[66] In her empirical research study of college students,

---

[65]Ibid., 28–9.

[66]Tubbs, *Small Group Interaction,* 98; Gorman, *Community That is Christian,* 130–2.

[67]Judee Burgoon, "Spatial Relationships in Small Groups," in Cathcart, Samovar, and Henman, eds., *Small Group Communication,* 241–54.

Judee Burgoon found that students overwhelmingly expressed a preference for a U-shaped or circular seating arrangement when asked what spatial arrangement would maximize participation, learning, and attention.[67] It is critical that group members be able to make eye contact with each of the other members. Sitting in a circle fashion is the best way to facilitate good eye contact and allow members to easily address one other.

The physical environment can also be enhanced by *avoiding environmental distractions.* Televisions and radios should be turned off. Pets, such as cats and dogs should be taken care of ahead of time—either put outside or in rooms where they will not be noticed. The host or hostess of the small group should respond to telephone calls, visitors, or disruptive children in a manner that creates as little disturbance as possible. Discussion groups would do well to avoid meeting in restaurants or other public places where noise and activity might interfere with the tasks of talking, attending, and listening.

Finally, it is important for the discussion leader to *pay attention to group size.* The effect of group size on member satisfaction, effectiveness of the group, and discussion patterns has been well documented. Hackman and Vidmar noted that members of discussion groups reported higher levels of disagreement in the group as the size increased.[68] Cartwright and Zander concluded that members find participation more satisfying and group processes more effective in smaller groups than in larger ones.[69]

---

[68]J. Richard Hackman and Neil Vidmar, "Effects of Size and Task Type on Group Performance and Member Reactions," in *Interpersonal Behavior in Small Groups,* Richard J. Ofshe, ed., (Englewood Cliffs, N. J.: Prentice-Hall, 1973), 285-99.

[69]Cartwright and Zander, *Group Dynamics,* 485-502.

[70]Joseph Luft, *Group Processes,* 23; Gorman, *Community That Is Christian,* 132; Tubbs, *A Systems Approach to Small Group Interaction,* 102; Brilhart and Galanes, *Effective Group Discussion,* 116; Elizabeth G. Cohen, *Designing Groupwork,* 73.

[71]Gorman, *Community That is Christian,* 132.

Experts on group discussions tend to agree that about five is the ideal number for achieving maximum participation and balance in group discussion—small enough for meaningful interaction, yet large enough to generate a variety of ideas.[70] Gorman emphasizes that as groups increase in size participation decreases, with the conversation centering on a talkative few who tend to speak to each other rather than to the whole group.[71] Tubbs observes that as groups grow beyond five, members tend to complain that they are not able to participate as much as they would like and that as the group increases in size, subgroups form, which may carry on annoying side conversations. As a group increases in size, there is less time available for each member to participate; as the group increases linearly, the potential number of interactions increases exponentially. For example, in a dyad only two relationships are possible; in a triad there are nine possibilities; however, when a group increases to eight, the number of possible interactions increases to over 1,000.[72]

Based on the results of research findings[73] and the observations of small-group discussion experts, it seems desirable to keep the group size to approximately five whenever possible so as to ensure optimum participation, satisfaction, and efficiency. It may be advisable to include a few more than five to allow for the inevitable absenteeism. Of course this optimal size depends on the type or nature of the group. While five might be ideal for a problem-solving or discussion group, certain work groups or other types of groups might perform better with a different number of members.[74]

Create a Warm Emotional Climate: For maximum effectiveness in the small-group tasks of self-disclosing, sharing, learning, and discussion, a warm emotional climate is crucial.[75]

---

[72]Tubbs, *A Systems Approach to Small Group Interaction,* 102–3.

[73]Hackman and Vidmar, "Effects of Size and Task Type on Group Performance and Member Reactions," 285–99; Cartwright and Zander, *Group Dynamics,* 485–502.

[74]Gorman, *Community That is Christian,* 132; Luft, *Group Processes,* 23; Tubbs, *A Systems Approach to Small Group Interaction,* 104.

[75]Luft, *Group Processes,* 127.

Lee's overview of relevant research indicates that a warm affective environment enhances the possibility of learning in all teaching-learning settings.[76] Gorman adds that cultivating a climate of security and belonging is a necessity if individuals are going to open themselves up to make changes.[77] What can the leader do to foster a sense of security in a group? What can be done to create a feeling of belonging? How can a group provide a warm emotional climate for learning, discussion, and self-disclosing? The following strategies can assist the small-group leader in effectively nurturing a satisfactory emotional climate:

- getting to know group members;

- making use of sharing questions;

- lowering the threat level; and

- creating a setting of mutual respect and collaboration.

First, a small-group discussion leader can begin to create a warm climate by *developing relationships with and getting to know each of the group members.* The group leader should arrive early, giving an opportunity to meet new members or build relationships with continuing members. It is imperative the discussion facilitator learn and use the first names of any attendees who are new. Lowman argues that learning participants' names is so effective at prompting interaction and rapport because it initiates personal contact immediately, yet does not seem forced, rushed, or intrusive.[78]

Another way the leader can create a warm and friendly climate for discussion and interaction is *through the use of sharing questions.*[79] Sharing questions are designed to encourage group members to tell others a little bit about themselves, and are usually used at the beginning of a particular group meeting.[80] These

---

[76]Lee, *The Flow of Religious Instruction,* 98–100.

[77]Gorman, *Community That Is Christian,* 114.

[78]Lowman, *Mastering the Techniques of Teaching,* 46.

[79]See the following chapter for more about sharing questions.

[80]Gorman, *Community That Is Christian,* 151.

types of questions nurture interpersonal relationships and help members get to know each other better. Examples of sharing questions are: "What is one memorable Christmas holiday you can remember? Why was it memorable?" and "What school teacher influenced you the most? How?"

Many adults have fears of learning or speaking in groups, even small groups. A facilitator should try to *make the group discussion experience as enjoyable and nonthreatening as possible.* The threat level of most youth and adults can be lowered by:

- avoiding calling on individuals for answers;

- encouraging honest efforts, even if answers are wrong;

- allowing group members to correct or challenge wrong answers;

- closely attending to any person who is speaking;

- allowing members to be silent if they so choose;

- protecting the privilege of every member to express his or her own opinion or feelings;

- keeping conflicts focused on issues, not on personalities;

- making every effort to be accepting and nonevaluative in reacting to comments by group members; and

- communicating the message that each member's thoughts are important and valued.

Finally, it is important to *create a setting of mutual respect and collaboration.*[81] Androgogy expert Malcom Knowles insists that any learning environment must exude a spirit of mutual respect. In such a setting, participants perceive that they bring a reservoir of experience to the group that is, itself, a rich resource for others' learning. They value the broad range of

---

[81]Westmeyer, *Effective Teaching in Adult and Higher Education,* 36; Knowles, *The Modern Practice of Adult Education,* 223.

differences as enriching and as such, the small-group experience is collaborative rather than competitive. Group members are eager to share what they know and can do, rather than restraining themselves for fear someone else might look better than they.[82]

HANDLING DIFFICULT SITUATIONS IN CHRISTIAN EDUCATION GROUP DISCUSSIONS

Christian education groups are made up of people. It goes without saying, then, that problems and difficult situations will be an inevitable part of the small group experience. It can be almost guaranteed that the Christian education group leader or facilitator one will encounter at least one of the problems or situations described below. Following are some difficult situations that might cause the facilitator the most concern.

Talkative and Dominant Members

One of the most common problems in small groups is the presence of the individual who is prone to answer most of the questions or dominate the discussion. He or she may interrupt and talk without ceasing on issues that may or may not be relevant to the group goal. Sometimes this person speaks in such an authoritative manner that other members hesitate to add anything to the discussion even if they find the opportunity to interject. How can you work with the dominant member? Seldom is there a need to create a tense, embarrassing situation in which the dominator has to be told not to talk so much. The resolution of the problem can usually occur rather naturally.[83] Consider these options:

- Call for the contribution of others in a nonthreatening manner with a comment such as, "What do the

---

[82]Knowles, *The Modern Practice of Adult Education*, 223

[83]Bergevin and McKinley, *Participation Training for Adult Education*, 86; Lowman, *Mastering the Techniques of Teaching*, 143–4.

rest of you think?" Pointedly encourage others to participate with statements like "Everybody's contribution is welcome!" or "I would like to hear from everyone."[84]

- Invite another group participant to respond with a statement like, "Bill, what thoughts do you have on this issue?" One must be careful to do this only if it is certain that that person will not feel intimidated or embarrassed by being called upon.

- Avoid making eye contact or giving the dominant person attention, limiting the opportunity for the individual to engage in discussion.[85]

- Politely interrupt the monopolizer and ask him or her to wrap up the thought.

If none of the above strategies are met with success, it may be necessary to talk to the dominator privately, explaining the importance of balanced group participation. Make sure this individual understands his or her input is welcomed, but that there must be sensitivity to the contributions of other group members.[86] Something like this could be said: "Sarah, I know you enjoy contributing to the discussion and I appreciate your eagerness to get involved in the group discussion. I'm concerned, however, that with your confidence and ability to articulate so clearly, you may be unwittingly stifling the contributions of others who are less confident. I wonder if you could help me out by limiting the length and frequency of your comments." It is extremely important that you acknowledge the overly talkative group member and show appreciation for his or her efforts to follow your suggestions.[87]

---

[84]Davis, *Tools for Teaching*, 79.

[85]Ibid.

[86]Ibid.

[87]Brookfield, *The Skillful Teacher*, 104.

Members Who Do Not Participate

In contrast to the dominant member is the silent member or the one who rarely participates in group discussion. First, it should be recognized that a silent person does not really hinder the Christian education group and the privilege to be silent should be recognized as much as the right to engage in discussion.[88] If the group, however, is made up primarily of nonparticipators, it makes for a rather difficult situation and can cause the small group to be unproductive. Some individuals find it extremely difficult to share personal or reflective thoughts of any kind, and they should be given the privilege of simply showing up and listening. The following suggestions, however, might help the facilitator to engage these individuals in discussion.[89]

- Make a general comment like, "We would like to hear from everyone," or "Everyone is welcome to participate."

- Look for nonverbal messages and sparks of interest. When an individual raises his or her eyebrows or suddenly looks at you, make a nonthreatening invitation to speak, such as, "Judy, were you going to say something?" or "Would you like to comment on that?" The member can then make the choice of responding or gracefully declining. Try to avoid putting a nonparticipator on the spot with a direct question such as, "John, would you like to comment on that insight?"

It may be helpful to spend some time with this person outside the small-group context. By getting to know the individual and finding out what interests him or her, two things might happen. First, the individual may feel more comfortable with the group as a result of the time spent together and second, a study or meeting might be shaped around that person's interests or needs. At the least, some discussion ques-

---

[88]Ibid., 108.

[89]Lowman, *Mastering the Techniques of Teaching,* 144.

tions based on his or her interests might be included in one or more group sessions.

• Brookfield proposes that discussions begin with comments along these lines: "I know that speaking in [group] discussions is a nerve-wracking thing and that your fear of making . . . fools of yourselves can inhibit you to the point of nonparticipation. I, myself, feel very nervous as a discussion participant and spend a lot of my time carefully rehearsing my contributions so as not to look like an idiot when I finally speak. So please don't feel that you have to speak in order to gain my approval. . . ."[90]

Getting Off Track

There is always the problem or danger in small-group discussion of getting off track or "rabbit trailing." It is more of a problem if there is a particular member who seems to be prone towards pulling the group away from study objectives. What can be done to keep a small-group discussion from drifting from the issue?[91]

• First, try making a polite verbal reminder to the group that the discussion has wandered too far away from the lesson plan or study topic. The facilitator could say something like, "That is an interesting thought, but we have left our topic. Let us try and get back to the issue at hand."

• Second, suggest to the party that is drifting that you and others would be interested in pursuing this issue after the formal discussion. Or, if it is a matter of significance, it could be the topic of discussion at a future time.

---

[90]Brookfield, *The Skillful Teacher*, 109.

[91]Lowman, *Mastering the Techniques of Teaching*, 142.

- It may be appropriate at times to allow the tangent to unfold. The facilitator might choose to follow the rabbit trail without saying anything, or he or she could ask the group if they would like to pursue this train of thought.

"Wrong" Answers

Handling factually wrong answers or responses is often a difficult responsibility of the facilitator. On one hand a discussion leader does not want to allow inaccurate statements to go unchallenged; on the other hand, it is important to allow members to explore possibilities, wrestle with issues, and even make mistakes. The facilitator certainly does not want to embarrass or cause an individual to "lose face." It is usually not appropriate to tell a small-group member his or her response is wrong. What is an appropriate response then?

- First, it is important to remember that any type of put-down or disapproval will discourage a small-group participant from speaking up or attempting to respond again.[92]

- Second, it is helpful to affirm the group member's attempt to answer the question or engage in the discussion. Comments like, "That's interesting" or "I never thought of it that way before" are ways of letting the participant know that comments are welcome.

- Third, the facilitator might ask the person to substantiate or back up what has been said. Often when asked to support an answer, an individual sees the fallacy in a certain response.

- Fourth, the facilitator could solicit a response from someone else. Comments like "What do the rest of you think?" or "Does anyone else have some information that would help us better understand the issue?" help

---

[92]Davis, *Tools for Teaching*, 80.

take the pressure off the facilitator of having to "correct" the false thinking.

- Finally, the discussion leader might rephrase the question or ask a further question that would clarify the thinking or stimulate further thought.

Silence

From time to time the small-group facilitator may experience a situation in which, after having asked a question, there is extended silence; no group participant wants to venture a response and what may be only a few seconds, seems like forever. Periods of silence may often be interpreted by group facilitators and members alike as something negative, even threatening. But silence in small-group discussions is a valuable component and necessary if ideas are to germinate and develop.[93] As John Dewey so aptly noted, "All reflection involves, at some point, stopping external observations and reactions so that an idea may mature."[94]

Writing from the perspective of the classroom, Brookfield proposes that students often complain that teachers rush through myriads of content without allowing them enough time to reflect on what is presented to them: "The period for mulling over that is reportedly needed for learners to make interpretive sense of what is happening to them is neglected."[95] The same could possibly be said of Christian education groups. Discussion group members often need time to ruminate over questions and statements that are made in the course of group interaction. How does the Christian education group facilitator respond to silence or a lack of response to a discussion question?

- First, as implied above, it is important not be afraid of silence.[96] The facilitator must resist the temptation to

---

[93]Chet Meyers and Thomas B. Jones, *Promoting Active Learning* (San Francisco: Jossey-Bass, 1993), 30.

[94]John Dewey, *How We Think* (Lexington, Mass.: Heath, 1910/1982), 210

[95]Brookfield, *The Skillful Teacher,* 50.

[96]Davis, *Tools for Teaching,* 86.

jump right in and answer the question for other group members. This only frustrates participants who are getting ready to respond.

- Group members must be given time to think through their responses. Perhaps the question is difficult and they need time to reflect on it; or maybe the question raises some sensitive issues, and the participants want to be very careful how they articulate their responses.

- Sometimes people do not answer because the question is unclear. If this appears to be the problem, the leader might ask something like "Did that question make sense?" or "Are you clear about what I am getting at?" If they indicate this is the case, the question should be rephrased. If group members are comfortable with their group, they will often volunteer this information without being asked.

CONCLUSION

This chapter has identified the fundamentals of effectively leading small-group discussions, the "procedural glue" that holds a group together. The chapter focused on the components of a good discussion (purpose, structure, leadership, communication, group involvement, and climate), and appropriate ways to handle difficult situations.

7

Nurturing Participation in Small Groups

MUCH of what has been dealt with to this point has been related to leadership behavior in Christian education groups. However, a significant amount of behavior that takes place in small groups might be considered nonleader-related. This includes all communication, roles, functions, and activities that occur outside the realm of leadership activity. It may not be appropriate to call this *followership* or *follower behavior*, because the designated leader may also participate in nonleader-type activities. This chapter will address group roles and functions, self-disclosure, expression of feelings and emotions, critical thinking, groupthink, and the effect of gender and cultural differences on Christian education group behavior.

CHRISTIAN EDUCATION GROUP ROLES AND ROLE FUNCTIONS

Sociologists who study small groups realize that group members maintain various roles and perform different role functions in the group context. Generally, considerable differentiation exists between members of Christian education groups, so that members carry out different tasks and are expected to accomplish different things for the group. Put another way, different members play different *roles*.[1] For example, group members may hold various roles, including discussion facilitator, host or hostess, or recorder.

---

[1]Johnson and Johnson, *Joining Together*, 20.

On the other hand, role *functions* are the specific behaviors role members exhibit in Christian education group activities. A further distinction must be made between *behaviors* and *behavioral functions*. For example, the story Phil tells in a group meeting is the behavior. The function of the behavior might be one of several, depending on how the story was told, the timing of the story, and what else was happening in the group. If it was a humorous story, it might serve to release tension; in a negative sense, it may have served to get the group off track.[2] The most successful Christian education groups are those that recognize and incorporate the unique and special abilities and contributions each member brings to the group.

Christian Education Group Roles

Group roles are divided into two main types: *formal* and *informal*. Most Christian education groups have formal or *positional* roles that are assigned or appointed to an individual and may carry a title. For example, a chairperson has the responsibility to call meetings, plan agendas, and delegate or coordinate the work of other group members; a discussion leader is responsible for facilitating group dialog; the host or hostess is called upon to provide a place for the group to meet and to take care of details such as refreshments.

Informal or *behavioral* roles, by contrast, are those unspecified parts people play that reflect their personality traits, behaviors, and habits in a small group. For instance, Em Griffin observed the following informal roles emerge over the course of a year in a small group in which he was involved.[3]

- *"The Mover*—the "can do" person who rolls up her sleeves and gets to work.

- *The Clown*—the jokester who keeps things from getting too serious.

---

[2]Brilhart and Galanes, *Effective Group Discussion*, 136.

[3]Adapted from Em Griffin, *Getting Together* , 21–2.

- *The Skeptic*—the one who raises tough questions just about the time the group's ready to get carried away. Often maligned, her doubts serve a valuable function.

- *The Technician*—the fellow who has expertise where you need it most. Sometimes this role floats from person to person as the task of the group changes.

- *The Encourager*—the warm soul who builds up others and makes them feel valuable. He or she is good at smoothing ruffled feathers and soothing bruised egos.

- *The Deviant*—the person who's different. He or she may hold back or suggest things that are off the wall.

- *The Nice Guy*—the foot soldier who does what is asked without grumbling. Not an initiator but someone with a sense of responsibility."

Role Functions of Group Members

The initial work on role functions in groups was carried out by Kenneth Benne and Paul Sheats, who reported multiple roles people commonly play in groups. They also described the functions or behaviors accompanying each role and classified them into three categories: task, maintenance, and individual.[4]

Task-Related Functions: Task functions are those that contribute to the achievement of the group goals:[5]

- *Initiating-contributing:* proposing or suggesting new ideas or a different way of viewing the group prob-

---

[4]Kenneth D. Benne and Paul Sheats, "Functional Roles of Group Members," in *Interpersonal Growth and Self Actualization in Groups*, eds. Raymond M. Maslowski and Lewis B. Morgan (n.c.: MSS Information, 1973), 151–9.

[5]Summarized from Benne and Sheats, "Functional Roles of Group Members," 151–9.

lem or goal. It may take the form of a new goal or through two chapters this month, instead of just one?); it may take the form of a suggested solution or way of handling a difficulty ("Perhaps if we meet at 7:30 on Thursday evening, we could all make the meeting); or it may include a new procedure for the group ("I think it would be good if we started our discussion group by praying for each other").

- *Information seeking:* asking for clarification or for authoritative information and facts pertinent to the issue being discussed ("I like the idea that our group get involved in the downtown mission; but I think we should get a lot more information about this particular organization before we go any further").

- *Opinion seeking:* looking not so much for facts related to the issue, but for clarification of the values pertinent to what the group is undertaking ("I would like to know how the rest of the group feels about getting involved with the downtown mission. Is this the kind of outreach that fits with our specific interests and goals?").

- *Information giving:* offering to the group generalizations or facts which are "authoritative" or relating his or her own personal experiences to the group's discussion ("I was involved in a similar kind of mission work in Chicago. I believe this is a worthy cause, especially when you consider the fact that there are reportedly over 5,000 street and homeless people in our city").

- *Opinion giving:* offering his or her opinion on statements made by other group members ("Frankly, I think you're way off on your numbers!").

- *Elaborating:* developing statements or suggestions made by group members in terms of examples or illustrated meanings, offering rationale for previously made suggestions, and endeavoring to deduce how a suggestion or idea would work out if adopted by the group ("I like what Susan said about meeting on Tuesday evenings at 7:30. Then the Wilsons could join our group again; and I don't work late on Tuesdays, so it makes it easier for me to get here on time. The only problem I possibly see is that. . . .").

- *Coordinating:* clarifying the relationship among various ideas, suggestions, and contributions; trying to pull suggestions and ideas together; or trying to coordinate activities of group members (Jeff volunteers to arrange for and coordinate a visit of his small group to the downtown mission).

- *Orienting:* defining the position of the group with regards to goals and purposes, raising questions about the direction the group discussion is taking, and reminding the group of departures from agreed upon goals or directions ("Aren't we distancing ourselves from our topic just a little? Our discussion subject is the responsibility of the Christian towards the poor, and we're talking about the role of the government in helping out Third-World countries. Could we get back on track?").

- *Evaluating: subjecting the group's accomplishments* to the standards previously established by group members ("About a month ago we agreed, as a group, to spend fifteen minutes of each meeting in prayer for each other. We're not really doing that").

- *Energizing:* prodding the group to decision or action, or attempting to stimulate the group to a higher level or quality of activity ("We've been talking about getting involved as a group with the downtown mission. I think it's time to quit talking, and do something concrete!").

- *Performing tasks:* contributing to the functioning of the group by performing routine tasks for the group such as handing out materials or rearranging furniture (Each week Julie makes sure she's the first one to arrive for her discipleship group, so she can help the hostess arrange the room appropriately).

- *Recording:* writing down suggestions, taking notes on group discussion, or making record of group decisions.

Maintenance-Building Functions: Maintenance, or group-building functions, are those that assist the Christian education group in sustaining harmonious relationships and a cohesive climate:[6]

- *Encouraging:* agreeing with, praising, and accepting the contributions of other group members ("I really appreciate how Julie comes early each week to set the chairs up and arrange the room for our study group").

- *Harmonizing:* mediating or peacemaking; attempting to mediate differences between others, reconciling disagreements, or relieving tension in conflict ("I'm really concerned that we are not so much addressing issues any longer, but rather we're taking shots at each other. I think it's okay to disagree, but let's avoid getting personal").

- *Compromising:* operating from within a conflict where his or her position or idea is involved; offering compromise by admitting error, yielding status, or coming halfway in moving along with the group ("I really wish we could keep our growth group meeting on Monday nights. However, I would support moving our meeting to Thursday evening if we could meet at 7:30 instead of our regular meeting time of 7:00").

- *Gatekeeping:* endeavoring to keep communication flowing freely by encouraging and facilitating the participation of others ("I noticed Jerry was starting to say something, I'd sure like to hear his response"); or

---

[6]Ibid.

by limiting the length of contributions so each member has an equal opportunity to contribute ("Since we only have a limited amount of time left before we have to draw our discussion to a close, I'd like to suggest we limit each comment to thirty seconds").

- *Standard setting:* expressing standards for the group to attempt to achieve or applying standards in evaluating the group's achievements ("I would suggest that we each have the respective chapter read before our discussion group meets each week, so that we're all better prepared to take part").

- *Following:* going along with group decisions, ideas, and activities more or less passively ("Whatever we decide is fine with me"); serving more as an audience than participant in group discussions and decision making.

Individual Roles: While task and maintenance behaviors are considered helpful to Christian education group development, individual roles are not. These behavior functions emerge when group members consider their personal needs as more important than those of the group. Frequently these self-centered behaviors take place as a result of a hidden agenda. An individual often has an unstated, perhaps even unconscious, reason for belonging to a group; or perhaps a member wants to achieve a private goal through the group.[7]

- *Withdrawing:* not participating; avoiding significant differences; refusing to get involved with conflicts; refusing to take a stand on issues; hiding feelings; giving little or no response to the comments of others.

- *Blocking:* preventing the progress toward group goals by continually raising objections ("I say we just keep meeting the same time we've always been meeting; we can't please everybody anyway, so why change?"); or by repeatedly bringing up the same topic or issue af-

---

[7]Ibid.

ter the group has considered and rejected it ("I know we decided last week to move our group meeting time to Thursday, but I still think we made the wrong decision. I want us to seriously reconsider the decision").

- *Status and recognition seeking:* garnering attention, bragging, and unduly calling attention to one's expertise or experience ("You know, I have more education than anyone else in the group"); playing games to elicit sympathy ("I guess I'll just have to quit coming if we change our meeting time"); switching the subject to an area of one's own personal expertise (Janelle continually attempts to introduce issues of eschatology to the discussion because of her personal interest in this area of theology).

- *Playing:* refusing to help the group with the task at hand; excessive joking, dramatizing, and goofing around; poking fun at small-group members who are serious about the group process ("Come on, you take this group too seriously; lighten up and have little fun"); interfering with the group's on-going work and interaction.

- *Acting helpless:* attempting to elicit sympathy from other members by continually needing help to complete a task ("I know I said I would, but I don't think I can provide refreshments next week unless I really get some help from the rest of you. I'm so busy and my husband never helps me with these kinds of things"); demonstrating inability for independent thought or action ("It's just a five-minute presentation, but I've never done this sort of thing before; will someone please do it with me?").

SELF-DISCLOSURE IN SMALL GROUPS

An indispensable ingredient of most all Christian education groups is *self-disclosure*. While disclosure should be expected in a small group, it often appears frightening or unsettling and is generally approached with uncertainty.

Self-disclosure presents group members with the dilemma of choosing between openly expressing thoughts and feelings, and concealing or distorting opinions, perceptions, and feelings. For example, a woman may not want to reveal that she had an abortion at one point in her life for fear of what other group members might think of her. Or a couple may not want to disclose some of the difficulties they are having in their marriage. Yet, if each member is not free to share personal thoughts and opinions, little is said and even less is accomplished in a small group. The question is not *whether* to reveal or conceal, but *how much* to reveal or conceal.[8] Other questions are more pertinent or of greater value: When is self-disclosure desirable?; How is it best done?; What should I disclose about myself?; or What hinders my self-disclosure?

What exactly is self-disclosure? Ronald Adler and Neil Towne define *self-disclosure* as the process of intentionally revealing significant information about oneself that would not normally be known to others.[9] Sidney Jourard, in his book on self-disclosure aptly titled *The Transparent Self*, sees it as "the act of making yourself manifest, showing yourself so others can perceive you."[10]

Several components of these definitions are worth expanding upon. First, self-disclosure must be deliberate. For example, if without much thought Christy mentions to her friend that she is thinking about quitting her job, it cannot really be considered disclosure. Second, information shared must be significant. Insignificant facts or opinions (that you like baseball or just subscribed to cable television) hardly count as points of disclosure.

Third, self-disclosure is that information not otherwise known by other group members. Telling the group about marital struggles that they are already familiar with does not count as self-disclo-

---

[8]Tubbs, *A Systems Approach to Small Group Interaction*, 211.

[9]Adler and Towne, *Looking Out Looking In*, 292.

[10]Sidney M. Jourard, *The Transparent Self*, rev. ed. (New York: D. Van Nostrand, 1971), 19.

sure. Finally, self-disclosure must by voluntary. Information that is revealed as a result of force or coercion cannot be considered as self-disclosure.

Benefits of Self-Disclosure

While the very thought of disclosing oneself to others elicits a spirit of fear and apprehension in many individuals, it has the potential to benefit individuals and groups in a variety of ways. In fact, argues David Johnson, communicating intimately with another person, especially in stressful times, appears to be a basic human need.[11]

Relationship Enhancement: Self-disclosure is requisite if relationships are to develop and remain healthy in a Christian education group. If individuals do not reveal how they feel to others, interaction remains limited and shallow, and group members simply do not get to know each other. Johnson reasons that without self-disclosure, close personal relationships cannot be fashioned. If one cannot reveal himself or herself, it is difficult to become close to others, and one cannot be valued by others for the person he or she is.[12] Em Griffin adds that self-disclosure usually draws us closer to those who listen, and that a certain amount of openness is a necessary precondition for intimacy.[13] Simply put, it is that we become known to others when we disclose of ourselves.

Tension Release and Inner Healing: Sometimes we disclose personal information just "to get it off our chests." People often go to counselors not so much for advice, but for someone to listen to them. There is a catharsis that takes place when we confess sins or actions we are ashamed of—the very act of disclosing brings relief or healing. Karl Mennenger, in his popular book, *Whatever Happened to Sin,* says unconfessed guilt feelings are hard to bear, and must be confessed to someone.[14]

---

[11]David W. Johnson, *Reaching Out* (Englewood Cliffs, N. J.: Prentice-Hall, 1972), 11.

[12]Ibid., 9.

[13]Griffin, *Getting Together*, 116.

[14]Karl Mennenger, *Whatever Became of Sin?* (New York: Hawthorn, 1973), 197.

Lynd rightly identifies the tremendous value of dealing with shame through self-disclosure: "If . . . one can sufficiently risk uncovering oneself and sufficiently trust another person to seek means of communicating shame, the risking of exposure can be in itself an experience of release, expansion, self-revelation, a coming forward of belief in oneself, and entering into the mind and feeling of another person."[15] Perhaps this is one of the reasons the New Testament author, James, instructs his readers to "confess your sins to each other" (Jas 5:16). Jourard states bluntly that alienation from one's real self arrests one's growth as a person.[16] The famous Swiss psychologist Paul Tournier admits that Christian confession leads to the same psychological liberation as do the best techniques of psychoanalysis.[17]

The Quaker writer Richard Foster recounts the time he went to a counselor friend to confess some sins and past activities he felt were hindering his spiritual walk with God. Upon receiving the confessions and self-disclosures, the wise friend took the piece of paper these sins and actions were written on, tore it into hundreds of tiny pieces and threw them in the wastebasket. The friend followed this symbolic act of absolution by praying a prayer of healing for all the sorrows and hurts of Foster's past. Foster describes the resultant effect on his life: "I cannot say I experienced any dramatic feelings. I did not. In fact, the entire experience was an act of sheer obedience with no compelling feelings in the least. But I am convinced that it set me free in ways I had not known before. It seemed that I was released to explore what were for me new and uncharted regions of the Spirit."[18]

Tournier warns against the dangers of withholding personal confession or disclosure. "The man who keeps secret his most

---

[15] Quoted Egan, *Face to Face* , 57.

[16] Jourard, *The Transparent Self*, 32.

[17] Paul Tournier, *The Healing of Persons* (New York: Harper and Row, 1965), 236.

[18] Foster, *Celebration of Discipline*, , 156.

painful memories, his bitterest remorse, and his most private convictions, must needs show also, in his whole demeanor and in all his relationships with other people, a certain reserve which they all intuitively feel. This reserve is contagious, and sets up an obstacle to the development of personal relationships."[19]

Self-Revelation: Another reason for self-disclosure is that we get to know ourselves.[20] In the process of letting others get to know us, we discover who we are. Griffin says, "Self-awareness is a by-product of the struggle to honestly expose my being to someone else."[21] Powell adds that in communicating things as freely and openly as possible, we will find a noticeable growth in our own sense of identity. It has come to be a psychological truism that we will understand only as much of ourselves as we have been willing to communicate to another.[22]

Jourard makes some strong statements in regards to the relationships between self-awareness and disclosure: "It seems to be another fact that no man can come to know himself except as an outcome of disclosing himself to another person. . . . When a person has been able to disclose himself utterly to another person, he learns how to increase his contact with his real self, and he may then be better able to direct his destiny on the basis of this knowledge."[23]

Self-Clarification: Sometimes an individual can clarify his or her beliefs, opinions, attitudes, feelings, and thoughts by talking about them with other members of the small group. It helps us sort out confusion and understand ourselves a little bit better.[24]

---

[19]Paul Tournier, *The Meaning of Persons* (New York: Harper and Row, 1957), 158.

[20]Jourard, *The Transparent Self*, 7.

[21]Griffin, *Getting Together*, 118.

[22]John Powell, *Why Am I Afraid To Tell You Who I Am?* (Allen, Tex.: Thomas More, 1998), 80.

[23]Jourard, *The Transparent Self*, 6.

[24]Adler and Towne, *Looking Out Looking In*, 6th ed., 304–5.

Personal Growth: The overall benefit of disclosing is that in having understood and communicated ourselves, we will grow and mature. Powell says that at the moment an individual realizes a negative pattern in his or her life, that person will find a way to change that pattern. For example, "If I consistently and honestly report the emotion of 'feeling hurt' by many small and inconsequential things, it will become apparent to me in time that I am hypersensitive and that I have been indulging myself in self-pity. The moment that this becomes clear to me, really hits me, I will change."[25] Powell may sound overly confident that this personal understanding will take place, but the dynamic is this: We allow our feelings or emotions to arise so as to be identified; we observe, report, and judge our emotional reactions; and finally we make the necessary adjustments for growth and change.[26]

Resistance to Self-Disclosure

Why do most people have such a difficult time disclosing to others? Why, inquires Julie Gorman, do we find revealing ourselves to others a frightening and psychologically threatening experience? We seem to find the prospect of revealing ourselves seems so unappealing and we flee self-exploration even in the presence of those who care for us. And when we do choose to self-disclose "we proceed cautiously, offering each item of personal information as a test to determine the safety of revealing ourselves further."[27]

The Fear of Rejection: One reason small-group participants tend to avoid self-disclosure is out of a fear of rejection. "If I am completely honest in revealing myself, people will get a picture of what I am really like, and they may not want any part of me." Powell proposes that individuals are afraid to tell others about themselves because they reason, "If I tell you who I am you may not like who I am, and its all that I have."[28]

---

[25]Powell, *Why Am I Afraid To Tell You Who I Am?*, 82.

[26]Ibid.

[27]Gorman, *Community That Is Christian*, 140.

[28]Powell, *Why Am I Afraid To Tell You Who I Am?*, 12.

Christian education group participants sometime fear disclosure because they think first in terms of revealing the worst. Then, if an individual tells other group members about incompetence in one area of life, perhaps they will assume similar incompetence or irresponsibility in other dimensions of life. This fear can be combated by encouraging group members to give balanced views of themselves, speaking alternately on strengths and weaknesses.[29]

Fear of Confidence Broken: There is also the very real possibility that what one has shared in the relative privacy of a small group will be revealed in public. There is a fear that what is disclosed in the intimacy of a small group may be fodder for gossip, which will be followed by further public embarrassment, ridicule, or even shunning. With that fear, many people are extremely protective of their inner thoughts, feelings, and personal experiences. For example, Frank wants to disclose to his Thursday morning support group that he really struggles with Internet pornography, but refrains from saying anything because he fears this may not stay within the context of the group.

Fear of Self-Awareness: As mentioned, self-disclosure is not only a way of communicating with others, it is a way to get to know oneself. But perhaps the latter is even the priority. Egan hypothesizes that many individuals flee self-disclosure because they fear gaining closer contact with themselves.[30] Larry Crabb agrees with Egan and suggests that the most frequently expressed fear of people when they look closely at their lives is this: "I am not sure I can make it if I face all that is inside of me."[31] However, he concludes that if we are to experience significant inner change and personal growth, a courageous and honest look inside is absolutely essential.[32]

---

[29]Egan, *Face to Face*, 56.

[30]Ibid., 53.

[31]Larry Crabb, *Inside Out* (Colorado Springs, Colo.: NavPress, 1988), 32.

[32]Ibid., 36–7.

Fear of Intimacy: The very act of revealing one's inner self leads to a measure of intimacy. In many varieties of small Christian education groups this intimacy is intense. Unfortunately for many individuals, the fear of intimacy overrides the benefits that might be gained from self-disclosure. For some people, insists Egan, the fear of human relations is greater than the fear of death. They prefer to ignore self-revelation in order to avoid intimacy; they skirt disclosure to evade closeness. One way to counteract this escape from intimacy is to engage in self-revelation or disclosure that is proportionate to the situation and involves minimal or reasonable risk taking. This is what should be expected in most Christian education groups.[33]

Fear of Over-Disclosure: Sometimes individuals lack discretion in self-disclosure. They may be so brutally honest that they offend others or make them feel uncomfortable. Over-disclosures may also say something about someone else (perhaps a spouse) that is better left unsaid ("My wife had an abortion when she was in her teens", or "My husband has a real problem with lust"). We may also risk boring people if we go on and on about a particular issue. Because of the abuses of self-disclosure or liberties some people take with opportunities for self-revelation, others may shy away from any interaction that involves personal sharing.

Fear of Change: One of the potential outcomes of self-disclosure is change. Self-disclosure brings to one's awareness areas of deficit, weaknesses, shortcomings, and sins. Consequently, self-awareness or declaration of what a person finds unacceptable in himself or herself brings commitment to change; avoiding change of behavior causes further pain and frustration. Egan carefully points out that "self-disclosure commits one to conversion, to the process of restructuring one's life; it demands that a person leave the security of his own house and journey into a foreign land, and most men balk at that. If one senses that conversion is impossible, then he must avoid self-disclosure."[34]

---

[33]Egan, *Face to Face*, 54.

[34]Ibid., 55.

But making a commitment to experience change is the very essence of most Christian education groups and the very core of Christian living. The apostle Paul admonishes, "Do not conform any longer to the pattern of this world, but be transformed by the renewing of your mind"(Ro 12:2). And when self-disclosure takes place in the context of a group, the pressure to change is even greater than in a one-on-one situation, for the demands and expectations are in the context of a community of individuals. But it is also in the safety of small community of supportive believers that transformation can be nurtured by following Paul's injunction to the church in Thessalonica: "Encourage one another and build each other up" (1Th 5:11). True community, posits Gorman, leads to growth.[35]

Establishing a Climate For Self-Disclosure

Before individual group members feel comfortable disclosing who they are or how they feel, they need to know that there is a safe emotional climate. If certain ingredients are not present, it is not likely a significant amount of self-disclosing will be accomplished. However, if they are present, group members will likely be more ready to reveal their inner selves.

It may take a while before such a climate is established. Group members will question themselves and others. "Who will disclose first?"; "How can we know others unless someone is willing to reveal himself or herself first?"; "How can we really trust group members?" And so, as Gorman insightfully suggests, we proceed with much caution, offering each bit of personal information as a test to determine the safety of disclosing ourselves further. Only as each item of revelation is safely received is more information divulged.[36] For self-disclosure to proceed with any amount of fluidity, some important ingredients must be present. These components include trust, risk, intimacy, and honesty.

Trust: Self-disclosure in a Christian education group occurs only after an attitude of trust, a central dynamic in

---

[35]Gorman, *Community That Is Christian*, 111.

[36]Ibid., 140.

face-to-face interaction, has been established.[37] While trust, the ability to place some of your security into the control of another person,[38] is clearly the most important ingredient for meaningful disclosure in a Christian education small group, the establishment of interpersonal trust is difficult to achieve.

How do participants in a small Christian education group demonstrate trustworthiness? First, interpersonal trust is built when it is clearly evident that members will not take advantage of the vulnerability of the one self-disclosing. Trustworthy behavior is "the willingness to respond to another person's taking risks in a way that ensures that the other person will experience beneficial consequences."[39]

Second, there must be a certain interpersonal warmth present. The expression of warmth towards another person in a relationship builds a high level of trust because it increases the other person's expectations that an individual will respond with support and acceptance when disclosure takes place.[40]

While trust is difficult to build, it is even more difficult to rebuild. Once group members have been betrayed or even feel they have been betrayed or taken advantage of, it is an arduous task to recover the trust that once existed. Thus, it is critical that a Christian education group protect that which has already been achieved. Continual dialogue, honesty, and respect for the other members is important in maintaining interpersonal trust.[41] Making a joke at the expense of another group member, laughing at an individual's self-revelation, moralizing about the person disclosing, or making an evaluative

---

[37]David W. Johnson, Roger T. Johnson, and Karl A. Smith, *Cooperative Learning: Increasing College Faculty Instructional Productivity*. ASHE-ERIC Higher Education Report No. 4 (Washington, D.C.: The George Washington University, School of Education and Human Development, 1991), 36.

[38]Richard Walters, *How to Be a Friend* (Ventura, Calif.: Regal, 1981), 102–3.

[39]Johnson, Johnson, and Smith, *Cooperative Learning: Increasing College Faculty Instructional Productivity*, 37.

[40]Johnson, *Reaching Out*, 47.

[41]Cragan and Wright, *Communication in Small Groups*, 178.

response to a self-disclosure all communicate rejection and will destroy some of the trust in the small group.[42]

Risk: If trust is to be built in a group it is essential that a certain amount of risk taking occurs.[43] Trusting behavior is the willingness to make one vulnerable through self-disclosure by *risking* either beneficial or harmful consequences.[44] However, we feel freer to share risky thoughts or feelings when we have established an atmosphere of trust and acceptance. So the question is: Which comes first? Do we risk in order to nurture trust or only when trust has been established?

Several factors influence the level of risk in sharing. Time is one variable. Usually past history is the safest time frame from which to disclose because there is nothing we can do about the events. Sharing of future plans, on the other hand, is more risky because we commit ourselves to following through with what we said we would do. The greatest risk is contained in the disclosure of present acts because they are open to scrutinization, evaluation, and are more capable of affecting present relationships.[45]

The focus or nature of the disclosure also affects the risk. Generally, disclosing feelings ("I can't take the tension and conflict in our home anymore; its tearing me up inside") is riskier than sharing life-related facts ("After my husband moves into his new position at work, which includes a substantial increase in salary, we're taking a trip to Europe"). Evaluative statements of ones self or others ("I hate myself for what I've done") take on a higher risk than non-evaluative statements ("We're thinking seriously of selling our business, since its increasingly difficult to make a satisfactory profit"). Finally, the number of receivers increases the risk factor in disclosure. The larger the group, the safer or less risky the subject must be.

---

[42]Johnson, *Reaching Out*, 47.

[43]Jourard, *The Transparent Self*, 5.

[44]Johnson, Johnson, and Smith, *Cooperative Learning: Increasing College Faculty Instructional Productivity*, 37.

[45]Gorman, *Community That Is Christian*, 144–5.

Intimacy: Intertwined with trust and risk is intimacy. To be intimate is to be closely associated, or very familiar, with another person. We feel freer to disclose risky thoughts or feelings when we have discovered a commonality with others. The very act of self-revelation creates some degree of intimacy which, in turn, promotes further self disclosure.

Honesty: Self-disclosure is not necessarily being brutally honest about ones feelings towards someone or revealing intimate details of the past. Rather, it is being open and forthright about reactions to present situations. Disclosing and being honest about the past is helpful only if it helps clarify why an individual is reacting a certain way in the present.

Guidelines for Self-disclosure

Self-disclosure in a small Christian education group can lead to new dimensions of communication, healthy community, and personal transformation. However to attain heightened levels of individual and group growth, self-disclosure must be entered upon with sensitivity and discretion. Adler and Towne offer the following guidelines for making self-disclosure a rewarding and positive small-group experience.[46]

First, *other persons must be important to the one disclosing.* Group participants should ask themselves two questions as they consider disclosing personal information:

- Are the relationships with other group members significant enough to warrant sharing personal aspects of my life?

- Do other members care enough for me to listen to my innermost thoughts and feelings?

Early stages of group development may not be conducive to some disclosures because group members have not developed close relationships. On the other hand some self-disclosure may be the path toward developing closer, more intimate relationships in the small group.

---

[46]Adapted from Adler and Towne, *Looking Out Looking In*, 305–8.

Second, *the risk of disclosure must be reasonable.*[47] It is of importance that each small-group member take a realistic look at the possible hazards or risks of self-disclosure. Even if the potential benefits are great, possible rejection or ridicule may be an invitation to trouble. Or the possibility of someone breaking confidence and sharing personal revelations outside the group may be greater than the possible benefits. Furthermore, blunt honesty about how one feels about someone else in the group may bring about serious interpersonal conflict.

Third, *the amount of disclosure must be appropriate.* It is usually not discreet or profitable to share too much personal information too soon. In most relationships, the process of revealing one's self is gradual, beginning with superficial and nonthreatening comments and slowly moving to a deeper level of sharing as trust and intimacy secured.[48] Even in close relationships the amount of personal information shared is relatively small when compared to non-intimate information. Besides being moderate in amount, self-disclosure should consist of a balance of positive and negative information.

Fourth, *the disclosure must be relevant.* Self-disclosure that is a long confession of current thoughts or a revelation of past events unrelated to the current discussion is inappropriate. Effective self-disclosure should be related to the topic of study or theme of the group meeting. Usually appropriate self-disclosure relates to the present—the here and now: "How am I doing now?" or "How am I feeling today?" There are times when it is important and relevant to bring up the past (for example, in support groups), but only as it relates to the present.

Fifth, *self-disclosure should be reciprocated.*[49] When an individual shares innermost feelings and thoughts to other group members, and realizes that self-revelation is not being reciprocated, he or she suddenly senses an imbalance in the relationship. There is a realization that the others know some-

---

[47]Luft, *Group Processes*, 68.

[48]Ibid., 67.

[49]Ibid.

thing about him or her, yet there is not similar information known about them, and this can be disconcerting. A Christian education group cannot function effectively without a balance of disclosing, as when only one or two group members do all the self-revealing while others remain silent.

Sixth, *the effect of disclosure must be constructive.* Self-revelation can be a damaging tool if not used with discretion and sensitivity. Comments made about friends or group members may be honest responses of how one feels about them ("Nathan talks too much in our group discussions") but it may also be a sure-fire way to disable them and destroy those relationships. It is of utmost importance to consider the effects of one's candor before opening up to others.

Levels of Interpersonal Sharing and Self-Disclosure

Self-disclosure can be further defined or better understood through the classification of the depths of interpersonal sharing. The following taxonomy describes five levels, or types, of sharing, beginning with the more superficial and moving to the most revealing level.[50] Small groups should endeavor to move toward the deeper levels of sharing. The five levels include (1) cliché conversation, (2) the reporting of facts, (3) the sharing of ideas and opinions, (4) disclosing feelings, and (5) confessional sharing.

Level One—Cliché Conversation: Clichés are actually the opposite of self-disclosing statements and often represent an unwillingness to share ourselves with others. Such conversation includes questions and comments that expect no thoughtful response from the others; it is simply a recognition that others are present.[51] Examples of cliché statements are:

- "Nice weather, isn't it?"

---

[50]A number of sources identify these levels of disclosure, including Powell, *Why Am I Afraid to Tell You Who I Am?*, 45–54; Icenogle, *Biblical Foundations for Small Group Ministry*, 76–7; Adler and Towne, *Looking Out Looking In*, 294–7.

[51]Icenogle, *Biblical Foundations for Small Group Ministry*, 76.

- "How has it been going?"

- "We'll have to get together sometime."

- "How about those Braves?"

Even remarks such as "How are you doing?" are not usually taken seriously or literally. If an individual responded to this question with a lengthy discourse on his or her health, private affairs, and personal problems, the person who asked the question might be quite surprised. Conversation that takes place before a small-group study or meeting tends to be at this level.

Level Two—Reporting Facts: The reporting of facts represents a minimal attempt at sharing with others. Information is being shared without too much personal reflection. However, to qualify as disclosure, they still must meet the criteria of being significant, intentional, and not otherwise known.

- "I'm going back to college in the fall."

- "We just bought some property and are ready to begin building a new house."

- "We are going to Europe for three weeks this summer."

While such information can be significant, revelation carries with it little risk of being rejected or threatened in any way. Nonetheless, disclosing such important information suggests a level of commitment and trust to the other group members that signals a desire to move the relationship to another level.[52]

Level Three—Sharing Ideas and Opinions: Still more revealing is the level of idea and opinion sharing. This demands more risk-taking on behalf of the one sharing because others have the potential to reject the idea or opinion.[53] Much group communication ends at this level. The following are examples of idea and opinion level statements:

---

[52]Adler and Towne, *Looking Out Looking In*, 295.

[53]Icenogle, *Biblical Foundations for Small Group Ministry*, 76.

- "I used to favor abortion, but now I believe it is wrong."
- "I believe that Christians should take a more active role in feeding the hungry!"
- "I believe that it is wrong for Christians to go to war!"

Level Four—Sharing Feelings, Values, and Emotions: At this level of sharing a group really gets to the point at which they are revealing things about themselves. They break through the facade, and share the feelings, values, attitudes, and emotions that make up the real face.[54] At this level individuals are looking for feelings in response to that which they have shared. Trust, a certain amount of intimacy, openness, and a willingness to take a risk are important ingredients in making this kind of small-group sharing possible. It involves the conveying of one's joys, sorrows, aspirations, fears, likes, dislikes, needs, dreams, desires, and burdens. Some examples of this level of sharing are:

- "I don't feel that God can ever forgive me for what I have done!"
- "I am distressed over the way my husband is treating me."
- "My wife is asking for a divorce—my heart is broken! I don't know if I can ever recover."
- "One day I hope to...."
- "When I retire, my dream is to...."

Level Five—Confessional Sharing: This level represents the deepest level of sharing—those words spoken only in the safest of relationships. Icenogle describes this level as follows: "This may be the stuff I might not even say to myself. These are the fears or hopes I may only share with God. Here are my deep wounds and crimes of my heart. Here is where my child-

---

[54]Ibid.

hood damages are hidden or repressed. Here is the stuff I share only when there is a gracious, compassionate and merciful listener facing me. Here is my most intimate self released only when I am in the face of a loving, forgiving, and compassionate person."[55]

The Use of Sharing Questions

An effective tool for encouraging self-disclosure, as well as enhancing group participation and relationship building in Christian education groups, is the sharing question. Sharing questions invite group members to tell something about themselves and are often used by Christian education groups to begin their times together. They are most helpful in the initial phase of group development when members are getting to know each other. They also serve as good icebreakers or tension relievers in that they often bring about laughter and friendly interaction.

Sharing questions can be thought of in terms of five main categories: past, present, future, affirmation, and accountability.[56] The threat, or intensity, of the types of questions moves from the low or nonthreatening past-tense questions to the highly demanding present-tense accountability questions.

Past-Tense Questions: Past-tense questions ask members to share one's history of the safe past. They are especially appropriate in the initial stages of a group when individuals are getting to know each other, when they are willing to risk relatively little in their disclosure. The following are examples of past-tense sharing questions:

- Where did you live when you were ten years old, and what is one strong memory you have of that time?

- Who was one influential person in your life and why?

---

[55]Ibid., 77.

[56]Unless otherwise noted, the following insights are summarized from Roberta Hestenes, *Using the Bible in Groups* (Philadelphia, Pa.: Westminster, 1983), 102–6. See also Gorman, *Community That Is Christian*, 151–4.

- What is one memorable vacation, and why is it memorable?

Present-Tense Questions: Usually asked after the group has been together for a while, present-tense questions invite people to share what is currently happening in their lives. They focus on the experiences and feelings that are a part of daily living; the very recent past may also be a part of these questions. The following are examples of present-tense sharing questions:

- What spiritual disciplines do you find to be the easiest or most difficult to follow?

- What do you do on a typical Saturday?

- What do you like about your job? What do you dislike?

- Where are you growing or changing in your life? What helps or hinders that process?

- What is one thing you worried about or struggled with this week?

Future-Tense Sharing Questions: These questions focus on what is ahead—usually the not so near future. They ask people to talk about their desires for change, their hopes and dreams, their expectations, and possibilities. Some examples of future-tense questions are:

- If you knew you could not fail and money was no problem, what one thing would you like to do in the next five years?

- What is one anxiety you have about the future, and how will you deal with it?

- What would you like people to say at your funeral?

- What is one dream or hope you have for the future?

- If you could change one thing about yourself or develop one quality that you do not have, what would it be?

Affirmation Sharing Questions: These types of questions invite group members to say something positive about each other. They help individuals to tell others why they are meaningful to them and why they are valued. These questions can be very important in building a sense of belonging and being cared for. They become especially appropriate in the final meetings of a group. Some examples of affirmation type questions are:

- What is one quality you admire or value in one or more of the group members?

- How have members been important or helpful to you?

- What spiritual gifts do you see present in one or more members of this group? How are those gifts being used in a helpful way?

Accountability Sharing Questions: These questions are asked when members promise to actively work at living out their Christian faith. Such sharing questions should be asked only when members have agreed to make themselves accountable to fellow group members. These types of questions might work best for closed groups where there is a high level of commitment. Some examples of accountability sharing questions are suggested here:

- What changes do you believe you should make in your actions or habits this week? How will you tackle these?

- How will you share the Good News this week, and with whom?

- What success (or difficulty) have you experienced this week in your attempt to follow Christ?

- How will you practice gratefulness to God this week?

Small-group leaders will find sharing questions more effective when certain procedures are adhered to. First, it is helpful to *keep the sharing process moving by going in a circle.*

This is the one type of group question to which it is appropriate that everyone responds, taking only a minute or two for each participant to answer. The facilitator can model by going first and demonstrating how he or she might like the question to be answered. While the intent is to have each person share, it is apropos to let members know that they can pass if they so choose. Participants might also reshape the question if it makes it easier for them to answer.

Second, *the best sharing questions are simple and uncomplicated.* Questions that do not require long explanations and can be answered in a brief period of time will elicit the most appropriate responses from group participants. For example, a question, such as, "What kind of heritage did your parents pass on to you and what kind of legacy would you like to bequeath to your children?" would require lengthy explanations, likely taking up a good part of a meeting. A simple query, such as, "What is one piece of heritage your parents passed on to you?" would serve much better as an opening sharing question.

Third, *sharing questions must be safe.* For instance, questions which obligate group members to confess sins ("What is one area of your life where you are failing God?") or reveal only negative things about themselves ("What is one spiritual discipline you are 'blowing' or not doing very well at?") can be threatening. Gorman says, "feelings of regret over the past where nothing can be done, or anger and depression over unfair treatment can color what goes on in the group for the rest of its life together."[57] Thus, the safeness of a sharing question is relative to the group itself.

In the initial stages of a Christian education group, when members are just getting to know each other, superficial questions that every member can easily answer without threat should be asked ("What do you like to do for fun?" or "What is your notion of an ideal vacation?"). Then, as the group matures and members feel more secure with one another, queries that call for more personal self-disclosure ("In what area of your spiritual life would you like to grow?") and thoughtful reflection ("If

---

[57]Gorman, *Community That Is Christian*, 152.

you were asked to define the term *Christian*, what would you say?") can be posed.

Fourth, *the best sharing questions are open-ended.* Questions that can be answered with a yes or no ("Did you go to Sunday School when you were a child?") or with one-word responses ("What is your favorite sport or game?") should be avoided. The purpose of sharing questions is to get members to talk a little bit about themselves so that others can get to know them better, something closed-ended questions fail to do. Often closed-ended questions can be transformed into open-ended inquiries by affixing "Why?" or "How?" ("Have you been influential in the spiritual development of another person? How?")

Fifth, *sharing questions should be inclusive.* In other words, questions should be framed in such a manner that they can be answered by each group member. For example, a question like "What college did you attend and what was your major?" eliminates the possibility of responses from those who did not attend college.

Sixth, *sharing questions do not call for the discussion of ideas or opinions* ("What is your opinion on the government's latest efforts to curb inflation?" or "How do you feel about Christians going to war?"). In the use of sharing questions, the facilitator is interested in permitting and encouraging individuals to talk about *personal* experiences and how they relate to those experiences. Opportunity to discuss ideas and opinions can be provided for in other ways during the small-group meeting.

Finally, it is good practice to *avoid the use of superlatives* such as *best, most,* or *worst* in sharing questions ("What is the most awesome thing God has ever done for you?" or "What is the funniest family story you can tell about you or your family members?"). Superlatives can force group members into making unnecessary evaluations or cause individuals to feel inadequate if their story does not match up to that of others. Usually it is better to use words like *significant, important,* or *difficult* ("What is one significant thing God has done for you in the past month?").

The Johari Window

One of the most helpful models for illustrating small-group self-disclosure is the Johari window (named after its creators, Joe Luft and Harry Ingram).[58]

The window classifies and describes awareness in interpersonal relationships according to four quadrants. The quadrants are called *open, blind, hidden,* and *unknown.*

Quadrant 1—The Open Area: This area represents behavior, motivation, and feelings known to both self and other group members. We feel free to share with others our views on weather, sports, current events, and other bits of nonthreatening information. For example, if Wendy comes to the group wearing a particular sweater, Jennifer might make a comment like, "I like your sweater; I don't think I've seen you in it be-

Figure 7.1
The Johari Window

	Known to Self	Not Known to Self
Known to Others	Area 1 Open	Area 2 Blind
Not Known to Others	Area 3 Hidden	Area 4 Unknown

[58]Luft, *Group Processes: An Introduction to Group Dynamics,* 59–69.

fore." To this, Wendy replies, "Oh yeah, I've worn it before, although I don't think you've seen me in it." The words express an open focus of exchange.

Quadrant 2—the Blind Area: This includes feelings, behaviors, and motivations that are known to others but that we are not aware of. In other words, we may reveal these things unintentionally or unwittingly. For example, group members are aware of the fact that Greg brags a lot about his abilities in a number of areas of life. But in a discussion on Christian humility, Greg says that he feels one of his strengths is being humble. In this case Greg is seemingly oblivious to his lack of humility, an oversight that is not lost on his fellow group members.

Quadrant 3—The Hidden Area: Hidden to others but known to self, this area is most likely to be changed by self-disclosure. It represents our feelings about ourselves that we know but find difficult to reveal to others. It includes fears, past experiences that are unpleasant ("I know none of you are aware of this, but when I was a seventeen-year-old teenager and unmarried, I got pregnant"), and fantasies. Relationship building is taking these things from the hidden area and bringing them into the open quadrant. These actions usually result in a reciprocal action made by others, thus establishing a basis for trust and growth in relationships.[59]

Quadrant 4—the Unknown: This quadrant points to the behaviors and motives of life that no one, neither the individual nor others, is aware of. Yet we can assume they exist because eventually some of these behaviors and motives become known, and we then realize that they were significantly influencing relationships all along.[60] For example, in a support group, Darla comes to the self-realization that she experienced serious rejection in early childhood that has affected interpersonal relationships in her adult years.

---

[59]Gorman, *Community That is Christian*, 147.

[60]Luft, *Group Processes: An Introduction to Group Dynamics*, 12.

The size of each of these quadrants increases or decreases according to the changes in relationships. For example, as disclosure takes place in a hidden area the open area increases while the hidden decreases. A change in any one of the quadrants will affect the other quadrants. The larger the first quadrant (open area) is, the better the communication will be. When quadrant one is small, however, there may be a high threat level, and communication is usually poor. As trust is developed among group members, awareness of hidden, open, and blind facets of relationships increases. Along with this awareness is a desire to move items from the hidden and blind quadrants into the open quadrant.[61]

EXPRESSING EMOTIONS IN SMALL GROUPS

It is difficult to talk about small-group communication without referring to the affective domain of feelings and emotions. While few sources on small groups so much as allude to the affect, it is a truism that feelings and emotions play an integral part in the interaction that takes place in every small group.[62]

However, there are mutually exclusive responses in American society in regard to the expression of emotions and feelings. On one hand, there are those who bear concern for the individuals who are unable to freely express their emotions and feelings in interpersonal relationships, the problem of emotional repression. On the other hand, there are those who think that feelings and emotions are somehow deified. This emotional overindulgence is evidenced in the proliferation of encounter and sensitivity groups that focus almost exclusively on the affective domain of feelings, emotions, sensory awareness, and touch.[63]

---

[61]Gorman, *Community That is Christian*, 148.

[62]Luft, *Group Processes: An Introduction to Group Dynamics*, 125–6; Johnson and Johnson, *Joining Together*, 497–8.

[63]Egan, *Face to Face*, 61; Gerard Egan, *Interpersonal Living* (Monterey, Calif.: Brooks/Cole, 1976), 71.

The appropriate recognition of emotions and the expression of feelings in a small-group encounter lies somewhere between repression and overindulgence. The expression of positive emotions such as love and concern for group members, as well as identification with others in hurt, pain, and discouragement are highly rewarding small-group experiences. Yet the meaningful expression of feelings and emotions is often more difficult to manage than other types of group communication.[64]

Reasons for Not Expressing Our Emotions

Powell reminds us that most interpersonal encounters are achieved through some sort of emotional communion such as empathy, tenderness, feelings of affection, or feelings of attraction.[65] Yet while people are usually comfortable and willing to share opinions and facts, they are often reticent to disclose how they feel. Why is this so? Adler and Towne offer several reasons.[66]

Social Rules: In North American society there are a number of unwritten social rules that discourage the open expression of most emotions or at least delineate certain parameters. For example, consider the following societal codes:

- men are not supposed to cry;

- it is more acceptable for women to be open with their emotions than men;

- being emotional is a sign of weakness.

Inability to Recognize Our Emotions: Many times individuals cannot share their emotions simply as a result of an inability to recognize them. Because of the social rules or family pressures to suppress certain emotions, capacity to identify them diminishes. For example, it may difficult for a man to cry if, for most

---

[64]Luft, *Group Processes: An Introduction to Group Dynamics*, 126.

[65]Powell, *Why Am I Afraid to Tell You Who I Am?*, 89.

[66]Adler and Towne, *Looking Out Looking In*, 6th ed., 124–5.

of his life, he has fulfilled the expectations of society that a man must hide his tears. Or, after years of denying one's anger, the ability to recognize that feeling may be next to impossible.

Fear of Self-Disclosure: Sharing our deepest emotions and feelings can be risky, thus we have certain fears of self-disclosing. Powell eloquently says, "A thousand fears keep us in the solitary confinement of estrangement. In some of us there is the fear of breaking down, of sobbing like a child. Others of us feel restrained by the fear that the other person will not sense the tremendous importance of my secret to me. We usually anticipate how deep the pain would be if my secret were met with apathy, misunderstanding, shock, anger or ridicule. My confidant might become angry or reveal my secret to others for whom it was not intended."[67]

Others May Feel Uncomfortable: Finally, we are often afraid that in being open and honest with our emotions, we will make others feel awkward or uncomfortable. So we are encouraged to suppress, deny, or ignore our personal feelings, especially if they are strong.

Guidelines for Expressing Feelings and Emotions in Small Groups

In spite of the dangers or fears of self-disclosure, the responsible sharing of feelings and emotions in Christian education groups is not only a worthy venture, it is, as mentioned above, indispensable to the success of a small group. But while emotions are a fact of life and an integral part of small-group experience, expressing them effectively is not such a simple matter.

It is clear how the unguarded release of negative emotions such as anger or rage, boredom, fear, and frustration could seriously damage small-group communication, harm interpersonal relationships, and hinder group development. Even the indiscriminate sharing of positive emotions such as joy, happiness, love, and affection can make members uncomfortable. On the other hand, if feelings and emotions are suppressed or discour-

---

[67]Powell, *Why Am I Afraid to Tell You Who I Am?*, 97.

aged, small groups can suffer in that members do not really get to know each other and individual growth is encumbered. The following suggestions, along with those given in the section on self-disclosure, can help Christian education group members to improve their effectiveness in expressing emotions and feelings.[68]

Being Aware of One's Feelings: The logical place to begin learning how to share personal feelings and emotions is to be aware of them. Unfortunately, as mentioned earlier, it is not always easy to recognize what our feelings are. Some people do not communicate clearly simply because they understate their emotions and fail to let others know how strongly they feel. For example, to say you're "annoyed" when a friend breaks an important promise would likely be an understatement. On the other hand, some people chronically overstate the strength of their feelings. To these individuals, everything is "wonderful" or "terrible."[69] Powell suggests that when we feel strong emotions, we should pay direct attention to the reaction by literally asking ourselves what we are feeling. Is it embarrassment? Is it fear? Is it anger?[70]

Choosing Words Carefully: It is important that one chooses the most appropriate language in describing his or her feelings. Unfortunately, many individuals have an impoverished vocabulary when it comes to expressing feelings, limiting their terms to those such as good, bad, great, or terrible. Small-group participants should be encouraged to explore broader possibilities in choosing words or phrases. Here are several ways to express a feeling verbally:

- through single words such as "I'm angry," "I'm depressed," or "I'm happy."

- by describing what is happening: "I feel like I'm losing the battle," "I feel like my world is slipping away," "I feel like I'm on top of the world."

---

[68]Adler and Towne, *Looking Out Looking In*, 127–9.

[69]Ibid., 123–4.

[70]Powell, *Why Am I Afraid to Tell You Who I Am?*, 90.

- by describing what you would like to do: "I feel like running away," "I feel like quitting," "I feel like giving you a hug."

Choosing the Appropriate Time for Sharing Feelings: Often the initial onset of strong emotions or feelings is not the appropriate time to verbalize what is inside. An initial reaction to something that angers or upsets can result in saying something later regretted. It is wise to delay the response, carefully thinking through the feelings so as to express them in a manner that is most likely to be well received by fellow group members.

CRITICAL THINKING IN CHRISTIAN EDUCATION GROUPS

Christian education groups, whether decision-making committees or study groups, are often called to engage in making important decisions or to better understand difficult issues. For example, an *ad hoc* committee might be charged with the task of reorganizing the Sunday school structure. In the process, age perimeters of groups will be changed, classes subsequently will be moved to different rooms, and teacher responsibilities will be adjusted. The changes and decisions involved in the restructuring procedure will affect a number of individuals in a variety of ways. Thus, decisions will demand careful, critical reflection.

Unfortunately, many small groups do not implement the kind of thinking and problem-solving skills necessary for making good decisions or effectively addressing difficult issues. Critical thinking is an important activity that can help Christian education groups make better decisions, increase the quality of group discussion, and better understand pertinent issues and content.

What Is Critical Thinking?

Descriptions of critical thinking abound, but one of the most helpful is offered by Galanes and Brilhart in their book on small-group discussion. They propose that critical thinking demands that a problem "be analyzed thoroughly, with as much relevant information as possible examined in the process of that analysis. Then, the solution must be developed on the basis of (1) *all* that information and (2) the best reasoning and logic that can be employed. Critical thinkers act *systematically,* not impulsively or instinctively."[71] Critical thinkers will not accept something as true simply because someone says so. They are willing to challenge information presented by raising questions about it; they are willing to confront other small-group members about their beliefs, opinions, ideas, and feelings.[72]

Stephen Brookfield, in his insightful book on developing critical thinkers, includes four components in his understanding of critical thinking. They are summarized as follows.[73]

- *Identifying and challenging assumptions:* Central to critical thinking is the task of attempting to identify the assumptions that lurk beneath our ideas, values, beliefs, and actions; assumptions that we often take for granted and allow to go unchallenged. Once assumptions are identified, they are examined for va-lidity and accuracy, and are cast off if and when they are found to be inappropriate (for example, "Women should be kept barefoot, pregnant, and in the kitchen"; "Christians should never allow themselves to be en-gaged in conflict"). New assumptions that fit more closely to their value system are then sought after.

- *Understanding and considering context.* Critical thinkers are aware that beliefs, values, practices, and actions are never context-free. What we regard as appropriate ways of behaving toward others, worshiping, or act-

---

[71]Galanes and Brilhart, *Communicating In Groups,* 93–4.

[72]Ibid., 96.

[73]Adapted from Stephen D. Brookfield, *Developing Critical Thinkers* (San Francisco: Jossey-Bass, 1991), 7–9.

ing politically reflects the culture and time in which we live. In other words, critical thinkers are contextually astute.

- *Imagining and exploring alternatives.* A component of critical thinking is the capacity to imagine and explore alternatives to thinking and living. Critical thinkers continually seek out better options to thoughts, ideas, and practices; they are not always content with current approaches or viewpoints to a particular matter.

- *Exhibiting a healthy, reflective skepticism.* Critical thinking includes a reflective skepticism towards claims to truth or authoritative explanations. For critical thinkers, simply because a practice, structure, or belief has existed for a long period of time does not mean that it is most appropriate for all time or for all situations. Because a president, Christian leader, educator, or small-group leader says something is right does not automatically make it so. The critical thinker carefully scrutinizes the words of those who appear to have all the answers to life's problems or dogmatically insist their viewpoint is the correct one.

The Benefits of Critical Thinking

For many Christians, however, especially those who find themselves in a more conservative camp, critical thinking can be perceived as threatening. They reason that since Scripture is the *authoritative* Word of God, it follows logically that it is sufficient to didactically transmit all knowledge and understanding of truth to others.[74] If we then proceed to teach Christians to be critical thinkers, they may fall into moral relativism, come to doubt their faith, indiscriminately challenge the teachings of the church, and perhaps reject God completely.

---

[74]Lawrence O. Richards, "Critical Thinking and Christian Perspective," in *Christian Education Journal* 15 (Fall 1994): 13–20.

But these fears are unfounded and unrealistic, and unnecessarily discourage careful scrutiny of scriptural understanding and application of God's Word to contemporary situations and issues. Richard Paul, one of the leaders in the contemporary critical thinking movement, suggests that individuals can develop their critical moral thinking within any tradition they choose—liberal, theistic, nontheistic, and conservative. Critical thinking, he goes on to propose, does not imply moral relativism for it "emphasizes the need for the same high intellectual standards in moral reasoning and judgment at the foundation of any bona fide domain of knowledge."[75] With these thoughts in mind, I offer the following benefits of critical thinking to small groups used in Christian education.

Better Decisions: For task groups (such as decision-making committees), the obvious benefit of critical thinking is making better decisions. Members of task groups who want to ensure that their decisions are the best that can possibly be made must engage themselves in critical thinking skills in every step of the decision-making process.[76]

Understanding Scripture and Doctrine: Another benefit of critical thinking is better understanding of the Scriptures and teachings of the church. The apostle Paul admonishes Timothy to be a worker "who correctly handles the word of truth" (2Ti 2:15). Knowing and understanding Scripture means asking tough questions, exploring possible answers, and searching for evidence to support assumptions. Private views of Scripture and our understanding of the nature of God must be carefully and critically evaluated in light of outside evidence, opinion, and scholarship.

Applying Scripture to Life Issues: The Bible was given to us neither for words to be memorized nor as fodder for intellectual debate. Rather, the inspired Word was given as a blueprint for life, for the application of principles to daily living and specific life situations. However, there are circumstances where the

---

[75]Richard Paul, *Critical Thinking: What Every Person Needs to Survive in a Rapidly Changing World*, 2nd ed. (Santa Rosa, Calif.: Foundation for Critical Thinking, 1991), 244.

[76]Brilhart and Galanes, *Effective Group Discussion*, 243.

Word of God gives guidance only, offering no specific commands. Today, for example, the whole field of biomedics presents us with difficult and complex situations that biblical writers were not confronted with. Even in Paul's day more mundane matters such as eating and drinking were subject to personal conviction and demanded serious reflection (Ro 14:1ff). To these issues Paul says, "Each one should be fully convinced in his own mind" (Ro 14:5). Rather than render judgment on one another (v. 4), Paul advises the Christians in Rome to exercise their liberty in Christ by applying the judicial mind to the issue itself. As Luther puts it, the meaning of these words is that "every man should be sure of his opinion or thoughts" concerning the particular controversial question.[77]

Spiritual Maturity and Faith Development: Finally, thinking critically is related to spiritual maturity and faith development. Theologically, it makes sense that the ability to think reflectively is critical to nurturing a mature faith. The Christian faith is one that involves both feelings and intellect, demanding one to "'love the Lord your God with all your heart and with all your soul and with all your mind'"(Mt 22:37).[78] In his first letter to the Corinthians, Paul reminds his readers that the spiritual person is able to make judgments about all things (1Co 2:15), which "implies an activity of the discriminating mind."[79] In the epistle to the Hebrews, the writer indicates that the immature believer can handle only milk, whereas the mature Christian can handle the meat or solid food (Heb 5:11ff.). The "milk" refers to the basic or elemental teachings of the divine oracles; those who have not matured beyond the stage of understanding simple truths are mere infants (5:13). By contrast, spiritually mature Christians are those "who by constant use have trained themselves to distinguish good

[77]Martin Luther, *Commentary on the Epistle to the Romans*, trans. J. Theodore Mueller (Grand Rapids, Mich.: Zondervan, 1954), 183.

[78]Eugene C. Roelkepartain, "The Thinking Climate: A Missing Ingredient in Youth Ministry," in *Christian Education Journal* 15 (Fall 1994), 53–63.

[79]F.W. Grosheide, *The First Epistle to the Corinthians* (Grand Rapids, Mich.: Eerdmans, 1980), 74.

from evil" (5:14). These believers, in the words of F.F. Bruce, "have built up in the course of experience a principle or standard of righteousness by which they can pass discriminating judgment on moral situations as they arise."[80] Christian maturity not only permits but clearly demands reflective thought applied to faith-related issues and the application of the intellectual capacity to draw conclusions from available evidence without annulling the "understanding of absolute truth upon which we must ultimately rest."[81]

Nurturing Critical Thinking in Small Groups

For Christians engaged in small groups, critical thinking includes the following elements:[82]

- asking difficult questions related to one's faith ("How can a loving and all-powerful God allow suffering and evil?");

- personally examining and exposing biases and questionable assumptions;

- revising perspectives which prevent or hinder the possibility of change;

- testing one's current beliefs and practice, as well as visionary alternatives, against biblical criteria;

- retracing the group's own steps of logic in pursuing and reaching conclusions.

These dimensions of critical thinking can be developed and nurtured in the context of the small group by implementing several strategies.

---

[80]F.F. Bruce, *The Epistle to the Hebrews* (Grand Rapids, Mich.: Eerdmans, 1964), 109.

[81]Kenneth O. Gangel and Christy Sullivan, "Mind Over Management: The Role of Critical Thinking in Educational Administration," in *Christian Education Journal* 15 (Fall 1994), 64–74.

[82]Robert Lay, "Introduction: Critical Thinking For Christian Education," in *Christian Education Journal* 15 (Fall 1994): 9–12.

Recognizing Counterproductive Behaviors: Nurturing critical thinking in the small group logically begins by recognizing behaviors that are counterproductive to critical thinking. Certain behaviors will surely hinder a small group's efforts to engage in reflective thinking. [83]

- *Impulsiveness:* Impulsive thinkers tend to jump to conclusions before all the pertinent information has been gathered and carefully evaluated. For instance, a small group may quickly select an outreach project because they were recently challenged with the notion that every group should be engaged in some sort of outreach. Unfortunately, they found out quickly that the undertaking was not only impractical, it was all but impossible for the group to do with the available resources. With patience, insightful research, and careful questioning, the group could have realized this and chosen a more appropriate outreach project.

- *Overdependence on Authority Figures:* One of the distinguishing traits of Judaism during the time of Christ was the authoritative role the Pharisees played in the life of the Jewish people. The average Jewish person did not think for himself or herself, but rather depended on the wisdom of the sages. Thus, explains Jacob Neusner, "Scripture, *mishna* [tradition], the sage—all three spoke with equal authority." [84] George Moore describes the importance of the Pharisees in the lives of the Jewish people: "They mediated to the people the knowledge of the law, impressed upon them by precept its authority, and set them the example of punctilious observance of its minutiae." [85] Uncritical thinkers are often more depen-

---

[83]Summarized from Galanes and Brilhart, *Communicating in Groups*, 112–6.

[84]Jacob Neusner, *Foundations of Judaism* (Philadelphia, Pa.: Fortress, 1989), 119.

[85]George Foot Moore, *Judaism in the First Centuries of the Christian Era*, vol. 1 (New York: Schocken, 1927/1971), 67.

dent on authority figures such as teachers, pastors, and small-group leaders. Small-group participants who frequently want to know what the leader thinks or says about a particular issue reflect a hesitancy to do independent thinking. Unfortunately, overly dependent people fail to mature into reflective thinkers who are capable of analyzing information when authority figures are not in their presence.

- *Lack of Confidence:* Sometimes individuals demonstrate overdependence on authority figures because they lack confidence in their own thinking skills. For instance, Michelle may possess information that is relevant, perhaps vital, to a better understanding of an issue, but is reluctant to speak up because she lacks the confidence to share her opinions. Consequently, failure to contribute to the group by expressing doubts, challenging faulty assumptions and conclusions, or offering information critical to understanding an issue contributes to poorer decisions or a less than satisfactory understanding of an issue.

- *Dogmatic or Inflexible Behavior:* Dogmatic people suffer from a lack of thinking skills because they have difficulties in listening to or understanding views, values, and ideas different from their own. William Perry, in his theory of intellectual and ethical development, describes these types of individuals as *dualistic* thinkers. Dualistic or dogmatic people tend to describe ideas only in bifurcated terms (black or white, right or wrong, good or evil).[86] They fail to recognize that not all issues or problems have simplistic answers or a single solution, and consider anyone who disagrees with them as misguided, stupid, or wrong. Those who are dogmatic by nature or who are dualistic thinkers

---

[86]William Perry, *Forms of Intellectual and Ethical Development in the College Years: A Scheme* (New York, N.Y.: Holt, Rinehart, and Winston, 1970), 79.

may find it difficult to function in small groups that esteem diversity of thought and critical thinking skills.

- *Unwillingness to Make the Effort to Think Critically:* Critical thinking will be difficult to facilitate in a small group if one or more group participants are unwilling to expend the effort to do so. Facilitating a framework for reflective analysis will be in vain unless group members possess the motivation to engage in criti-cal thinking.[87]

Encouraging the Asking of Questions: Small-group facilitators can inspire group members to exercise critical thinking skills by encouraging them to ask questions and explore possibilities beyond the obvious or known. The nonthreatening climate of a small group should motivate participants to question their assumptions, face their doubts, seriously reflect on matters of faith, and actively pursue answers to difficult questions. Roehlkepartain suggests that leaders ask themselves a few of questions in order to evaluate the thinking climate of their particular setting, such as: When an individual asks a question is he or she affirmed or discounted? Is it safe to ask any question without being considered an infidel? Are questions discouraged or encouraged in my group?[88]

Encouraging Sound Reasoning and Well-Supported Conclusions: Too often Christians accept simplistic answers to difficult questions or fail to provide solid evidence for their conclusions. To encourage critical thinking in small groups, leaders or facilitators should ask members to articulate their thinking or reasoning in clear, well-thought-out and well-supported conclusions. Good thinkers assert a claim only when they have enough evidence to back that claim up.[89]

Encouraging Perspective-Taking: Critical thinkers recognize that varying points of view exist on issues, especially those that

---

[87]Chet Meyers, *Teaching Students to Think Critically* (San Francisco: Jossey-Bass, 1986), 8.

[88]Roelkepartain, "The Thinking Climate: A Missing Ingredient in Youth Ministry," 61–2.

[89]Paul, *Critical Thinking,* 131.

are controversial in nature. Effective small-group facilitators will encourage group members not only to respect other points of view, but to understand clearly where the other person is coming from. The leader can enhance perspective-taking by playing "the devil's advocate" (purposefully taking an opposing viewpoint), as well as introducing multiple viewpoints, ambiguity, and disagreements of authoritative sources ("How do you respond to the opposing view that says . . . ?").[90]

Building on Group Members' Experience: Small-group facilitators can help group members think reflectively by encouraging them to relate what they are learning in group discussions to their own life experiences. It is helpful to initiate this strategy by building on past learning and experiences members bring into the group ("What disciplines or traditions are valued in the religious circles you have been a part of? Which of these cannot be clearly supported by Scripture?"). This can be continued by enabling them to gradually broaden their frame of reference and integrate new information into their frameworks of thinking and practice ("What are some ways we can apply Jesus' notion of servant leadership to our personal and business lives?").

GROUPTHINK IN CHRISTIAN EDUCATION SMALL GROUPS

Christian education groups can sometimes fall into a state of what has been earlier identified as *groupthink.* Groupthink refers to the tendency of cohesive groups *not* to critically examine all elements of a decision or problem the group is working through. It often occurs because the small group is shortcutting the critical thinking process, failing to allow group participants to express doubts, challenge assumptions, engage in healthy conflict, or examine all of the available information. [91] In other instances a group tries to coerce an individual to think the thoughts of the majority if he or she desires to continue to be a group member. In this case the group has

---

[90]John Chaffee, "Teaching for Critical Thinking," *Educational Vision* 2 (1994): 24.

[91]Galanes and Brilhart, *Communicating In Groups,* 224–5.

moved into a sort of reverse tyranny, where the group is trying to control the individual.[92] When groupthink occurs, decisions are often flawed, and conclusions may be faulty because information has not been examined carefully. Small-group members may have doubts, but they tend to keep these reservations to themselves for fear of being on the receiving end of some sort of retribution from other group members.

Symptoms of Groupthink: The term groupthink was coined by Irving Janis, who has conducted extensive analysis of a number of major decisions by policy-making groups. He and others have found that groupthink occurs in highly cohesive groups under pressure to achieve a consensus on issues or important decisions. Here are three important symptoms that might help a Christian education group leader spot groupthink.[93]

One symptom of groupthink is that *the small group overestimates its power and ability.* There may be an illusion of invulnerability, shared by most or all of the members of the group. This creates excessive optimism and encourages the group to take extreme risks or overestimate the chances for the program to succeed. For example, a Christian education group confidently proposes as an outreach project, to spearhead an effort to purchase a piece of property and building in the inner city and start a Boys and Girls Club. They feel they have the personnel and resources to effectively develop the project, feel the church congregation will surely back them, and are confident the community and authorities will welcome their ambitions with open arms. In reality they find they may have underestimated their own capabilities, do not have support from their congregation, and run into strong opposition from the community and city council.

A second symptom of groupthink is that *the group becomes close-minded.* In this case there are collective efforts to close

---

[92]Icenogle, *Biblical Foundations for Small Group Ministry,* 72.

[93]Summarized from Irving Janis, *Groupthink,* 174–5; Galanes and Brilhart, *Communicating in Groups,* 225–7.

the small group off to any warnings or information that might be contrary to a preferred course of action. Or the group may stereotype the views of outside figures as too uninformed or foolish. The group will then not have to pay any attention to what these other individuals have to say. For example, a church cell group is facilitated by a man who has become disgruntled with the church and certain church policies, and uses the group as a platform to air his grievances. As group members become inclined to side with him and agree with his assessments, there develops a group mentality that biases their evaluation of information, refuses to look open-mindedly at all the relevant information, and considers only information that supports their viewpoints.

And finally, *group members experience pressures to conform*, demonstrated in the following manners:

- There is a self-censorship of deviations from the apparent group consensus, reflecting each member's inclination to minimize the importance of his or her doubts and counterarguments. In other words, if every other group member is in favor of a decision or viewpoint, one will tend to suppress any doubts or fears. For example, in his heart Doug disagrees with the rest of the group members on their view of how the church should respond to homosexuals. He hesitates to voice his opinion because the other members are so vociferous on the matter that he does not want to jeopardize his relationships with them. Unfortunately self-censorship often prevents differing opinions from being presented, a situation which is detrimental to the group's ability to wrestle with issues or to solve problems.

- There may also be a shared illusion of unanimity concerning judgments conforming to the majority view. This results partly from self-censorship of deviations and is reinforced by the false assumption that silence means consent. In the above illustration, other group members may falsely assume that Doug agrees with them and supports their view on how the church should respond to homosexuals.

- There is direct pressure on any member who expresses strong disagreement with any of the group's ideas, decisions, or commitments. It is made clear that this type of dissension is perceived as disloyalty: "Bill, why are you going against us? The rest of us feel it is a good idea."

- There is an emergence of self-appointed mind guards who protect the group from any information that might counter or contrast their shared views. For example, members may deliberately prevent outsiders from addressing the group or they may even withhold any contrasting viewpoints that have been discovered through research or talking with parties outside the small group.

Preventing Groupthink: As mentioned earlier, certain Christian education groups are particularly susceptible to groupthink. Groups with members who are in high need for affiliation (group members are afraid that by disagreeing they will offend others and subsequently lose favor with them), those which are highly cohesive (are under pressure or aspire to achieve consensus), and those who have an autocratic leadership style (a forceful and influential leader who commands adherence) will be prone to groupthink. However, the dangers of groupthink can be minimized by incorporating a number of strategies:[94]

- *Encourage disagreements:* Group facilitators should encourage each group member to be a reflective evaluator who welcomes disagreements and criticisms. It is important for leaders to model a willingness to

---

[94]Tubbs, *A Systems Approach to Small Group Interaction*, 161; Brilhart and Galanes, *Effective Group Discussion*, 266-8.

receive opposing points of view by welcoming criticism or disagreements of their own ideas.

- *Withhold facilitator preference:* Group facilitators should refrain from revealing their preferences to the group at the outset of the session. It is typical for small-group members to yield to the wishes or preferences of the leader, consequently any efforts to search out and identify the best options or other viewpoints are impaired.

- *Explore the issue outside the group context:* Group members should be encouraged to discuss the issue, group processes, and/or potential decisions with trusted associates outside the group, and then share the responses of others with the small group. For example, the aforementioned group that endeavored to establish the Boys and Girls Club would have done well to explore the possibility with other church members, as well as members and leaders in the community. Consequently, they would have garnered some valuable information on the feasibility of the project and the support they may or may not have received from the church and community.

- *Bring outside experts into the group:* Outside experts should be called in periodically to discuss their viewpoints with the group. These outsiders should be encouraged to disagree with the group's assumptions and decisions.

- *Reassess the issue or decision:* After the initial decisions have been reached, the group should readdress the conclusions at a later date, giving participants an opportunity to allow their ideas to incubate.

The problem of groupthink may not be an issue for every Christian education small group. It likely exists in study groups or discussion groups where members are given little freedom to think for themselves and diverse theological or philosophical opinions are not warmly welcomed. Groupthink might also be an issue for decision-making task committees. If a group suffers from groupthink it will more than likely make an incomplete survey of the potential information and possible options, as well as a less than thorough assessment of the information and ideas made available to them. The group's search and assessment procedures will surely be biased. Groupthink illustrates the value of healthy small group conflict. To avoid such conflict circumvents or ignores two of the very reasons for engaging in small-group discussion: effective decision making and the drawing of sound conclusions.

CONCLUSION

Christian education small-group leaders and facilitators face special challenges in understanding the way individuals behave in the context of small groups. This chapter explored the various dimensions of small group participation and behavior. It addressed group roles and functions, self-disclosure, expression of feelings and emotions, critical thinking, and groupthink.

8

Gender and Cultural Differences

CHRISTIAN education groups are often heterogeneous in nature—that is, they are diverse in terms of age, gender, education, ethnicity, socioeconomic background, and religious background. Culturally, Canadians and Americans tend to affirm the notion that heterogeneous groups are more productive and growth-producing than homogeneous groups.[1] However, though diversity in group membership may bring a richness to understanding issues and provide greater possibilities for problem solving, heterogeneity may lead to a number of problems in communication and becoming a group. Simply put, it would be naive to ignore the differences individuals bring to a Christian education group. While all of the individual differences members bring to a small group are of consequence, none impact group communication and process as profoundly as do gender and culture, the foci of this chapter.

GENDER DIFFERENCES IN CHRISTIAN EDUCATION SMALL GROUPS

Many stereotypical assumptions and biases exist in regard to gender differences. Some of these assumptions might generally prove true, while others are unfounded and inaccurate. One of the best-selling books of the 1990s was John Gray's *Men Are from Mars, Women Are from Venus*. In this popular manual on communication, Gray contends that "not only do men and women communicate differently but they think, feel, perceive, react, respond, love, need, and appreciate differently. They almost seem

---

[1]Cragan and Wright, *Communication in Small Groups,* 142.

to be from different planets, speaking different languages and needing different nourishment."[2]

In a more academic tone, psychologist and researcher Carol Gilligan insists that women do indeed speak *in a different voice* than men. While a man expresses his identity in achievement and independence, she argues, a woman defines who she is in the context of relationships.[3] Gorman suggests that both of these factors, achievement and relationships, are at the very core of small groups and small-group communication.[4] This raises many possible questions in regard to gender and communication in small groups. Are there differences in how men and women relate in small groups? Do men and women communicate differently? Do men and women play different roles in small groups?

Different Reasons for Communication

Men and women appear to communicate for significantly different reasons. Women talk with their friends and others primarily for intimacy, understanding, and empathy, whereas men communicate for the sharing of information and problem solving.[5] Linguist Deborah Tannen argues that in conversation men are typically oriented toward facts, while women are oriented toward talk as a means of connection.[6] In other words, she argues, men use fact-oriented talk or conversation to preserve independence

---

[2]John Gray, *Men Are From Mars, Women Are From Venus* (New York: HarperCollins, 1992), 5.

[3]Carol Gilligan, *In a Different Voice* (Cambridge, Mass.: Harvard University Press, 1982), 160.

[4]Gorman, *Community That is Christian* (Wheaton, Ill.: Victor, 1993), 241.

[5]Adler and Towne, *Looking Out Looking In*, 185; Deborah Tannen, *That's Not What I Meant* (New York: William Morrow, 1986).

[6]Deborah Tannen, *You Just Don't Understand: Women and Men in Conversation* (New York: Ballantine, 1990). Not all research confirms gender-linked communication patterns. Mary-Jeanette Smythe and Jasna Meyer, "On the Origins of Gender-Linked Language Differences: Individual and Contextual Explanations," in *Differences That Make a Difference*, eds. Lynn H. Turner and Helen M. Sterk (Westport, Conn.: Bergin and Garvey, 1994), 51-60, found no difference in patterns of interaction, and suggest Tannen's interpretations of social interaction as being simplistic.

and to negotiate and maintain status (e.g., seeing discussion or conversation as a contest, an opportunity to increase status in the eyes of group members). Women, on the other hand, use talk to express intimacy and connect with others.[7]

Given these differences, how do men and women effectively communicate with each other in small groups? First, both men and women need to broaden their assumptions regarding conversation. They must "take each other on their own terms rather than applying the standards of one group to the behavior of the other."[8] Women will continue to misjudge men if they apply the principle of connectedness to small-group discussion, and men will misjudge women if they apply the standards of fact-giving and status to discussions. Both fact-giving and connectedness are legitimate standards for assessing small-group dialogue.[9]

Second, they must learn to adapt to each other's style of conversation. Men might exhibit greater interest in establishing connections and negotiating relationships, making fewer interruptions to seize conversational control. Women could learn assertiveness skills and expand their opportunities to be heard without losing their sensitivity to the significance of connection.[10]

In mixed groups, such differences may cause some frustration and conflict in that what appeals to one of the genders may not be satisfactory to the other. Nonetheless, cross-gender conversations often run smoothly because women are willing to accommodate to the topics men raise.[11]

Gender Differences in Self-Disclosure

Generally speaking, men in American society tend to have more trouble disclosing inner thoughts and feelings or per-

---

[7]Tannen, *You Just Don't Understand: Women and Men in Conversation*, 24–5.

[8]Ibid., 120.

[9]J. Dan Rothwell, *In Mixed Company*, 27.

[10]Ibid.

[11]Adler and Towne, *Looking Out Looking In*, 186.

sonal information than do women.[12] Men seem to be more concerned with information or facts, whereas women are more inclined to share affective information and engage in self-disclosure.[13] A female student of mine reported an interesting observation in regard to two small groups she had the opportunity to lead and consequently compare—one an all female group and another, all males (except for herself). In the all-female group, the participants tended to move quickly over content-related questions and spent a good part of the hour on personal reflection questions. In the male-dominated group, participants spent a good deal of time on the content-oriented dimension of the session, and glossed over questions that required personal disclosure.

Why do men and women differ significantly in their ability or willingness to divulge personal information about themselves? Jourard notes that "The male role . . . will not allow man to acknowledge or to disclose the entire breadth and depth of his inner experience to himself or to others. Man seems obliged, rather, to hide much of his real self . . . from himself and others."[14]

Even as children, boys are usually praised for their mastery at games and sports, while girls are affirmed in their success in relationships with others. Boys are expected to hide their feelings because "men don't cry," while little girls are encouraged to show their feelings and emotions. As little boys grow into men, they may fear being rejected or ridiculed if they violate culturally determined expectations of gender-appropriate behaviors. Women, on the other hand, exhibit expressive behaviors because they continue to receive approval and reinforcement for high levels of disclosure.[15]

---

[12]Valerian J. Derlega and Alan L. Chaikin, "Norms Affecting Self-Disclosure in Men and Women," *Journal of Consulting and Clinical Psychology* 44 (3:1976): 376–80; Brian S. Morgan, "Intimacy of Disclosure Topics and Sex Differences in Self-Disclosure," *Sex Roles* 2 (2:1976): 161–6.

[13]Cragan and Wright, *Communication in Small Groups,* 139; Jourard, *The Transparent Self,* 35.

[14]Jourard, *The Transparent Self,* 35.

[15]Derlega and Chaikin, "Norms Affecting Self-Disclosure in Men and Women," 376–80.

Consequently, small-group facilitators may find it easier to engage men in interaction if the discussion is focused more on, as Morgan terms it, low-intimacy items (e.g., current events or theological issues). Women may be more prone to talk if the heart of the interaction is related to high-intimacy items (personal problems or inner issues such as love, loneliness, and inferiority feelings).[16]

Gender Differences in Listening

An impression that is commonly held is that men generally do not listen as well as women. At this point, however, research is inconclusive as to who are better listeners. According to a literature review by Pearson, West, and Turner, some studies suggest men and women do not differ in their listening abilities; a few indicate women are superior; and others propose that men are the better listeners.[17]

Perhaps men and women listen *differently:* Women listen to understand something they did not previously understand, while men listen to find out how to solve a problem. This goal orientation is illustrated in Richard Halley's classic study on listening. College students were instructed to listen to one of two stories read simultaneously. When tested on the stories, it was discovered that the men were able to extract more information than the women. The females were more easily distracted by the irrelevant, while the goal-oriented males were able to focus on certain elements.[18]

Here are other findings on gender differences in listening:

- Women hear more of a message because they reject less of it, while the male derives a more coherent

---

[16]Morgan, "Intimacy of Disclosure Topics and Sex Differences in Self-Disclosure," 161–6.

[17]Judy Cornelia Pearson, Richard L. West, and Lynn H. Turner, *Gender and Communication*, 3rd ed. (Dubuque, Ia.: Brown, 1995), 35.

[18]Richard D. Halley, "Distractibility of Males and Females in Competing Aural Message Situations: A Research Note." in *Human Communication* 2 (1975): 79–82.

meaning from it because he restructures it in terms of his own goals.[19]

- Men have shorter attention spans than women.[20]

- Females may be better at reading and decoding nonverbal messages.[21]

- Women give more nonverbal and verbal listening signals than do men.[22]

- The verbal signals men and women give when listening have different meanings. For example, women use "yeah" to indicate "I understand you," while men tend to say "yeah" when they are in agreement with the speaker.[23]

Gender and Role Functions

Leadership is also affected by the gender dynamics of a small group. Ernest and Nancy Bormann determined that men tend to resist the leadership of a woman, no matter how capable she might be. They also found, with the rise of the women's movement, a similar attitude on the part of some women. In other words, certain women, as a matter of principle, have refused to cooperate with the leadership of a man.[24] Some women, therefore, may have difficulty attaining small-group leadership responsibilities in some church circles. More conservative denominations or movements which perceive women in leadership or teaching positions over men as unbiblical may prohibit women from leadership capacities in mixed-gender groups. The greatest struggle women may

---

[19]Judy Pearson, Lynn Turner, and William Todd-Mancillas, *Gender and Communication,* 2nd ed. (Dubuque, Ia.: Brown, 1985), 39.

[20]Andrew Wolvin and Carolyn Coakley, *Listening,* 4th ed. (Dubuque, Ia.: Wm. C. Brown, 1992), 141.

[21]Wolvin and Coakley, *Listening,* 141; Gorman, *Community That Is Christian,* 253.

[22]Tannen, *You Just Don't Understand,* 142.

[23]Ibid.

[24]Bormann and Bormann, *Effective Small Group Communication,* 52.

have in leading Christian education small groups is the negative perception churches and some males have of women as leaders, assuming that they are less competent or desirable as leaders. There may be a tendency to relegate women to other roles, such as recorder or hostess, because those are traditional roles women have played in the male-dominated work environment.[25]

In actuality, the relational, cooperative, and interpersonal skills and tendencies more frequently associated with women may make them very effective in facilitating and nurturing small group interaction. On the other hand, many women could learn from men to accept conflict and difference without seeing it as a threat to group intimacy and interdependence.[26]

CULTURAL DIFFERENCES IN CHRISTIAN EDUCATION GROUPS

Small groups are not limited in use to North American or Western cultures. Jim and Carol Plueddemann remind us that world-wide urbanization has led to new small group structures virtually everywhere in the world. Small groups play an important role in all societies.[27] Furthermore, multicultural diversity continues to grow in the United States and Canada, as well as in other urban centers of the world. This means that in North America, small groups will become increasingly diverse in ethnic and cultural make-up. Learning about cultural differences is essential for small-group leaders who will be involved in small groups cross-culturally or in ethnically diverse Christian education groups. Group dynamics, values and attitudes, as well as preferences for learning and leadership styles will differ from culture to culture.[28]

Individuals leading small groups in a cross-cultural context or leading groups with people from more than one culture need to be aware of different cultural values and attitudes. Cultural differences

---

[25]Cragan and Wright, *Communication in Small Groups*, 139.

[26]Gorman, *Community That Is Christian*, 257–8.

[27]Plueddemann and Plueddemann, *Pilgrims in Progress*, 116.

[28]Ibid.

can cause certain problems in group dynamics and the socialization of a small group. Plueddemann and Plueddemann describe potential problems when small-group members fail to recognize cultural differences: "[Cultural] values sink below the level of our awareness and we take them for granted. So when people from different cultures get together for a small group, . . . there might be interpersonal friction without anyone knowing precisely why. Unnecessary misunderstandings can arise in cross-cultural small groups about leadership styles, conflict management techniques, and group goals. Confusion can even arise over the tone of voice or hand motion of another person in the group."[29]

It would be pointless, if not impossible, to compile a list of differing values and attitudes that cross the endless numbers of cultures and subcultures. People who lead small groups with members from other cultures, however, must learn some general principles and adapt these to fluid conditions. There are a number of helpful classification schemes that identify and describe the value orientations of different cultures.[30] One insightful taxonomy is proposed by missiologist Marvin Mayers, whose classification includes twelve basic cultural values (six contrasting pairs), and is particularly helpful in understanding cross-cultural small-group behavior:[31]

---

[29]Plueddemann and Plueddemann, *Pilgrims in Progress*, 116.

[30]For example, Florence R. Kluckhohn and Fred L. Strodtbeck, *Variations in Value Orientations* (Evanston, Ill.: Row, Person, 1961); S.H. Schwartz, "Universals in the Content and Structure of Values," in *Advances in Experimental Social Psychology*, vol. 25, ed. M. Zanna (New York: Academic Press), 1–66. Edward T. Hall makes a helpful distinction between *high-context* and *low-context* cultures. In a high-context culture people pay special attention to the concrete world around them (e.g., the atmosphere of the room, sounds, smells, nonverbal messages); most of the message is in the physical context or internalized in the person. People who are members of low-context cultures, on the other hand, pay more attention to ideas and abstract concepts , and the bulk of information is vested in the verbal code [Edward T. Hall, *Beyond Culture* (Garden City, N.Y.: Anchor, 1977), 91]. For a helpful application of Hall's context theory to small groups, see Plueddemann and Plueddemann, *Pilgrims in Progress*, 120–1.

[31]Marvin Mayers, *Christianity Confronts Culture* (Grand Rapids, Mich.: Zondervan, 1974), 151–5.

Small-group facilitators whose familiarity with cross-cultural communication is limited, may err in perceiving these classification polarities as pure and distinctly held by individuals of particular cultures. It is important to recognize that these contrasting cultural values are not hard and fast, and individuals may land on a continuum somewhere in between the extremities of:

- *dichotomizing* versus *holistic;*

- *declarative* versus *interrogative;*

- *time-oriented* versus *event-oriented;*

- *goal-conscious* versus *interaction-conscious;*

- *prestige ascribed* versus *prestige achieved;*

- *vulnerability as weakness* versus *vulnerability as strength.*

Dichotomizing versus Holistic

The *dichotomizer* tends to polarize life in terms of black and white, right and wrong, here and there, myself and the other. For example, Mayers describes North American persons as tending "to be more particularistic with greater attention to detail, to linear sequence, to a sequential type of organization."[32] Consequently, in small-group discussions dichotmizing persons may tend to speak directly and pointedly to a subject, not afraid to evaluate the other group member's ideas or positions.

A *holistic* person derives satisfaction in the integration of life and thought; parts have a vital function within the whole. For example, proposes Mayers, the Filipino appears to have an absence of logical thought and consequently would use "euphemism extensively to talk around a subject rather than speak directly to the point of a subject."[33] For most Asians, harmony

---

[32]Ibid., 158.

[33]Ibid.

of the group (a dimension of holism) is highly regarded, thus they tend to share their opinions in indirect manners.[34]

Peter Chang makes a rather similar distinction between linear and nonlinear thinking and cleverly illustrates the difference between the two modes with the following word picture: "In an American meal, one has steak, potatoes, and peas placed separately on the plate; whereas in chop suey everything is mixed together. The latter is not without organization, but only organized differently."[35] Linear thinkers are by and large "analytical, objective, logical, and systematic," whereas nonlinear thinkers see the whole of a picture.[36]

Small-group facilitators should expect dichotomizers or linear thinkers to prefer systematic doctrinal studies. In addition, they will be more prone to debating each other's ideas and challenging assumptions of other group members. By contrast, holistic or nonlinear individuals might find narrative or imaginative sections of the Bible more suited to their likings. A topic related to everyday life, such as family living, may be preferred over a doctrinal study. There may be more of a tendency to spend time sharing personal stories and experiences, at the expense of substantive content study.[37]

Chang proposes that a balanced combination of linear and nonlinear thinking is helpful in small-group Bible studies, since linear thinking alone has its handicaps: "in Bible study, objectivity [or linear thinking] avoids the danger of reading one's own mind into the text, but the empathetic approach [or nonlinear thinking] leads the whole person into the passage instead of remaining aloof while analyzing it."[38]

---

[34]Cathcart, Samovar, and Henman, 306–15.

[35]Peter S.C. Chang, "Steak, Potatoes, Peas and Chopsuey—Linear and Non-linear Thinking." In *Missions & Theological Education in World Perspective*, eds. Harvie M. Conn and Samuel F. Rowen (Farmington, Mich.: Associates of Urbanus, 1984), 113–23.

[36]Ibid., 113.

[37]Plueddemann and Plueddemann, *Pilgrims in Progress*, 121.

[38]Chang, "Steak, Potatoes, Peas and Chopsuey—Linear and Non-Linear Thinking," 122.

Declarative versus Interrogative

A *declarative* person seeks an expert to give advice in crisis or educational settings. Thus, in a learning experience much emphasis is placed on the responsibility of the instructor as the expert to dispense information. For instance, Johng Ook Lee proposes that "many Asians have been reared under the British-American system of education. The teacher is an authority, and what he says is important. Therefore, lecture is a popular method of instruction. Students also have a great respect for teachers and are sometimes fearful of them."[39] Consequently, in small group discussions, where the leader's responsibility is to facilitate discussion rather than teach didactically, declarative-oriented individuals may have difficulty engaging themselves. They tend to fear and avoid group participation and will likely be hesitant about asking questions or may be apprehensive when called upon to respond to a question or statement. If, however, the small-group facilitator takes the time and makes the effort to build relationships with these group members, declarative individuals will be more apt to engage in group discussion.[40]

An *interrogative* person will expect to select an answer to the question from a number of alternatives. Satisfaction comes from the process of considering possibilities to questions or problems, and selecting an alternative. These individuals tend to be frustrated with didactic teaching styles. Consequently small-group discussion opportunities, where reflective thinking and exploring possibilities are germane to the whole process, will be much more appealing to them than to the declarative persons.

Time-Oriented versus Event-Oriented

Clearly, time is viewed differently by people of different cultures, a variety of time systems have been described by an-

---

[39]Johng Ook Lee, "Asian Americans," in *Christian Education: Foundations for the Future*, eds. Robert E. Clark, Lin Johnson, and Allyn K. Sloat (Chicago: Moody, 1991), 384–9.

[40]Ibid., 388.

thropologists and sociologists.[41] Cultures may be labeled as either time-oriented or event-oriented. Individuals from *time-oriented* cultures (such as the dominant cultures of the United States and Canada) are highly concerned with time and punctuality. They adopt a linear, schedule-driven approach to time and tend to focus on doing one thing at a time. Usually the time stated is the time intended. In the context of small-group meetings, this type of person will be concerned with punctuality in starting and ending and will seek to accomplish the most possible in the time allotted.

In *event-oriented cultures,* by contrast, people are not so concerned with time frames and will come together without a rigidly planned or detailed schedule. Thus a small-group leader in an event-oriented society may need to be less concerned about starting or finishing a small-group meeting on time. Putting too much emphasis on punctuality and schedules may cause frustration on behalf of the leader when group members show little concern or respect for such a value. In addition, people from event-oriented cultures will be more concerned with relationships and what is going on between people in the Christian education small group than when the meeting begins and finishes.

Goal-Conscious versus Interaction-Conscious

Cultures are also made up of *goal-conscious* and/or *interaction-conscious* individuals. Goal-conscious people are concerned with definite goals and with reaching those goals. In a Christian education small group, achieving identified goals becomes a priority over interpersonal relationships. Consequently, small groups that are comprised primarily of people who are goal-conscious will be more task-oriented. These groups will, for example, want to cover a certain amount material in a particular time frame or will concentrate on completing particular projects.[42]

---

[41]For example, see Edward T. Hall and Mildred Reed Hall, *Hidden Differences: Doing Business With the Japanese* (New York: Anchor,1987), 16–27; Kluckhohn and Strodtbeck, *Variations in Value Orientations,* 13–4.

[42]Plueddemann and Plueddemann, *Pilgrims in Progress,* 121.

Interaction-conscious individuals are more interested in nurturing relationships with others than achieving group goals. They will sacrifice a goal for the sake of conversation and break rules if they interfere with the involvement with another person. Small groups that consist of interaction-conscious members will see their purpose as primarily to build interpersonal relationships and to nurture community.

Prestige Ascribed versus Prestige Achieved

Persons who feel that prestige is *ascribed* and confirmed by the social group will show respect in keeping with the prescriptions of prestige determined by the group or society. They see rank and formal credentials as important, and are willing to sacrifice to achieve them. Thus, in terms of small-group leadership, one with higher status (e.g., credentials) will hold much authority over group members with lower status.[43] It may be difficult to expect lay people to be considered as small-group leaders in these cultures, since formal credentials (such as a seminary degree or certificate of ordination) are held in such high regard.

Those who feel prestige is *achieved* will tend to ignore formal credentials. They will work to achieve prestige in their own eyes rather than to seek status in society. In the context of the small group, authority is earned by the individual through personal efforts; authority is temporal and is contingent upon continued performance. Since formal credentials are less important to achievement-oriented cultures, lay people will be readily recruited to serve as small-group leaders.

Vulnerability as Weakness versus Vulnerability as Strength

Jourard emphasizes the distinction between people who are *transparent* and those who are *opaque*. Transparent people are readily willing to fully, spontaneously, and honestly disclose their experiences, inner thoughts, and feelings to others. By

---

[43]Ibid.

contrast, opaque individuals hide themselves to others, rarely offering a glimpse of what is going on inside.[44]

We might expect that people from dissimilar cultures would differ in the amount and nature of self-disclosure they feel is appropriate in interpersonal communication.[45] In some cultures, vulnerability is perceived as a *weakness,* consequently individuals will not expose their weaknesses or tell stories about their mistakes. They have a tendency to speak vaguely about areas of life that are personal. Those persons from cultures that emphasize vulnerability as a *strength,* are willing to tell stories about themselves exposing weaknesses and to talk freely about very personal areas of life.[46]

Research by Dean Barnlund concerning the differences between Japanese and Americans on interpersonal encounters illustrates this distinction: "Among Japanese there is substantially less disclosure of inner experience while among Americans substantially greater disclosure on all topics and with all persons. Where the former share their private thoughts in only a general way, among the latter these are revealed much more completely. Americans, for example, reveal themselves more completely on the most superficially explored topics than do the Japanese on all but the safest and most completely explored topics of conversation.[47]

How does this play out in small-group interaction? Obviously, individuals from cultures that see vulnerability as a strength will find it less difficult to share inner thoughts and feelings. By contrast, those from cultures that view vulnerability as a weakness will tend to be shy about personal

---

[44]Jourard, *The Transparent Self,* 3–5.

[45]Dean C. Barnlund, "Verbal Self-Disclosure: Topics, Targets, Depth," in *Towards Internationalism,* eds. Elise C. Smith and Louise Fiber Luce (Rowley, Mass.: Newbury House, 1979), 83–101.

[46]Summarized from Meyers, *Christianity Confronts Culture,* 149–54.

[47]Barnlund, "Verbal Self-Disclosure: Topics, Targets, Depth," 99–100.

self-disclosure. Furthermore, when individuals from different cultures interact, intimacy and self-disclosure are sometimes inhibited.[48]

Three factors may encourage self-disclosure when communication becomes intercultural in a Christian education group. The first factor is the ability of group members to respect one another's values, without which one cannot adapt his or her communicative behavior to the other system.[49] A second factor is similarity; that is, there is a need for group members to observe similarities in background and lifestyle (for example, we are all students or we attend the same church), as well as likenesses in attitudes and values. A third factor is involvement, measured by the efforts of group members to take or make the time to interact and increase intimacy.[50]

CONCLUSION

The differences individuals bring to a small group are a blessing. Gender and cultural diversity, especially, bring a richness to understanding issues and variety in the nature of communication that takes place. Diversity, however, is also a likely source of communication problems and can hinder group processes if not handled carefully.

---

[48]Harry C. Triandis, *Culture and Social Behavior* (New York: McGraw-Hill, 1994), 232.

[49]K.S. Sitaram and Lawrence W. Haapanen, "The Role of Values in Intercultural Communication," in *Handbook of Intercultural Communication,* eds. Molefi Kete Asante, Eileen Newmark, and Cecil A. Blake (Beverly Hills, Calif.: SAGE, 1979), 147–60.

[50]Triandis, *Culture and Social Behavior,* 233.

9

Implementing Small Groups

SMALL groups are the building blocks of society. Primary groups such as the family and work groups are rudimentary devices of socialization and chief sources of social harmony. In like manner, Christian education groups constitute the basic units or building blocks for the congregation. It is in smaller groups that people are built up in their faith, equipped for significant roles in the congregational life of the church or parish, and unleashed for service to others.

But simply recognizing the merit of, and urgent need for, small groups in the Christian education ministry of the church is not sufficient to get groups started or implement a strategy for building people up through groups. Small groups are made up of people, and people are complex. Consequently, implementing small groups means there must be prayerful and thoughtful response to questions related to purpose, organization, and human needs. In establishing healthy Christian education groups, Christian educators must make critical choices that will determine the success or failure of the groups.

CHOICES TO BE MADE
To successfully get a Christian education small group off the ground, a number of pertinent questions must be asked, considered, and eventually resolved by potential group members.

What Is the Nature of the Group?
Earlier, we categorized four major types of groups (relational, influence, content, task) and further identified a variety

of small groups in each of these categories. Anyone considering starting or leading a Christian education group must make a decision as to what kind of a group he or she would like to lead or be involved in. Will it be a support group for single adults? A divorce recovery support group? A study of denominational distinctiveness? A Bible study? A discipleship group for teenagers? A prayer group? A noon-hour discussion group for businessmen? Once a general type of group is determined, interested participants can prayerfully consider additional group options.

Should the Group Be Open or Closed?

One of the initial issues to be resolved is whether the Christian education group will open or closed. Both types have advantages and disadvantages. An open group is designed to accept new members at any time and is valuable in assimilating people into the church and reaching the unchurched. In addition, the open approach can prevent exclusiveness and inwardness. On the other hand, allowing a group to be open to all comers can impede self-disclosure and group intimacy.

Some small-group proponents, especially those advocating cell groups, are adamant about keeping groups open. Dale Galloway, for instance, declares closed groups are restricted, dead-end, and do not fulfill the Great Commission.[1] Carl George is equally emphatic: "Show me a nurturing group not regularly open to new life, and I will guarantee that it's dying. If cells are units of redemption, then no one can button up the lifeboats and hang out a sign, 'You can't come in here.'"[2] Lyman Coleman encourages openness by suggesting groups place an empty chair in the group circle serving as a reminder that the group is always accessible to other strugglers.[3] Cell groups,

---

[1]Dale Galloway, *The Small Group Book* (Grand Rapids, Mich.: Fleming H. Revell, 1995), 150.

[2]Carl G. George, *Prepare Your Church for the Future* (Grand Rapids, Mich.: Revell, 1991), 99.

[3]Coleman and Scales, *Serendipity Training Manual*, 79.

content-oriented groups, outreach groups, and recovery groups often work well under the open principle.

Closed groups have a fixed, or limited, membership and are appropriate for nurturing long-term, intimate relationships and encouraging self-disclosure. They allow members the opportunity to develop a high degree of vulnerability, trust, and openness. The drawbacks of closed groups are that they foster cliquishness and exclusivity, limit outreach opportunities, and do not allow for the incorporation of new church or parish members into a group.

Discipleship groups, training groups, counseling groups, and encounter groups often function best as closed. Jesus' group, the Twelve, serves as a biblical model of a closed group. Churches and Christian education departments should not feel constrained to limit themselves to either closed or open groups; a well-balanced ministry will include both types. Some groups allow themselves to be open for a period of time at the beginning (perhaps a month) then close, creating sort of an open/closed hybrid variety.

What Size Should the Group Be?

Many small-group experts agree that groups function best with somewhere between three and twelve members.[4] It must be reemphasized that as a group increases in membership the number of possible relationships expands exponentially. Neal McBride reminds us that a group of twelve has the potential of sixty-six different relationships. Just increasing the group by three people boosts the number of possible relationships to 105.[5] It is easy to see that for the sake of growing meaningful relationships and providing for balanced interaction, it is better to keep groups relatively small.

Should the Group Be Short-Term or Ongoing?

There is no preferred set time a Christian education group should be in existence. Some task or study groups meet for the

---

[4]For example, see Jeffrey Arnold, *Starting Small Groups* (Nashville, Tenn.: Abingdon, 1997; McBride, *How to Build a Small Groups Ministry*, 81; George, *Prepare Your Church for the Future*, 125-6.

[5]McBride, *How to Build a Small Groups Ministry*, 81-2.

period of time necessary for completing a task or studying a particular book. Relationship-oriented groups, in order to be successful, need to meet for a minimum of a year. For the most part, groups should have a stated time limit, as people may feel uncomfortable about committing themselves to a group lacking clear time perimeters. For instance, McBride encourages group to meet for one year.[6] Bringing groups to a close and forming new ones helps prevent ingrownness and stagnation. Cell groups usually exist for an indefinite period of time, but retain a dynamic lifeline by growing, dividing, and continually reproducing new groups.

Should the Group Be Clergy or Lay Led?

Who should lead small Christian education groups? Small-group experts are generally in agreement that groups should be led primarily by lay people. Hadaway, Wright, and DuBose suggest that one of the amazing aspects of the home cell movement is the phenomenal rate at which leadership is developed, in that "small home-centered groups provide the intimate atmosphere . . . conducive to maximum leadership development."[7] Comiskey insists that the transforming of lay people into lay leaders is the force behind the cell group explosion.[8] Ware advocates that "group leadership seems particularly adaptable to the gifts lay people bring to the church, and the group will more likely flourish if leadership comes from grass roots rather than if it is handed down or directed by a church official."[9] Vandenakker observes that important to the lay-facilitated Roman Catholic SCCs, is the "renewed understanding of the laity's role in the life of the church."[10]

Does that mean clergy play no role in the small-group strategy of the church or Christian education department? Most

---

[6]Ibid., 85

[7]Hadaway, Wright, and Dubose, *Home Cell Groups and House Churches*, 200-1.

[8]Comiskey, *Home Cell Group Explosion*, 57.

[9]Ware, *Connecting to God* , 8.

[10]Vandenakker, *Small Christian Communities and the Parish* , 162.

certainly not. Clergy can and should play a dynamic role in recruiting, equipping, and supervising small groups. Their task is to carry out the injunction of the apostle Paul in Ephesians 4:11–12: "to prepare God's people for works of service."

When Should Christian Education Small Groups Meet?

Churches and Christian education programs should offer small-group opportunities on days and times that provide for maximum participation. In today's busy world, many adults wish to be in small groups but cannot find time due to schedule conflicts. Offering group experiences at a variety of different times increase the possibility of parish or church members to get involved in small group Christian education opportunities.

Some churches have all their groups meet at the same time on the same night. This eliminates involvement of those who are unable to attend at the specified time, but is an attractive alternative for churches where:[11]

- most of the adults tend to be employed in the same business or industry;

- a high measure of supervision and structure is desired by the church leaders;

- group meetings have replaced traditional meetings such as prayer meeting or the Sunday evening service;

- supervision or a quality program is offered for the children so parents are freed to participate in the small groups.

Where Should the Groups Meet?

While groups can meet any place they choose, for the most part small group experts agree that the ideal locale for meetings is the home.[12] Homes provide a comfortable and relaxed

---

[11]McBride, *How to Build a Small Groups Ministry,* 85–6.

[12]See, for example, McBride, *How to Build a Small Groups Ministry,* 86; Vandenakker, *Small Christian Communities and the Parish,* 173.

atmosphere that is especially conducive to fellowship and interpersonal communication.

Some groups like to meet in restaurants over breakfast or lunch. These settings can work well as long as the business of the restaurant is not a distraction to the group. For some churches, the church or parish itself offers the best location for small group meetings. If this is the case, the facilitator or group leader must be sure that classrooms are conducive to a relaxed, informal meeting.

What Are the Components of a Successful Christian Education Group?

The components that make up a Christian education group will depend, to a large degree, on its nature or primary purpose. For example, the basics of a support group for single mothers will differ somewhat from those of a Bible study group. But most groups will include dimensions of the Christian life of the early church, described by Luke:

> They devoted themselves to the apostles' teaching and to the fellowship, to the breaking of bread and to prayer. Everyone was filled with awe, and many wonders and miraculous signs were done by the apostles. All the believers were together and had everything in common. Selling their possessions and goods, they gave to anyone as he had need. Every day they continued to meet together in the temple courts. They broke bread in their homes and ate together with glad and sincere hearts, praising God and enjoying the favor of all the people. And the Lord added to their number daily those who were being saved (Ac 2:42–7).

From this biblical model of Christian community, at least four components of small group life can be delineated: worship, nurture, community, and outreach.[13]

---

[13]Ron Nicholas, "The Basics of Small Group Life." In *Small Group Leaders' Handbook*, ed. Ron Nicholas (Downers Grove, Ill.: InterVarsity Press, 1982), 34–47.

Worship: Worship is the active, human response of praise and thanksgiving to God, whereby His worth is declared.[14] Members of the early church "were filled with awe" (2:43) and engaged in "praising God" (2:47). Small groups can worship God through prayer, the singing of hymns or praise songs, or the reading passages of worshipful Scripture.

Nurture: The early Christians were also nurtured by the apostles' instruction (2:42). In Christian education small groups, nurture will come, for the most part, in the form of Bible study. In fact, Bible study is the most critical element in the life of a healthy Christian education group. In inductive Bible study,[15] small-group members can appreciate the joy of discovering the truth of Scriptures for themselves as they delve into the Word to answer carefully constructed questions. However, while the Bible should be the primary source of study content, small-group members can also be nurtured by reading and discussing good Christian books and small-group curricula.

Community: The Christians in the early church became a community through the experiential process of sharing and caring for one another. They had everything in common, they met together in the temple courts, they broke bread together in their homes, and ate meals together (2:44–6). A major task of any Christian education group is community or group building, a process that takes considerable time, effort, and commitment. The community-building goals of a small group are relatedness and interdependence; being knit together in love and built up as whole people.[16] Community building occurs in small groups when mem-

---

[14]Robert E. Webber, *Worship: Old and New* (Grand Rapids, Mich.: Zondervan, 1982), 11–2; Ronald Allen and Gordon Borror, *Worship: Rediscovering the Missing Jewel* (Portland, Ore.: Multnomah, 1982), 16.

[15]Inductive method of study is described by Richards and Bredfeldt as an impartial and objective approach to the text of Scriptures that follows a three-step process of observation, interpretation, and application [Richards Bredfeldt, *Creative Bible Teaching*, 63].

[16]Nicholas, "The Basics of Small Group Life," 37; Gorman, *Community That Is Christian*, 98.

bers share their needs, pray for one another, confess their sins and shortcomings, bear one anothers' burdens, encourage each other to identify and develop their spiritual gifts, and carefully listen to each other. While community-building is essential to the healthy development of a group, if a group does little else than group building, it will become ingrown and codependent.

Outreach: A small-group dynamic that will serve as a safe-guard from becoming too ingrown or self-serving is outreach. Mission or service to others through acts of kindness and love is essential for the success and health of a group. In the early church the Christians gave generously to anyone who had a need, and as a result people were saved and added to the church daily (2:45, 47). Christian education groups can perform acts of outreach such as praying for people in need, supporting missionaries, raising money for a relief project, working in a soup kitchen, and having studies for people seeking God.

LAUNCHING A CHRISTIAN EDUCATION GROUP

Christian education small groups do not simply appear on the scene. They take careful planning, thoughtful consideration, and perseverance. There are a number of logical steps to be taken in getting a group off the ground.

- First, approval from the pastor, director of Christian education, or appropriate church leadership must be secured. Some church leaders may provide opposition or resistance to the implementation of small Christian education groups. They may fear heresy may creeping into the group, or the small group becoming a clique or renegade assemblage. They may have had a bad experience with small groups in the past, or fear that they will in some way lose control of parishioners.[17]

- Second, the many details discussed above ("Choices To Be Made") must be tentatively decided upon: What will be the nature of the group? Will it be open or

---

[17]E. Stanley Ott, *The Vibrant Church* (Ventura, Calif.: Regal, 1989), 132–3.

closed? When and where will the group meet? Will the group be ongoing or will it have a predetermined life span? Additional questions to ask are What do we do with children? How often do we meet? Will the group be homogeneous (e.g., same age, gender, marital status) or heterogeneous (e.g., mixed ages, men and women, single and married)? Once the group is under way, some necessary adjustments can be made to group procedures.

- Third, the nature of leadership must be determined. The alternatives for leading small group meetings described earlier in the book are (1) the designated leader, (2) rotated leadership, (3) or shared leadership.

- Fourth, it is important to secure an initial date for the group meeting. If prospective group members do not commit to a firm starting point, it is entirely possible the group will never get off the ground.

- The final step in establishing a Christian education group is to recruit members for the small groups. There are two approaches one can take. The private approach is to personally invite individuals to be part of the group. The public approach is to invite any interested members from the congregation or community to join. If more than ten or twelve express interest, form two or more groups.

Once a group has been formed, members will want to affirm the choices that were tentatively made earlier in the process of starting a group. Some Christian education groups will choose to express their choices and options in the form of a covenant or contract.

CONCLUSION

The small group serves as a wonderful option for doing Christian education. While groups must not be considered as a panacea for all the ills or shortcomings of a church, they can most assuredly be employed for Christian nurture, community building, spiritual care of believers, and outreach. But small groups do not just happen. They must be carefully planned for; important choices must be made and formal questions related to structure and format must be resolved. Getting a dynamic Christian education group off the ground will take careful planning and hard work, but the rewards and benefits are well worth the efforts.

Index of Scripture References

Index of Proper Names